THE END OF EDUCATION

PEDAGOGY AND CULTURAL PRACTICE

Edited by Henry Giroux and Roger Simon

Recognizing that pedagogy begins with the affirmation of differences as a precondition for extending the possibilities of democratic life, the series analyzes the diverse democratic and ideological struggles of people across a wide range of economic, social, and political spheres.

1. *The End of Education: Toward Posthumanism*, William V. Spanos

THE END OF EDUCATION

Toward Posthumanism

WILLIAM V. SPANOS

PEDAGOGY AND CULTURAL PRACTICE
V O L U M E   1

University of Minnesota Press
Minneapolis London

Published by the University of Minnesota Press
2037 University Avenue Southeast, Minneapolis, MN 55414
Printed in the United States of America on acid-free paper

Library of Congress Cataloging-in-Publication Data

Spanos, William V.
    The end of education : toward posthumanism / William Spanos.
      p. cm. — (Pedagogy and cultural practice ; v. 1)
    Includes index.
    ISBN 0-8166-1955-7
    1. Education, Higher—United States—Philosophy. 2. Humanism.
3. Education, Humanistic—United States—History—20th century.
4. Education, Higher—United States—Curricula—History—20th
century.   5. Educational change—United States—History—20th
century. 6. Educational anthropology—United States. I. Title.
II. Series.
LA227.4.S64 1993
370.11'2'0973—dc20

92-6292
CIP

The University of Minnesota is an
equal-opportunity educator and employer.

For my daughter, Stephania,
Golden Helmet,
who knows dispersal
and sings its measure

Will this mean the end of Civilization As We Know It?

Ishmael Reed, "Jes Grew,"
sung by Taj Mahal, from the album *Conjure*

CONTENTS

Acknowledgments xi

Introduction xiii

1   Humanistic Understanding and the Onto-theo-logical Tradition:
The Ideology of Vision 1

2   Humanistic Inquiry and the Politics of the Gaze 25

3   The Apollonian Investment of Modern Humanist Educational
Theory: The Examples of Matthew Arnold, Irving Babbitt,
and I. A. Richards.. 65

4   The Violence of Disinterestedness: A Genealogy of the
Educational "Reform" Initiative in the 1980s 118

5   The University in the Vietnam Decade: The "Crisis of
Command" and the "Refusal of Spontaneous Consent" 162

6   The Intellectual and the Posthumanist Occasion: Toward
a Decentered *Paideia*... 187

Notes 223

Index 271

This book was instigated by the publication of the Harvard Core Curriculum Report in 1978 and was intended to respond to what I took to be an ominous educational reform initiative that, without naming it, would delegitimate the decisive, if spontaneous, disclosure of the complicity of liberal American institutions of higher learning with the state's brutal conduct of the war in Vietnam and the consequent call for opening the university to meet the demands by hitherto marginalized constituencies of American society for enfranchisement. The book has undergone three versions since then. The first took the form of a monograph commissioned, along with three others, by Clifford Clark, then president of the State University of New York at Binghamton. He intended them to initiate a local debate on the existing undergraduate curriculum. Unlike the other reports, which subscribed in some degree or other to the "reforms" advocated by the Harvard Core Curriculum Report, my differential monograph met with institutional indifference. Prompted by the ideological implications of this indifference, I expanded my argument and sent the manuscript (in the fall of 1980) to a prestigious Ivy League university press for consideration. Although two prominent scholars in the field of contemporary theory recommended it for publication (with revisions), it was, after an extended period of time, finally rejected by the press on manifestly ideological grounds: "Given the long-standing emphasis on general education at X University, it was felt that an attack on the Harvard Core Curriculum was, in a very real sense, an attack on the educational system espoused by X University. As an organ of the university, the Press is in a delicate position, one which the committee felt should not be jeopardized by undertaking publication of this work." The third version, published here, constitutes an extension and deepening of the theoretical argument based on one of the readers' reports, and addresses the rapidly developing history of the "reform" movement initiated by the Harvard Report, of which the fate of the second version is a telling instance.

It will be understood, therefore, why I owe my deepest gratitude to Terry Cochran and Biodun Iginla, former and present editors at the University of Minnesota Press, for their openness to my oppositional project, despite the increasing institutional resistance to postmodern or, as I prefer, posthumanist theory and practice. Though I do not want to impute their support of *The End of Education* to a solidarity with my critique of the humanist university, I do want to say that their support as editors for alternative discourses such as my own is an exemplary instance of what I take to be an intellectual imperative in a time when the emancipatory energies in the university are being threatened in the name of "free speech."

There are, of course, many others, too numerous to identify, who have contributed significantly to the enrichment of my argument and my intellectual life in the errant process of "completing" this book. I hope that some of them will recognize the occasion of their contribution in my text. It would be remiss on my part, however, if I did not acknowledge my unnameable debt to the *boundary 2* editorial collective—Jonathan Arac, Paul Bové, Joseph Buttigieg, Nancy Fraser, Margaret Ferguson, Michael Hays, Daniel O'Hara, Donald Pease, and Cornel West—and, in a different way, to Biodun Iginla and Jim Merod for providing the occasions for the kind of antagonistic dialogue that dislocates (and vitalizes) thinking. Finally, I also want to express my gratitude to those students, undergraduate and graduate, who, in the years of my labor to produce this book, came into my classes in fear and trembling or with indifference, discovered their constituted identities in the process, and left as comrades in the struggle against injustice: not least Philip Armstrong, Christina Bacchilega, Erica Braxton, Giovanna Covi, Ann Higginbottom, Katrina Irving, Sandra Jamieson, Lara Lutz, Patrick McHugh, Jeannette McVicker, Cynthia Miecznikowski, Peter Mortenson, Rajagiop Radhakrishnan, David Randall, Deborah Reiter, Madeleine Sorapure, Judith Sumner, and Wei Wang. Their presence insistently redeemed my teaching in an otherwise alienating academic environment. Finally, I want to thank Ann Klefstad for her superb copyediting of my idiosyncratic manuscript. She has made my writing more readable without annulling its philosophically grounded errancy.

Parts of chapters 3 and 4 of this book constitute much revised and expanded versions of essays published in *boundary 2* ("The End of Education: The Harvard Core Curriculum Report and the Pedagogy of Reformation," vol. 10, Winter 1982) and in *Cultural Critique* ("The Apollonian Investment of Modern Humanist Education: The Examples of Matthew Arnold, Irving Babbitt, and I. A. Richards," vol. 1, Fall 1985). I wish to thank the editors of these journals for permission to reprint.

In the aftermath of the Vietnam War, a massive educational reform movement was initiated in 1979 by Harvard University (marked by the adoption of the Harvard Core Curriculum Report). Such reform was theorized by prominent American humanists, by conservatives such as William Bennett, Walter Jackson Bate, and Allan Bloom, and by liberals such as E. D. Hirsch and Wayne Booth. This reform movement has as its purpose the recuperation of not only the humanist curriculum that was "shattered" by the protest movement in the 1960s but also the discourse of disinterestedness now called into question by the theoretical discourses that have come to be called "postmodern" or "poststructuralist," but which this book prefers to call "posthumanist." The dominant liberal humanist wing of this reform movement by and large passes over the historically specific moment that precipitated the crisis of higher education: exposure by various student constituencies of the complicity of the university with the relay of power structures conducting the war in Vietnam. Rather, it concentrates on the disabling "randomness" of higher education: what the Harvard Core Curriculum Report called "the proliferation of courses" that, in the name of relevance, had "eroded" the traditional general education program. The reform projects of E. D. Hirsch, Wayne Booth, and Gerald Graff, among others, distinguish themselves from the narrow pedagogical authoritarianism and political conservativism of humanists such as Bennett, Bate, Kramer, Bloom, and more recently Roger Kimball, Dinesh D'Souza, and David Lehman. But this opposition is only — and conveniently — apparent. Despite the radical problematization of the enabling principles of the humanist university, the dominant liberal discourse of the reform movement is at one with the conservative wing in its reaffirmation of the humanist tradition — of the *anthropologos* — as the point of departure for its pluralist curricular reform initiative. To put it another way, the reformers' commitment to the sovereign subject and the principle of disinterestedness (that truth is external to and is the adversary of power) obscures what the Vietnam decade disclosed: the complicity of truth and power, of knowledge production and the dominant sociopolitical order. Indeed, the so-called liberal reform initiative renders its opposition to the conservative humanists' overt call for the imposition of a curriculum consonant with the state's goals a disarming hegemonic strategy.

My purpose is to demonstrate this complicity between the liberal and conservative reform initiatives, and the complicity of both with what Althusser has called the (repressive) state apparatuses. I argue that the benign pluralism of contemporary liberal humanism constitutes a strategy of incorporation that, whatever its explicit intentions, operates to reduce the subversive threat of the emergent differential constituencies (whether bodies of marginalized texts or marginalized social groups) by accommodating them to the humanist core or center; that is, the anthropologos. In thus disarming the inevitable resistance precipitated by overt exclusionary tactics, the liberal reformist strategy of incorporation is far more sociopolitically economical than that of the conservative humanist project. In short, the renewed appeal to disinterested inquiry by liberal humanists in the university is ultimately intended to recuperate the lost authority of humanism by way of a more subtle practice than heretofore of what Antonio Gramsci, Louis Althusser, Raymond Williams, and Edward Said have called hegemony. In Foucault's rhetoric, such hegemony constitutes a microtechnology of the disciplinary society intended to make those on which it is practiced the bearers of their own oppression.

Since the content of a text includes what it does not say as well as what it does say, I want first to make clear what this book is not. It is not intended to constitute a critique of particular organizational and programmatic aspects of the modern humanist university. Nor is it intended to articulate concrete alternative modes of institutional organization and curricular programming. Although the book makes a number of gestures in both directions—on the one hand, an extended critique of the general education program adopted by Harvard University in the aftermath of World War II and of the core curriculum adopted by Harvard after the Vietnam War, and, on the other, a proposal for an alternative idea of the intellectual that involves specific recommendations about the teacher/student relationship and the organization of the curriculum—my primary intent is to deconstruct the educational theory and institutional practice of modern humanism with a view to making explicit the *ideological relay* hidden in them and the emancipatory pedagogical possibilities this relay has hitherto repressed. It is my claim that, despite the persuasive critiques of aspects of humanist inquiry by the practitioners of various types of postmodern or poststructuralist theory (of its understanding of the subject and of textuality, cultural production, gender and race relations, sociopolitical formations, and so on), these critiques have been limited by a vestigially disciplinary orientation. As a result, they have been easily accommodated by the institution. Since, in other words, the discourse of humanism has successfully resisted critique, I attempt here to articulate a theoretical basis for the projection of specific organizational and programmatic alternatives that is more adequate to the task of critique than that provided by contemporary theory.

The fundamental purpose of this book, then, is to show that the disinterestedness of humanist inquiry is grounded in a metaphysics—a perception of the temporality of being (*physis*) from the end or from a superior position above (*meta*)—that either coerces or accommodates the differences that temporality disseminates. This anthropological metaphysics manifests itself in an analogous accommodational political practice whose coercions are concealed in the illusion of individual sovereignty. Appropriating Heidegger's de-structive hermeneutics, chapter 1, "Humanist Understanding and the Onto-theo-logical Tradition," thus demonstrates the ultimate continuity of the onto (Greek)-theo (medieval)-logical (humanist) tradition that resides in the constellation of metaphors this metaphysical tradition has privileged, naturalized, and inscribed in the discourse and practices of knowledge production. The central metaphors are these: the *panoptic eye* (and its light) and the affiliated figure of the *centered circle*, the benign connotations of which obscure the will to power informing them. A crucial preparatory aspect of this demonstration—one enabled by Heidegger's genealogy of technology—

is the disclosure of the complicity between "philosophical" inquiry (by which I mean the humanities in general) and scientific inquiry. It will be an important purpose of the following chapter to suggest that the assumption of an adversarial relationship between the so-called Two Cultures has disabled every radical critique of the dominant cultural and sociopolitical orders; that is, every critique of post-Enlightenment modernity.

This is not to suggest that Heidegger's destructive hermeneutics *as such* is adequate to the task of radical critique. Although the opening chapter contends that his incipient understanding of being as an indissoluble continuum from the ontological through the textual and cultural to the sociopolitical helps create a basis for radical critique, it also acknowledges that Heidegger's limitation of his interrogation largely to the site of ontological inquiry had disastrous consequences when he intervened directly in German politics. To put this in terms of the metaphorics privileged by the ontotheological tradition, Heidegger's destruction of the discourse of the centered circle does not get beyond demonstrating the disabling consequences of modern metaphysical thinking (of anthropology, i.e., the discourse of Man) for inquiry: to think meta-physically, as in fact humanists do, is to *overlook*, and thus to spatialize or structure, time, and eventually to *forget* the ontological differences time disseminates.

Michel Foucault's historically specific political analysis of the Panopticon and panopticism can be read as a corrective, or rather as an extension, of Heidegger's disclosure of the will to power informing the circular philosophical discourse privileged by the ontotheological tradition in general and by the humanist tradition in particular. Thus chapter 2, "Humanist Inquiry and the Politics of the Gaze," undertakes a new interpretation of Foucault's genealogy of the modern bourgeois capitalist disciplinary society in *Surveiller et punir* (*Discipline and Punish*). Foucault traces its origins back to the Enlightenment's obsession with optics, which culminates in Jeremy Bentham's Panopticon, or "Inspection House": the centered, circular architectural structure that enabled the reformation and normalization of a variety of social deviants by means of constant surveillance, and not by means of force. Eventually, a pervasive panoptic discursive practice (in workplaces, in medical and psychiatric practices, and not least in educational institutions) inscribed the centered circle into the body politic at large. In short, what Heidegger interpreted as a negative limitation of the circular humanistic discourse of modernity—as the *over*looking and forgetting of difference throughout ontology—becomes in Foucault a positive or productive potential of power relations: the *supervision* and disciplining of difference thoughout the whole of society.

This, however, is not to suggest that Foucault's genealogy of modern knowledge/power relations supersedes Heidegger's destruction of the philosophical discourse of humanist modernity. In tracing the genealogy of the disciplinary society back to the epistemic break that first precipitated and then privileged the discursive practices of both reason and the natural sciences in the Enlightenment, Foucault inadvertently reinscribes the inadequate terms of the two cultures debate. He allows the practice of the humanities (philosophy, literature, literary criticism, etc.), precisely the target of

Heidegger's critique, to escape the charge of complicity with the disciplinary society. Reading Foucault against the grain, however, chapter 2 also shows that, despite his emphasis on the Enlightenment as the origin of the panopticism of modernity, his discourse in fact betrays the fundamental continuity between the sociopolitical disciplinary uses to which the post-Enlightenment put the panoptic diagram (and the panoptic gaze it enables) and the will to power informing the figure of the centered circle (and the visual sense) privileged by the ontotheological tradition at large.

Rereading Foucault with Heidegger, in other words, foregrounds Foucault's insistent, however underdeveloped, awareness that the Panopticon (the historically specific institution) "is a diagram of a mechanism of power reduced to its ideal form; . . . it is in fact a figure of political technology that may and must be detached from any specific use." In thus thematizing the *figurality* and the *polyvalency* of the Panopticon, this comparative analysis of Heidegger's and Foucault's discourses enables a reconciliation of destructive hermeneutics and genealogy. It suggests that ontology and sociopolitics constitute an indissoluble relay, however unevenly developed in any historically specific occasion, and this points to a theoretical orientation that is more adequate than Heidegger's or Foucault's, or any of the other postmodern discourses, to the task of a radical critique of the existing conditions of knowledge/power relations in late capitalism. More specifically, in suggesting that the centered circle/panoptic diagram informs the "disinterested" or "objective" discursive practices of the humanist disciplines as well as those of the empirical sciences, such a reconciliation of Heidegger's destruction and Foucault's genealogy dispels the pervasive and disabling notion (represented by Gerald Graff and Fredric Jameson, among others) that the modern university is defined by a radical heterogeneity. It thus enables the perception of the accommodational function of anthropological inquiry and of the complicity of its different parts in the reproduction of the dominant sociopolitical order. In short, it enables an irresistible critique of hegemony.

The next three chapters address the reform initiative undertaken in the 1980s in response to the crisis of higher education precipitated by what William Bennett refers to as the "shattering of the humanities" during the Vietnam decade. Focusing on the ideological uses to which the metaphorics of the centered circle and the panoptic gaze are put, these chapters constitute a genealogy first of the *theory* and then of the *institutional practices* of the modern humanist university—its abiding commitment to disinterested inquiry, to general education (the core curriculum or common body of indispensable knowledge), and to the principle that the university constitutes a value-free (apolitical) space.

Chapter 3, "The Apollonian Investment of Modern Humanist Educational Theory," undertakes a destructive analysis of the *theoretical* discourse on higher education undertaken by three exemplary and influential humanists, concentrating, above all, on their common call for the recuperation of the classical "Greek" model. The theoretical initiatives of these humanists coincide with the three previous major institutional reform movements in the modern period: Matthew Arnold's reform imperative responded to the crisis precipitated by the emergence of a working-class consciousness, Irving Babbitt's to the crisis of the collapse of Europe and the victory of the Bolshevik Revolution, and that of I. A. Richards to the emergence of the Soviet Union as a superpower. This analysis discloses the fundamental continuity of the metaphorics of the centered circle and panoptic gaze in their apparently diverse rhetorics. It reveals the will to power over a relay of sociopolitical "otherness" (ranging unevenly from the working class through women, gays, and racial and ethnic minorities to Third World peoples) that informs these writers' so-called disinterested discourses. As the historically specific moments of their theoretical interventions suggest, the various humanisms of these writers betray a fundamental complicity with state apparatuses—a complicity I will disclose in Arnold's advocacy of "culture," Babbitt's advocacy of "the classical measure," and Richards's advocacy of "the synoptic university."

The final section of this chapter extends the destructive reading of Arnold's, Babbitt's, and Richards's theoretical discourses on education, focusing on the affiliation between their mutual appeal to the classical Greek *paideia* and the metaphorics of the centered circle/panoptic gaze informing their humanism. Appropriating Heidegger's distinction between the Greek understanding of truth as *a-letheía* (dis-closure) and the Roman understanding of truth as *veritas* (the adequation of mind and thing), this section reveals that the classical *paideia* theorized and sponsored by these leading humanist intellectuals does not, in fact, have its origins in Greek culture but in the decisive Roman *representation* of Greek culture (mediated by what is usually called the Enlightenment or the Augustan Age). It shows that the humanist educational project is founded not on the originative and "errant" thinking of Greece, but on the secondary or derivative (and calculative; i.e., "politically correct") thinking of the Romans, which represents being as a relay of reified and hierarchized binary oppositions subsumed under the primary opposition between civilization and barbarism. The Roman *paideia*, as Heidegger repeatedly demonstrates (and as Foucault's reiterated invocation of "the Roman reference" in his genealogy of the origins of the disciplinary society implies), involves *eruditio et institutio in bonas artes*: scholarship and training in good conduct.

This is a crucial moment in the argument of *The End of Education*. In tracing the genealogy of humanism to a Roman origin, it suggests the degree to which, despite what Arnold calls its "discourse of deliverance," the humanist *paideia*—its celebration of culture against anarchy—is implicated in the imperial political project. The anthropologos informing humanist inquiry, which orders and domesticates the force and threat of differential knowledge in terms of its fixed and permanent center (core) and in the name of correctness is simultaneous with the metropolis, which orders and domesticates the force (threat) of the barbarian provinces in terms of the capital and in the name of civilization. The centered circle and the sur-veillance (and normalization) of deviations inform both projects. What is in varying degrees implicit in the texts of Arnold, Babbitt, and Richards is shown in the conclusion to be explicit in the cultural criticism of T. S. Eliot, who, despite different ideological emphases, is more or less universally recognized as one of their company. In short, this phase of the analysis of the educational discourses of Arnold, Babbitt, and Richards suggests that the humanist *paideia* each espouses in response to the crisis in education precipitated by their particular historical occasion was ultimately, however unevenly explicit, intended to reproduce an imperial or colonial political economy.

Chapter 4, "The Violence of Disinterestedness," repeats this genealogical project by examining modern institutional practice in America. To prepare the ground for the critique of the massive educational reform movement initiated in 1978 by Harvard University, the first part of this chapter focuses on the two watershed institutional reform initiatives in this century, which gave shape to the idea of the general education program that has served as the essential and (until recently) unexamined measure of undergraduate study in American colleges and universities: one undertaken by Columbia University following World War I and the Bolshevik Revolution, and another sponsored by Harvard University following World War II at the beginning of the Cold War era. This genealogy of the institutional practice of general education in America, the programmatic inscription of "a common body of knowledge," discloses its origins in historically specific sociopolitical reaction. In the case of the Columbia initiative, we find the origins of the inordinately influential General Honors and Contemporary Civilization courses instituted in 1919 in the War Issues Course mandated for all colleges and universities by the federal government during World War I. The aim was to combat, here and abroad, the "menace to democracy" posed first by the "barbarous Huns" and then, after the war, by the "Reds." In the case of the general education program instituted by Harvard University in 1945 (the program articulated in *General Education in a Free Society*, better known as "The Harvard Redbook" and largely modeled on the Columbia courses), we find its origins in the Cold War.

The second part of this chapter reads the apparently innocuous—and extremely influential—discourse of the Harvard Core Curriculum Report of 1978 in the light of the preceding genealogy, a project justified by the report's overtly stated purpose to reestablish the general education program that was "eroded by the proliferation of courses" in the interim. The report strategically makes no reference to the historical circumstances that precipitated this "proliferation" (the student, civil rights, and feminist protest movements during the Vietnam decade), using instead a rhetoric invoking the self-evident universal values of the core curriculum. The analysis of the historically specific occasion from which the report emerged, however, makes quite clear that the sociopolitical agenda informing the earlier, more overtly ideological reform movements also informs this recent institutional effort to recuperate the core curriculum. No less than the others, however more accommodational than before, the report constitutes an effort on the part of the cultural memory to recuperate the "American heritage" in the face of the crisis precipitated by the emergence of hitherto excluded or marginalized constituencies in the wake of the United States' use of massive technological power in

Vietnam in the name of the "free world." And, as the analysis of the rhetoric of the Core Curriculum Report suggests, the metaphorics of the centered circle/panoptic gaze inexorably determine the programmatic shaping of all differential knowledges activated by the discursive explosion in the Vietnam decade.

In thus disclosing the contradiction informing the discursive practices of disinterested inquiry and of the liberal university, this genealogical history of American higher education in the twentieth century points not only to the "end of education" but also to the positive possibilities of a new and posthumanist theory of higher education commensurate to the decentered social, cultural, and historical realities of postmodernity.

Chapter 5, "The University in the Vietnam Decade," begins to explore these possibilities once they are released from anthropological structuration. It constitutes a symptomatic reading of the multisituated student protest movement which is intended to provide the context for the posthumanist theory of pedagogy articulated in the final chapter of the book. Whereas the reform movement of the 1980s represents the student resistance within the framework of the narrative of the American cultural memory, this chapter interprets the student uprising as a *spontaneous* exposure of the contradictions inhering in the theory and practice of the humanist university: the socially constituted character of the principle of "disinterested inquiry" and the "autonomous" university as, in Althusser's term, ideological state apparatuses. The chapter reads the students' exposure of the complicity of the university with the military-industrial complex and their demand for "relevance" as (in Gramsci's resonant terms) the decisive refusal of spontaneous consent to the discursive practices of North American hegemony. These constitute the culminating moment of the epistemic break that brings modernity (the legacy of the Enlightenment) to its fulfillment/end.

Beyond the positive contribution of the spontaneous student protest movement, this chapter goes on to analyze the failure of that movement to effect productive changes in the university commensurate with the knowledge explosion precipitated by the events of the Vietnam decade. My argument focuses on the two general phases of the protest movement: the existential, which, in resorting to the principle of authenticity—of self-identity or the self-present subject—disabled an effective collective practice; and the Marxist, which, in resorting to the essentialism of the (economic) base/superstructure model, failed to realize the degree to which cultural production (the humanities) was implicated with the "knowledge industry" in serving the military-industrial complex. The conclusion drawn is that the protest movement's failure to effect lasting changes in the structure of the university was the consequence of its resistance to theory or, more accurately, *its failure to theorize hegemony*: the affiliation between cultural and material production and their relation to state power, between the ideology of "disinterested" humanist discourse (and the sovereign subject) and the ideology of "objective" empirical scientific discourse. Put alternatively, the protest movement failed to theorize what Foucault calls the repressive hypothesis. It did not recognize that the discourse of truth/beauty is an *agency*, not an adversary, of power.

In analyzing the failure of the protest movement to theorize the ideological agenda of the university, this chapter accounts for the remarkable success of the reform initiative of the 1980s in its effort to recuperate the core curriculum. But in thematizing the network of constituencies this agenda was ultimately intended to dominate—the affiliations overlooked by the protest movement—my intention is to lay the ground for an adequate theorization of the differential but affiliated relay of forces released by the self-destruction of the university in the 1960s and early 1970s.

This task is undertaken in chapter 6, "The Intellectual and the Posthumanist Occasion." This chapter delimits the theorization of educational imperatives disclosed by the knowledge explosion and by the irruption of the multiplicity of hitherto repressed historical subjects in the Vietnam decade to the role of the intellectual vis-à-vis (1) scholarship/criticism; (2) pedagogy; and (3) the curriculum. This chapter repeats the argument for understanding the differential knowledges precipitated by the decentering of the anthropological circle, not as discrete and autonomous, but as an indissoluble (however unevenly developed and asymmetrical) relay of discrete knowledges. Despite this decisive decentering, the practitioners of various versions of posthumanist theory in the academy—deconstructionists, genealogists, neo-Marxists, new historicists, feminists, black critics, and so on—have not entirely succeeded in breaking from the disciplinary parameters established by the tradition of higher education. This failure, not incidentally, explains why their discourses have been easily institutionalized, and further, why they, however inadvertently, fulfill the productive and hegemonic ends of the disciplinary logic of division and mastery (the logic that constituted the "sovereign subject" and the "sovereign discipline"). An adequate theorization of the multisituated student protest movement demands that the oppositional intellectual recognize the affiliative bonds between the specific sites of repressed and alienated forms of knowledge. What is needed is a *specifically engaged but collaborative* practice. By this I mean a practice that, without reinscribing itself in the paradigm of the general or universal or leading intellectual, thwarts the division of labor invented by the disciplinary society to annul collective intellectual practice and to extend and deepen the discreet operations of hegemony by producing knowledge/power.

The second section of the final chapter then attempts to theorize the implications of this idea of the oppositional intellectual for pedagogy in the classroom. It invokes a crucial traditional binary opposition strangely overlooked (despite its centrality in Nietzsche) by oppositional intellectuals such as Althusser, Foucault, and Derrida in their efforts to think the events of May '68: that between maturity and adolescence, age and youth. In keeping with the idea of the scholar/critic who is both specific (or organic) and general in a way that overcomes the respective limitations of both an orthodox Marxism, which minimizes specific struggles in privileging the general intellectual, and the Foucauldian orientation, which minimizes collective struggle in privileging the situated intellectual, my argument posits the specific space of the contemporary university as a microcosm of the world at large. That is, it represents the educational institution as a site in which the different student constituencies—women, racial and ethnic minorities, the gay community, the working class, Third World students, and so on—reflect specific yet affiliated sociopolitical constituencies, once excluded but since the Vietnam period increasingly accommodated by the dominant sociopolitical order. Thus I am calling for a decentered pedagogy that, in understanding youth at once as an organically collective "other" and as differential instances of this collective other, empowers students to think and speak from both subject positions. In dismantling the centered pyramidal structure—and its supervisory metaphorics—concealed by the pluralism of traditional liberal pedagogical practice, it enables a truly dialogic pedagogy: a reciprocally destructive learning process in which, in Paolo Freire's terms, the oppositional teacher becomes a student and the interested student a teacher. This destructive pedagogy—which, following Heidegger, I also call a pedagogy of repetition (*Wiederholung*)—is thus capable of facilitating the emergence of both the youthfulness of youth and the differential sociopolitical energies youth embodies from the cultural identity (the consensus) into which the amnesiac teleological pedagogy of the cultural memory would submerge them.

This chapter, and the book, concludes with a theorization of the implications for the curriculum precipitated by the decentering of the anthropological center. Just as it mandates the breaking of the pyramidal structure determining the hierarchical relationship between teacher and student, so also it mandates the disruption of the pyramidal structure of the core curriculum with a view to liberating the differential forces that it had colonized. This does not mean the randomizing of the curriculum, the unleashing of a multitude of discrete and autonomous course offerings, which would simply reproduce the situation that has enabled the recuperative project of the traditionalist reformers. It means, rather, the dislocation of the core from its transcendental "center elsewhere" into the arena of the free play of criticism. More specifically, it means the genealogical critique or destruction of the (socially constituted) narrative history that produced the canon; in Nietzsche's terms, it means the "use of history to resolve the problem of history." Accordingly, this new materialist practice, which "brushes history against the grain," entails the imperative to work politically for the establishment of courses reflecting the knowledge that has been excluded or misrepresented by the canon. *At the same time, this new practice precludes the accommodation and domestication of this differential knowledge by the institution in the name of pluralism or diversification.* As important as opening up the curriculum is in the oppositional intellectual's struggle to achieve the truly social democratic educational potential disclosed by the decentering of the anthropologos, this chapter claims that such an opening is not enough. To utilize history to overcome history, the oppositional intellectual, of whatever critical persuasion, has the responsibility of gaining a commanding view of history and its multiple coercions, not in the sense of a panoptic mastery, but in the genealogical sense of their socially constituted origins and ideological ends. In this the intellectual repeats the destructive process already at work in scholarly/critical inquiry and in pedagogy. The "commanding view," according to this alternative, becomes not a pre-conception that specific inquiry will confirm, as in the case of the traditional perspective, but a forestructure that the leap into the hermeneutic circle will always already deconstruct, that is, it will always already disclose the cultural, social, and historical differences that the traditional curriculum would accommodate to its core or center.

This imperative is underscored by recent history, specifically the events in Central and Eastern Europe in 1989 and the Gulf War in 1991. The collapse of Stalinist Marxism and the decisive defeat of a tyrannical dictator have been interpreted by the agencies of knowledge production and the information media in the Western capitalist nations, most notably in the United States, as the "fall of Communism" or the "triumph of democracy": indeed, as the emergence of a "new world order" determined by the relay of ontological principles subsuming the discourse of Man and the Western liberal democratic tradition. This representation of contemporary global history has already gone far in effacing the memory of the Vietnam War, a forgetting synecdochically suggested by the reduction of the healthy crisis of the American cultural identity (defined by its self-ordained global "errand in the wilderness") precipitated by the United States' brutally executed, if finally abortive, intervention in Vietnam to the "Vietnam Syndrome": a collective psychological sickness that the decisive defeat of Saddam Hussein cured (what President George Bush announced in the wake of victory as "kicking the Vietnam Syndrome"). Equally ominous, it has simultaneously enabled a massive counter-offensive against posthumanist theory at large (and the minimally multicultural pedagogical practices it in part has enabled in the university). Reenforced by the disclosure and publicizing of the Nazi affiliations of Martin Heidegger and Paul de Man, this revisionary initiative represents emancipatory discourse as a practice of "political correctness" or "new McCarthyism of the Left." It is no accident that the humanist exponents of "our cultural heritage" now justify their counteroffensive against those intellectuals who would remember Vietnam—and the "wound" it opened up in the American psyche—by representing the revolt of the peoples of Eastern Europe and the "coalition" of Western industrial nations against Iraq as symptoms of a worldwide discovery and embracing of the principles, values, and cultural products of America.

To counter this increasingly reactionary momentum, an oppositional discourse and practice can no longer, as in the past, rely either on a Marxist critique that continues to be determined by the base/superstructure model or on a poststructuralist critique that remains vestigially disciplinary. The task contemporary history has assigned oppositional intellectuals is that of thinking contemporary power relations in terms of a relay extending throughout the indissoluble continuum of being, from the ontological (the anthropologos) through the cultural (the discourse of Man) to the economic and sociopolitical (the practices of consumer capitalism, patriarchy, and racism). Only such a transdisciplinary mode of critical thinking can enable effective resistance to and subversion of the neoimperialism that masks itself in the hegemonic discourse of the "new

ONE

Humanistic Understanding and the Onto-theo-logical Tradition

The Ideology of Vision

> If you have form'd a Circle to go into,
> go into it yourself & see how you would do.
>
> William Blake, "To God"

> Apollo, the god of all plastic energies, is at the same time the
> soothsaying god. He who (as the etymology of the name
> suggests) is the "shining one," the deity of light, is also ruler
> over the beautiful illusion of the inner world of fantasy.
>
> Friedrich Nietzsche, *The Birth of Tragedy*

I

In 1974 at the behest of Derek Bok, the new president of Harvard University, a faculty committee chaired by the new dean of arts and sciences, Henry Rosovsky, undertook a "major review of the goals and strategies of undergraduate education at Harvard."[1] In 1978, when it had become clear that "there was wide agreement that the proliferation of courses [in the previous decade] had eroded the purpose of the existing General Education Program" (RCC, p. 1), the task force submitted its Report on the Core Curriculum to the Harvard faculty. This report, the members of the committee believed, was grounded in "a standard [of education] that meets the needs of the late twentieth century" (RCC, p. 2). After a brief period of deliberation, the Harvard faculty adopted the report on May 2, 1978. The mass media, on the basis of the report's promise to renew American cultural and sociopolitical life, inflated the curricular reform at Harvard into an educational event of national significance.

As if waiting for such a commanding sign from the *pharmakos*, colleges and universities throughout the country began to follow suit. This recuperative momentum in higher education—in which the "reformation" of the humanities curriculum was compared to the recuperation of the good health the nation apparently lost during the turbulent decade of the Vietnam War—received institutional impetus by Walter Jackson Bate, the eminent Kingsley Porter Professor of English at Harvard, in an essay entitled "The Crisis in English Studies," published in 1982 in the *Harvard Magazine* (an alumni journal). In this essay he appealed to the administrators of the university for executive support for the effort of the humanist "survivors" of the catastrophic Vietnam War decade to recuperate the *litterae humaniores* in the face of the literary profession's "self-destructive" course, a course, according to Bate, precipitated by the intervention of theoretical discourse in literary studies in the late 1960s.

> The subject matter—the world's great literature—is unrivaled. All we need is the chance and the imagination to help it work upon the minds and characters of the millions of students to whom we are responsible. . . . The number at first may seem small. But much can be done if one has a really committed and talented nucleus. . . . Small as it is, a larger fraction of it than I can remember consists of gifted young people who really *care*, who are ready to face difficulties and to make sacrifices in order to recapture some understanding of the centrality and larger values of humane letters. At Harvard we have been trying to take advantage of this. . . . But we shall need the help of the administrators in the years ahead.[2]

The recuperative process came to culmination—and its hidden ideological agenda into clear focus—in the report on the state of the humanities in education published in November 1984 by William J. Bennett, chairman of the National Endowment for the Humanities and, subsequently, secretary of education in the Reagan administration. In this report, significantly entitled "To Reclaim a Legacy," Chairman Bennett, like the Harvard task force and Walter Jackson Bate (whose jeremiad he invokes), deplored the disarray into which higher education—especially the teaching of the humanities—had fallen during the 1960s and called for the restoration of a curriculum that would guarantee the reclamation of "our" cultural heritage in behalf of its "rightful heirs":

> Although more than 50 percent of America's high school graduates continue their education at American colleges and universities, few of them can be said to receive there an adequate education in the culture and civilization of which they are members. Most of our college graduates remain shortchanged in the humanities—history, literature, philosophy, and the ideals and practices of the past that have shaped the society they enter.
> The fault lies principally with those of us whose business it is to educate these students. We have blamed others, but the responsibility is ours. . . . It is we the educators—not scientists, business people, or the general public—who too often have given up the great task of transmitting a culture to its rightful heirs.
> Thus, what we have on many of our campuses is an unclaimed legacy, a course of studies in which the humanities have been siphoned off, diluted, or so adulterated that students graduate knowing little of their heritage.[3]

What the Harvard task force and Bate tactically leave unsaid, Bennett says explicitly: that the disintegration of the humanities was the consequence of a "collective loss of nerve and faith on the part of both faculty and administrators during the late 1960s and early 1970s."[4] To put this critical initiative positively, the massive institutional effort inaugurated by Harvard University to recuperate the core curriculum betrays its complicity with the state's effort to recuperate the good health the nation apparently lost during the turbulent decade of the Vietnam War because of the civil rights, feminist, and student protest movements. And this "healing of the wound," as it came popularly to be called, means essentially the recuperation of a national consensus:

> Great works, important bodies of knowledge and powerful methods of inquiry constitute the core of the humanities and sustain the intellectual, moral and political traditions of our civilization. If we neglect, as we have been neglecting, this essential core and rationale of the humanities, if we permit the fragmentation of the humanities to continue, then we will jeopardize everything we care about.[5]

Who is this "we" with whom Bennett identifies himself and the future fate of young Americans? Is it an accident that, just as Bate addresses his recuperative discourse to Harvard University administrators and alumni, Bennett addresses his, in the above quotation, to the readers of the *Wall Street Journal*?

II

It is the genealogy of this naturalized "we" that I will pursue. What follows, in other words, will interrogate the massive educational reform movement initiated by Harvard University in the aftermath of the Vietnam War. My aim is to make explicit that movement's informing assumptions about the nature of human understanding, the university, culture, and beyond these civil and political society. As such, I intend to look at higher education in order to advance the contemporary countermemory's general project of demystifying humanist modernity. Unlike the recollective cultural memory to which the Harvard reformers and those universal intellectuals they have relegitimated appeal, the memory informing this study is not synoptic. It is, rather, historically specific, *apparently* empirical, and explicitly genealogical: one that proffers a decentered mode of procedure, focusing on the differences, details, and particulars that the institutionally dominant mode of inquiry, in its normalizing appeal to a synoptic disinterestedness, necessarily overlooks.

Both in its method and content, this book will call into question what I take to be the privileged metaphysical or logocentric assumptions inscribed in the humanistic paradigm that the Harvard reform project aims to recuperate in behalf of contemporary higher education. *Especially in what it leaves unsaid*, the Harvard report (and the discursive practices it has enabled) constitutes a reactionary effort of the "saving remnant" to recuperate a nonexistent golden age of higher education. In doing so, it not only precludes the possibility of educating American students to confront the enormously complex problems facing them but also lends cultural legitimacy to historically specific economic and sociopolitical power structures. I do not intend, in other words, to relegate the past to nullity; I wish to retrieve positive possibilities forgotten by the perennial commitment to the center and its structures, by the privileging of *the* enabling metaphysical principle: *that identity is the condition for the possibility of difference and not the other way around.*

In recollecting "that time," *in illo tempore,* the Harvard Core Curriculum Report forgets the witness of the immediate past (the crisis of the university in the 1960s, the decade of the Vietnam War). Even more significantly, it also overlooks the momentous historical rupture in the Western tradition. I am referring to the epistemological break enacted, as Derrida has observed, in the decentering discourses of Nietzsche, Freud, and Heidegger, which rendered definitively visible the always absent presence hitherto obscured by the various and insistent efforts in the history of the West to recuperate a determining center when such a center was menaced by historical events.

> If we wished to choose several "names," as indications only, and to recall those authors in whose discourse this occurrence has kept most closely to its most radical formulation, we doubtless would have to cite the Nietzschean critique of metaphysics, the critique of the concepts of Being and truth, for which were substituted the concepts of play, interpretation, and sign (sign without present truth); the Freudian critique of self-presence, that is, the critique of consciousness, of the subject, of self-identity and of self-proximity or self-possession; and, more radically, the Heideggerian destruction of metaphysics, of onto-theology, of the determination of Being as presence.[6]

To be more specific, the curricular reforms outlined in the Harvard Core Curriculum Report too easily assume the ameliorative virtue of the humanistic tradition. Overlooking the origins of the "over-optioned" curriculum in the student protest movement during the decade of the Vietnam War, the report finds a purely negative institutional situation—educational anarchy—and thus an obvious need to restore a former ideal model of liberal education. The report seeks to redefine this model so it can accommodate the disruptive currents within its comprehensive horizon. In so doing, the report thus minimizes, if it does not deliberately suppress, the growing suspicion that the privileged instrument (to borrow from Heidegger's hermeneutic rhetoric) that has shaped and authorized Western culture, including the idea of the university since Plato and Aristotle, has broken down. I mean, of course, the epistemological method and rhetoric of the ontotheological tradition, which, as Heidegger, Derrida, and Foucault among others have in their various ways persuasively shown, subsumes the late classical age (onto-), the medieval period (theo-), and the Renaissance and after, including the modern age of technology (logical).

Thus the report indicates little awareness that the breaking of this privileged epistemological instrument has precipitated not only a crisis situation in Western culture at large but also a number of related "post-Western" modes of inquiry (destructive, deconstructive, genealogical, neo-Marxist, feminist, etc.) and of artistic production (especially in literature) that call into question the alleged naturalness of the received instrument and the cultural discourse, including that of higher education, that it has inscribed in the Western institutions. Assuming the naturalness—the universality—of its mode of inquiry, the report thus blinds itself to the positive ways of relating to the decentered condition of modern men and women opened up by what traditionalists have pejoratively called "postmodern theory." The destructive impulse in philosophy and the arts (and more recently in legal studies) does not manifest itself in a purely negative act of hermeneutic violence, as too readily assumed by academy humanists. As the case of Heidegger's seminal dialogue with Kant in *Kant and the Problem of Metaphysics* (1951), it also manifests itself as an essentially positive impulse of retrieval (*Wiederholen*). In de-stroying the tradition, this negative discourse discloses—opens up—that primary significance closed off or covered over and eventually forgotten by purely logical structures in the name of the dominant term within the binary logic of metaphysics. As Heidegger puts it in *Being and Time*:

> If the question of Being is to achieve clarity regarding its own history, a loosening of the sclerotic tradition and a dissolving of the concealments produced by it is necessary. We understand this task as the *de-struction* [*Destruktion*] of the traditional content of ancient ontology which is to be carried out along the *guidelines of the question of Being*. This de-struction is based upon the original experiences in which the first and subsequently guiding determinations of Being were gained.
>
> This demonstration of the provenance of the fundamental ontological concepts, as the investigation which displays their "birth certificate," has nothing to do with a pernicious relativizing of ontological standpoints. The de-struction has just as little the *negative* sense of disburdening ourselves of the ontological tradition. On the contrary, it should stake out the positive possibilities of the tradition, and that always means to fix its *boundaries*. These are factually given with the specific formulation of the question and the prescribed demarcation of the possible field of investigation. Negatively, the de-struction is not even related to the past: its criticism concerns "today" and the dominant way we treat the history of ontology, whether it be conceived as the history of opinions, ideas, or problems. However the de-struction does not wish to bury the past in nullity; it has a *positive* intent. Its negative function remains tacit and indirect.[7]

If we are to gain new understanding of the essentially logocentric assumptions inscribed in the "disinterested" and "value-free" humanistic discourse of the Harvard Core Curriculum Report and, more important, in what it leaves unsaid about the educational imperatives of our historically specific occasion, it will be necessary to develop at some length what I take to be the essential project of this postmodern countermemory, which has as its broad purpose the de-struction of the ontotheological tradition in general, and its modern allotrope, what Michel Foucault has called "the disciplinary society," in particular.

III

Beginning with Nietzsche's genealogical critique of traditional historiography[8] and Husserl's phenomenological call to "return to the things themselves" (*zu den Sachen selbst*), this de-structive confrontation with the Western tradition vis-à-vis knowledge interprets the crisis of modernity as having its source in the hardening of what I have elsewhere called the metaphysical will to spatialize time.[9] To put it provisionally for the sake of orientation, this is the will to domesticate and thus minimize by *object*ifying the threatening uncanniness of *physis*, of things-as-they-are *as* be-*ing* (Heidegger's term is *die Unheimlichkeit*, the etymology of which points to the source of uncanniness), the will that, with the rise in the Renaissance and the Enlightenment of a humanism grounded in empirical reason and science, becomes an obsession to *dominate* nature, to force "her" to yield in every sense of the word to "Man's" desire. It is, as Heidegger puts it in an essay on Nietzsche's *Thus Spoke Zarathustra*, the "spirit of revenge against the transience of time," which begins with Plato's determination of "the earthly, the earth and all that is part of it," as *"me on*, non-being"[10] and culminates in the enframing (*Ge-stell*) of modern technology, which, in re-presenting being, transforms the earth—the mystery—into "standing reserve" (*Bestand*).[11]

To be more specific, the de-struction discloses that the Western tradition, since the time of the late classical Greek philosophers—and especially after Bacon, Descartes, and the revival of Roman humanistic education in the Renaissance—has increasingly interpreted the *logos* in the Aristotelian sentence "Man is the animal who is endowed with *logos*" "as 'reason,' 'judgment,' 'concept,' 'definition,' 'ground,' or 'relationship.' "[12] In so doing this "onto-theo-logical" tradition has covered over and eventually *forgotten* its origin in *legein* (to talk),[13] which itself is (un-)grounded in human being's radical temporality: in nothingness, in the absence of presence or, in terms that mediate Heidegger's "ontological difference" and Derrida's *differance*, in the difference that temporality always already disseminates, the difference that, in always already deferring presence, activates *interest*—and the metaphysical will to recuperate a lost origin.[14] To put Heidegger's genealogy in Derrida's terms, to which I will return, the de-struction discloses that the Western tradition at large, despite the apparent variations, has been a logocentric tradition, one based on a philosophy of presence—the mystified assumption of an original Identity (the Word, the Transcendental Signified) that has been dispersed with the "fall" into time. This logocentric/recuperative interpretation of human being thus results eventually in the total acceptance of the *secondary* or *derived* (constructed) notion of truth as correspondence—as agreement of the mind with its object of knowledge (Aristotle's *homoiosis*, Saint Thomas's *adequaetio intellectus et rei*).[15] Its hermeneutic corollary is the specular propositional language of assertion (judgment)—as original, natural, and self-evident.

Since judgment (i.e., propositional correctness or accuracy of correspondence) is the goal of the relationship between the inquiring mind and its object, the epistemological impulse behind the traditional notion of truth is to wrest the object (thing or human being) out of its existential, temporal context, the context of the lived world, of *differance*, to render it a *pure and shareable or consensual presence*. In so re-presenting time, human being as interpreter reduces his or her temporal being-in-the-world to a detemporalized and dedifferentiated series of "now points." It assumes, that is, the inauthentic stance of an "awaiting [*Gewärtigen*] which forgets and makes present."[16] Metaphysical thinking suspends and thus spatializes the temporal process, coerces the differences that temporality disseminates into an identical whole that can be seen all at once, as presence, from above. In thus reifying time, in thus bringing time to light, as it were, thinking and the thinking subject achieve "objectivity," the essential comportment (prior to being) of humanistic inquiry, indeed, of humanistically educated men and women; a dis-stance from the originative experience of the object which allows a thinking self to become a privileged observer, one who, from this disengaged distance, merely looks at or, rather, "*overlooks*"[17] synchronically the lived experience of being-in-the-world, as if it were a completed narrative. It is in thus separating the subject and object that the sedimented traditional understanding of truth as correspondence— the understanding of truth that, as I will suggest, continues to inform humanistic pedagogy—becomes static and visual. The interpretive expression of this "truth" becomes a constituted and *interested* "disinterestedness," a representation from the (preconceived) end. In Michel Foucault's more recent version, the secondariness of correspondence constructs an "archival" system of discourse.[18]

However, this "objectivity" is a fiction in a further sense. For the notion of correspondence conceals the fact that in this scheme of things mind (the subject) conveniently presupposes a rational or logocentric whole—a preestablished and preknown world order created by the infinite mind of God (which is made in Man's image)—that is *ontologically prior to physis* and thus is the measure of judgment. In other words, a de-struction of the epistemological instrument of the Western ontotheological tradition discloses that despite the surface differences between its positivist and idealistic variations—supplements, according to Derrida—the essential impulse informing its ontology has been increasingly to close off, re-present, or spatialize time as a means of transforming the differential essence of being (what Heidegger calls nothingness [*das Nichts*] in *Being and Time* and later *die Erde* [the earth]) into a certain identity. For what the de-struction discovers is that within the "self-evident" and privileged *logos-as-ratio* of the traditional understanding of truth is inscribed a more fundamental and inclusively "self-evident" ontological concept: the *logos* as eternal essence, *the Logos*, variously invoked in the history of Western ontology as "the Word," "the One," "the unmoved mover," "the beginning," "God," "the alpha and omega," "the absolute idea," "the final cause," "the principle of causality," "identity," or as Heidegger (and Derrida) have focalized it for our occasion, the *logos* as "permanent presence."[19] The de-struction, in other words, makes explicit—and here I take issue with a certain emphasis in Foucault—that Western thought does not constitute a history of radical disruptions in the ways of understanding, but rather a series of recuperative supplements—"of substitutions of center for center"[20]—that replaces one form of logocentrism, the authority of whose discourse has been discovered to be groundless, for another. It discloses that Western thought, from Plato through Saint Thomas to Descartes, Locke, Kant, Hegel, Bentham, and modern positivist science (especially in its technological allotrope) has been essentially a *metaphysical* tradition, in which, according to its familiar medieval formulation, essence precedes (is ontologically prior to) existence. Eternity precedes time; the one precedes the many; identity precedes difference.

The epistemology of the Western tradition and its practice and elaboration in higher education has grounded and continues to ground the meaning of being *meta-ta-physica*: from "beyond-what-is as such"[21] both in the related sense of *after* and *above*, from the specular distance of an end or *télos*. This epistemology has reified being, reduced verbal be-ing and its differential force to nominal Being, to a visually appropriatable super thing (*summum ens*) at rest, which comprehends (includes, contains, and determines) the motion of all things (including human being). In the rhetoric Heidegger uses in his destruction of the Platonic turn (his critique of the traditional concept of truth as idea or visual model, or as a determining methodology, i.e., as center or core, should be remarked):

> This transformation of unconcealment (*a-letheía*) by way of distortion to
> undistortion and thence to correctness [in the tradition], must be seen as one
> with the transformation of *physis* [being] to *idea*, of *logos* as gathering to *logos*
> as statement. On the basis of all this, the definitive interpretation of being
> that is fixated in the word *ousia* now disengages itself and comes to the fore.
> It signifies being in the sense of permanent presence, already-thereness.
> What actually has being is accordingly what always is, *aei on*. Permanently
> present [according to the metaphysical tradition] is what we must go back to
> in comprehending and producing: the model, the *idea*. Permanently present is
> what we must go back to in all *logos*, statement: it is what lies-before,
> *hypokeimenon, subjectum*. From this standpoint of *physis*, emergence, what
> was always there is the *proteron*, the earlier, the a priori.[22]

To appropriate a more recent rhetoric, the de-struction discloses the thought of the ontotheological tradition to be grounded in the principle that identity is the condition for the possibility of difference. It is this founding theoretical principle of metaphysics that enabled the technology of power: the scientific, economic, and sociopolitical "tables" allowing for the classification, distribution, hierarchization, supervision, and regularization of anatomical, monetary, and human differences within the enclosed space of the same. According to Foucault, these emerged, like mutations in the rational/scientific age of the Enlightenment, as the essential instruments of the modern disciplinary society, the society that harnesses knowledge to power, that pursues learning for the essential purpose, however benign in appearance, of reducing the potentially disruptive energies of differential human being to "docile and useful bodies":

> The first of the great operations of discipline is . . . the constitution of
> "*tableaux vivants*," which transform the confused, useless or dangerous
> multitudes into ordered multiplicities. The drawing of "tables" was one of the
> great problems of scientific, political and economic technology of the
> eighteenth century: how one was to arrange botanical and zoological gardens,
> and construct at the same time rational classifications of living beings; how
> one was to observe, supervise, regularize the circulation of commodities and
> money and thus build up an economic table that might serve as the principle
> of the increase of wealth; how one was to inspect men, observe their
> presence and absence and constitute a general and permanent register of the
> armed forces; how one was to distribute patients, separate them from one
> another, divide up the hospital space and make a systematic classification of
> diseases: these were all twin operations in which two elements—distribution
> and analysis, supervision and intelligibility—are inextricably bound up. In the
> eighteenth century, the table was both a technique of power and a procedure
> of knowledge. It was a question of organizing the multiple, of providing
> oneself with an instrument to cover it and to master it; it was a question of
> imposing upon it an "order." . . . Tactics, the spatial ordering of men;
> taxonomy, the disciplinary space of natural beings; the economic table, the
> regulated movement of wealth.[23]

However more sophisticated its theoretical articulation and effective its practical elaborations, the disciplinary table that emerges pervasively in the eighteenth century with the triumph of empirical science is fundamentally a spatialization of temporality: a visual image—a re-presentation—projected by a transcendental and teleological eye in which every thing and every event—known and unknown—is assumed to have its proper name and place in a larger, inclusive whole. The meaning and use of difference, in other words, is determined by the ontological priority of identity. The "microphysics of power" of the modern disciplinary society Foucault so brilliantly describes constitutes a historically specific manifestation of the essential principle that has defined

Western theory and practice, culture and sociopolitical organization, from its origins in classical antiquity.

This modification of Foucault's genealogy of the disciplinary society, this linking of Heidegger's ontological interrogation of the Western philosophical tradition at large with Foucault's interrogation of the post-Enlightenment West is important for my argument about modern educational theory and practice. As I will show more fully in the next chapter, it undermines the modern humanists' potential appeal to Foucault's discourse in their effort to recuperate the classical tradition — the *litterae humaniores* — in the face of the triumph of instrumental reason and the scientific education it has privileged over the humanities. The reform initiative of the Harvard core curriculum has emerged out of the debate over the respective roles in Anglo-American higher education of the humanities and the sciences initiated by Matthew Arnold and Thomas Henry Huxley at the end of the nineteenth century. This old but still productive debate was extended into the present by beleaguered humanists such as Irving Babbitt, F. R. Leavis (in his polemic against C. P. Snow), Lionel Trilling, and I. A. Richards (and the New Critics). To read Foucault's genealogy in the light of Heidegger's destruction, in other words, is to recognize that this debate is a familial quarrel, innocently irrelevant at best, because neither pole addresses itself to the ontological source of the crisis.

It is of paramount importance to emphasize that in thus grounding the be-ing of being in presence, metaphysical inquiry relegated becoming or, better, the differences time always already disseminates, to the status of the *apparent*. This distance of "objectivity" or "disinterestedness," "detachment" and "impartiality" (terms interchangeably privileged by scientists and humanists alike), metaphysics assumes, will *bring to light* and *focalize* the oneness of multiplicity, the linear and progressive directionality — the narrativity, as it were — of apparent erraticness, of accident or chance, that immediacy or, rather, *interest* (from *interesse*: to be in the midst, to care) obscures from view.[24] It is this metaphysical imperative, which reduces difference to identity, forces the particular into its *proper* place by means of spatialization, that has since Plato endowed privileged status on *visual perception* over the other senses in the pursuit of knowledge. To evoke what has been represented as a postmodern discourse, the structuralization of time has determined knowledge production in the Western tradition at large.

The rational eye of classical philosophers (from Plato to Leibniz, Kant, Hegel, and Bentham) and historiographers (from Thucydides and Polybius to Ranke and Dilthey) assumes that the eccentric course of time and history can be comprehended (in Hegel's sense) by disinterested observation. The empirical eye of the classical scientist or psychologist assumes with Newton that the fragmentary and accidental nature of physical or psychological evidence constitutes traces or clues, the gaps between which will eventually be filled to form the closed "whole picture." (I am thinking, for example, of Linnaeus's anatomical classifications, Mendeleev's periodic table, and a certain aspect of Freud's psychoanalysis of neurosis.) The objective eye of the classical realist novelist (whether Fielding, Defoe, Balzac, Thackeray, Zola, or Dreiser) assumes that the fortuitous events of human life can be narrated in a linear and progressive sequence toward an end that is always there from the beginning; i.e., can be re-presented in the form of time transformed into a circle. The inclusive (or ironic) imagination of the classical (or humanist) poet—from Virgil through Dante and Donne to T. S. Eliot—assumes that the disparity between things and between events in the temporal/spatial world will yield a subsuming and satisfying system of correspondences or myths for its supervisory gaze.

To put all this in terms that point to the project of education, de-struction ultimately makes explicit that the Western ontotheological tradition has assumed too unquestioningly that human beings exist in some kind of fallen state and therefore that the essential purpose of learning is self-evidently *recuperative*: to regain the heights—and the mental and spiritual well-being—from which they have fallen into the disease of time. It has assumed that the catastrophic fall was, in one way or another, a fall from the unity of being, oneness, totality, enlightenment, presence, eternity, truth, into division, multiplicity, nothingness, darkness, absence, time, error. As the postmodern counter-memory would put this paradigmatic Western structure, the tradition has assumed that the fall from the in-difference of perceptual wholeness was a dispersal of identity into difference (*differance*), in which presence is infinitely deferred and thus in which men and women exist in anxious and interested longing for the lost origin, for enlightenment. Nor is this diagnosis of the discourse of Western man restricted to postmodern philosophers such as Nietzsche, Heidegger, Derrida, Lacan, Foucault, Lyotard, Kristeva, and so on. It is also that of postmodern writers such as Samuel Beckett, Eugène Ionesco, Thomas Pynchon, and Charles Olson, to name only a few of those who have been explicit about it:

> Muthologos has lost ground since Pindar
> the odish-man sd: "poesy
> steals away men's judgment
> by her *muthoi* taking this crack
> at Homer's sweet-versing

> "and a blind heart
> is most men's portion." Plato
> allowed this divisive
> thought to stand, agreeing

> that *muthos* is false, *Logos*
> isn't—was facts. Thus
> Thucydides.

> I would be a historian as Herodotus was, looking
> for oneself
> for the evidence of
> what is said. . . . [25]

IV

Since Plato's allegory of the cave, but especially since the Roman appropriation of Greek thinking, the purpose of Western education (whatever its historically specific permutations) has been to lead Man (*ex ducere*) out of the darkness and depths of his fallen/temporal condition and into the universal light. As such, this is a nostalgic and recuperative (and patriarchal) activity intended to recover the homeland, the "lost" origin: to generate by means of the recollective memory a re-ascent to those lambent Olympian heights of certainty from which he has fallen into darkness, an essentially aesthetic (fictional) remembrance of prelapsarian origins beginning from the vantage point of an end (metaphysically). To focus the metaphorics of the eye (and its light) privileged by this metaphysical process, learning has meant to re-collect the dispersed tenses of time into its primal state as self-present, visible, and inclusive image.

This historical continuity, which begins with Plato's "correction" of Heraclitus, is what Heidegger implies in calling the Western tradition ontotheological. Whether Greek (onto-), medieval (theo-) or humanist (logo-), the theory and practice of education in the West, like philosophical and literary discourses, has been logocentric: a process oriented by a fixed, abiding and luminous Word willfully devoted to the reduction of time to a totalized circle, the center of which, as Derrida puts it, "is elsewhere" and thus "beyond the reach of play"[26] — and criticism. To put this analysis in terms of the Neitzschean metaphorics common to Heidegger, Derrida, Foucault, and other postmodern theorists of knowledge production, the theory and practice of education in the ontotheological tradition has been Apollonian, its purpose the domestication of the obscure Dionysiac force by bringing it to light, identifying its parts within a comprehensive and visible structure, and putting it to social use.

This model of humane learning, enabled by the formulation of the human condition as fallen, has been central to the Western tradition at large, despite the historically specific permutations effected by idealistic or empirical representations of the text of being. It is a model that has its origin in Plato's affirmation of a retro-spective memory as the essential agency of remembering the "truly real" world of Forms that the pre-existent soul loses sight of and eventually forgets in its birth (death) into the unreal and errant life of dispersed time:

> It is impossible for a soul that has never seen the truth to enter into our
> human shape; it takes a man to understand by the use of universals, and to
> collect out of the multiplicity of sense impressions a unity arrived at by a
> process of reason. Such a process is simply the recollection [anamnesis] of
> the things which our soul once perceived when it took its journey with a god,
> looking down from above on the things to which we now ascribe reality and
> gazing upward towards what is truly real. That is why it is right that the soul
> of the philosopher alone should regain its wings; for it is always dwelling in

memory as best it may upon those things which a god owes his divinity to dwelling upon. It is only by the right use of such aids to recollection, which form a continual intuition into the perfect mystic vision, that a man can become perfect in the true sense of the word. . . . Whole were we, unspotted by all the evils which awaited us in time to come, and whole and unspotted and changeless and serene were the objects revealed to us in the light of the mystic vision. Pure was the light and pure were we from the pollution of the walking sepulchre which we call a body to which we are bound like an oyster to its shell.[27]

This circular model is also inscribed in Hegel's enormously influential philosophy of the history of spirit. I quote from M. H. Abrams's summary account of the role of *Er-Innerung* (which means not only "internalization," as Abrams suggests, but, as Kierkegaard insistently demonstrates, "re-collection" in the sense of forcing the eccentricity of temporal process into the closed and centered circle—the fold, as it were) in the circuitous educational journey to *Wissenschaft* in *Phenomenology of Spirit* not simply for convenience. For Abrams's sympathetic—and disablingly innocent—analysis of Hegel's recollective approach to knowledge is the basis of his affirmation of the *essential* historical continuity of Western culture, from humanistic Christianity to Romantic humanism (Saint Augustine to Hegel, Schiller, Fichte, Schlegel, and even Marx and Nietzsche, for example; and in literature, from Dante to Romantics such as Wordsworth, Coleridge, Blake, and Shelley, and to post-Romantics or Modernists such as T. S. Eliot, Wallace Stevens, and D. H. Lawrence). Hegel provides the basis of Abrams's understanding of canon formation and of his more recent paradigmatic defense of the Western humanistic scholarly and critical tradition against the deconstructive criticism of Jacques Derrida, Paul de Man, J. Hillis Miller, Joseph Riddel, and others:[28]

Now, *Wissenschaft* is no other than the total dialectic of truth which is embodied in Hegel's own philosophical system, so that the tortuous educational journey of the spirit ends in the event toward which it has been unknowingly pointing from the beginning: its *accomplished* shape in the consciousness of the philosopher Hegel. But Hegel also says, the way by which consciousness reaches this goal of total self-knowledge [Identity or Self-Presence], or "the knowledge of [the object] as itself", is *by recollecting, reliving, and so "grasping,"* its own temporal past from the beginning up to the present, "in the form of shapes of the consciousness." (Hegel hyphenates the first occurrence of the word for recollection, *Er-Innerung*, in order to bring out the pun on "remembering" and "internalizing.") And this process by which consciousness recollects, reparticipates in, *assimilates* and so comes to *comprehend its identity* in its own past, as Hegel shows in a concluding reprise of his entire book, is precisely the history of evolving consciousness that has just been recollected and narrated in the *Phenomenology* itself, in the mode of a spiritual journey. "Thus," as Hegel says in his conclusion, "the goal which is absolute knowledge, or spirit knowing itself as spirit, has for its road [*Weg*] the recollection [*Er-Innerung*] of the spirits [*Geisten*], as they are in themselves, and as they carry out the organization of their realm.[29]

The inscription of the specular/circular (metaphysical) model has not been restricted to the discourses of humanistic idealism, as the previous examples might suggest. Heidegger has persuasively argued, in his aptly titled essay "The Age of the World Picture" (*Weltbild*), that the full implications of this model for knowledge at large culminate in the re-presentational discourse, prepared by Descartes, of the modern age of technology:

> Knowing, as research [which includes the human (in this case, historiographical) and physical sciences], calls whatever is to account with regard to the way in which and the extent to which it lets itself be put at the disposal of representation. Research has disposal over anything that is when it can either calculate it in its future course in advance or verify a calculation about it as past. Nature, in being calculated in advance, and history, in being historiographically verified as past, becomes, as it were, "set in place" [*gestellt*]. Nature and history become the objects of a representing that explains. . . . Only that which becomes object in this way *is*—is considered to be in being. We first arrive at science as research when Being of whatever is, is sought in such objectiveness.
>
> This objectifying of whatever is, is accomplished in a setting before, a representing, that aims at bringing each particular being before it in such a way that man who calculates can be sure, and that means be certain, of that being. We first arrive at science as research when and only when truth has been transformed into the certainty of representation. What it is to be is for the first time defined as the objectiveness of representing, and truth is first defined as the certainty of representating, in the metaphysics of Descartes. . . . The whole of modern metaphysics taken together, Nietzsche included, maintains itself within the interpretation of what it is to be and of truth that was prepared by Descartes.[30]

As the affiliation between the discourses of Plato, Hegel, Descartes, and the age of technology suggests, Western (official) educational theory and practice has been, with marginal(ized) but telling exceptions, a continuous or continuously *reconstructed* tradition. Apparent historical dissimilarities have in fact been substitutions or displacements of one organizing center for another, undertaken to contain the disruption of knowledge explosions. What Derrida says about the "whole history of the concept of structure"—that "[it] must be thought of as . . . a linked chain of determinations of the center," which, whatever the names given to it ("*eidos, arché, telos, energeia, ousia . . .*

consciousness, God, man, and so forth") designates an invariable presence—applies to the whole history of the Western *paideia*.

Whether grounded in Plato's philosophical idealism or Cicero's or Quintilian's Roman humanism; in Saint Augustine's psychobiographical or Saint Thomas's providential cosmic Christianity; Pico della Mirandola's or Marsilio Ficino's neo-Platonism; Francis Bacon's or René Descartes's or Jeremy Bentham's scientific humanism; Kant's or Hegel's Romantic or "natural supernatural" humanism; Matthew Arnold's or Irving Babbitt's or I. A. Richards's synoptic classicism; whether it is informed by the *studia humanitatis* of the Roman *paideia*, the trivium and quadrivium of the medieval schools, or the arts and sciences configuration of fields of the modern university, Western educational theory and practice, like philosophy and literature (especially literary criticism) has always assumed a prior unity of knowledge (and Being) inhering in the apparently dispersed, disseminating, and duplicitous multiplicity or difference of temporal being: what the Harvard Core Curriculum Report innocently—and pejoratively—calls "proliferation."

Despite the historically specific ruptures in the *epistème* calling the "naturalness" of the preceding paradigm into question, Western education has thus always reaffirmed a nostalgic and recuperative circuitous educational journey back to the origin. More specifically, it has always had as its essential purpose the domestication of new knowledge by resorting to the itinerary of the recollective cultural memory. I mean a memory taking the hermeneutic form of a "disinterested" suspension of the essentially uncertain temporal process and an insistent *looking back over* the past mediated by archival authority in search of the underlying universals informing the *apparently* discontinuous traces thrown up in and by time. It is this amnesiac recollective educational journey— epitomized by Dante's recuperation of Virgil (History) in *The Divine Comedy*[31]—that will enlighten the benighted student or disciple in the nether world and thus bring him or her, as errant prodigal, into the higher original region, the lost home. In the affiliated psychological terms epitomized by I. A. Richards's educational texts, it is a circuitous journey that will cure the sickness of desire, bring the diseased consciousness into the balanced and inclusive state of repose—the well-roundedness, as it were, of sanity and normalcy. In the sociopolitical terms epitomized by the Roman *paideia*, it is a circuitous journey that will render the errant student a good citizen. Whether the ideal model of mind is the philosopher king's, the Roman statesman's, the Christian saint's, the empirical detective's, or the liberally educated humanist's—humanists whose judgments are guided by "the best that has been thought and said [by Western Man]"—the Western *paideia* has been fundamentally, though with increasing assurance of its self-evidence, i.e., with greater forgetfulness, enabled above all by the colonization of a more originative Greek thinking—grounded in a recollective, a metaphysical or spatial, perception. It has always been inscribed by a metaphorics intended to annul anxiety and desire: to bring the student into a state of Apollonian repose.

This is the "conclusion" that Heidegger draws (tentatively, since his disclosure is inhibited by the vestigial remains of visualism in his version of phenomenology) in his destruction of the philosophical discourses of the ontotheological tradition. It is a conclusion reinforced by Michel Foucault, above all, in his analysis of the panoptic gaze,[32] and by Jacques Derrida, especially in his early essay "Force and Signification," which, taking its point of departure from Heidegger's (and Nietzsche's) interrogation of the privileged status accorded to Apollonian vision at the expense of Dionysiac force in the pursuit of knowledge, calls into question what he refers to interchangeably as the "heliocentrism" or "photology" of Western philosophy at large. Since Derrida's focus in this important essay, concerned with the privilege accorded to light and the eye over darkness by the logocentric tradition, has been unfortunately overlooked in favor of that accorded to speech over writing by his American followers in their effort to rethink the question of textual interpretation, the passage is worth quoting at some length:

> *To comprehend* the structure of becoming, the form of a force [read "temporality"], is to lose meaning by finding it. The meaning of becoming and of force, by virtue of their pure, intrinsic characteristics, is the repose of the beginning and the end, the peacefulness of a spectacle, horizon or face. Within this peace and repose the character of becoming and of force is disturbed by meaning itself. The meaning of meaning is Apollonian by virtue of everything within it that can be seen.
>
> To say that force is the origin of the phenomenon [Derrida here is alluding to the etymological source of the word, i.e., φώς, light] is to say nothing. By its very articulation force becomes a phenomenon [a picture seen]. Hegel demonstrated convincingly that the explication of a phenomenon by a force is a tautology. But in saying this, one must refer to language's [i.e., metaphysical language's] peculiar inability to emerge from itself in order to articulate its origin, and not to the *thought* of force. Force is the other of language without which language would not be what it is.
>
> In order to respect this strange movement within language, in order not to reduce it in turn, we would have to attempt a return to the metaphor of darkness and light (of self-revelation and self-concealment) *the founding* metaphor of Western philosophy as metaphysics. The founding metaphor not only because it is a photological one—and in this respect the entire history of our philosophy is a photology, the name given to a history of, or treatise on, light—but because it is a metaphor. Metaphor in general, the passage from one existent to another, or from one signified meaning to another, authorized by the initial *submission* of Being to the existent, the *analogical* displacement of Being, is the essential weight which anchors discourse in metaphysics, irremediably repressing discourse into its metaphysical state. . . . In this heliocentric metaphysics, force, ceding its place to *eidos* (i.e., the form which is visible for the metaphorical eye), has already been separated from itself in acoustics.[33]

The assimilative/recollective/visual (Apollonian) orientation, needless to say, has advanced Western knowledge about and power over "nature" beyond the wildest expectations of the late Greeks and Romans. But in the process and precisely because of the inherent secondary or constituted (distanced) status of disinterested observation, it has forgotten and alienated that which is more primordial than "nature": being, or rather the be-ing of being.[34] That is what I take Derrida to mean by "force" in the above passage. In recollecting the differences that temporality disseminates from the "infinitely negative" distance[35] — the "hovering" (Kierkegaard) or "free-floating" (Heidegger) of the spatial perspective — the metaphysical eye, however diverse its historically specific forms, achieves the advantage of such distance, of seeing *physis* as measurable *shape*, where immediately, "it" appears to be sheer contingency. This appropriation of *physis* as a geo-metry enabled by the overlooking metaphysical eye is manifest, for example, in Plato's absolutely original/final and fully established and determined Republic, which mirrors — re-presents — the transcendental realm of Ideal Forms; in Saint Augustine's prefigurative/providential history; in Hegel's circuitous history of the absolute spirit. But in the "blindness of its insight," to adapt Paul de Man's phrase,[36] the distanced Platonic or spatializing or, even better, aesthetic eye (for a metaphysical interpretation is, finally, a work of the esemplastic imagination) tends to *overlook* the dislocating, the disconcerting, contradictions, accidents, discontinuities, discordances, aporias, gaps (the *differance*) — even in its own rhetoric — in search of the inclusive (epiphanic) or en-cyclo-pedic whole, the enlightened *circle of Being*.[37] In thus shaping the be-ing of being into a satisfying structure or figure or picture made in Man's image, a re-presentational fiction that *places* us properly in the context of identity (the narrative of the *arché* or *télos*), Being defuses the force of temporal difference, of our occasion, by way of the satisfaction of fulfillment ("the repose of the beginning and end, the peacefulness of a spectacle, horizon or face") and annuls the very interest (care or desire) that originally generates the being-question. What Derrida says in the following decisive passage (to which I will return in chapter 2) about the "ultra-structuralist" interpretive strategy of the literary critic Jean Rousset applies as well not only to the interpretation of literary texts but to the representation of being itself in the entire ontotheological tradition:

> For the sake of determining an essential "Corneillean movement," does one
> not lose what counts? Everything that defies a geometrical-mechanical
> framework — and not only the pieces which cannot be constrained by curves
> and helices, not only force and quality, which are meaning itself, but also
> *duration*, that which is pure qualitative heterogeneity within movement — is
> reduced to the appearance of the inessential for the sake of this essentialism
> or teleological structuralism.[38]

To introduce a metaphor that will become increasingly important in my text, the spatializing eye enables Western Man to colonize or rather to colonialize (and pacify) the "other," which, *as* other, always threatens to disrupt the hegemonic aspirations of the West. The privileged spatializing eye enables not simply the domination of being as such, but of being understood as an indissoluble continuum or force field that includes the entire lateral spectrum from the ontological through the cultural to the sociopolitical site. Heidegger, for example, points precisely to this lateral relay—this simultaneous colonization of the ontological difference and the "other" worlds enabled by the spatializing gaze—when, in response to a Japanese interlocutor's observation that the modern East's great temptation is "to rely on European ways of representation and thus concepts," he adds: "That temptation is reinforced by a process which I would call the complete Europeanization of the earth and man."[39] And what Heidegger only suggests in passing, Edward Said fully articulates in his brilliant critique of Orientalism as a re-presentational discourse that has been the essential academic/pedagogical instrument in the West's sustained effort to dominate the Orient.

> I believe it needs to be made clear about cultural discourse and exchange
> within a culture that what is commonly circulated by it is not "truth" but
> representations. It hardly needs to be demonstrated again that language itself
> is a highly organized and encoded system, which employs many devices to
> express, indicate, exchange messages and information, represent, and so
> forth. In any instant of at least written language, there is no such thing as a
> delivered presence, but a *re-presence*, or a representation. The value, efficacy,
> strength, apparent veracity of a written statement about the Orient therefore
> relies very little, and cannot instrumentally depend, on the Orient as such.
> On the contrary, the written statement is a presence to the reader by virtue
> of its having excluded, displaced, made supererogatory any such *real thing* as
> the "Orient." Thus all of Orientalism stands forth and away from the Orient:
> that Orientalism makes sense at all depends more on the West than on the
> Orient, and this sense is directly indebted to various Western techniques of
> representation that make the Orient visible, clear, "there" in discourse about it.[40]

It is through this ability to colonize difference that the spatializing eye becomes the agent par excellence of the "spirit of revenge" against the dislocating transience of time which, according to Nietzsche's genealogy, constitutes the origin and driving force of Western nihilism.[41] This re-presentational gaze (and the *image* of being it constructs) is not simply an agency of ontological domination; it is also an instrument of cultural and sociopolitical repression. It is, to refer to two recent exemplary discourses that thematize the power informing and enabled by this spatial metaphorics, *both* the representational "calculative thinking"—"the technological method"—that "enframes" and reduces the differential things of this earth and its differential temporal processes into "standing reserve" or "stockpile" (Heidegger)[42] *and* the panoptic technology that produces the "disciplinary society" (Foucault).[43] This, notwithstanding Fredric Jameson's identification of postmodernism with the logic of late capitalism, is the testimony of contemporary theory and literary production at large.

The term "technological method" should not be taken, as it invariably is by professors of the humanities (I think of the example of F. R. Leavis) to refer simply to the limitations of positivistic scientific inquiry. The vicious circularity of technological method has been inscribed in all the disciplines. It is not only the classical physical sciences that privilege method — the mode of research that in beginning from the end predetermines the questions it can ask and the answers it receives and in doing so, as Gadamer has persuasively demonstrated, alienates rather than discovers truth.[44] Method is privileged also by the humanities: literary criticism, history, philosophy, and so on. Here, for example, in a discursive practice as innocent of its implications as that of the Harvard Core Curriculum Report, is a classic and still influential statement of the "technology" of reading espoused by the New Criticism, an interpretive method that, despite its loss of theoretical authority, continues to enjoy privileged status in introductory undergraduate courses in "practical criticism" or "literary analysis" everywhere in the academy.[45] Although the author is ostensibly attempting to define the modernity of modern poetry against the linear narrative sequence of realism, this should not obscure recognition that he is also and more fundamentally defining the hermeneutics of the New Critics (who, of course, took as their model the lyrical poem) or, more accurately, their formalist representation of such modernist poems as Ezra Pound's "In a Station of the Metro," W. B. Yeats's "Sailing to Byzantium," T. S. Eliot's "Sweeney Among the Nightingales," and Wallace Stevens's "Anecdote of the Jar." Nor should we take at his word the author's all-too-easy assumption that this "spatial form" and the interpretive method it enabled constitutes a revolutionary departure from the linear/narrative mode of perception generally characterizing the poetic and interpretive practices of Western writers and critics since the "dissociation of sensibility" in the Renaissance; since, that is, the rise of positivistic science:

> Esthetic form in modern poetry . . . is based on a space-logic that demands a complete re-orientation in the reader's attitude towards language. Since the primary reference of any word-group is to something inside the poem itself, language in modern poetry is really reflexive: the meaning-relationship is completed only by the simultaneous perception in space of word-groups which, when read consecutively in time, have no comprehensible relation to each other. Instead of the instinctive and immediate reference of words and word-groups to the objects or events they symbolize, and the construction of meaning from the sequence of their references, modern poetry asks its readers to suspend the process of individual reference temporarily until the entire pattern of internal references can be apprehended as a unity.[46]

What I am suggesting, at the risk of premature misunderstanding, is that *both* classical science *and* classical idealism, both causal and spatial interpretive practices, both the scientific and humanistic *paideias* sponsored by the "adversary" Two Cultures, are determined by the impulse to spatialize (or reify) time. However ironic the oversight, it is no accident that, in his effort to distinguish Modernist from traditional realist form, Joseph Frank recuperates the very term Henri Bergson uses to characterize the procedures and goals (and limitations) of empirical science:

> The main object of science is to forecast and measure: now we cannot forecast physical phenomena except on condition that we assume that they do not endure as we do; and, on the other hand, the only thing we are able to measure is space. Hence the break here comes about of itself between quality and quantity, between true duration and pure extensity. But when we turn to our conscious states [characterized by *durée réele*] we have everything to gain by keeping up the illusion through which we make them share in the reciprocal externality of outer things because this distinctness, and at the same time this solidification, enables us to give them fixed names in spite of their instability and distinct ones in spite of their interpenetration. It enables us to objectify them, to throw them out into the [sequential] current of social life.[47]

In this series of false oppositions, that is, both terms are oriented by a metaphysical or logocentric perspective that *looks back* retrospectively from the end (in both senses of the word)—from after or above the temporal process, "future anteriorly," in the resonant phrase Althusser applies to "tendentious" humanist (Hegelian) readers of the young Marx's texts.[48] In their re-collective projects, both thus exclude or repress or forcibly accommodate the differences that would disrupt the identity of that which is being produced, interpreted, or explained (taught). Both, in short, are inscribed by the spatial model of the centered circle. As such, both become agencies of the will to power over temporality and difference. There is, in this fundamental respect, no difference—as the affiliated metaphorics of power and making visible suggest— between the scientific method proffered by Francis Bacon to his contemporaries in the face of the death of Elizabeth as the means of "putting nature on the rack to make her yield up her secrets" and the "mythic method" proffered by T. S. Eliot as a means of giving "a shape and a significance" to the fragmented modern world, the world disintegrated by World War I:

> In using the myth [of *The Odyssey*], in manipulating a continuous parallel between contemporaneity and antiquity, Mr. Joyce is pursuing a method which others must pursue after him. . . . It is simply a way of controlling, of ordering, of giving a shape and a significance to the immense panorama of futility and anarchy which is contemporary history. . . . Instead of narrative

method, we may now use the mythical method. It is, I seriously believe, a step toward making the modern world possible for art.[49]

Of this same nature is the structuralist method profferred by Claude Lévi-Strauss in the aftermath of World War II "to reduce apparently arbitrary data . . . to a meaningful system":

What is the virtue of reduction either of scale or in the number of properties? It seems to result from a sort of reversal in the process of understanding. To understand a real object in its totality we always tend to work from its parts. The resistance it offers us is overcome by dividing it. Reduction in scale reverses this situation. Being smaller, the object as a whole seems less formidable. By being quantitatively diminished, it seems to us qualitatively simplified. More exactly, this quantitative transposition extends and diversifies our power over a homologue of the thing; and by means of it the latter can be grasped, assessed and apprehended at a glance. A child's doll is no longer an enemy, a rival or even an interlocutor. In it and through it a person is made into a subject. In the case of miniatures, in contrast to what happens when we try to understand an object or a living creature of real dimensions, knowledge of the whole precedes knowledge of the parts. And even if this is an illusion, the point of the procedure is to create or sustain the illusion, which gratifies the intelligence and gives rise to a sense of pleasure which can already be called aesthetic on these grounds alone.[50]

However different the mode of inquiry they espouse and the historical context from which they emerge, these synecdochical passages represent a significant continuity spanning the centuries of modernity. To recall Derrida, they constitute "a series of substitutions of center for center," "a linked chain of determinations of the center," in which "successively and in regulated fashion the center receives different forms or names." And in each case knowledge is understood in terms of visibility and power, that is, as an agency of certitude on the basis of which "anxiety," whether it takes the form of ontological decentering (absence of presence) or cultural proliferation (a knowledge explosion) or sociopolitical upheaval, "can be mastered."

If, therefore, the postmodern interrogation of modern humanistic education is to achieve effectiveness, the constructed ontological continuity discovered by the destruction of the ontotheological tradition to underlie the historically specific differences between classical antiquity, medieval Europe, and the postindustrial West needs to be marked. It has been the insistent claim of humanists in general since the Enlightenment that, in rejecting the Word of God in favor of the mind of mortal Man, humanism posits a *dis-interested* and *natural* mode of inquiry in its pursuit of knowledge. Humanism, according to this representation, is thus immune to the charge of constructing the

truth by the coercion of the real. Understood in the context disclosed by the destruction of the ontotheological tradition, however, such a claim and justification becomes at
least problematic. Humanistic inquiry in general appears to be at odds with Christian
inquiry (theology), and yet it is fundamentally the same in one crucial respect: the illuminating narrative it articulates is determined by a Transcendental Signified beyond
the reach of the free play of criticism. It simply substitutes the anthropo-logos for the
theo-logos. As Foucault puts this complicity between God and Man (in an essay on
Nietzsche that seems to contradict or qualify his analysis of Western history as a series
of radical epistemic breaks):

> The lofty origin [of the humanist historian whom the antihumanist genealogist
> mocks] is no more than "a metaphysical extension which arises from the
> belief that things are most precious and essential at the moment of birth." We
> tend to think that this is the moment of their greatest perfection, when they
> emerged dazzlingly from the hands of a creator or in the shadowless light of a
> first morning. The origin always precedes the Fall. It comes before the body,
> before the world and time; it is associated with the gods, and its story is
> always sung as a theogony. But historical beginnings are lowly: not in the
> sense of modest or discreet like the steps of a dove, but derisive and ironic,
> capable of undoing every infatuation. "We wished to awaken the feeling of
> man's sovereignty by showing his divine birth: this path is now forbidden;
> since a monkey stands at the entrance."[51]

In disclosing the similarities between theological discourse and anthropological discourse, I do not want to minimize the difference between them. But the difference is
not the radical one all too easily assumed by the modern practitioners of humanist inquiry. The difference, rather, is a matter of the *visibility* of the metaphysics, specifically
of the ontological priority of identity over difference; or to put it in terms of the metaphorics I am interrogating in this text, of the center (and the power informing it) over
the periphery that determines both discourses. The great achievement of the humanist
problematic[52] was to conceal—to render invisible—the "center elsewhere" it appropriated from medieval Christianity. It not only made its discourse and its institutions
invulnerable to criticism; it also enabled the extension of its hegemony.

Furthermore, to interpret the history of the Western tradition as a series of
epistemic breaks, as some postmodern theorists do, lends itself to the purposes of the
advocates of the *litterae humaniores* in their debate with the proponents of scientific
education. Thus, for example, Foucault's genealogy of the disciplinary society—his attribution of its origins to the epistemic break that produced the Enlightenment—has
made it possible for humanists to misread his analysis of the technology of power.
Foucault's emphasis upon tables, anatomical diagrams, classificatory procedures, and
the panoptic spatial arrangements brought to fruition by Bentham's Panopticon creates

an analysis restricted to the cultural effects of post-Enlightenment positivistic science. In thus minimizing the continuity of the Western tradition—its narrative of history—in favor of historical mutations, certain aspects of postmodern theory have been used to validate and even reinforce the false and secondary opposition between the humanities and the sciences, thus reinscribing in contemporary terms the very old *querelle des anciens et modernes.*

I do not want to discount the historically specific variations of educational theory and practice in Western history. They are crucial. But it is especially important to thematize these as historically specific variations *within* the ontotheological tradition: to make explicit the ontological ideology—the will to power over being enabled by metaphysics and its recollective eye—that subsumes the various discourses (whether humanistic or scientific) determining educational practice in Western history: Plato's *Republic*, Cicero's *De Oratore*, Augustine's *De Doctrina Christiana*, Hugh Saint Victor's *Didascalion*, Thomas Aquinas's *Summa theologica*, Campanella's *City of the Sun*, Elyot's *Boke of the Governour*, Francis Bacon's *Advancement of Learning*, Diderot's (et al.) *Encyclopédie*, Hegel's *Phenomenology of Spirit*, Humbolt's *Über die innere und aussere Organisation der höheren wissenschaftlicher Anstalten in Berlin*, Schiller's *On the Aesthetic Education of Man*, Matthew Arnold's *Culture and Anarchy*, T. H. Huxley's essays on science and education, C. P. Snow's *Two Cultures*, F. R. Leavis's *Two Cultures?*, John Dewey's *Experience and Education*, Robert Hutchins's *Higher Learning in America*, I. A. Richards's *Speculative Instruments*, the so-called Harvard Red Book (*General Education in a Democratic Society*), to name but a handful of historically influential texts. For, as I have suggested, such a thematization does not only demystify the opposition between the humanities and the classical sciences that continues to legitimate the institutions of learning that, in turn, reproduce the dominant culture. It also calls into question the vestigially disciplinary approaches taken by various contemporary theorists in their critique of the dominant culture. However persuasive their disclosures, these discourses of the countermemory minimize the effectiveness of their critique of the institutions of learning by tending to situate their interrogations at relatively particular sites. To put it another way, these discourses take one or another site to be the base of superstructural epiphenomena—for example, the question of being (Heidegger), language (Derrida), historical discursive formations (Foucault), the textual subject (Lacan), the material economy (Althusser), and gender (Cixous).

If there is anything that postmodern theory *in general* has disclosed, it is that power since the Enlightenment has been increasingly hegemonic. Power does not reside in any particular formation, but is always already distributed throughout the indissoluble continuum of being from ontological representations through cultural and sociopolitical relations, however overdetermined certain apparatuses of power may be at any specific place and occasion. This disclosure of the postmodern countermemory is especially crucial at the present historical conjuncture, in which the "revolutions" in Eastern and Central Europe—the self-destruction of a sociopolitical order characterized by a more or less direct and visible use of power justified by a base/superstructure economic model of history—is being represented in Europe and especially in America as the triumph of (humanistic) democracy over communist totalitarianism. To portray the revolution and the end of the Cold War in the traditional disciplinary terms of a base/superstructure model, whether the base is understood as the forces of material production or the political order or even the cultural formation, is to leave the ontological ground of such a representation intact. Because the institutions of higher learning are collectively the Western capitalist state's essential agency for the reproduction of the sovereign individual and the transmission of the repressive hypothesis—the metaphysical assumption that knowledge (as *adequaetio intellectus et rei*) is the essential adversary of power—the postmodern critique of the dominant sociopolitical formation (what Foucault calls the "disciplinary society") must be utterly transdisciplinary.

As modern history bears sad witness, a model of critical inquiry such as Heidegger's, which has its determining base in the ontological question, is inadequate to the critique of the complex relay of power relations characterizing the contemporary historical conjuncture. But it is also the case that a model of critical inquiry grounded in one or another of the more visible "political" sites that treats the ontological site as a superstructure is far from adequate to this task. This, as I will show, is the testimony of the event of the Vietnam War, a witness remarked by the political transformation of Eastern Europe, especially by its representation as the triumph of truth over power.

Two

Humanistic Inquiry and the Politics of the Gaze

> How many [teachers] (the majority) do not even begin to suspect
> the "work" the system (which is bigger than they are and
> crushes them) forces them to do, or worse, put all their heart
> and ingenuity into performing it with the most advanced
> awareness (the famous new methods!). So little do they suspect
> it that their own devotion contributes to the maintenance
> and nourishment of this ideological representation of the School,
> which makes the School today as "natural," indispensable,
> useful and even beneficial for our contemporaries as the Church
> was "natural," indispensable and generous for our
> ancestors a few centuries ago.
>
> Louis Althusser, "Ideology and Ideological State Apparatuses"

> Any attempt to "soften" the power of the oppressor in deference
> to the weakness of the oppressed almost always manifests
> itself in the form of false generosity; indeed, the attempt never
> goes beyond this. In order to have the continued opportunity
> to express their "generosity," the oppressors must perpetuate
> injustice as well. An unjust social order is the permanent fount of
> this "generosity," which is nourished by death, despair, and
> poverty. That is why the dispensers of false generosity become
> desperate at the slightest threat to its source.
>
> Paolo Friere, *Pedagogy of the Oppressed*

I

In the preceding chapter, I situated my inquiry into the pedagogy of humanism at the site of ontology in order to suggest the continuity between the various historically specific representations of reality (and the educational discourses transmitting them) in the ontotheological tradition, the tradition, in more familiar terms, that has come to be called "the West." To put it another way, my ontological focus was intended to thematize the metaphysics that "worldly" critics all too insistently overlook or minimize in their interrogation of the dominant culture of the present historical conjuncture: the hegemony of what has been variously called humanism, bourgeois capitalism, the consumer society, *la sociètè de la spectacle*, late capitalism, the age of the world picture, or the disciplinary society.

I did not want to suggest that the historically specific conjuncture is irrelevant to the critique of modern educational theory and practice. On the contrary, this relative indifference to the historical occasion results in the essential limitation of Derridian deconstruction. Its tendency to understand discourse as textuality—as a transhistorical base to epiphenomenal superstructural phenomena—paradoxically reduces the text's historically specific difference and the *difference* it makes in the world, to an indifferent *differance*.[1] This relative indifference to the historicity of discourse, one need hardly add, also results in the essential weakness of Heidegger's destructive hermeneutics. In tending to limit the interrogation of the ontotheological tradition to the question of being (*die Seinsfrage*) it overlooks the affiliation between philosophy and sociopolitical formations. In this and the following chapters I want to situate my inquiry into the educational discourse of modern humanism at the site of sociopolitics.

Several adversarial theoretical discourses are competing for authority in the interrogation of the dominant culture and the sociopolitical formations it legitimates: the discourses of textuality, of psychoanalysis, of ontology, of feminism, of critical genealogy, of neo-Marxism, to name only the most prominent. Vestigially bound by the old rules of disciplinary discourse, each of these interpretive strategies *tends* to assume a base/superstructure model. Each, that is, assumes that the site at which it situates its own inquiry constitutes the determining ground of all the other (superstructural) regions of knowledge, which thus tend to be represented as epiphenomenal. Understood in terms of the questions they have raised in their common demystification of the humanist discourse of the dominant culture—questions about consciousness, language, culture, gender, race, society, politics (about which the "value-free" problematic of humanism is necessarily blind)—a different understanding of the base/superstructure model suggests itself.

According to my reading of the destruction—a reading I believe is latent in Heidegger's destructive hermeneutics—the sites that the base and superstructure include are not in essence hierarchically ordered but laterally equiprimordial. They exist along an indissoluble and interpenetrating force field of lived experience, unevenly developed at any historically specific moment. Such critical destruction understands the constituted history of "the West" as a *process of reconstitutions*, a process characterized by periods of relative stability all along the lateral field of forces that undergo destabilization when their internal contradictions surface as disruptive events or, in Foucault's phrase, "discursive explosions."[2] These, in turn, are *accommodated* by the substitution of another constituted center. In this process of accommodation to the "new" center, a particular historical conjuncture overdetermines one or more discursive sites at the expense of the visibility of the others. (It is in this sense that one could say that the lateral field of forces is always unevenly developed at any historically specific moment in the tradition.) As a consequence of this historical overdetermination, it *appears* that the overdetermined site (or sites) is determinant of the less visible ones: that it constitutes the base that shapes its superstructural manifestations.

This, to take one of the most obvious and crucial examples, is how Marx and Engels tended to read the historically specific conjuncture in which they lived and wrote. With the rise of capital and the material productive mechanisms in the European nation-states, it was the material economy that became overdetermined. That overdetermination seemed to Marx and Engels, however insistent their qualifications, to constitute the base of and for such superstructural phenomena as language, culture and its institutions, gender relations, law, and sociopolitical formations. This insight, always problematic in Marx's and Engels's discourse, was institutionalized by their more doctrinaire ephebes. It became "Marxism": a historical determinism grounded in the means of production and a discursive practice of "social realism" that profoundly minimized the active roles played by the subject, culture, language, and social, political, and gender formations in the dominant order's effort to legitimate and extend its hegemony.

In the twentieth century, however, following the collapse of imperialism during World War I and the accommodation of the new and essentially disruptive knowledge it released within the inclusive network of information theory and retrieval technologies, the economic site as defined by Marx and Engels, and as defined more rigidly by the discourse of social realism (i.e., Stalinism), lost its privileged status in favor of the newly overdetermined discursive site. This crisis of Marxism, I suggest, explains the massive and essentially positive effort on the part of neo-Marxist and other "worldly critics" of the post-War West—from Gramsci and the Frankfurt School through Althusser, Poulantzas, Macherey, and Jameson to Foucault, Kristeva, Lyotard, Habermas, Williams, and Said—to readjust the Marxist base/superstructure model to accommodate itself to this overdetermined site.[3] One recognizes this strategy of accommodation, for example, in the otherwise valuable revisionist Marxism of Louis Althusser, which criticizes Marxist economism as an "analytico-teleological" theory that recuperates Hegelianism and which attempts to give semi-autonomy to superstructural overdeterminations. But the metaphysics of even Althusser's anti-Hegelian Marxism is betrayed by his insistence on the determination of the superstructure by the modes of production "in the last instance."[4] It is this determinism inhering in the base/superstructure model that Raymond Williams finds in the discourse not only of "vulgar" Marxists but also in that of recent revisionist Marxists like Althusser:

> In the transition from Marx to Marxism, and then in the development of
> expository and didactic formulations, the words used in the original
> arguments were projected, first, as if they were precise concepts, and
> second, as if they were descriptive terms for observable "areas" of social life.
> The main sense of the words in the original arguments had been relational,

but the popularity of the terms tended to indicate either (a) relatively enclosed categories or (b) relatively enclosed areas of activity. These were then correlated either temporally (first material production, then consciousness, then politics and culture) or in effect, forcing the metaphor, spatially (visible and distinguishable "levels" or "layers"—politics and culture, then forms of consciousness, and so on down to the "base.")[5]

Williams's awareness of the disabling disciplinary aspects of the Marxist critique of the postindustrial West precipitates his own revision of the Marxist project, a revision that collapses the hierarchical and temporally sequential distinction between base and superstructure in favor of the absolute *indissolubility* of the relationship between the base and superstructural formations. It is a revision, in other words, that rejects the base/superstructure *model* (and its secondary or derivative thinking) on the grounds of its reductive spatialization (and disciplining) of temporal phenomena (its appropriation of the metaphysical principle that identity—here, economy—is the condition for the possibility of difference—the individualized superstructural sites) in favor of a historical materialism understood as "specific indissoluble real processes."

What is fundamentally lacking, in the theoretical formulations of this important period, is any adequate recognition of the indissoluble connections between material production, political and cultural institutions and activity, and consciousness. . . . What is wrong with [these formulations] is [their] description of these "elements" as "sequential," when they are in practice indissoluble: not in the sense that they cannot be distinguished for purposes of analysis, but in the decisive sense that these are not separate "areas" or "elements" but the whole, specific activities and products of real men. That is to say, the analytic categories, as so often in idealistic thought, have, almost unnoticed, become substantive descriptions, which then take habitual priority over the whole social process to which, as analytic categories, they are attempting to speak. Orthodox analysts began to think of "the base" and "the superstructure" as if they were separable concrete entities. In doing so they lost sight of the very processes—not abstract relations but constitutive processes—which it should have been the special function of historical materialism to emphasize.[6]

Indeed, if Williams's more originative definition of the relationship between base and superstructure includes the ontological site, it would coincide with the point I have been making about the equiprimordiality of the various sites in the force field of being. In other words, the Heideggerian notion of the continuum of being—if we understand "continuum" as a lateral relationship of forces and "being" as be-*ing*, as temporality (or more specifically, as the differences that temporality disseminates) rather than as a transcendental (or derived) category—provides the context for a material theory of historical inquiry capable of reconciling the ontological and the sociopolitical critiques of the dominant order without either recuperating a teleological or metaphysical origin or discounting the repressive power inhering in the spatial metaphorics privileged by the ontotheological tradition. I am, of course, referring to the perennial metaphorics of the panoptic eye, of light and darkness, of the centered circle, which continues to exert its silent and invisible power everywhere in the present historical conjuncture, not only in the classical physical and social sciences, as Foucault, for example, tends to imply, but also—and most discreetly—in the discursive practices of the liberal arts. Because critique is interested, it must focus on the overdetermined site that generates interest; in the case of the present conjuncture, on the positivist technology of information retrieval. But to do so without recognition of the ideological linkage at work in all the sites is to weaken the effectiveness of critique.

Understood in the context of this destructive reading of history, then, the temporal "progress" of Western civilization (including the educational paradigms it has elaborated) has involved the eventual exploitation of the indissoluble relationship between visual (spatial) perception of things-as-they-are and cultural, economic, and sociopolitical power. To be more specific, what from the beginning of the Western tradition was a tentative, discontinuous, and unevenly developed intuition of this relationship coalesced in the *epistème* variously called the Enlightenment, the Age of Reason, bourgeois capitalism, the *epistème*, according to Michel Foucault, that constituted the subject (the individual) in order to facilitate the achievement of sociopolitical consensus (identity). To put it another way, this "progress" has involved the eventual recognition of the integral relationship between the perennially and increasingly privileged figure of the centered circle as the image of beauty and perfection and the centered circle as the ideal instrument of a totalized sociopolitical domination. Post-Renaissance humanists, that is, intuited the inherent "strength" (which from a destructive perspective discloses its essential weakness) of the older metaphysical epistemology: its ability to *see* or re-*present* the differential temporal process as *integral* and *inclusive* picture (table, blueprint, design) or, negatively, to lose *sight* of and forget difference, in the pursuit of the certainty (distance) of logocentric order. As a result, they transformed the oversight of the metaphysical perspective into a pervasive methodological or disciplinary instrument for the discreet coercion of difference into identity all through the field of forces that being comprises, from the ontological and epistemological sites through language and culture (*paideia*) to economics and sociopolitics (gender, family, state). More accurately, the intuition of the power inhering in visualization enabled the humanist tradition to harness difference (the individual entity) to the purposes of normalization and utility.

This "speculative instrument" (a resonant phrase used by I. A. Richards to epitomize his vision of the modern university), which has its origins in Western antiquity, has inscribed its visual/recollective interpretive imperative into all phases of Western culture. It continues in the present to serve the dominant social formation that benefits most from the circumscription and colonization of the earth: the computerized capitalist establishment.

Heidegger limited his destructive hermeneutics by and large, though not exclusively, to the philosophical discourses of the ontotheological tradition. For him, the destruction of the priority accorded to the spatializing eye by the Western philosophical tradition took the form of the disclosure of its ontological *limitations*: that metaphysical inquiry resulted in the distortion of "truth," in an "overlooking," "leveling," and "forgetting" of the ontological difference, the difference that temporal being always already disseminates. As a consequence of his focus on the ontological site, he remained relatively blind to its emancipatory potential at the site of sociopolitics. Heidegger's blindness, needless to say, had unfortunate consequences for his understanding of his historically specific German occasion. In the period of his rectorship of Freiburg University and for some time after, he did apply his destructive hermeneutics to the domain of German politics. But his failure to think its sociopolitical imperatives concretely and deeply resulted in his support of a totalitarian regime that he interpreted to be emancipatory. Despite his own tendency to represent the ontological site as a base, however, Heidegger's insistence in *Being and Time* on the equiprimordiality of the constitutive structures that make up being-in-the-world, specifically *Dasein*'s state of mind (*Befindlichkeit*), understanding (*Verstehen*), and discourse (*Rede*), suggests that the temporality of being-in-the-world is not a base to superstructural epiphenomena: "The phenomenon of the *equiprimordiality* of [these] constitutive items," he writes, "has often been disregarded in ontology, because of a methodologically unrestrained tendency to derive everything and anything from some simple 'primal ground.' "[7] This suggests that the temporality of being-in-the-world is an always transforming, unevenly developed field of forces encompassing all the "regions" between ontology and sociopolitics. It thus becomes possible to recognize that wherever (and whenever) one situates inquiry, whether at the site of being, of the subject, of gender, of law, of culture, of education, or of the sociopolitical formation, one is also inquiring into all the other sites.

More specifically, it becomes possible to conceive of destructive hermeneutics as an emancipatory practice occurring all along the continuum of being, from ontology to sociopolitics. In other words, though Heidegger chose to interrogate the dominant order at a site that his historical occasion had underdetermined, this does not invalidate his disclosures, nor does it disable his destructive hermeneutics as a means of simultaneously interrogating those overdetermined sites, especially the sociopolitical, that Heidegger himself by and large neglected or misrepresented. Indeed, as the following unremarked moment in "Letter on Humanism" suggests, such a passage from ontological to sociopolitical critical practice is latent in Heidegger's destructive effort to reinsert being in historicity:

Homelessness is coming to be the destiny of the world. Hence it is necessary to think that destiny in terms of the history of Being. What Marx recognized in an essential and significant sense, though derived from Hegel, as the estrangement of modern man has its roots in the homelessness of modern man. This homelessness is specifically evoked from the destiny of Being in the form of metaphysics and through metaphysics is simultaneously entrenched and covered up as such. Because Marx by experiencing estrangement attains an essential dimension of history, the Marxist view of history is superior to that of other historical accounts. But since neither Husserl nor—so far as I have seen till now—Sartre recognizes the essential importance of the historical in Being, neither phenomenology nor existentialism enters that dimension within which a productive dialogue with Marxism first becomes possible. . . . No matter which of the various positions one chooses to adopt toward the doctrines of communism and to their foundations, from the point of view of the history of Being it is certain that an elemental experience of what is world-historical speaks out in it.[8]

In the specific terms of my destructive inquiry at the site of contemporary education, recognition of the temporality of being as a lateral continuum or field of forces makes explicit the "affiliations" (in Edward Said's term)[9] between the inactive epistemological oversight, leveling, and forgetting of difference by inquiring *metá-tá-physicá* and the active (if largely rarefied) repression, territorialization, and colonization of the sociopolitical "other" enabled by the supervisory panoptic machinery of our overdetermined disciplinary society. In other words, such a recognition makes possible a productive dialogue between Heidegger's ontological critique and the worldly critics', especially Foucault's, secular critiques of the modern West; between, that is, the former's de-struction of the ontotheological tradition and the latter's genealogical history of the disciplinary society.

I am suggesting, in short, the following historical narrative enacted by the inscribed tendencies of the grave "objective" metaphysical eye to *overlook* deviations: what Blake called the disconcerting "minute particulars," Heidegger "ontological difference" (or the temporality of being), Derrida "*differance*," and Foucault "the singular event." This oversight, which has as its vantage point a Transcendental Signified (the logocentric One, as it were) inevitably, however erratically, became in time (during the Enlightenment) a willful, indeed *mono*maniacal obsession of rationality to name, comprehend, and control the potentially disruptive mystery of difference, which, in turn, precipitated the generalized calculative reformative cultural and sociopolitical strategy of *sur-veillance* or *super-vision*. The centered circle, the figure of beauty/perfection idealized by the post-Socratics, came to be understood and utilized in the modern world as the discreet figure of sociopolitical power. However outrageous it may at first seem to the innocent and well-intentioned disinterested humanist or liberally educated man or woman, this disciplinary strategy—this technology of power—which has as its end the coercive re-formation of de-formed entities or, what is the same thing, the re-center-ing of the de-centered center and thus of ec-centric or err-atic being, in the name of the logocentric norm (the guardian eye) of bourgeois humanism and the consumer cap-italist power structure—has been the real agenda informing the "disinterested," "lib-eral" discourse of the post-Enlightenment university.

That norm is also the real agenda inscribed in the apparently innocuous, highly con-sensual project to recuperate the core curriculum initiated by the Harvard faculty in the aftermath of the Vietnam War. The thesis I am suggesting is significantly strengthened when this reformist project is understood to constitute an effort to recuperate for "the last third of the twentieth century"[10] the highly disciplinary "synoptic" idea of the uni-versity envisioned by the (English) philosopher/literary critic I. A. Richards, in his con-tribution to the establishment of the general education program at Harvard in the 1940s, the period of the Cold War.[11] Richards's synoptic idea of the university, as I will show in chapter 3, had as its model the "inclusive" and "autonomous" poem impervi-ous to the ironies of historicity: the transcendental poetics he developed as a literary critic was instrumental in establishing literary study as a rigorous (New Critical) disci-pline in North America.

II

It is not the explicit intention of Michel Foucault's genealogical analysis of the theory and practice of humanist society in *Surveiller et punir* (1975) to extend the scope of Heidegger's destructive hermeneutics. Indeed, Foucault seems to reject an under-standing of Western history in terms of continuity—of an ontotheological tradition—though the too easy acceptance of this dissociation by those Foucault has influenced has obscured the affinities between his thought and that of Heidegger. These affinities may, in fact, be a matter of influence, as Foucault's remarks in his last interview suggest.

> For me Heidegger has always been the essential philosopher. I began by
> reading Hegel, then Marx, and I set out to read Heidegger in 1951 or 1952;
> then in 1952 or 1953—I don't remember any more—I read Nietzsche. I still
> have here the notes that I took when I was reading Heidegger. I've got tons
> of them. And they are much more important than the ones I took on Hegel
> and Marx. My entire philosophical development was determined by my
> reading of Heidegger. I nevertheless recognized that Nietzsche outweighed
> him. I do not know Heidegger well enough: I hardly know *Being and Time*
> nor what has been published recently. My knowledge of Nietzsche certainly is
> better than my knowledge of Heidegger. Nevertheless, these are the two
> fundamental experiences I have had. It is possible that if I had not read
> Heidegger, I would not have read Nietzsche. I had tried to read Nietzsche in

the fifties but Nietzsche alone did not appeal to me—whereas Nietzsche and Heidegger: that was a philosophical shock. But I have never written anything on Heidegger, and I wrote only a very small article on Nietzsche. . . . In the end for me there are three categories of philosophers: the philosophers that I don't know; the philosophers I know and of whom I have spoken; and the philosophers I know and about whom I don't speak.[12]

A rereading of Foucault's text in the context of Heidegger's interrogation of the founding metaphorics of the Western philosophical tradition—the light/darkness opposition or, what has always been another version of the same thing, the centered circle/periphery, which privileges the first term as the figure of the beautiful (and utopian)—goes far to support an interpretation of modern educational institutions as ideological state apparatuses constituted not simply to legitimate and extend (by producing knowledge) the hegemony of the logocentric discourse of metaphysics but also and simultaneously to reproduce the dominant cultural and sociopolitical orders.[13] Because it exposes the relationship between power and knowledge inscribed in the "disinterested" and "humane" discourse of post-Enlightenment "liberal" society, *Surveiller et punir*[14] is an epoch-making text in the history of penalogy and also in that of educational discursive practices. It is thus worth considering at some length, even at the risk of recovering by-now-familiar ground, what its thematization of this disciplinary optics is capable of disclosing about the sociopolitical imperatives concealed behind the humanistic rhetoric of "deliverance" (Matthew Arnold's term)[15] that justifies the modern institutions of liberal learning.

Foucault traces the genealogical origins of the supervisory schema informing the disciplinary society to the Enlightenment. For him, its emergence constitutes something like an epistemic break with prior and less efficient technologies of sociopolitical control. He is, of course, remarkably persuasive in suggesting that this schema has determined and continues increasingly to invest every facet of life in modern Western societies, from the everyday lives of ordinary men and women through material and cultural production and consumption to the history-making agendas of those who administer civil and political societies. What I am suggesting, however, is not simply that this schema long precedes the historical conjuncture in which Foucault locates its origin, that it is a latent possibility of the metaphysical mode of inquiry, of the circle that has its "center elsewhere," of the binary light/darkness opposition privileged by the post-Socratic Greeks and the republican and imperial Romans. I am also suggesting that this disciplinary supervisory schema came to be theorized and practiced considerably earlier than the Enlightenment. It can, as I have suggested elsewhere,[16] be seen in the utopian discourses of the humanist Renaissance. We find this schema, for example, in Campanella's *City of the Sun* (1623), in which the ideal Platonic/Christian city is represented in terms of a circular and radial geometry that was theoretically intended to represent in microcosmic form the beauty, the harmony, the integration, and the permanence of a heliocentric macrocosm supervised by a transcendental deity or Being, and to produce a private and collective form of life that reflected this ideal, an *urbis* mirroring the *orb*. This supervisory schema was not restricted to the utopian discourse of Renaissance "poetic" humanists. Through the rediscovery and mediation of the Roman Vitruvius's *Ten Books of Architecture* (first century B.C.) in the fifteenth century, the radially organized circular city, posited as the ideal design both for defense and for the health of its citizens, became an architectural and city planning tradition. That tradition led inevitably from the circular city modeled on the Christian humanist figure of beauty, order, and perfection (Filarete, 1400-1469; Giocondo, c. 1435-1515; Cataneo, ?-1569; Cerceau the Elder, 1500-1584; Daniel Speckle, 1536-1589; etc.) through the circular fortress cities of the seventeenth and eighteenth centuries (Pietro Sardi, Errard de Bar-le-Duc, 1554-1610, and, above all, Vauban, 1633-1707) to the disciplinary manufactory (Claude-Nicholas Ledoux's Arc-et-Senan, 1775-1779) and city (Ledoux's Chaux) to the Paris of Baron Haussmann.

In thematizing a process in which the humanist figure of beauty gradually and unevenly manifests the potential for domination latent in it—a process that parallels within architectural design what occurs within philosophy and literature—this synecdochical history suggests a significant modification of Foucault's genealogy of the disciplinary society. According to his emphasis, its origins rest in the Enlightenment and it is given its enabling impetus by empirical science. There is, I submit, an affiliative relationship, however muted, between the panoptic polis of the post-Enlightenment and the circular cities of the Renaissance humanists. These cities drew their inspiration not only from the medieval theo-logians (Saint Augustine's *City of God*, for example) but also from the onto-logians of classical antiquity (Plato's *Laws* and *Timaeus*, for example). The microphysical techniques of power enabled, according to Foucault, by the emergence of the panoptic schema in the Enlightenment are more scientific, more complex, more ordinary, and less visible than the mathematical techniques of supervision and discipline enabled by the "poetic" humanist Tommaso Campanella's circular/ cosmic City of the Sun. And the uniform life of docile and useful bodies produced by the geometry of panopticism is far more various than the monochromatic uniformity of social life produced by the geometry of Campanella's Platonic heliocentrism. They do have in common, fundamentally, both the polyvalent diagram of the centered circle and, as the following passage on genetics from the *City of the Sun* makes clear, the supervisory procedures and disciplinary end that this perennially ideal figure is intended to achieve.

> Since both males and females, in the manner of ancient Greeks, are completely naked when they engage in wrestling exercises, their teachers may readily distinguish those who are able to have intercourse from those who are not and can determine whose sexual organs may best be matched with whose [*e quali membra con quali si confanno*]. Consequently, every third

night, after they have all bathed, the young people are paired off for intercourse. Tall handsome girls are not matched with any but tall brave men, while fat girls are matched with thin men and thin girls with fat men, so as to avoid extremes in their offspring. On the appointed evening, the boys and girls prepare their beds and go to bed where the matron and senior direct them. Nor may they have intercourse until they have completely digested their food and have said their prayers. There are fine statues of illustrious men that the women gaze upon. Then both male and female go to a window to pray to God of Heaven for a good issue. They sleep in separate neighboring cells until they are to have intercourse. At the proper time [when the most favorable astronomical conditions obtain], the matron goes around and opens the cell doors.[17]

This brief synecdochical retrieval of the history of the disciplinary uses to which the figure of the circle was put in architecture and urban planning is important for my purposes; it makes plain that such uses were thought long before Claude-Nicholas Ledoux's construction of the salt plant at Arc-et-Senan near Besançon (1775-1779), where Foucault locates their origins.

If Heidegger fails to perceive the possibility of a sociopolitical critique of the modern disciplinary society because he puts the emphasis of his critique at the ontological site, Foucault (and especially those sociopolitical critics he has influenced) fails to perceive the possibility of an ontological critique of the disciplinary society; the degree, that is, to which the model of the circle as beauty/power has been already inscribed in the consciousness of the disinterested humanitarian reformers who culminate in Jeremy Bentham and his Panopticon. To fix the disruptive emergence of the supervisory schema in the Enlightenment suggests that the repressive ideology informing its ostensibly benign purposes is coincidental with the emergence of empirical science, applied technology, the bourgeois class, and capitalism, a context from which liberal humanists can all too easily disengage their "poetic" anthropology in the context of the debate between the Two Cultures. On the other hand, to recognize the always reconstituted "continuity" of the supervisory schema, to trace its fulfilled version in the post-Enlightenment back through the idealized circular cities to the generalized polyvalent image of beauty privileged by Plato and the post-Socratics (and, as I will suggest, harnessed politically in the form of the opposition between metropolis and provinces, *Homo romanus* and barbarian, to the Roman pursuit of empire) suggests, first, how strongly the relationship between spatial perception of temporal difference and sociopolitical power is inscribed in the Western consciousness at large. It suggests also the continuing complicity of modern humanism—its classical mode of "disinterested" inquiry, the philosophical and literary texts it privileges, and its educational institutions—with the disciplinary society on which such sociopolitical thinkers as Gramsci, Althusser, Foucault, Adorno, Said, and others focus their critique of modernity.

According to Foucault's genealogical analysis, then, the relationship between the spatializing eye or "disciplinary gaze"[18] and power, supervision, and discipline assumed overt theoretical articulation and practical expression during the Enlightenment and increasingly thereafter, when the "universal" (Western) possibilities of humanistic education began to become manifest.[19] The reformers of the brutal aristocratic punitive machinery were not essentially committed to humanitarian principles. They were more interested in the formulation of a more efficient and "economic" penal system:

> It was not so much, or not only, the privileges of justice, its arbitrariness, its archaic arrogance, its uncontrolled rights that were criticized; but rather the mixture of its weaknesses and excesses, its exaggerations and its loopholes, and above all the very principle of this mixture, the "super-power" of the monarch. The true objective of the reform movement, even in its most general formulations, was not so much to establish a new right to punish based on more equitable principles, as to set up a new "economy" of the power to punish, to assure its better distribution, so that it should be neither too concentrated at certain privileged points, nor too divided between opposing authorities; so that it should be distributed in homogeneous circuits capable of operating everywhere, in a continuous way, down to the finest grain of the social body. The reform of criminal law must be read as a strategy for the rearrangement of the power to punish, according to modalities that render it more regular, more effective, more constant and more detailed in its effects; in short, which increase its effects while diminishing its economic cost . . . and its political cost. (*DP*, pp. 80-81)

What the early reformers of the Enlightenment were ultimately searching for, that is, was not a penal system that cared for the otherness of the antisocial others, but one that diminished the economic wastefulness of the indiscriminate irregularities and, equally important, diminished the political visibility of power; they sought a system that internalized, distributed, and saturated power in and throughout society in order to increase productivity (of knowledge as well as of capital goods) and to decrease the threat of revolt to which an identifiable power—a visible sovereign center—is necessarily exposed. They were groping for a generalized and generalizable system capable of annulling the "force" of the alienated other, and able to produce "docile and useful bodies." As Foucault states the fully developed agenda of the post-Enlightenment:

> The historical moment of the disciplines was the moment when an art of the human body was born, which was directed not only at the growth of its skills, nor at the intensification of its subjection, but at the formation of a relation that in the mechanism itself makes it more obedient as it becomes more useful, and conversely. What was then being formed was a policy of coercions that act upon the body, a calculated manipulation of its elements, its gestures,

its behaviour. The human body was entering a machinery of power that explores it, breaks it down and rearranges it. . . . Thus discipline produces subjected and practiced bodies, "docile" bodies. Discipline increases the forces of the body (in economic terms of utility) and diminishes these same forces (in political terms of obedience). In short, it dissociates power from the body; on the one hand, it turns it into an "aptitude," a "capacity," which it seeks to increase; on the other hand, it reverses the course of the energy, the power that might result from it, and turns it into a relation of strict subjection. If economic exploitation separates the force and the product of labor, let us say that disciplinary coercion establishes in the body the constricting link between an increased aptitude and an increased domination. (*DP*, p. 138)

Foucault situates the reformers' search for such a "new 'economy' of the power to punish" in the Enlightenment, specifically in the technology of optics it was developing to facilitate its achievement of knowledge of and power over nature: "Side by side with the major technology of the telescope, the lens and the light beam, which were an integral part of the new physics and cosmology, there were the minor techniques of multiple and intersectional observations, of eyes that must see without being seen; using techniques of subjection and methods of exploitation, an obscure art of light and the visible was secretly preparing a new knowledge of man" (*DP*, p. 71).[20] There is no doubt that their appropriation of the new science of optics and its technologies were instrumental in preparing this "new knowledge of man." But the historical specificity of Foucault's genealogy should not obscure the legacy of the ontotheological tradition in this process, not least, given my focus on the genealogy of modern American knowledge production, the optics inscribed in the theology of Calvinist Protestantism. For it is quite clear, despite Foucault's emphasis on an overdetermined science and technology, that the Enlightenment's war of reason against "wastefulness" (and deviance) in behalf of sociopolitical and material economy coincides with the Calvinist/Protestant work ethic. I am referring not simply to the ethic that, according to Max Weber, gave rise to the "spirit of capitalism" in general, but to the specific Puritan ethic that determined the educational imperatives of the American college: the ethic that was rationalized and enabled by the austere pro*vid*ential history represented, as the etymology suggests, in the image of the absolutely hidden, inscrutable, and supervisory eye of the Calvinist God. This last is, in Weber's resonant rhetoric, the "transcendental being," "beyond the reach of human understanding," who, with "His quite incomprehensible decrees has decided the fate of every individual and regulated the tiniest detail of the cosmos from eternity."[21]

What, according to Foucault, lay more immediately but not unrelatedly at hand as architectural/methodological models for these "observatories of human multiplicity" (*DP*, p. 170) was, significantly, the hospital, the insane asylum, the workshop, the elementary classroom, and above all, the military camp, modeled (not incidentally, as I will show), on the camp structure of the Roman legions. In these spaces, as in a plague town (*DP*, p. 147), time was enclosed, partitioned, functional, serial, and thus immobile or frozen: arranged to achieve optimal supervision under "the scrupulously 'classificatory' eye of the master" (*DP*, p. 17)[22] of a prolific and proliferating world assumed to be naturally deviant—or, on another level, "prodigal" or "fallen" and "dispersed." It was an economy of space/time designed to eliminate confusion and waste and to rechannel the force of living bodies from the vantage point of a preestablished judgmental norm: a center or core, as it were.[23] In the military camp (derived from the Roman legions), for example, which, according to Foucault, provided "an almost ideal model" for these emergent observatories, geometry and supervision combined to ensure discipline.

> The camp is the *diagram of a power* that acts by means of general visibility.
> For a long time this model of the camp *or at least its underlying principle* was
> found in urban development in the construction of working-class housing
> estates, hospitals, asylums, prisons, schools: the spatial "nesting" of
> hierarchical surveillance. . . . The camp was to the rather shameful art of
> surveillance what the darkroom was to the great science of optics. (*DP*,
> pp. 171-72. My emphasis.)

Thus, according to Foucault, a whole "new" spatial problematic emerges: that of an architecture that would assure the ends of discipline by rendering visible those on whom power acted. It was to be "an architecture that is no longer built simply to be seen (as with the ostentation of palaces), or to observe the external space (cf. the geometry of fortresses),[24] but to permit an internal, articulated and detailed control— to render visible those who are inside it; in more general terms, an architecture that would operate to transform individuals: to act on those it shelters, to provide a hold on their conduct, to carry the effects of power right to them, to make it possible to know them, to alter them. Stones can make people docile and knowable" (*DP*, p. 172).

"Or at least its underlying principle": Read in the context of the destruction of metaphysics—the ontotheological tradition—in the previous chapter, Foucault's analysis of the historically specific sociopolitical conjuncture giving rise to such disciplinary architectural experiments suggests, in fact, how deeply the affiliation between spatial perception and power, center and circle, was inscribed in the Western consciousness by the time of the Enlightenment. (It should not be forgotten, for reasons that will become more explicit in the next chapter, that the Enlightenment, especially in England, France, and, with a Protestant twist, America,[25] was, as the disciplinary reformers' appropriation of the camp structure of the imperial Roman legion suggests, an age that appropriated classical Rome—*Homo romanus*—as its essential cultural and sociopolitical paradigm.) It was inevitable, therefore, however ironic, that the quest of an age for such a functional economy of space—an economy that served both as agency of surveillance and correction (reformation) according to the humanistic norm—would culminate at the end of the century in an architectural model of the ideal prison, a prison that, in reflecting its cosmology (metaphysics) and its epistemology—truth as *adequaetio intellectus et rei*—as well as its symbolic figuration—the centered circle—precisely and concretely epitomized the logocentric perspective of the ontotheological tradition. It was inevitable, in other words, that the Enlightenment (as the very name suggests) should discover an architectural model for "educating" men (and women) in which "the spatial nesting" of military surveillance becomes *sur*-veillance; supervision, *super*-vision.

Nor is it accidental, I think, that this structural model—this trope—inscribed as a deep structure in the Western consciousness should have been inferred from the philosophical tradition by a humanist who contributed significantly to the triumph of technology and to rendering the modern period the "age of the world picture," a thinker who brings the tradition beginning with Plato's privileging of the eye, the recollective memory, and, by extension, the hierarchized *polis* supervised by the encompassing (synoptic) gaze of the guardians, to its fulfillment—and end. I am referring, of course, to Jeremy Bentham and his epochally revolutionary Panopticon or "Inspection House." In "reversing the principle of the dungeon," which the *ancien regime* intended "to deprive of light and to hide" (*DP*, p. 200), and in recognizing that "full lighting and the eye of a supervisor captured better than darkness, which ultimately protected," Bentham's centered circular architectural design brings the visual/disciplinary machinery, articulated and thematized during the Enlightenment—the taxonomic table, the "evolutive" time of genesis, the examination, and the spatializing structures—into absolute symmetry with the supervision enabled by the metaphorics that privileged space and light over time and darkness.

Bentham's Panopticon was not simply intended to enable a generalized supervision of the prison inmates. It was also intended to eliminate communication between them (which, applied to the context of pedagogy, inhibits the dialogic act that disperses the monologic Word of the teacher), to annul their potentially disruptive force, and, by gaining knowledge about them, to facilitate their correction. Bentham wanted his architectural design to operate on human beings in the same way the scientific tables of the Enlightenment operated on natural phenomena. He wished it to effect the disciplinary transformation or re-collection of amorphous and wasteful deviation into a collective of discrete and thus knowable entities which had their *proper places* in the larger whole. In short, he wanted his Panopticon to transform a multitude into subjected subjects, the willing transmitters of the normative power that rendered them docile and useful instruments of the dominant sociopolitical formation. Thus the individual's cell was arranged to impose on him or her an "axial visibility," but the separated cells within the peripheric building implied "a lateral invisibility" which "is a guarantee of order," for this arrangement abolished "the crowd, a compact mass, a locus of multiple exchanges, individuality merging together, a collective effect," transforming it into "*a collection of separated individualities*. From the point of view of the guardian, it is replaced by a multiplicity that can be numbered and supervised; from the point of view of the inmates, by a sequestered and observed solitude" (Bentham, pp. 60-64) (*DP*, p. 201; my emphasis).

Further, according to Foucault, Bentham "envisaged not only venetian blinds on the windows of the central observation hall, but, on the inside, partitions that intersected the hall at right angles and, in order to pass from one quarter to another, not doors but zig-zag openings; for the slightest noise, a gleam of light, a brightness in a half-opened door would betray the presence of the guardians." In this way the Panopticon would accomplish in practice Bentham's guiding principle: that power should be visible and unverifiable. "Visible: the inmate will constantly have before his eyes the tall outline of the central tower from which he is spied upon. Unverifiable: the inmate must never know whether he is being looked at at any moment; but he must be sure that he may always be so." This spatial economy would induce in the errant inmates as its primary effect "a state of conscious and permanent visibility that assures the automatic functioning of power. So to arrange things that the surveillance is permanent in its effects, even if it is discontinuous in its actions; that the perfection of power should tend to render its actual exercise unnecessary; that this architectural apparatus should be a machine for creating and sustaining a power relation independent of the person who exercises it; in short, that the inmates should be caught up in a power situation of which they are themselves the bearers" (*DP*, p. 201). Behind this post-Enlightenment disciplinary practice lies, it should now be evident (even though Foucault does not refer to it overtly), the principle and figurative extensions that, according to Heidegger, enable Western metaphysics: (1) the principle that *Identity is the condition for the possibility of difference and not the other way around*; (2) the transcendental eye (and its light) that this principle must necessarily privilege; and (3) the metaphorics of the centered circle that it precipitates to do its discreetly repressive work.

Bentham's Panopticon brings to fulfillment the coercive potential latent in metaphysical "oversight" *and*, by way of this excess, makes explicit the disciplinary genealogy of the idea and practice of the modern synoptic humanist university that the metaphysical tradition authorized and elaborated. A careless reader of Foucault might object that Bentham's model applies essentially to a historically specific and appropriate architectural instance within modern Western society: the reformatory prison. But such an interpretation is what Foucault's genealogical scholarship insistently denies. This is suggested by the passages I have quoted from *Surveiller et punir* which, in relating the metaphorics of vision/power informing the disciplinary technology of the emergent penal institution to the metaphorics of vision/power informing the discourse of truth/beauty in the ontotheological tradition at large, disclose (often against themselves) the degree to which the generalized disciplinary model—the *figure* of the centered circle—had been inscribed, prior to Bentham's historical occasion, in the institutions of Western culture. As I have provisionally noted, it is also suggested by Foucault's insistent, however muted, reference to the *principle* underlying the concrete architectural instances: the military camp, we recall, "is a *diagram* of power that acts by means of general visibility." But it is most clearly suggested in Foucault's analysis of Bentham's Panopticon itself, where he shows that Bentham conceived it as a *generalized* structural model that was separable from any concrete and particular practice, thus implying the affiliation of his utilitarian discourse with the metaphysical tradition at large.

> [The Panopticon] is the diagram of a mechanism of power reduced to its ideal form; its functioning, abstracted from any obstacle, resistance or friction, must be represented in a pure architectural and optical system: it is in fact a figure of political technology that may and must be detached from any specific use.
>
> It is polyvalent in its applications; it serves to reform prisoners, but also to treat patients, to instruct schoolchildren, to confine the insane, to put beggars and idlers to work. . . .
>
> Whenever one is dealing with a multiplicity of individuals on whom a task or a particular form of behaviour must be imposed, the panoptic schema may be used. It is—necessary modifications apart—applicable "to all establishments whatsoever, in which, within a space not too large to be covered or commanded by buildings, a number of persons are meant to be kept under inspection." (Bentham, p. 40) (*DP*, pp. 205-6.)

Letting Bentham's rhetoric do his critical work, Foucault writes of the panoptic schema:

> It is a way of obtaining from power "in hitherto unexampled quantity," "a great and new instrument of government . . . ; its great excellence consists in the great strength it is capable of giving to *any* institution it may be thought proper to apply it to" (Bentham, p. 66). . . . Bentham's Preface to *Panopticon* opens with a list of the benefits to be obtained from his "inspection-house": "*Morals reformed—health preserved—industry invigorated—instruction diffused—public burthens thus lightened—*Economy seated, as it were, upon a rock—the gordion knot of the Poor-Laws not cut, but untied—all by a simple idea in architecture!" (Bentham, p. 39) (*DP*, pp. 206-7)

Foucault is not restricting the polyvalency of the spatial/visual diagram to scientific uses. He is thinking as well about the uses to which it has been and can be put by "poetic" humanists. This becomes clear in an interview entitled "The Eye of Power" that followed the publication of *Surveiller et punir*, where he identifies Bentham's "liberal scientific" (technological) project with Rousseau's liberal "lyrical" project: the pedagogy of "self-fulfillment":

I would say Bentham was the complement to Rousseau. What in fact was the Rousseauist dream that motivated many of the revolutionaries?

It was the dream of a transparent society, visible and legible in each of its parts, the dream of there no longer existing any zones of darkness, zones established by the privileges of royal power or the prerogatives of some corporation, zones of disorder. It was the dream that each individual, whatever portion he occupied, might be able to see the whole society, that men's hearts should communicate, their vision be unobstructed by obstacle, and that opinion of all reign over each. . . .

Bentham is both that and the opposite. He poses the problem of visibility, but thinks of a visibility organized entirely around a dominating, overseeing gaze. He effects the project of a universal visibility which exists to serve a rigorous, meticulous power. Thus Bentham's obsession, the technical idea of the exercise of an "all-seeing" power, is grafted on to the great Rousseauist theme which is in some sense the lyrical note of the Revolution. The two things combine into a working whole. Rousseau's lyricism and Bentham's obsession.[26]

Bentham's Panopticon, that is, is but an overdetermined instance of the practical uses to which the panoptic diagram was put in the post-Enlightenment. Eventually, as Bentham prophesied, it would come to be fully applied to the medical hospital, the psychiatric clinic, the educational institution, and finally to society at large. It would, in Foucault's terms, become a generalized, all-encompassing, and comprehensive—a hegemonic—"panopticism," which, however unevenly developed at any particular site, would traverse the entire lateral continuum of being, from being itself through culture and cultural institutions to sociopolitical formations. It would constitute "the disciplinary society":

There are two images . . . of discipline. At one extreme, the discipline blockade, the enclosed institutions, established on the edges of society, turned inwards towards negative functions: arresting evil, breaking communications, suspending time. At the other extreme, with panopticism, is the discipline-mechanism: a functional mechanism that must improve the exercise of power by making it lighter, more rapid, more effective, a design of subtle coercion for a society to come. The movement from one project to the other, from a schema of exceptional discipline to one of a generalized surveillance, rests on a historical transformation: the gradual extension of the mechanisms of discipline throughout the seventeenth and eighteenth centuries, their spread throughout the whole social body, the formation of what might be called in general the disciplinary society. (DP, p. 209)

III

All through the period witnessing the rise of the modern American university, especially since the Cold War, commentators on higher education, critics and historians like Richard Hofstadter, Laurence Vesey, Daniel Bell, and most recently Gerald Graff, have characterized the university in terms of its radical heterogeneity, criticizing it for its lack of a unified and common purpose or praising it for its pluralism. Thus, for example, Graff observes in his institutional history of English departments:

> Although the turn of the century saw the imposition of a uniform canon of English literature, traditionalists complained that the curriculum had all but dissipated the civic potential of the canon by breaking it up into such disconnected fragments that students could get no clear sense of its unity. Far from being organized on a centralized logocentric model, the American university is itself something of a deconstructionist, proliferating a variety of disciplinary vocabularies that nobody can reduce to the common measure of any metalanguage. This in fact is one of the reasons why such institutions are so hard to change.[27]

In opposition to this common and disabling reading—a reading that fails to recognize the homologous continuity between sociopolitical and ontological ideology as the last chapter will suggest—I want to claim that the apparent heterogeneity of the vocabularies of the American university obscures a fundamental singularity. However invisible and unthought by administrators, faculty, students, and historians, the polyvalent panoptic diagram thematized on the ontological level by Heidegger and on the sociopolitical level by Foucault traverses the heterogeneous structure of the modern "pluralist" university. It saturates the domain of higher education from the physical organization of institutional and classroom space to the "spiritual" space of inquiry and knowledge transmission: the "author function," research, journals, learned societies, conferences, hiring, professional advancement, and both pedagogical theory and practice. The university as we know it has its historically specific origins in the Enlightenment and reflects and contributes to "the gradual extension" and "spread" of the mechanisms of discipline "throughout the whole social body." I am primarily concerned about the way the panoptic diagram organizes spiritual space. Since there is a fundamental homological relationship between the structures of spiritual and physical space, I want first to suggest how the panoptic diagram functions as a discreet agency of disciplinary power in the latter.

For the sake of economy, I will focus on two synecdochical and continuous sites of this structure: the compartmentalization of the field of knowledge into departments and, even more discreetly, the separation of students in the classroom. The separation of the indissoluble continuum of being/knowledge into more or less autonomous disciplines, or departments, operates precisely like Bentham's Panopticon. The panoptic machinery produces *subjects*, in both senses of the word: it individualizes an assumed abnormal multiplicity of young men and women, who as a whole constitute a threat to the power of the normal (dominant and monologic) culture, in order to gain better knowledge and thus greater power over them. Its function is to annul the possibility of insurrection by producing sovereign individuals who are subjected to the monologue of normalcy or consensus. Similarly, the physical and intellectual separation of the indissoluble continuum of knowledge into disciplines housed in separate and separated departments operates ultimately to produce teachers and students who, assuming themselves to be free inquirers, are in fact subjected to the monologic discourse of the "pluralist" uni-versity and the dominant late capitalist social formation of which it is a microcosm. It is no accident, therefore, that professors and students of the several disciplines not only know little about what goes on in departments outside their own, but actively resist the intrusion of other bodies of knowledge in the name of the autonomy (sovereign individuality) and privileged status of their own.[28] Nor should the fact that interdisciplinary study has been insistently encouraged in higher education at least since World War II constitute an objection to this charge of disciplinarity. For if departments do acknowledge the value of interdisciplinary study, it is always *their* discipline that constitutes the condition of the intelligibility of the others. This explains the resistance of English departments to those "philosophical" discourses that humanist English professors have pejoratively identified as "theory," one of the essential purposes of which is to dissolve the hierarchical partitions among the disciplines. The constitution of the autonomous department, like the constitution of the sovereign individual by the panoptic machinery, annuls the possibility of interrogating or contesting the dominant monoglossic discourse inherent in dialogic exchange (*Auseinandersetzung*). Heteroglossia, as Bakhtin observed in tracing the genealogy of the novel to its origins in the centrifugal discourse of the carnival of the low or repressed, is revolutionary and threatens the "completeness" (the assumed inclusive, totalized, and matured state) of the dominant social formation.[29]

Similarly, it is no accident that the organization of space in the typical classroom or lecture hall locates the teacher at the head of the class and the students in linear or curved rows directly facing him or (occasionally) her. In this institutionalized economy of space all eyes are compelled by and directed upwards toward the gaze of the standing custodian of the knowledge to be transmitted. It is thus a panoptic economy that, in privileging the gaze of the teacher, centers and elevates him or her to a position of dominance (and transforms the teacher's words into a Transcendental Signified) in relation to the periphery below (the students and their words). Further, such a spatially compelled optics makes it very difficult for students to look at, to get to know, and thus to carry on real dialogue with each other, a kind of dialogue that might call the teacher's authority into question. Despite the proximity of bodies, the hold the teacher's gaze has on the eyes of the students enabled by this spatial economy in effect *isolates* the students from each other. As a result of this invisible partitioning and supervision, they become "sovereign individuals" in the context of an ontologically prior identity.[30] Thus, like the economy of departmental space, which separates knowledge into disciplines, this discreet economy of classroom space guarantees the legitimacy and enhances the disciplinary power of the monologic cultural Word that speaks through the authoritative voice of the teacher. What Foucault says about the disciplines in general applies as well to classroom space:

> In this task of adjustment, discipline had to solve a number of problems for which the old economy of power was not sufficiently equipped. It could reduce the inefficiency of mass phenomena: reduce what, in a multiplicity, makes it seem less manageable than a unity; reduce what is opposed to the use of each of its elements and of their sum; reduce everything that may counter the advantage of number. That is why discipline fixes; it arrests or regulates movements; it clears up confusion; it dissipates compact groupings of individuals wandering about the country in unpredictable ways; it establishes calculated distributions. It must also master all the forces that are formed from the very constitution of an organized multiplicity; it must neutralize the effects of counter-power that spring from them and which form a resistance to the power that wishes to dominate it: agitations, revolts, spontaneous organizations, coalitions—anything that may establish horizontal conjunctions. Hence the fact that the disciplines use procedures of partitioning and verticality, that they introduce, between the different elements at the same level, as solid separations as possible, that they define compact hierarchical networks, in short, that they oppose to the intrinsic, adverse force of multiplicity the technique of the continuous, individualizing pyramid. They must also increase the particular utility of each element of the multiplicity, but by means that are the most rapid and least costly, that is to say, by using multiplicity itself as an instrument of this growth. (*DP*, pp. 219-21)

The economy of classroom space forces a binary opposition between the teacher (colonizing center) and students (colonized periphery). Like the pyramidal opposition between guardian and inmates of Bentham's Panopticon, the hierarchized opposition of maturity and youth in the classroom compels the pedagogical relationship into an opposition of normalcy and deviance, a capital (of civilized citizens) and province (of barbarians) and reduces learning to re-formation/civilization. No matter the intention of those involved, this opposition is between oppressor and oppressed, as Paolo Friere has persuasively argued.[31]

Missing in Foucault's analysis of modern panopticism is overt reference to the ultimate ontotheological origins of this historically specific diagram of discreet power in which the subject who is subjected is constituted. To thematize what his discourse leaves unsaid, it is therefore worth invoking Heidegger's more inclusive ontological critique of the modern age, particularly its viciously circular calculative thinking. For Heidegger the triumph of humanist anthropology (and therefore of panopticism) at the end of the eighteenth century precipitated the "age of the world picture" (*die Zeit des Weltbildes*):

> The interweaving of these two events, which for the modern age is decisive—that the world is transformed into a picture and man into *subjectum*—throws light at the same time on the grounding event of modern history. . . . Namely, the more extensively and the more effectively the world stands at man's disposal as conquered, and the more objectively the object appears, all the more subjectively, i.e., the more importunately, does the *subjectum* rise up, and all the more impetuously, too, do observation of and teaching about the world change into a doctrine of man, into anthropology. It is no wonder that humanism first arises where the world becomes picture. . . . Humanism, therefore, in the more strict historiographical sense, is nothing but a moral-aesthetic anthropology. The name "anthropology" as used here . . . designates that philosophical interpretation of man which explains and evaluates whatever is, in its entirety, from the standpoint of man and in relation to man. . . .

> The fundamental event of the modern age is the conquest of the world as picture. The word "picture" [*Bild*] now means the structured image [*Gebild*] that is the creature of man's producing which represents and sets before [*des vorstellenden Herstellens*]. In such producing, man contends for the position in which he can be that particular being who gives the measure and draws up the guidelines for everything that is.[32]

Remarkably like Foucault's analysis of the panopticism of the disciplinary society, Heidegger's analysis of the age of the world picture exposes the "calculative thinking" (*rechnende Denken*) of anthropological representation (*Vorstellung*) that constitutes the subject as a "technological" consciousness. In turn, this subject "enframes" (*Ge-stell*) *physis* in its own fixed image. The subject thus reduces the dynamic and "proliferating" processes of *physis*, including other human beings, not simply into knowable objects, but into objects "standing in reserve" (*Bestand*), into "docile and useful bodies," as it were.[33] This technological achievement of humanistic recollection, this anthropological version of metaphysical *oversight*, is a forgetting of the be-ing of being with a vengeance, an amnesia no less repressive than the technology of supervision in the disciplinary society.

Foucault situated the articulated form of the panoptic diagram in the Enlightenment, which overdetermined the empirical sciences. The discreetly repressive operation of this disciplinary diagram, however, was not limited to this site, as his discourse—especially in *The Birth of the Clinic* and *Discipline and Punish*—seems to suggest. It was also applied to the sites of classical philosophy, literature, and the arts privileged by the cultural memory of modern humanism. In thus obscuring its "universality," Foucault's genealogy obscured a deeper ideological apparatus informing the disciplinary ideology of a sociopolitical formation overdetermined by a model of knowledge production having its immediate source in scientific/technological investigation: the metaphysical ideology that privileges the centered circle and its affiliated optics. It is this practically polyvalent (idealized) spatial diagram (the ideology of domination concealed behind the figure of beauty and perfection), inscribed in the discourses of the physical and human sciences and in the institutional practices of the dominant culture, that contemporary secular critics of modern power relations all too often overlook even as their critical discourses, like Foucault's, circle more or less unthought around this constellation of metaphors, this imaginary real. I am referring above all to those "new historicists" whom Foucault has influenced (Stephen Greenblatt, Sacvan Bercovitch, Frank Lentricchia, Jonathan Arac, and Donald Pease, for example) but also to those neo-Marxist critics (Raymond Williams, Jean Baudrillard, Pierre Bordieu, Fredric Jameson, Terry Eagleton, Stuart Hall, Jürgen Habermas, Ernesto Laclau, and Chantal Mouffe, for example), and to those otherwise diverse feminist critics of the discursive practices of Western patriarchy (Julia Kristeva, Hélène Cixous, Gayatri Spivak, Juliet Mitchell, Pamela McCallum, for example) whose oppositional discourses are directed against the cultural hegemony of contemporary late capitalist culture.

Foucault's unevenly developed discourse inadvertently reinscribed the false opposition between the natural sciences and the humanities that, despite Nietzsche's and Heidegger's disclosure of the origins of modern empirical science in the *ressentiment* of the ascetic/speculative perspective, has determined cultural discourse on knowledge production in the West since the Renaissance (of Roman antiquity): the discourse epitomized in Anglo-American modernity by the Two Cultures debate that has extended from Matthew Arnold and Thomas Henry Huxley through F. R. Leavis and C. P. Snow to the present. If Foucault, in focusing his critique of modernity on the production of (cultural) discourse, challenges the orthodox Marxist base/superstructure model of interpretation—in which the material economy is determinative "in the last instance"—he nevertheless reinscribes his interpretive practice in a version of the base/superstructure model. Foucault's discourse, that is, has made it easy for many of his academic followers to further subordinate the "lyrical" humanist discourse of the ontotheological tradition (the *litterae humaniores*) to the "hard" humanist discourse of post-Enlightenment science. As a consequence of this reductive separation and hierarchization, politically left-oriented critics of modernity, neo-Marxists, and even those influenced by Foucault's genealogy of the disciplinary society, continue in practice to identify the "regime of truth" with the scientific/technological/capitalist establishment while minimizing the role that literature, philosophy, the arts, and the institutions that transmit their "truths," play (in English departments and university presses) in the repression of the relay of sociopolitical "others" that constitute being-in-the-world.

Therefore the thematization of Foucault's undeveloped understanding of the Panopticon as "a diagram of a mechanism of power reduced to its ideal form" is an important project of the postmodern countermemory, especially for its interrogation of the deceptively "heterogeneous" discourse of the institution of higher learning in late capitalism. A Foucauldian genealogy of the modern disciplinary society that overlooks the circular/specular diagram inscribed in the discourses of modern producers of culture is no less vulnerable to criticism than a Heideggerian destruction of the ontotheological tradition that fails to recognize its historically specific, worldly manifestations. Both critiques are blinded by their (partial/disciplinary) insights.

IV

In specifying the applications of the polyvalent "diagram of a mechanism of power reduced to its ideal form," Foucault does not say that it can also be used as a means of disciplining the deviance of words, of recuperating the prelapsarian Word from its "fallen" state. But his argument (especially his passing references to pedagogy) implicitly suggests this. If we take, with Heidegger, discourse (*Rede*) to be equiprimordial with our radical historicity (*Befindlichkeit*) and our understanding (*Verstehen*),[34] we can say that the panoptic model and its disciplinary economy can be appropriated for the production, deployment and transmission of knowledge germane to the humanities: in the case of literature, such a model can be appropriated for the making and interpretation of literary texts and the formation of canons and curricula.

Foucault in fact traces the genealogy of the realistic novel to the emergence of supervisory, disciplinary, and knowledge-producing technology: the table, the examination, the exercise, and on a more practical level, the police (*DP*, 193-94).[35] And his insight is persuasive.[36] If, however, to take one of any number of instances in Western literary history, we recall the typological or figural hermeneutic strategy of the Patristic Biblical exegetes (and its application by writers such as Dante), we may perceive too that the panopticism of post-Enlightenment literary discourse is a historically specific and overdetermined manifestation of an economy of power that has informed the production and, above all, the interpretation (consumption) of literary texts in the Western tradition at large: this economy has informed the organization of language (the essential deviance of *logoi*, i.e., the *différance* of writing), of historically specific literary texts, and of the institutional agencies for transmitting the knowledge these contain. The scriptural Text (the totalized Book) narrated by the Biblical exegetes (no less, however more overtly, than for Balzac, Flaubert, and James) was enabled by a "future anterior" perspective on temporality that, like God's all-seeing and encompassing eye watching the fall of a sparrow or the flight of a recalcitrant Jonah, facilitated the assimilation (coercion) of the historically alien texts of the Old Testament, the differentiated texts of non-Christian writers (Virgil's "Fourth Eclogue" and *The Aeneid*, for example), and the singular events of history at large (the *"pax"* of the Augustan Empire, for example) into the totalized and plenary framework of the New Testament, in order to legitimate and relegitimate (as in the case of the American Puritans' exegetical project) the Word—and the authority and power of the institutional *ecclesia*:

> Figural interpretation establishes a connection between two events or persons, the first of which signifies not only itself but also the second, while the second encompasses or fulfills the first. The two poles of the figure are separate in time, but both being real events or figures, are within time, within the stream of historical life. Only the understanding of the two persons or events is a spiritual act, but this spiritual act deals with concrete events whether past, present, or future, and not with concepts or abstractions; these are quite secondary, since promise and fulfillment are real historical events, which have either happened in the incarnation of the Word, or will happen with the second coming. Of course purely spiritual elements enter into the conceptions of the ultimate fulfillment, since "my kingdom is not of this world"; yet it will be a real kingdom, not an immaterial abstraction; only the *figura*, not the *natura* of this world will pass away . . . and the flesh will rise again. Since in figural interpretation one thing stands for another, since one thing represents and signifies the other, figural interpretation is "allegorical" in the widest sense. But it differs from most of the allegorical forms known to us by the historicity of the sign and what it signifies.[37]

Like the re-presentation of "reality" in the fiction and interpretive practice of the post-Enlightenment, typological or prefigurative Biblical interpretation is determined by the panoptic gaze and the centered circle that is its tropological corollary. In both, the gaze and the circle function to supervise and discipline the differential words of the "fallen" world from a center elsewhere—a providential eye, as it were—and to legitimate and extend the hegemony of the dominant sociopolitical formation. The difference is that the eye of power is *visible* and thus vulnerable to criticism in the typology of the custodians of the theologos, whereas it is out of sight in the representational practice of the modern custodians of the anthropologos.

Indeed, Foucault says as much in the following passage demonstrating the complicity of modern literary criticism in general with Saint Jerome's exegetical methodology as a particular corollary of the prefigurative determination of God's authorship of the providential narrative of history:

> In [modern] literary criticism, the traditional methods for defining an author— or, rather, for determining the configuration of the author from existing texts—derive in large part from those used in the Christian tradition to authenticate (or to reject) the particular texts in its possession. Modern criticism, in its desire to "recover" the author from a work, employs devices strongly reminiscent of Christian exegesis when it wished to prove the value

of a text by ascertaining the holiness of its author. In *De Viris Illustribus*, Saint Jerome maintains that homonymy is not proof of the common authorship of several works, since many individuals could have the same name or someone could have perversely appropriated another's name. The name, as an individual mark, is not sufficient as it relates to a textual tradition. How, then, can several texts be attributed to an individual author? What norms, related to the function of the author, will disclose the involvement of several authors? According to Saint Jerome, there are four criteria: the texts that must be eliminated from the list of works attributed to a single author are those inferior to the others (thus, the author is defined as a standard level of quality); those whose ideas conflict with the doctrine expressed in the others (here the author is defined as a certain field of conceptual or theoretical coherence); those written in a different style and containing words and phrases not ordinarily found in the other works (the author is seen as a stylistic uniformity); and those referring to events or historical figures subsequent to the death of the author (the author is thus a definite historical figure in which a series of events converge). Although modern criticism does not appear to have these same suspicions concerning authentication, its strategies for defining the author present striking similarites. The author explains the presence of certain events within a text, as well as their transformations, distortions, and their various modifications (and this through an author's biography or by reference to his particular point of view, in the analysis of his social preferences and his position within a class or by delineating his fundamental objectives). *The* author also constitutes a principle *of unity in writing* where any unevenness of production is ascribed to changes caused by evolution, maturation, or outside influences. In addition, the author serves to neutralize the contradictions that are found in a series of texts. *Governing this function is the belief that there must be—at a particular level of an author's thought, of his conscious or unconscious desire—a point where contradictions are resolved,* where the incompatible elements can be shown to relate to one another or to cohere around a fundamental and originating contradiction. Finally, the author is a particular source of expression who, in more or less finished forms, is manifested equally well, and with similar validity, in a text, in letters, fragments, drafts, and so forth.[38]

Foucault says here that the interpretive procedure determining authorship or, more precisely, "the configuration of the author from existing texts," in the modern period is inscribed by an anthropological version (a supplement) of the theological hermeneutics enabled by the belief in God as creator/author of a teleological narrative of presence in which historically specific contradictions are understood as prefigurative of the eschatalogical end. Modern humanistic interpretive practice, according to Foucault, is determined by the same spatial/panoptic trope that secured the authority of the medieval world view—and the church—against the disruption of "heresy": the pro-*vid*-ential model of history. Jerome's exegetical method justifies the exclusion of deviant texts from or accommodation to the Christian canon, by assuming that an author is one who, in being a "certain field of conceptual coherence," reflects in his temporally articulated texts the coherence of God's teleological temporal *design*. So too the modern literary critic's understanding of authorship as self-identical consciousness ("the principle of unity") reflecting the "mind of Europe" justifies the exclusion of deviant or "inferior" texts from the humanistic canon, and also the rationalization of textual contradictions ("any unevenness of production") in an author's temporally articulated body of work in terms of "evolution, maturation or outside influence." Like the *Logos* of Patristic exegesis, the (Apollonian) anthropocentric *logos* of modern humanist interpretation—whether it goes by the name of historicism, New Criticism, myth criticism, criticism of consciousness, or structuralism—domesticates and discreetly pacifies the (Dionysiac) force by measuring it against or accommodating it to its "providential design," or hegemonic circular geometry.

This is precisely the critique Derrida registers against the "structuralism" of Jean Rousset in drawing out the metaphorics of "preformationism" determining Rousset's interpretation of Corneille's authorship. In thematizing the pervasive inscription of the privileged metaphorics of spatialization (the centered circle) and the devaluation of difference in Rousset's text, the passage forcefully demonstrates the complicity of the Apollonian anthropologos of modern humanistic literary criticism (and pedagogy) with the theologos against temporality (duration) and Dionysiac force:

> Not only does the geometric structure of *Polyeucte* mobilize all the resources and attention of the author, but an entire teleology of Corneille's progress is coordinated to it. Everything transpires as if, until 1643, Corneille had only a *glimpse*, or anticipated the *design* of, *Polyeucte*, which was still in the shadows and which would eventually coincide with the Corneillean *design*, thereby taking on the dignity of an entelechy toward which everything would be in motion. Corneille's work and development *are put into perspective* and interpreted teleologically on the basis of what is considered its *destination, its final structure. Before Polyeucte*, everything is but a sketch in which only what is missing is due consideration, those elements which are still *shapeless* and lacking as concerns the perfection to come, or which *foretell* this perfection. . . . After *Polyeucte*? It is never mentioned. Similarly among the works prior to it, only *La galérie du palais* and *Le Cid* are taken into account, and these plays are examined, in the style of preformationism, only as structural *prefigurations* of *Polyeucte*. . . .
>
> Further, for the sake of determining an essential "Corneillean movement," does one not lose what counts? Everything that defies a geometrical-

mechanical framework—and not only the pieces which cannot be constrained by curves and helices, not only force and quality, which are meaning itself, but also *duration*, that which is pure qualitative heterogeneity within movement—is reduced to the appearance of the inessential for the sake of this essentialism or teleological structuralism. . . . Everything transpires as if everything within the dynamics of Corneillean meaning, and within each of Corneille's plays, *came to life with the aim of final peace*, the peace of the structural *energeia: Polyeucte*. Outside this peace, before and after it, movement, in its pure duration, in the labor of its organization, can itself be only sketch or debris. Or even debauch, a fault or sin as compared to *Polyeucte*, the "first impeccable success." Under the word "impeccable," Rousset notes: "*Cinna* still sins in this respect."

Preformationism, teleologism, reduction of force, value and duration—these are one with geometrism, creating structure.[39]

Despite the ruptures in Western history that have produced different epistemic configurations, the production and consumption of literature (and of all the humanities) has been characterized by a supervisory hermeneutics intended to annul the force that would jeopardize the authority of the dominant structure. By means of this generalized interpretive model, each *epistémé* has attempted to recuperate by re-formation or accommodation an always already dispersing (falling) historical *logos* or center in the name of one privileged Transcendental Signified or another, which valorizes and legitimates for all times only those texts that fulfill its formal imperatives, its *promised* end. In each *epistémé* the historically specific dominant culture and its educational institutions have tried to maintain the continuity of Western literature in the face of philosophical, religious, cultural, and sociopolitical disruptions by measuring the new literary production against its particular ideal, normative model, or master narrative. Whatever the historical moment in the ontotheological tradition (though increasingly from the Renaissance of Roman classicism to the advent of institutionalized literary studies at the end of the nineteenth century), the classic or, as it is now called, the masterpiece, is that text that *assimilates* and *universalizes* the threatening play of difference precipitated by the historical rupture by locating it within a new identical totality. In the term Derrida exposes in his critique of Rousset, the masterpiece is "impeccable," conforming in all its details to the structural imperatives of the *epistémé's* original or "sacred Book," the text whose "story is always a theogony." Masterpieces contribute to the preservation of the canon—the "simultaneous order" of the European literary tradition, as T. S. Eliot remarks—and of the cultural and sociopolitical hegemony it reflects in microcosmic form.

The texts that deviate radically from this logocentric norm or master narrative are included by exclusion: they become, like the madman in Foucault's analysis of Enlightenment reason (sanity), the measure of what the masterpiece is not:

The poet must win our imaginative consent to the aspect of human experience he presents, and to do so he cannot evade his responsibility to the beliefs and presuppositions of our common experience, common sense, and common moral consciousness. . . . The artist's cost of failure in this essential respect is demonstrated by the writing of accomplished craftsmen in which the substance is too inadequately human to engage our continuing interest, or which require our consent to positions so illiberal or eccentric or perverse that they incite counterbeliefs which inhibit the ungrudging "yes" that we grant to masterpieces.[40]

This transcendental gesture of exclusion in the name of consensus, this suprahistorically sanctioned prejudice against the grotesque or ludic play of "monstrous" texts in the name of a privileged "common sense" by prominent guardians of the monumental literary history of humanism (from Matthew Arnold through Irving Babbitt, to T. S. Eliot, I. A. Richards, E. D. Hirsch, Walter Jackson Bate, Allan Bloom, William Bennett, and Roger Kimball), repeats in the present historical conjuncture a gesture that the official custodians of culture have made in the name of high seriousness, by and large more forcefully, throughout the history of the Western literary tradition.

This is not only the testimony of Foucault, whose genealogy by way of Nietzsche mocks the "solemnities of the [lofty] origin" of the cultural monument, which, coming "before the body, before the world and time," is associated with the gods and whose "story is always sung as a theogony":

The new historian, the genealogist, will know what to make of this masquerade. He will not be too serious to enjoy it; on the contrary, he will push the masquerade to its limit and prepare the great carnival of time where masks are constantly reappearing. No longer the identification of our faint individuality with the solid identities of the past, but our "unrealization" through the excessive choice of identities. . . . Taking up these masks, revitalizing the buffoonery of history, we adopt an identity whose unreality surpasses that of God who started the charade. "Perhaps, we can discover a realm where originality is again possible as parodists of history and buffoons of God." In this, we recognize the parodic double of what the second of the *Untimely Meditations* called "monumental history": a history given to reestablishing the high points of historical development and their maintenance in a perpetual presence, given to the recovery of works, actions, and creations through the monogram of their personal essence. But in 1874, Nietzsche accused this history, one totally devoted to veneration, of barring access to actual intensities and creations of life. The parody of his last texts serves to emphasize that "monumental history" is itself a parody. Genealogy is history in the form of a concerted carnival.[41]

It is also the testimony of Mikhail Bakhtin in his several genealogies of the novel, beginning with his "unacceptable" doctoral dissertation, *Rabelais and His World*. Like Nietzsche and Foucault, he demonstrates that, from antiquity to the present, the custodians of high culture—"the *agelasts*" (those incapable of laughter)—have insistently tried to repress and marginalize the heteroglossic, contemporaneous, temporally open, indeterminate, and always threatening because "degrading" parodic genres of the "lowly folk" in the name of the cultural monuments that reflect and legitimate the "finished" sociopolitical formations.[42] And like Nietzsche and Foucault, as well as Heidegger and Derrida, it is in terms of the binary opposition between center and periphery that Bakhtin bears witness against the teleologies of high culture:

> In general, the world of high literature in the classical era was a world
> projected into the past, on to the distanced plane of memory, but not into a
> real, relative past tied to the present by uninterrupted temporal transitions; it
> was projected rather into a valorized past of beginnings and peak times. This
> past is distanced, finished and closed like a circle. This does not mean, of
> course, that there is no movement within it. . . . But within this time,
> completed and locked into a circle, all points are equidistant from the real,
> dynamic time of the present; insofar as this time is whole, it is not localized
> in an actual historical sequence; it is not relative to the present or to the
> future; it contains within itself, as it were, the entire fullness of time. As a
> consequence all high genres of the classical era, that is, its entire high
> literature, are structured in the zone of the distanced image, a zone outside
> any possible contact with the present in all its openendedness . . .
> contemporaneity as such (that is, one that preserves its own living
> contemporary profile) cannot become an object of representation for the high
> genres.
>
> Contemporaneity was reality of a "lower" order in comparison with the
> epic past. Least of all could it serve as the starting point for artistic ideation
> or evaluation. The focus for such an idea of evaluation could only be found in
> the absolute past. . . . The temporally valorized categories of absolute
> beginning and end are extremely significant in our sense of time and in the
> ideologies of past times. The beginning is idealized, the end is darkened. . . .
> This sense of time and the hierarchy of times described by us here permeate
> all the high genres of antiquity and the Middle Ages. They permeated so
> deeply into the basic foundation of these genres that they continue to live in
> them in subsequent eras—up to the nineteenth century, and even further.
>
> This idealization of the past in high genres has something of an official air.
> All external expressions of the dominant force and truth (the expression of
> every thing conclusive) were formulated in the valorized-hierarchical category

of the past, in a distanced and distant image (everything from gesture and clothing to literary style, for all are symbols of authority). . . .

Contemporaneity, flowing and transitory, "low," present — this "life without beginning or end" was a subject of representation only in the low genres. Most importantly, it was the basic subject matter in that broadest and richest of realms, the common people's creative culture of laughter.[43]

This resistance of officialdom to the de-gradations of ephemerality or, as Foucault would put it, this insistence on grading or pyramidal ranking, in the name of an absolute and hierarchized time, I submit, explains the insistent appeal of the custodians of "our heritage" to the masterpiece in the effort to recuperate the core curriculum by English (and other) departments in the aftermath of the Vietnam decade. For the privileging of the masterpiece on the grounds of its "high seriousness" and "universality" not only obscures its origins in a Trancendental (and patriarchal) Signified that is constituted by the dominant social formation to produce the (subjected) subject. As "masterpiece," it also becomes a discreetly disarming means of excluding *play* (laughter, difference, *jouissance*), of refusing "our consent" to deviant ("illiberal, eccentric, or perverse") texts (and media) that might "incite counterbeliefs." In short, the privileged masterpiece becomes an ideological instrument of the dominant culture that functions to repress the historically specific difference of the "lower" classes, women, blacks, third world peoples, homosexuals, and youth.

This privileging of the masterpiece also explains the tacit prejudice of these custodians of high culture against the "popular arts," a prejudice that on occasion manifests itself in the form of an astonishing reduction and irrational contempt, a form that in fact parodies the very "right [Platonic] reason" in whose self-righteous image it is articulated. A case in point is Allan Bloom's grotesque diatribe against "barbaric" and "orgiastic" rock music, the "gutter phenomenon" to which the youth culture has become increasingly "addicted" since its emergence in the "catastrophic" 1960s:

Picture a thirteen-year-old boy sitting in the living room of his family home doing his math assignment while wearing his Walkman headphones or watching MTV. He enjoys the liberties hard won over centuries by the alliance of philosophical genius and political heroism, consecrated by the blood of martyrs; he is provided with comfort and leisure by the most productive economy ever known to mankind; science has penetrated the secrets of nature in order to provide him with the marvelous, lifelike electronic sound and image reproduction he is enjoying. And in what does progress culminate? A pubescent child whose body throbs with orgasmic rhythms; whose feelings are made articulate in hymns to the joys of onanism or the killing of parents; whose ambition is to win fame and wealth in imitating the drag-queen who makes the music. In short, life is made a nonstop, commercially prepackaged masturbational fantasy.

. . . The continuing exposure to rock music is a reality, not confined to a particular class or type of child. One need only ask first-year university students what music they listen to, how much of it and what it means to them, in order to discover that the phenomenon is universal in America, that it begins in adolescence or a bit before and continues through the college years. It is *the* youth culture and as I have so often insisted, there is no other countervailing nourishment for the spirit. . . . With rock, illusions of shared feelings, bodily contact and grunted formulas, which are supposed to contain so much meaning beyond speech, are the basis of association.[44]

The point is that these popular arts have become more fundamental to postmodern life than the written word (as this medium is transmitted in schools) for good reason. However co-opted by the culture industry of late capitalism, these popular arts, especially rock and roll, repeat symptomatically the parodic and de-grading heteroglossic project of the "lowly" arts of the carnival in a postindustrialist disciplinary society in which knowledge production has become the principal means of grading, normalizing, and pacifying its citizens, and enhancing the hegemony of the dominant culture.[45]

More often, however, since the dislocating force of the "monstrous" cannot be tolerated even within an incarcerated space, the disciplinary society includes ex-orbitant texts in the canon by overlooking or supervising their disruptive centrifugal eccentricities, by assimilating or reforming their differential force within the ever-expanding panoptic and centripetal framework of the tradition. This strategy of accommodation becomes generally and provisionally thematized when one considers, for example, the domestication of radically deviant texts like *Moby-Dick* and *Pierre, Madame Bovary, The Waste Land, Lady Chatterley's Lover, Ulysses, Paterson,* and *Watt* under the scrutiny of the gaze that familiarized and "harmonized" their disorienting and disconcerting immediacy and contemporaneity. This accommodational and pacifying operation of the modern custodians of the anthropologos has its genealogical origins, not in nature, but in the theologos and the providential history it enabled. It is, however "lighter" its oppressive power, the same clerical interpretive operation practiced by the church fathers in their effort to accommodate the Old Testament to the New, Virgil's paganism (the *Fourth Eclogue* and *The Aeneid*) to Christian spiritualism, the radically disruptive parodic text of carnival (for example, the *Coeni Cyprianus*) to the Christian year.[46]

This disciplinary hermeneutics is fundamental to the literary and pedagogic discourse of modern humanism in general, conservative or liberal. It is epitomized, for example, in Matthew Arnold's inaugural address as Professor of Poetry at Oxford in November 1857, in which he exhorts his audience of students, faculty, and institutional dignitaries to reclaim the legacy of classical Greek literature; for this humanistic body of writing (as Arnold [mis-]read it from his Victorian perspective) "is, even for modern times, a mighty agent of intellectual deliverance":

> But first let us ask ourselves why the demand for an intellectual deliverance arises in such an age as the present, and in what the deliverance itself consists? The demand arises, because our present age has a copious and complex present, and behind it a copious and complex past; it arises, because the present age exhibits *to the individual man* who contemplates it the spectacle of a vast multitude of facts awaiting and inviting his comprehension. The deliverance consists in man's comprehension of this present and past. It begins when our minds begin to enter into possession of the general ideas which are the law of this vast multitude of facts. It is perfect when we have acquired that harmonious *acquiescence of mind which we feel in contemplating a grand spectacle that is intelligible to us,* when we have lost that impatient irritation of mind which we feel in the presence of an immense, moving, confused spectacle which, while it perpetually excites our curiosity, perpetually baffles our comprehension.[47]

When we read this representative passage from a writer whose cultural discourse enabled the educational practice of modern humanism in England and North America in terms of the critique of the disciplinary diagram, we begin to understand Arnold's appeal to "deliverance" to justify his argument for reclaiming the classical heritage in a way different from what has been subsequently taken. "Deliverance" in his text means constraint. It means the encompassing and containment of the heterogeneous energies released by a discursive explosion. It means visualizing and reifying the whole amorphous panorama of apparent "futility and anarchy which is contemporary history" from the distanced panoptic vantage point of a universal norm.

If, further, we construe Arnold's reference to "the copious and complex present" in historically specific terms, it comes to mean not simply the intellectual confusion— "the [bewildering] multitude of voices counselling different things" to writers of the present age[48]—but also the sociopolitical "confusion" precipitated by the demand for electoral reform, the right of public assembly, and better wages and working conditions in the wake of the midcentury knowledge explosion in Victorian England. We therefore begin to understand Arnold's "mighty agency of [individual] intellectual deliverance" as a recuperative agency serving the discreetly repressive sociopolitical purposes of the disciplinary society. Intellectual deliverance is achieved when the individual acquires "that harmonious acquiescence of mind which we feel in contemplating a grand spectacle that is intelligible to us." As Terry Eagleton wryly observes in his genealogy of the rise of English studies at the end of the nineteenth century:

> Literature was in several ways a suitable candidate for this ideological enterprise [hitherto undertaken by religion]. As a liberal, "humanizing"

pursuit, it could provide a potent antidote to political bigotry and ideological extremism. Since literature, as we know, deals in universal human values rather than in such historical trivia as civil wars, the oppression of women or the dispossession of the English peasantry, it could serve to place in cosmic perspective the petty demands of working class people for decent living conditions or greater control over their own lives, and might even with luck come to render them oblivious of such issues in their high-minded contemplation of eternal truths and beauties. English, as a Victorian handbook for English teachers put it, helps to "promote sympathy and fellow feeling among all classes"; another Victorian writer speaks of literature as opening a "serene and luminous region of truth where all may meet and expatiate in common," above "the smoke and stir, the din and turmoil of man's lower life of care and business and debate." Literature would rehearse the masses in the habits of pluralistic thought and feeling, persuading them to acknowledge that more than one viewpoint than theirs existed—namely, that of their masters. It would communicate to them the moral riches of bourgeois civilization, impress upon them a reverence for middle-class achievements, and, since reading is an essentially solitary, contemplative activity, curb in them any disruptive tendency to collective political action. It would give them a pride in their national language and literature: if scanty education and extensive hours of labour prevented them personally from producing a literary masterpiece, they could take pleasure in the thought that others of their own kind—English people—had done so. The people, according to a study of English literature written in 1891, "need political culture, instruction, that is to say, in what pertains to their relation to the State, to their duties as citizens; and they need also to be impressed sentimentally by having the presentation in legend and history of heroic and patriotic examples brought vividly and attractively before them." All of this, moreover, could be achieved without the cost and labour of teaching them the Classics: English literature was written in their own language, and so was conveniently available to them.[49]

The promise/fulfillment structure informing Arnold's rhetoric of deliverance is not simply the inclusive circular structure of a providential narrative that brings "acquiescence of mind" in the "comprehended" end. It is also the structure of the narrative of the "saving remnant": the narrative that enabled the hermeneutics of Virgil, of the Patristic exegetes, and of the American Puritans, and thus the legitimation of the political and spiritual hegemony of the Roman, the Holy Roman, the British, and the American empires. For this narrative of the saving remnant, however invisible the rhetoric of deliverance renders it, is the justifying fiction inscribed in the recuperative discourse of modern humanism at large. In it, the humanist, like Virgil's Aeneas, Saint Augustine's Saint

Paul, Cotton Mather's Governor Winthrop, fictionalizes himself as a relic or seed-bearer whose preordained mission in the face of the disintegration of the Old City it had previously colonized is to replant the seed, to cultivate it and bring it to fruition within the cultivated and colonized circle. It is no accident that Arnold himself and his progeny often appeal to this narrative in their recuperative discourses. In "Numbers; or the Majority and the Remnant," for example, in which he gives advice to an American audience intended to forestall the impending "anarchy" incumbent on the emergence of a working-class consciousness that threatens Great Britain and its heritage, Arnold writes:

> The remnant!—it is the word of the Hebrew prophets also, and especially is
> it the word of the greatest of them all, Isaiah. Not used with the
> despondency of Plato, used with far other power informing it, and with a far
> other future awaiting it, filled with fire, filled with hope, filled with faith, filled
> with joy, this term itself, the remnant, is yet Isaiah's term as well as Plato's.
> The texts are familiar to all Christendom. "Though thy people Israel be as
> the sand of the sea, only a remnant of them shall return." Even this remnant,
> a tenth of the whole, if so it may be, shall have come back into the purging
> fire, and be again cleared and further reduced there. But nevertheless, "as a
> terebinth tree, and as an oak, whose substance is in them, though they be
> cut down, so the stock of that burned tenth shall be a holy seed."
>   Yes, the small remnant should be a holy seed; but the great majority, as in
> democratic Athens, so in the kingdoms of the Hebrew nation, were unsound,
> and their State was doomed.[50]

Similarly, to cite the example of a more recent humanist addressing the "crisis of English studies," M. H. Abrams's discourse is inscribed by the disciplinary diagram that both justifies and is justified by the narrative of the saving remnant, especially in his virtually scriptural retrospective (panoramic) history of Romanticism, *Natural Supernaturalism* (1971). In this comprehensive humanist text, Abrams takes Hegel's recollective circular paradigm in *The Phenomenology of Spirit* as point of departure and overlooks or represses all the historical gestures that disrupt it, most notably Kierkegaard's critique of Hegel's *Er-Innerung* (memory) and its economy of sublation (*Aufhebung*) and the contemporary antimetaphysical discourses it in large part enabled: above all, those of Heidegger, Sartre, Merleau-Ponty, Derrida, Althusser, and Foucault. Thus Abrams discovers the "circuitous journey" through differential time to be the informing and re-forming model for Western literature at large:

> Much of what distinguishes writers I call "Romantic" derives from the fact
> that they undertook, whatever their religious creed or lack of creed, to save
> traditional concepts, schemes, and values which had been based on the
> relation of the Creator to his creatures and creation, but to reformulate them
> within the prevailing two-term system of subject and object, ego and non-

ego, the human mind or consciousness and its transactions with nature. Despite their displacement from a supernatural to a natural frame of reference, however, the ancient problems, terminology, and ways of thinking about human nature and history survive, as the implicit distinctions and categories through which even radically secular writers saw themselves and their world, and as the presuppositions and forms of their thinking about the condition, the milieu, the essential values and aspiration, and the history and destiny of the individual and of mankind.[51]

Approaching Arnold's and Abrams's humanistic texts from either Heidegger's ontological or Foucault's sociopolitical standpoint, it is obvious that, as Abrams's title itself suggests, they constitute exemplary instances traversing the history of modern literary studies of the *covert* policing activity of a disciplinary society shaped by a Transcendental Signified; they appeal to and are enabled by the apparent benignity of the panoptic diagram: the circle whose center is beyond the reach of the free play of criticism. In proffering his humanistic *paideia*, Arnold appeals to the classic in the name of deliverance. But on closer examination, it turns out that the study of the classics is actually intended to annul the force of desire of a colonized or territorialized otherness. Abrams appeals to the legacy of Western Romantic literature in the name of humanity. But on closer examination it turns out that the study of this legacy is actually intended to speak for or annul the voices of those who, in deviating from the humanistic norm, threaten the hegemony of the anthropologos: of those whose art "is too inadequately human to engage our continuing interest, or which requires our consent to positions so illiberal or eccentric or perverse that they incite counterbeliefs which inhibit the ungrudging 'yes' that we grant to masterpieces." In Arnold and Abrams, the commitment to the "free will" of the individual is produced by the dominant discourse inscribed by the viciously circular ontological and sociopolitical principle that identity is the condition for the possibility of difference. In Arnold and Abrams, men and women are, in Foucault's phrase, "subjected sovereignties":

By humanism I mean the totality of discourse through which Western man is told: "Even though you don't exercise power, you can still be a ruler. Better yet, the more you deny yourself the exercise of power, the more you submit to those in power, then the more this increases your sovereignty." Humanism invented a whole series of subjected sovereignties: the soul (ruling the body, but subjected to God), consciousness (sovereign in a context of judgment, but subjected to the necessities of truth), the individual (a titular control of personal rights subjected to the laws of nature and society), basic freedom (sovereign within, but accepting the demands of an outside world and "aligned with destiny"). In short, humanism is everything in Western civilization that restricts *the desire for power*: it prohibits the desire for power and excludes the possibility of power being seized. The theory of the subject (in the double sense of the word) is at the heart of humanism and this is why our culture has tenaciously rejected anything that could weaken its hold upon us.[52]

V

The displacement of the medieval theologos by humanist recuperation of the late Greek and Roman ontologos in the form of Enlightenment reason did not constitute a revolutionary interrogation of logocentric power in the name of a presuppositionless mode of inquiry, but the naturalization of the Word's—the center's—supernatural status. Making the constituted *logos* natural—which is to say, self-evident—makes it invisible, an absent presence. As in Foucault's analysis of the concealment of the hitherto visible power of the sovereign by the disciplinary technology of the Enlightenment, it *puts out of sight* what the Greco-Roman and especially the Christian *epistèmés* merely put out of reach of the free play of criticism. The "presuppositionless" problematic of humanistic literary studies thus not only bases itself on an inviolable panoptic "center elsewhere" but, unlike the problematics of the late Greek and Roman and of the medieval Christian cultures, also, by the sleight of hand that renders coercion benign, makes this enabling center and the supervisory power informing it seem like deliverance: difficult, if not finally impossible, to critically engage. Nevertheless, this privileged center—the Transcendental Signified—is no less present in the discourse of modern (liberal) humanism, imposing from the end—from its impregnable "little Quebec"[53]—its repressive power, at the site of the literary text and also, however unevenly, at the sites of the subject, of gender, of race, of ethnicity, of culture, of sociopolitics.

There is, then, a fundamental affiliation between the literary history theorized and practiced by "poetic" humanists from Arnold to Abrams and the empirical sciences which, according to a certain emphasis in Foucault's genealogy, was responsible for the establishment and reproduction of the disciplinary society. No less than the "objectivity" of the sciences, against which it has insistently affirmed the alternative of a delivering culture, the "disinterestedness" of the *litterae humaniores* is a panopticism that has worked to discipline deviance. This, in fact, is what Foucault implies in the following passage on Nietzsche's genealogy of the humanist historiography, where he traces the origins of its disinterested discourse back to metaphysics, that mode of inquiry that spatializes time and bends its differential force into the figure of the circle, which paradoxically is attributed to Egypt:

> Nietzsche's criticism, beginning with the second of the *Untimely Meditations*, always questioned the form of history that reintroduces (and always assumes) a suprahistorical perspective; a history whose function is to compose the finally reduced diversity of time into a totality fully closed upon itself; a

history that always encourages subjective recognitions and attributes a form of reconciliation to all the displacements of the past; a history whose perspective on all that precedes it implies the end of time, a completed development. The historian's history finds its support outside of time and pretends to base its judgments on an apocalyptic objectivity. This is only possible, however, because of its belief in eternal truth, the immortality of the soul, and the nature of consciousness as always identical to itself. Once the historical sense is mastered by a suprahistorical perspective, metaphysics can bend it to its own purpose and, by aligning it to the demands of objective science, it can impose its own "Egyptianism."[54]

Nietzsche's and Foucault's uses of the term "Egyptianism," and my appropriation, invoke a deliberate and resonant ironic play on the binary opposition constituted in antiquity by late (Hellenic) Greek and Roman intellectuals to define and establish their "democratic" or "republican" hegemony over Egyptian "pharaohism" (or "Asiatic despotism"). The opposition was later appropriated by Western humanists at large, though the second term underwent topographical expansion and eventually came to be encoded in a cultural rhetoric that effaced its geographical origins, and was used to define their "civil" and "liberal" identities against all "barbarism" or "alien" cultures and thus to legitimate the Occident's cultural—and sociopolitical—colonization of their space. Nietzsche and Foucault redirect this enabling Western binary formula against itself: "classical" Greek humanism is an Egyptianism.[55]

Always latent in the discursive practice of classical humanism, this policing action that I call "Egyptianism" becomes manifest at times of crisis, at historically specific moments when the questions its problematic cannot ask—to which it is blinded by its insight—become explicit. The will to power inherent in the disinterested discourse of humanism asserts itself overtly when the differences contained, comprehended, and circumscribed by the invisible anthropologos become explicit as epistemic ruptures or "discursive explosions" that expose its inherent contradictions: the interest of its disinterestedness. This self-destructive movement, in which, under the pressure of historical crises, the hidden center is compelled to disclose itself overtly as an "Egyptianism" that implicates it with sociopolitical power, has been the essential pattern of institutional curricular reform movements in North American higher education in the twentieth century. We encounter it during and immediately after World War I (the period of the Red Scare), after World War II (the period of the Cold War), and most tellingly during the Vietnam War and its aftermath.

VI

The discovery by means of Heidegger's destruction and Foucault's genealogy of the centered circle/panoptic diagram as the enabling metaphorics of the repressive ontotheological tradition, culminating in the age of the world picture or alternatively the panopticism of the post-Enlightenment disciplinary society, makes persuasively clear that this disciplinary panopticism is a constituted ideology deeply inscribed in the consciouness of the modern West at large. In fact, the panoptic perspective as a mode of inquiry, whether it takes the form of "objective" science or "disinterested" humanism, determines the practice of the dominant culture all along the continuum of being: not only at the site of ontological discourse but also at the sites of sexual, cultural, and sociopolitical relations. Despite the rhetoric of liberation characterizing the discourse of humanism, the privileged centered circle precipitated by the mystified *logos* as its visual model, no less than the more recent "objective" discourse of classical science, is a disciplinary instrument of the will to power over the differences that time disseminates, an Apollonianism brought up to date. And despite the historical ruptures of the last century, especially those precipitated by the Vietnam War, and despite the postmodern critique of humanism (the discourse and its institutions, which privilege the sovereign subject), this coercive panoptic logocentrism continues in the name of the disinterested pursuit of (transhistorical) truth and beauty to constitute the authorizing ground of both the custodians of culture and the institutions of learning they represent.

This disclosure prepares us to perceive that the massive contemporary effort on the part of educational institutions to recuperate a core curriculum in the face of the "proliferation" of knowledge precipitated by the events of the Vietnam decade reveals an educational institution that in the name of Apollo will continue to perpetuate a careless calculative/disciplinary thinking based on and serving the disciplinary dictates of the Western panoptic will to power: the futile attempt of Western Man to achieve technical mastery over being's prolific mystery. In short, as they gesture back nostalgically to the lost origin, such attempts point forward to the end of thinking and the exhaustion of language as the "house of being":

> When thinking comes to an end by slipping out of its element it replaces this loss by procuring a validity for itself as *techné*, as an instrument of education and therefore as a classroom matter and later a cultural concern. By and by philosophy becomes a technique for explaining from highest causes. One no longer thinks; one occupies himself with "philosophy." In competition with one another, such occupations publicly offer themselves as "-isms" and try to offer more than the others. The dominance of such terms is not accidental. It rests above all in the modern age upon the peculiar *dictatorship* of the public realm. . . . Language thereby falls into the service of expediting communication along routes where objectification—the uniform accessibility of everything to everyone—branches out and disregards all limits. In this way language comes under the dictatorship of the public realm which decides in advance what is intelligible and what must be rejected as unintelligible. . . .

The widely and rapidly spreading devastation of language not only undermines aesthetic and moral responsibility in every use of language; it arises from a threat to the essence of humanity. A merely cultivated user of language is still no proof that we have as yet escaped the danger to our essence. These days, in fact, such usage might sooner testify that we have not seen and cannot see the danger because we have never yet placed ourselves in view of it. Much bemoaned of late, and much too lately, the downfall of language is, however, not the grounds for, but already a consequence of, the state of affairs in which language under the dominance of the modern metaphysics of subjectivity almost irremediably falls out of its element. Language still denies us its essence: that it is the house of the Truth of Being. Instead language surrenders itself to our mere willing and trafficking as an instrument of domination over beings.[56]

The disclosure of the interestedness of the discourse of humanism, of its arbitrary naturalness, also prepares us to perceive the complicity between the massive theoretical and institutional effort to recuperate the core curriculum and the modern disciplinary society. Far from countering the interested rapacity of the power structure that would achieve hegemony over the planet and beyond, the Apollonian educational discourse and practice of modern humanism in fact exists to reproduce its means and ends.

THREE

THE APOLLONIAN INVESTMENT OF MODERN HUMANIST EDUCATIONAL THEORY

THE EXAMPLES OF MATTHEW ARNOLD, IRVING BABBITT, AND I. A. RICHARDS

> The disclosure of being as such is simultaneously and intrinsically
> the concealing of being as a whole. In the simultaneity
> of disclosure and concealing errancy holds sway.
> Errancy and the concealing of what is concealed belongs
> to the primordial essence of truth.
>
> Martin Heidegger, "On the Essence of Truth"

> There is no center, but always decenterings, series that register
> the halting passage from presence to absence,
> from excess to deficiency. The circle must be abandoned
> as a faulty principle of return.
>
> Michel Foucault, "Theatrum Philosophicum"

I have suggested in the previous chapters that a destructive genealogy of humanism discloses its discourse of deliverance to be, in fact, a logocentrism that precipitates a binary logic—being/time, identity/difference, order/chaos, and so on—in which the first term is not simply privileged over the second, but is endowed with the authority and power to colonize the latter or to relegate it, in Thomas Pynchon's resonant term, to preterition. Far from being a mode of disinterested inquiry, humanism was discovered to be a naturalized version of the supernatural *Logos*. Its discourse is governed by a center, beyond the reach of free play, from which its panoptic I (eye) can spatialize and enframe, reify and comprehend ("take hold of," "grasp," "manage") the be-*ing*—the difference—that being-as-temporality always already disseminates.

In the different but fundamentally related terms suggested by Michel Foucault's genealogy of the disciplinary society, humanism comes to be understood as an intellectual and cultural legitimation of the dominant economic, social, and political power structures, which reproduces the world in its own image; it assimilates and circumscribes the other to the central proper self of capitalistic man. It comes to be recognized as an ideological apparatus that reduces the vital forces of difference in all their specific manifestations — from consciousness through gender and class to nature itself — to docile and efficient instruments of hegemonic power. Governed by the supervisory economy of this binary logic, the history of humanistic education since the Renaissance has been, therefore, a re-collective history undertaken in the name of presupposition-less inquiry. It has been a history of subtle and imperceptible coercion and pacification of the multiple differences precipitated by historically specific knowledge explosions that dis-integrate the existing "common (singular) body of humanistic knowledge" and threaten the dominant social consensus. As such, this history has been one of complicity with sociopolitical power.

This chapter is intended to contribute to the writing of this unwritten disciplinary history by doing "hermeneutic violence," as it were, to the theoretical humanistic discourses that have given shape to the liberal arts curricula of the Anglo-American institutions of higher learning in the modern period. More specifically, I will undertake a de-struction of the educational discourse of three exemplary humanists, Matthew Arnold, Irving Babbitt, and I. A. Richards, in order to disclose the will to power — the disciplinary imperative — that informs their commitment to "disinterested" inquiry. This assemblage is not as incongruous or arbitrary as it may seem at first glance. For each critic, as I will show, has had a continuing and significant, if not immediately visible, impact in this century on the idea and practice of liberal education at such bellwether institutions of higher learning as Harvard University, and also, and more important, an influence on the idea and practice of culture in the bourgeois capitalistic Anglo-American world at large.

I

Interpreted in terms of the prescriptive binary oppositions of metaphysics, Michel Foucault's analysis of panopticism as a "Benthamite physics of power"[1] might be taken to constitute an interrogation of spatial perception restricted exclusively to scientific positivism. Such an interpretation would thus provide "poetic" humanists — humanists professing the *litterae humaniores*, the humanities — with an unjustifiable justification for their idealistic alternative to the sciences regarding the question of knowledge and learning. Bentham's utilitarian panoptic schema is the culturally dominant manifestation of the metaphysical will to power over being in our historical conjuncture. But as Heidegger's destruction of the ontotheological tradition suggests, in disclosing, for example, the affiliation between Hegel and Descartes, both idealistic and empirical, subjective and objective, are derivative modes of inquiry that spatialize time from a *telos*. Panopticism, that is, is endemic not only to modern positivistic education but also to the modern humanistic alternative to positivism. I am referring, of course, to the idealistic *Bildung* that begins to assert itself in the Romantic period in Germany with Winckelmann's, Goethe's, and Schiller's apotheosis of aesthetic culture,[2] but that, because of the dominance of bourgeois capitalistic political and cultural values and the decadence of an aristocratic system, did not assume broadly effective authority in the Anglo-American world until the latter part of the nineteenth century with the enactment of electoral reforms and the democratization of educational opportunity to ward off social stratification.

It was, by and large, the success of John Stuart Mill's appeal to the therapeutic effects of "poetry" in a materialist society and, above all, Matthew Arnold's sustained effort to recuperate the classical tradition in the face of the seductive challenge of a revisionary utilitarian curriculum based on "objective science" and sponsored by such politically liberal heirs of Jeremy Bentham and the elder Mill as T. H. Huxley and Herbert Spencer[3] that assured a fundamental and privileged place for the humanities in higher, especially undergraduate, education in England and America. And it was also their success that enabled the affiliative continuity between their humanistic educational thought and that which has determined educational praxis up through the twentieth century to the present: that of Irving Babbitt, Paul Elmer More, the Cambridge Group (including E. M. W. Tillyard, H. M. Chadwick, M. D. Forbes, I. A. Richards, and later F. R. Leavis), Robert Hutchins, the authors of *General Education in a Free Society* (the so-called Harvard Redbook to which I. A. Richards also contributed), Jacques Barzun, Lionel Trilling, and, after the disruptions and dispersal of this tradition in the 1960s, Gerald Graff, M. H. Abrams, Wayne Booth, Walter Jackson Bate, the authors of the Harvard Core Curriculum Report, Allan Bloom, E. D. Hirsch, Roger Kimball, David Lehman, and Dinesh D'Souza.[4] The difference, finally, between the two "antithetical" approaches, or cultures, as they have come to be called—one emphasizing the physical sciences and the other the liberal arts—is not ontologically substantive. As Heidegger's and Gadamer's persuasive disclosure of the complicity between the propositions of empirical science and of idealism suggests,[5] both are affiliated supplements—supplements that, as Derrida's understanding of the term reminds us, always already disclose the absence of the privileged center they would reinstate—of a logocentrism that assumes the priority of a secondary or derivative (archival) mode of inquiry. It is simply that the sedimented humanistic rhetoric of deliverance—a rhetoric that identifies itself as against science as Freedom opposes Necessity—conceals and puts out of reach of the free play of criticism the panoptic model and its coercive, disciplinary manipulations more successfully than does positivism. What I am suggesting is perhaps best expressed by Francis Bacon, an admired forebear of modern scientific and poetic humanists alike: "The End of Our Foundation," his spokesman in *The New Atlantis* says, "is the knowledge of Causes and secret motions of things; and the enlarging of the bounds of Humane Empire, to the effecting of all things possible."[6]

Behind the innocent rhetoric of liberation—of disinterested inquiry, of sweetness and light—these humanists would implement against the mechanical abstractions of empirical science, lies the privileged, authorizing, and coercive image (*eidos, Bildung*) of metaphysics that also informs the Panopticon of the positivist Jeremy Bentham: the *centered circle* or, to appropriate the presiding and influential ontological metaphor of

T. S. Eliot's late metaphysical poetry, "the still point in the turning world." Though ostensibly justifying the liberal arts against the reifying consequences of an emergent "scientific education," each of these humanists, no less than their scientific counterparts, understands the knowledge context in terms of the binary logic of metaphysics: the one/many; presence/absence; identity/difference; eternity (universality)/time; permanence/ephemerality; objectivity/subjectivity; truth/error and its consequent binary ethical metaphorics: light/darkness; health/sickness; stability/volatility; purpose/drift; economy/waste; growth/decay; Apollo/Dionysus—in short, culture or anarchy.

For all their romantic warnings against abstraction and necessity, they understand the real danger to be the (Dionysiac) dispersal and proliferation of classical (Apollonian) knowledge; that is, the emergence of difference activated by the definitive rupture of the Western tradition and the decentering of the anthropologos in the modern world. Assuming, like Plato or Aquinas or Hegel, a disruptive violence against an authorizing origin—a fall from one kind of eternity or another into time—they perceive the ensuing diaspora as a fundamentally negative condition, the remediable cause of anxiety and perplexity. They thus prescribe the restoration of a holistic, integral, harmonious, balanced, closed, inclusive, total, and reassuring domain of knowledge grounded in what Derrida has called "a philosophy of presence"—a prelapsarian or universal and timeless norm or center. This hidden center is the sedimented word of Man, that is, the humanistic tradition, which is the naturalized supplement of the supernatural tradition of the Word of God. This "naturalized supernaturalism"—making the anthropologos (the self-identical ego of Man) the condition for the possibility of difference—is *the* constant of the discourse of modern Western humanism from its supplemental origins in German Romantic classicism to the present. It is the fundamental point of departure of Schiller's influential *On the Aesthetic Education of Man* (written in response to the Reign of Terror in France):

> The subject matter of activity . . . or the reality which the supreme
> Intelligence creates out of itself, must first be *received* by Man, and he does
> in fact receive it as something external to himself in space and as something
> changing within himself in time, through the medium of perception. This
> changing substance in him is accompanied by his never-changing ego—and to
> remain perpetually himself throughout all change, to turn every perception
> into experience, that is, into unity of knowledge, and to make each of his
> manifestations in time a law for all time, is the rule which is prescribed for
> him by his rational nature. Only as he alters does he *exist*; only as he remains
> unalterable does *he* exist. Man conceived in his perfection would accordingly
> be the constant unity which amidst the tides of change remains eternally the
> same.
>
> Now although an infinite being, a divinity, cannot *become*, we must surely

call divine a tendency which has for its infinite task the proper characteristic of divinity, absolute realization of capacity (actuality of all that is possible) and absolute unity of manifestation (necessity of all that is actual). Beyond question Man carries the potentiality for divinity within himself; the path to divinity, if we may call a path what never reaches its goal, is open to him in his *senses*.[7]

This humanization of the theologos is also, to recall the passage celebrating the humanistic literary tradition, the determining historical principle of M. H. Abrams's *Natural Supernaturalism* (written in response to the crisis precipitated by the disruption of the Vietnam decade):

> Much of what distinguishes writers I call "Romantic" derives from the fact that they undertook, whatever their religious creed or lack of creed, to save the traditional concepts, schemes, and values which had been based on the relation of the Creator to his creatures and creation, but to reformulate them within the prevailing two-term system of subject and object, ego and non-ego, the human mind or consciousness and its transactions with nature. Despite their displacement from a supernatural to a natural frame of reference, however, the ancient problems, terminology, and ways of thinking about human nature and history survived.[8]

What Derrida says about the logocentric tradition in general applies as well to the discourse of modern humanism:

> The concept of centered structure is in fact the concept of a play based on a fundamental ground, a play constituted on the basis of a fundamental immobility and a reassuring certitude, which itself is beyond the reach of play. And on the basis of this certitude anxiety [in the face of dispersal] can be mastered, for anxiety is invariably the result of a certain mode of being implicated in the game, of being caught by the game, of being as it were at stake in the game from the outset. And again on the basis of what we call the center (and which, because it can be either inside or outside, can also indifferently be called the origin or end, *arché* or *télos*), repetitions, substitutions, transformations, and permutations are always *taken* from a history of meaning [*sens*]—that is, in a word, a history—whose origin may always be reawakened or whose end may always be anticipated in the form of presence.[9]

Thus, like positivistic science, humanistic education, despite its appeal to the disinterested "play of mind," assumes a preordained norm immune to the assaults of temporal process and becomes essentially re-formist and disciplinary.

II

Through the black rushing smoke-bursts,
Thick breaks the red flame;
All Etna heaves fiercely
Her forest-clothed frame.

Not here, O Apollo,
Are haunts fit for thee

Matthew Arnold, "Callicles' Song," *Empedocles on Etna*

In his celebrated essay, "The Function of Criticism at the Present Time," Matthew Arnold, following Schiller, affirms "disinterestedness" as the measure for English criticism if it is "to avail itself of the field now opening to it, and to produce fruit for the future":

> The rule may be summed up in one word—*disinterestedness*. And how is criticism to show disinterestedness? By keeping aloof from what is called the "practical view of things"; by resolutely following the law of its own nature, which is to be a free play of the mind on all subjects which it touches. By steadily refusing to lend itself to any of those ulterior, political, practical considerations about ideas, which plenty of people will be sure to attach to them, which perhaps ought often to be attached to them, which in this country at any rate are certain to be attached to them quite sufficiently, but which criticism has really nothing to do with. Its business is, as I have said, simply to know the best that is known and thought in the world, and by in its turn making this known, to create a current of true and fresh ideas.[10]

In thus giving privileged status to disinterestedness in the pursuit of knowledge in the human sciences—impartiality toward, detachment and distantiation from, the immediate historical context—Arnold established the central and inviolable tenet of modern Anglo-American humanistic inquiry and educational theory and practice. More than any of the other values he reiterated over and over again in his prose, this one gained him his identity as the father of the most influential humanists of the modern period—those as diverse as Irving Babbitt, Lionel Trilling, F. R. Leavis, I. A. Richards, Walter Jackson Bate, and even T. S. Eliot—indeed, as the founder of modern humanism as an institution. A destructive reading of his discourse, especially of *Culture and Anarchy* (1869), discloses that Arnold's appeal to the disinterested play of consciousness against the partiality of interested inquiry and his apotheosis of culture over anarchy (whether literary or sociopolitical) conceal, in fact, the perennial nostalgia for a lost origin: the center beyond the reach of free play and the circle it precipitates to enframe and stabilize the differential and volatile "objects" under scrutiny and to master anxiety.

Given his commitment to the binary logic of the Western metaphysical tradition, Arnold's confrontation in *Culture and Anarchy* with an "epoch of expansion"[11]—the dislocating intellectual, cultural, social, and political irruptions of the industrialized nineteenth century—takes the inevitable form of re-collection and re-action. He represents the disintegration of theological doctrine and sanctions, sociopolitical hierarchies, and classical humanistic educational goals in the face of the proliferation of scientific, anthropological, sexual, geological (and thus Biblical) knowledge as essentially negative phenomena. For Arnold, the increasing demand for electoral reforms, educational opportunities, and a more equitable distribution of wealth are manifestations of the decadence. And the emergence of modern languages and their literatures are manifestations of the disintegration of culture. For all his rhetorical references to "'revolution by due course of law'" that "we are on our way to" (*CA*, pp. 135-36), these emergencies constitute for him symptoms of an incipient catastrophe—a fall from a concentrated state of ideal unity or equilibrium of forces ("Hellenism") grounded in the absolute origin (*arché*), into an apparently ungrounded ("provincial") and immiscible pluralism, an expansive and unbalanced anarchy. Such anarchy threatens the very well-being of Western Man, both individually and collectively. It is a precipitous momentum to which even the institutions of learning contribute their energies:

> And even the institutions, which should develop these ["culture, and the harmonious perfection of our whole being, and what we call totality"], take the same narrow and partial [Hebraist] view of humanity and its wants as the free religious communities take. Just as the free churches of Mr. Beecher or Brother Noyes, with their provincialism and want of centrality, make more Hebraisers in religion, and not perfect men, so the university of Mr. Ezra Cornell, a really noble monument of his munificence, yet seems to rest on a misconception of what culture truly is, and to be calculated to produce miners, or engineers, or architects, not sweetness and light. (*CA*, pp. 244-45)

So inscribed is the mystified paradigm of the centered circle in Arnold's consciousness that it precludes any intuition of the possibility that the explosion of hitherto repressed knowledge in nineteenth-century England and the ensuing cultural/political dispersal may have been in large part the consequence of the perennial humanistic effort to contain the expansive play of difference in being, language, culture, and society within the comprehensive orbit of humanism. Arnold's problematic blinds him to the possibility that interest, properly understood—decolonized, as it were—is the authentic agent of the free play of mind, the dialogical process that, *interesse* ("in the midst"), always makes a difference in the world.

Thus, beginning with the metaphysical binary interpretation of the open and disconcerting ambiguities, the mystery of being-in-the-world—culture or anarchy, civility or barbarism, sanity or madness, light or darkness, and, perhaps, West or East—Arnold meets the challenge of proliferation by substituting a "new" (which is, in fact, an older) center for the divine *Logos* that the intellectual and political history of his century had decentered and rendered untenable. Without ever pausing to interrogate the fundamental ideological assumptions of the old broken instrument (ontotheology) or the ideological sources of his commitment to disinterested inquiry—the imperative "to see life steadily and to see it whole"[12]—he insistently reaffirms the abiding "touchstones" of the logocentric humanistic mind. It becomes "the best that has been thought and said in the world [by which, as the omission of reference to any other makes clear, he means the *Western* world]" (*CA*, p. 233).[13] This recentering, this restoration of a common body of knowledge grounded on the anthropologos, is, according to Arnold, the one thing necessary (*CA*, p. 123; *porro unum est necessarium, CA*, pp. 176-91) for recuperating from the "social disintegration," the totalized and totalizing harmony of culture and the "aerial ease, clearness, and radiancy" of the "sweetness and light" (*CA*, p. 167) it promises even for the emergent working class.

The site of this recuperative activity is not, as it is usually understood to be, restricted simply to the site of culture per se. For this "one thing necessary," this enlightening and saving normative discipline, is discovered to be "the principle of authority" that, however unevenly developed, necessarily and simultaneously extends into and comprehends knowledge at all the sites on the continuum of being, from being itself to language, culture, and sociopolitics. Culture as right reason becomes the principle of authority for the recuperation of the "Establishments" (*CA*, p. 238), those institutions reflecting the mainstream of national life (*CA*, p. 249) that were disintegrating under the hammers of the emergent class-consciousness of the proletariat:

> Now, if culture, which simply means trying to perfect oneself, and one's mind as part of oneself, brings us light, and if light shows us that there is nothing so very blessed in merely doing as one likes, . . . that the really blessed thing is to like what right reason ordains, and to follow her authority, then we have got a practical benefit out of culture. [This is in response to the positivist charge that Arnold's "culture" was a dilettante's evasion of the sociopolitical imperatives of the human world.] We have got a much wanted principle, a principle of authority, to counteract the tendency to anarchy which seems to be threatening us.
>
> But how to organize this authority, or to what hands to entrust the wielding of it? (*CA*, p. 123)

And the too-assured (because logically "necessary") answer Arnold gives to these questions provoked by the threatening darkness of class conflict—an answer whose tautological argument is invariably overlooked in the selective mnemonic process of those sympathetic humanist commentators who identify Arnold with disinterested inquiry—is "to rise above the idea of class to the idea of the whole community, *the State*" (*CA*, p. 134).

In a democracy of "ordinary selves" which "do not carry us beyond the ideas and wishes of the class to which we happen to belong," we are "separate, personal, at war" (*CA*, p. 134). In contrast to the anarchic multiplicity and darkness of such a partial or decentered orientation, Arnold's "State," "so familiar on the Continent and to antiquity" (*CA*, p. 117), derives from the "best self," the "proper," cultured self, through which "we are united, impersonal, at harmony":

> We are in no peril from giving authority to this, because it is the truest friend we all of us can have; and when anarchy is a danger to us, to this authority we may turn with sure trust. Well, and this is the very self which culture, or the study of perfection, seeks to develop in us; at the expense of our old untransformed self, taking pleasure only in doing what it likes or is used to do, and exposing us to the risk of clashing with every one else who is doing the same! So that our poor culture, which is flouted as so unpractical, leads us to the very ideas capable of meeting the great want of our present embarrassed times! We want an authority, and we find nothing but jealous classes, checks, and a deadlock; culture suggests the idea of *the State*. We find no basis for a firm State-power in our ordinary selves; culture suggests one to us in our *best self*. (*CA*, pp. 134-35)[14]

Arnold's use of the first person plural pronoun in this passage—indeed, in his discourse at large—ostensibly refers to every individual member of the human community ("we all of us"). But close attention to the particular contexts of this usage reveals that, in fact, it refers to *no one in particular*. The "we" as "our best self" is the suprahistorical abstract standard or representational model (*arché* and *télos*) that Arnold derives from the texts privileged by the Western (humanistic) tradition and that he would impose, by way of "the State," as the measure of human practice in the volatile historical world of late nineteenth-century England. To put it another way, attention to the referential slides in Arnold's use of the inclusive first person plural pronoun discloses, in fact, a magisterial "we," speaking to and in behalf of the members of the culturally and sociopolitically dominant classes threatened by the emergent class consciousness and newly discovered desires of those whom the privileged have traditionally repressed: the "Populace," as Arnold contemptuously calls them:

> But that vast portion, lastly, of the working class which, raw and half-developed, has long lain half-hidden amidst its poverty and squalor, and is now issuing from its hiding-place to assert an Englishman's heaven-born privilege of doing as he likes, and is beginning to perplex us by marching where it likes, meeting where it likes, bawling what it likes, breaking what it likes,—to

this vast residium we may with great propriety give the name of *Populace*. (*CA*, p. 143)

The "we" that simultaneously speaks in the interest of the privileged minority and "for" the "vast residuum" of the weak is, in fact, a "we" that differentiates itself from the "other" in order to contain and pacify "them." As the "organ of our collective best self, our national right reason" (*CA*, p. 136), Arnold's "State" thus becomes the dominant culture's teleologically justified agency of forcing the imperfect "ordinary" (real) selves of the Barbarians, Philistines, and Populace toward their actualization and fulfillment in the (hierarchical) "*best self* and of punishing those who fail or resist" (*CA*, p. 117): the state, Arnold writes, is "the nation in its collective and corporate character, entrusted with stringent powers for the general advantage, and controlling individual wills in the name of an interest wider than that of individuals" (*CA*, p. 117). For all his seductive rhetoric about the sweetness and light of the state as our best self, this, finally, is what Arnold means by his reiterated assertion that the state is "our [true] centre of light and authority" (*CA*, p. 134).[15] If "we" cannot persuade the historically subordinated, who are beginning to act in behalf of their newly awakened consciousness of their deprivations, that culture or the "best self" is an end far more enriching than food, clothing, shelter, enfranchisement, then this state, which embodies culture and the best self, has the right, indeed the obligation, to use its repressive apparatuses against them.

The liberal humanist rhetoric that reiteratively equates light (knowledge) and authority (power) thus betrays Arnold's alleged disinterestedness to conceal a center elsewhere — the "*paramount* authority of a *commanding* best self, or right reason" (*CA*, p. 147; my emphasis) — which is both immune to the free play of criticism and actively determinative in the disposition, distribution, and grading of everything in time and space that it surveys. It is no accident that one of Arnold's most repeated maxims is "*Semper aliquid certi propenum*": "Always some certain end must be kept in view." And since this center of light and authority, this disinterested "best self," is "the State," his discourse also suggests that such a state is, finally, the re-collective or panoptic, and thus disciplinary, state. It is the state that actualizes in history the metaphysical consciousness that assumes the end to be ontologically prior to process, identity prior to difference, and justifies the coercion of anything that threatens to decenter the center, to anarchize the *arché*, as it were. There is, then, no room in the metaphysical or speculative space of Arnold's problematic for the ontological, linguistic, cultural, and sociopolitical questions — questions related to the second terms of the relay of binary oppositions — that would disrupt its still movement. His viciously circular problematic exists to colonize such questions by determining their proper place in the larger design of "our best self." "Humanism," to recall Foucault, "invented a whole series of subjected sovereignties: the soul (ruling the body, but subjected to God), consciousness (sovereign in a context of judgment, but subjected to the necessities of truth), the individual (a titular control of personal rights subjected to the laws of nature and society), basic freedom (sovereign within, but accepting the demands of an outside world and 'aligned with destiny'). In short, humanism is everything in Western Civilization that restricts the desire for power."

Arnold's "State," in other words, is not simply a state of mind, a mental model for the ordering of consciousness, of philosophical and literary discourse, of culture, as we have been led to think by his humanistic progeny's tendency to restrict Arnold's discourse to the site of culture. It is also and simultaneously a political state. It is, as the naturalized supernatural metaphorics of his discourse suggest, an idealized representation of the "main stream of the national life" of nineteenth-century England: the liberal middle-class/capitalistic allotrope of the ontological state that is designed to annul and domesticate the class consciousness of the working class and, when that proves impossible, to repress its overt disruptive manifestations in the name of "right reason" and the state of "perfection" it promises. This becomes grimly manifest in the Conclusion of *Culture and Anarchy*. Because it brings to explicit resolution the binary metaphorics of circle/panopticism/power informing Arnold's humanism (and, as we shall see, the Roman model informing his appeal to the literature of Greece), it warrants quoting at length:

> For we have seen how much of our disorders and perplexities is due to the disbelief, among the classes and combinations of men, Barbarian or Philistine, which have hitherto governed our society, in right reason, in a paramount best self; to the inevitable decay and break-up of organisations by which, asserting and expressing in these organisations their ordinary self only, they have so long ruled us; and to their irresolution, when the society, which their conscience tells them they have made and still manage not with right reason but with their ordinary self, is rudely shaken, in offering resistance to its subverters. But for us,—who believe in right reason, in the duty and possibility of extricating and elevating our best self, in the progress of humanity towards perfection,—for us the framework of society, that theatre on which this august drama has to unroll itself, is sacred; and whoever administers it, and however we may seek to remove them from their tenure of administration, yet, while they administer, we steadily and with undivided heart support them in repressing anarchy and disorder; because without order there can be no society, and without society there can be no human perfection.
>
> With me, indeed, this rule of conduct is hereditary. I remember my father, in one of his unpublished letters written more than forty years ago, when the political and social state of the country was gloomy and troubled, and there were riots in many places, goes on, after strongly insisting on the badness and foolishness of the government, and on the harm and dangerousness of

our feudal and aristocratic constitution of society, and ends thus: "As for rioting, the old Roman way of dealing with *that* is always the right one; flog the rank and file, and fling the ringleaders from the Tarpeian Rock!" (*CA*, pp. 222-23)[16]

We discover in Arnold's privileged principle of "disinterested inquiry" not the promised "sweetness and light," but the gall and darkness (for the underprivileged) it would alleviate in the name of the recuperation of culture, the naturalized supernatural state or earthly paradise of the nostalgic humanistic consciousness. In Nietzsche's and Foucault's terms, we discover humanistic "disinterest" to be an "Egyptianism," an instrument of repression (Arnold's own word) not simply of something as philosophically abstract as ontological errancy, but also as politically concrete as social protest in behalf of the right to vote:

And this opinion of the intolerableness of anarchy we can never forsake, however our Liberal friends may think a little rioting, and what they call popular demonstrations, useful sometimes to their own interests and to the interests of the valuable practical operations they have in hand, and however they may preach the right of an Englishman to be left to do as far as possible what he likes, and the duty of his government to indulge him and connive as much as possible and abstain from all harshness of repression. And even when they artfully show us operations which are undoubtedly precious, such as the abolition of the slave-trade, and ask us if, for their sake, foolish and obstinate governments may not wholesomely be frightened by a little disturbance, the good design in view and the difficulty of overcoming opposition to it being considered, — still we say no, and that monster-processions in the streets and forcible irruptions into the parks, even in professed support of this good design, ought to be unflinchingly forbidden and repressed; and that far more is lost than is gained by permitting them. Because a State in which law is authoritative and sovereign, a firm and settled course of public order, is requisite if man is to bring to maturity anything precious and lasting now, or to found anything precious and lasting for the future. (*CA*, p. 223)

Arnold, we should recall, is alluding generally to the massive workers' rallies organized in July 1866 by the Reform League (under the radical leadership of Edmond Beales, Charles Bradlaugh, and Lt. Col. Lothian Sheffield Dickson) in behalf of electoral reform. The central event to which Arnold refers is what he calls the "Hyde Park riots." On July 23, 1866, the Reform League organized a massive protest demonstration to be held at Hyde Park, which was prohibited by the Commissioner of Police, Sir Richard Mayne, under the instructions of the Home Secretary, Spencer Walpole, and the Conservative cabinet. Determined to hold their meeting, the workers defied the prohibition, broke down the iron railings, and entered the park. Although the government called out troops, an engagement did not occur and the demonstration took place.[17]

In the concluding pages of *Culture and Anarchy*, where he returns specifically to the theme of education, Arnold assumes, in the rhetoric of the detached magisterial "we," an assurance that must certainly have its source in what Foucault would call the panoptic gaze of the "general [universal] intellectual":

> Every one is now boasting of what he has done to educate men's minds and to give things the course they are taking. Mr. Disraeli educates, Mr. Bright educates, Mr. Beales educates. We, indeed, pretend to educate no one, for we are still engaged in trying to clear and educate ourselves. But we are sure that the endeavour to reach, through culture, the firm intelligible law of things, we are sure that the detaching ourselves from our stock notions and habits, that a more free play of consciousness, an increased desire for sweetness and light, and all the bent which we call Hellenising, is the master-impulse even now of the life of our nation and of humanity, — somewhat obscurely perhaps for this actual moment, but decisively and certainly for the immediate future; and that those who work for this are the sovereign educators. (*CA*, p. 229)

Understood in terms of the logocentrism that authorizes the panoptic geometry of the centered circle, Arnold's dream of restoring the Hellenistic spirit to modern educational theory and practice turns out to be inadequate to the challenge of the Bethamism of T. H. Huxley and Theodore Spencer—of science and capitalism and the liberal sociopolitical superstructure that these sanction, energize, and elaborate. Finally, his poetic humanism turns out to be complicitous with them, and not simply in the sense of inculcating an aloof quietism. Arnold's humanistic educational project does not represent an alternative to scientific positivism. It constitutes, rather, a replication on a different register of the Enlightenment's transformation of metaphysical oversight into a calculative panopticism. Despite its humane pretensions, it becomes in fact a mechanism of supervision, domination, and mastery—of re-formation—grounded in an anthropological norm established in the image of the dominant bourgeois capitalistic culture: the "best" as "proper self." It becomes, in other words, a *polyvalent* optics designed to assimilate and pacify the difference that Arnold represents as errant, deviant, eccentric: "monstrous," not simply at the ontological site but all along the continuum of being, especially at the sites of culture and sociopolitics. As Edward Said puts it:

> Even as an ideal for Arnold, culture must be seen as much for what it is not and for what it triumphs over when it is consecrated by the State as for what it positively is. This means that culture is a system of discriminations and evaluations . . . for a particular class in the State able to identify with it; and it also means that culture is a system of exclusions legislated from above but

enacted throughout its polity, by which such things as anarchy, disorder, irrationality, inferiority, bad taste, and immorality are identified, then deposited outside the culture and kept there by the power of the State and its institutions. For if it is true that culture is, on the one hand, a positive doctrine of the best that is thought and known, it is also on the other a differentially negative doctrine of all that is not best. If with Michel Foucault we have learned to see culture as an institutionalized process by which what is considered appropriate to it is kept appropriate, we have also seen Foucault demonstrating how certain alterities, certain Others, have been kept silent, outside or — in the case of his study of penal discipline and sexual repression — domesticated for use inside the culture.[18]

Committed with such sovereign certitude to his enlightening problematic, it was inevitable that Arnold should have failed to *see* that his insistent panoptic prescription to "see life steadily and to see it whole" as a "cure"[19] for the threat of anarchy was, in fact, grounded on the assumption that "life" was informed by a *presence* that transformed high seriousness into an undeviating will to power and inquiry into an inclusive panoptic or spatializing economy, the function of which was to reduce the infinite play of difference to the comprehensive circle of identity. To put it another way, it was inevitable that his humanistic insight should blind him to the fact that "disinterestedness" — "the free play of consciousness" — was, in Derrida's words, a "play . . . constituted on a fundamental immobility and a reassuring certitude which itself is beyond the reach of play," and that therefore such a "master-impulse even now of the life of our nation and of humanity" could only legitimate, indeed reinforce, the hegemonic aspirations of the English (and European) middle class and exacerbate the social and political disruptions he was trying to remedy.

Despite the different reality to which contemporaries or near contemporaries like Dickens, Dostoevsky, and Melville (and the Young Hegelians, Kierkegaard, Marx and Engels, and Nietzsche) were bearing witness, Arnold's Apollonian vision precluded awareness of the repressive praxis authorized by the imperative of high seriousness. It also precluded the possibility that the "confusion" and "perplexity" he said he saw everywhere in this centrifugal age of expansion — in language, culture, society, government — were, in fact, irruptions of the contradictions inherent in his discourse of deliverance, the retaliation of an alienated being (the other) against the enlightened logic of reification, against the Western eye's will to power over its energies: in short, of a repressed Dionysus against the privileged Apollo, the god of high seriousness.

III

> The true Greek . . . put his final emphasis, as befitted a child of
> Apollo, not on intoxication but on the law of measure and

MODERN HUMANIST EDUCATIONAL THEORY

sobriety—on preserving the integrity of his mind, to render
literally the Greek word for the virtue that he perhaps prized
most [Σωφροσυμη]. One must indeed remember that alongside
the Apollonian element in Greek life is the orgiastic or Dyonisiac
[sic] element. But when Euripides sides imaginatively with the
frenzy of Dionysus, as he does in his "Bacchae," though
ostensibly preaching moderation, we may affirm that he is falling
from what is best in the spirit of Hellas and revealing a kinship
with the votaries of the god Whirl.

Irving Babbitt, *Rousseau and Romanticism*

In an example closer to the North American context, the figure of the centered circle
also informs the discourse on higher education of Irving Babbitt, the professor of
French literature who, in the first decades of the century, attempted to transplant Matthew Arnold's recuperative archival message into the Harvard garden, which the
"Rousseauistic" president, Charles William Eliot, had allowed to go to seed by intro-
ducing the elective system. Like Arnold in *Culture and Anarchy*, Babbitt in *Literature
and the American College* (1908) represents the present as a fall from a previous golden
age (classical Greece and the Renaissance) into a proliferating anarchy, and pictures
himself as one of the saving remnant. The contemporary situation, according to Babbitt, is the result of a deracination of a prior fixed center—an ideal and static state of
organic unity and balanced sanity—into a degenerative or decadent *kinesis*. Greece,
for example, "having lost its traditional standards through the growth of intellectual
skepticism, fell into a dangerous and excessive mobility of mind because of its failure to
develop new standards that would unify its life and impose a discipline upon the individual."[20] Similarly, the modern age comes "at the end of an era of expansion" (*LAC*,
p. 219) characterized by intellectual and political deviance whose exorbitance threatens
to unleash a material and spiritual barbarism that will overwhelm the circle of the *polis*.
Under the impetus of the "scientific naturalism and humanitarianism" (*LAC*, p. 35) of
Francis Bacon and, above all, the "sentimental naturalism" (*LAC*, p. 35) of Jean-
Jacques Rousseau, whose anticlassical "eccentricity" (*LAC*, p. 228) instigated "the
most powerful insurrection the world has ever seen against every kind of authority"
(*LAC*, p. 184), the present age has fallen out of orbit.[21] "Now, as then [the Renais-
sance]," Babbitt observes, in a rhetoric that goes beyond Arnold's usually "soft" authority, "there is a riot of so-called originality. In the name of this originality art is
becoming more and more centrifugal and eccentric. As the result of our loss of standards . . . we are inbreeding personal and national peculiarities and getting farther and
farther away from what is universally human" (*LAC*, pp. 219-20, 230). This "eccentricity," it is important to emphasize, is not simply a matter of idiosyncratic behavior.
For Babbitt, the meaning of this key word resonates back and forth from the spatial

figure—the geometry, as it were—informing its etymology. What he literally visualizes when he uses the word is an action that takes place outside the circumference of a circle, the peripheric border of an enclosure. This is implicit everywhere in *Literature and the American College*, but it is most explicitly stated in *Rousseau and Romanticism* (1919):

> The Rousseauist tends . . . to repudiate the very idea of an ethical centre along with the special forms in which it had got itself embedded. Every attempt, whether humanistic or religious, to set up some such centre, to oppose a unifying and centralizing principle to expansive impulse, seems to him arbitrary and artificial. He does not discriminate between the ethical norm or centre that a Sophocles grasps intuitively and the centrality that the pseudo classicist hopes to achieve by mechanical imitation. He argues from his underlying assumption that the principle of variation is alone vital, that one's genius and originality are in pretty direct ratio to one's eccentricity in the literal meaning of the word; and he is therefore ready to affirm his singularity or difference in the face of whatever happens to be established.[22]

This proliferation of new knowledge and consequent differentiation of personal and cultural characteristics—this expansive decentering—has its ultimate historical source, according to Babbitt, in the triumph of the moderns in the *querelle des anciens et modernes*. In a way that recalls Arnold and, as we shall see, remarkably anticipates not only I. A. Richards but Walter Jackson Bate and Allan Bloom, Babbitt attributes the dangerous "centrifugal" or "expansive" momentum that is taking us "farther and farther away from what is universally human"[23] to the Romanticists' development of the historical method, "which has proven so powerful a *solvent* of both Christian and classical dogma" (*LAC*, p. 185; my emphasis). In discovering the strange and virtually immiscible languages and cultures of the Far East, their inordinate "study of origins" has become the "means of undermining the classical orthodoxy" and its archivalized (and ethnocentric) rules of discourse and thus has precipitated cultural anarchy.

> The revelation of remote times and countries that were plainly cultivated, and yet in a way so strangely different from our own, had in it a potent suggestion of the new doctrine of relativity; it taught men to see
>
> > "Beyond their passion's widest range
> > Far regions of eternal change."
>
> It helped him to feel that there was no standard of taste, as the classicists maintained, but a multiplicity of standards, each one justified by the special circumstances of its age and environment. (*LAC*, pp. 190-91)

Assuming (his version of) the Greek standard and its binary metaphysical structure to be unquestionably natural and right, Babbitt like Arnold (though more dogmatically) would thus return to "classical Greece" and its luminous idea of human being. For, as he says in *Rousseau and Romanticism*, "in the life of no other people perhaps does what is universal in man shine forth more clearly from what is only local and relative." For Babbitt, that is, the one needful thing in a world threatened by anarchy is the recuperation of Apollonian man: that representative (central) Man purged of and "set above the local and relative" and thus capable of "detect[ing] this abiding element through all the flux of circumstance; in Platonic language, [seeing] the One in the Many." Though Babbitt appeals to Aristotle in his representation of Greece, it is the authority of Matthew Arnold's Victorian (English middle-class and, as I will suggest, imperialist) Aristotle that he is really invoking. Babbitt, that is, recalls Arnold's distinction between the interested and erratic "ordinary self" and the "disinterested" center of light and authority, the "best self"—the polyvalent rule of propriety proper to the proper self:

> Like all the great Greeks Aristotle recognizes that man is the creature of two
> laws: he has an ordinary or natural self of impulse and desire and a human
> self that is known practically as a power of control over impulse and desire. If
> man is to become human he must not let impulse and desire run wild, but
> must oppose to everything excessive in his ordinary self, whether in thought
> or deed or emotion, the law of measure. This insistence on restraint and
> proportion is rightly taken to be of the essence not merely of the Greek
> spirit but of the classical spirit in general. The norm or standard that is to set
> bounds to the ordinary self is got at by different types of classicists in
> different ways and described variously: for example, as the human law, or the
> better self, or reason . . . or nature.[24]

Finally, this Victorian/Greek standard of the "best self" informs Babbitt's definition of humanism in *Literature and the American College*:

> We may perhaps venture to sum up the results of our search for a definition
> of humanism. We have seen that the humanist, as we know him historically,
> moved between an extreme of sympathy and an extreme of discipline and
> selection, and became humane in proportion as he mediated between these
> extremes. To state this truth more generally, the true mark of excellence in
> a man . . . is his power to harmonize in himself opposite virtues and to
> occupy all the space between them. . . . By his ability thus to unite in himself
> opposite qualities man shows his humanity, his superiority of essence over
> other animals. (*LAC*, p. 22)

As the military metaphors suggest, what this achieved equilibrium of qualities means in practice is the hierarchization of Western binary logic, in which "selection" and "discipline" colonize and pacify "sympathy" or any other "impulse" or "desire" that threatens order. Like Arnold's, Babbitt's humanism does not deny difference; rather, it makes identity the condition for its possibility.

The classical humanism Babbitt would have higher education inculcate in the young, in other words, is a recollected ethnocentric humanism purged not only of its later "humanitarian" accretions but also, if more discreetly, of the new, "solvent" knowledge of remote times and nations: precisely those "others" (as opposed to "us") precipitated by the "historical method" (if not by the dynamics of temporality) and now precipitating the disruptive "mobility of mind," the "multiplicity of standards," and the deviant and eccentric intellectual and sociopolitical behavior that characterizes the modern age and threatens the well-being of humanity at large. Babbitt, unlike Arnold, expresses unusual interest in the question of East-West relations. Having studied Sanskrit and Pali at Harvard and the Sorbonne and translated the Buddhist *Dhammapada* from the Pali,[25] Babbitt, in a late text such as "Buddha and the Occident" (1927), even criticizes Western imperialism and its assumption of cultural superiority over the East.[26] But Babbitt's essential project vis-à-vis the Orient is from the beginning "classical." His purpose is to counter what he mistakenly takes to be the Romantic poets' and philosophers' tendency to read the newly discovered artifacts of Oriental culture as further justification for their commitment to the local, the strange, the exotic (i.e., to multiplicity and thus to the relativity of standards) by accommodating Oriental thought and art, especially their will to transcend the temporal and local occasion, to his version of classical Greek humanism. Thus, for example, his insistent interpretation of Buddha's *dhamma* as "human law, as one may render it, in contradiction to the law of physical nature";[27] his preference for the early Buddhism of the Pali canon ("the basis of the form of religion known as the Hinayana or Small Vehicle, which prevails in Ceylon, Burma, and other countries") over the texts of the Mahayana or Great Vehicle ("which, variously modified, prevails in Thibet, China, Korea, and Japan");[28] and his privileging of Buddhist "religion" and the "humanism of Confucious" over the Taoism of Lao-tzu and Chuang-tzu, which he compares with the "Rousseauism" of the Romantics.[29] Babbitt's representation of the Oriental texts he addresses, in other words, is essentially European. Like the texts of so many nineteenth- and early twentieth-century Western students of the Orient—Lane, Renan, Massignon, Gibb, for example—his is what Edward Said would call "Orientalist."

Given Babbitt's insistent invocation of "rule," "standard," "norm"—the human "law of Measure"—it is no accident that he should privilege "representative human nature," which, in turn, precipitates an opposed rhetoric of otherness culminating in the "monstrous":

> Having decided what is normal either for man or some particular class of men
> the classicist takes this normal "nature" for his model and proceeds to imitate

it. Whatever accords with the model he has thus set up he pronounces natural or probable, whatever on the other hand departs too far from what he conceives to be the normal type or the normal sequence of cause and effect he holds to be "improbable" and unnatural or even, if it attains an extreme of abnormality, "monstrous."[30]

This all-encompassing term, which we have also encountered in Arnold's discourse, suggests not only the humanist's anxiety in the face of difference, but also, as the etymology of the word implies, his ultimate commitment to a self-leveling and homogenizing process that reduces the self to a "visible invisibility"—a dedifferentiated difference—in order to neutralize its susceptibility to violence from without. In Heidegger's terms, Babbitt's representational humanism ends in the production of "public man": *Das Man.*[31]

It was, according to Babbitt, the "ordinary self," the "spontaneous play of impulse and temperament" unleashed by Rousseau and the cult of Romantic genius that precipitated the crisis of modern man. To achieve balance and sanity, Babbitt, like Arnold, calls for a reinstitution of the "best self." Thus Babbitt's principle of impartiality, like Arnold's, is an interested disinterest, the disciplinary panoptic measure of the anthropologos.

> Man is a creature who is foredoomed to one-sidedness, yet who becomes humane only in proportion as he triumphs over this fatality of his nature, only as he arrives at that measure which comes from tempering his virtues, each by its opposite. The aim, as Matthew Arnold has said in the most admirable of his phrases, is to see life steadily and see it whole. (*LAC*, p. 23)

Grounded in an unmoving center that simultaneously shapes what it encounters in the world yet remains immune to the assaults of history, Babbitt's measure thus authorizes, indeed demands, a "sense of form and proportion," "fastidious selection," "restraint," and, above all, "discipline." This centered standard constitutes the means and end of Culture:

> The very heart of the classical message, one cannot repeat too often, is that one should aim first of all not to be original, but to be human, and that to be human one needs to look up to a sound model and imitate it. The imposition of form and proportion upon one's expansive impulses which results from this process of imitation is, in the true sense of that much abused word, culture. Genuine culture is difficult and disciplinary.[32]

And it is, of course, the function of undergraduate education to instill the (privileged) young with this recuperative measure, for which "there was never greater need . . . than there is today, and especially in this country" (*LAC*, p. 179): "In general, education should represent the conservative and unifying element in our national life. Its function is not, as is so often assumed, merely to help its students to self-expression, but even more to help them to become humane; . . . [The end of college education] is to supply principles of taste and judgement and train in sanity and centrality of view; to give background and perspective, and inspire, if not the spirit of conformity, at least a proper respect for the past experience of the world" (*LAC*, pp. 240-42).

The parallel with Arnold's classical humanism—and Bentham's Enlightenment utilitarianism—should by now be obvious. However "humane" the humanistic rhetoric that invests it, Babbitt's one needful thing in the face of a rampant Rousseauism is, finally, a totalitarian ideology: a panoptic instrumental measure based on an absolute origin which allows life to be *seen* steadily and *seen* whole. (One should not overlook the binary metaphysics of sobriety/inebriation and its integral affiliation with that of space/time in this Arnoldian formula.) As such it justifies the coercive circumscription and re-formation of the intemperate "natural" impulses of the "ordinary self" to deviate, the difference that characterizes the other (which Babbitt's binary logic compels him to interpret as the fatal Adamic "one-sidedness" of human beings), for the sake of saving Man from the fallen state of dispersal (into particular men and women not as sovereign subjects, but beings-in-the-world):

> For most practical purposes, the law of measure is the supreme law of life, because it *bounds and includes* all other laws. . . . Greece is perhaps the most humane of countries, because it not only formulated clearly the law of measure ("nothing too much"), but also perceived the avenging nemesis that overtakes every form of insolent excess (ὕβρις) or violation of this law.
> (*LAC*, p. 24; my emphasis)[33]

As in Arnold's discourse, moreover, Babbitt's measure is informed by an ideology that is not limited to the cultural site, but extends into and affects every other site on the continuum of being, particularly, as we shall see, the sites of gender and of sociopolitics.

Given his relentlessly undeviating commitment to the centrality and circumscribing inclusiveness of the "law of measure," it was inevitable that Babbitt should interpret President Charles Eliot's antipatriarchal and antiarchival introduction and encourage-ment of the elective system at Harvard as essentially "Rousseauistic." It is difficult to determine whether Eliot's elective system was truly democratic since it was accom-modational; that is, it was designed in some degree to absorb an expanding student population, and to readjust the classical bent of Harvard University and American higher education at large to fit the social imperatives of a society being overdetermined by science, technology, and industrialization. Further, Eliot's elective system was even-tually transformed into a cultural apparatus that harnessed the new knowledge produc-tion to the disciplinary society. This became quite clear in the project of the Harvard Redbook in the Cold War period. It did, however, open up the classical (gentlemen's) curriculum and its institutional space to students from hitherto excluded social strata, and thus it created the tension between ideas that a Henry Adams, attuned to the pro-liferation of knowledge accompanying the decentering of the classical center in the late nineteenth century, found wanting.[34] In Babbitt's eyes, therefore, Eliot's opening up of the closed undergraduate curriculum to historical differences precipitated by an "era of [intellectual and sociopolitical] expansion" simply carried the disintegrative effects of a certain avant-garde painting and fiction into the domain of *paideia*:

> President Eliot speaks as a pure Rousseauist in a passage like the following:
> "A well-instructed youth of eighteen can select for himself a better course of study than any college faculty, or any wise man who does not know him. . . . Every youth of eighteen is an indefinitely complex organization, the duplicate of which neither does nor ever will exist." There is then no general norm, no law for man, as the humanist believed, with reference to which the individual should select; he should make his selection entirely with reference to his own temperament and its (supposedly) unique requirements. The wisdom of all the ages is to be as naught compared with the inclination of a sophomore. Any check that is put on this inclination is an unjustifiable constraint, not to say an intolerable tyranny. Now inasmuch as the opinions of even a "well-instructed youth of eighteen" about himself and his own attitudes are likely to shift and veer this way and that according to the impressions of the moment, we may, perhaps, designate the system that would make these opinions all-important, "educational impressionism." This inordinate exaltation of the individual sense as compared with the general or common sense of mankind scarcely ante-dates Rousseau. (*LAC*, pp. 47-48)

Nor was it accidental that, against this infected and contagious "educational impres-sionism" which fed the decadent "centrifugal and eccentric" impulse of modern (Rous-seauistic) man and exacerbated the breakdown of traditional hierarchical structures, Babbitt, like Arnold, should invoke the "healing Hellenic spirit" and reaffirm the study of the classics—a canonical core curriculum, as it were—which embody "the seasoned and matured experience of a multitude of men, extending over a considerable time, as to the studies they actually found helpful and formative" (*LAC*, p. 82). Given his "law of measure," it was inevitable that Babbitt should privilege literary texts that represent (and reproduce) the "proper" essence of (Western) Man to himself and should endorse a teleological history of literature that excluded, as inessential to or disruptive of this essence, the interested and relevant expression (occasioned by repressed desire) of the differences that time disseminates: "When books like the Greek and Latin classics have survived for centuries after the languages in which they are written are dead, the presumption is that these books themselves are not dead, but rather very much alive—that they are less related than most other books to what is ephemeral and more related to what is permanent in human nature. By innumerable experiments the world slowly winnows out the more essential from the less essential and so gradually builds up standards of judgment" (*LAC*, pp. 82-83). As Babbitt says elsewhere in his text, the classics constitute a "golden chain of masterpieces which link together into a simple tradition the more permanent experiences of the race; books which so agree in essentials that they seem, as Emerson puts it, *to be works of one all-seeing gentleman*" (*LAC*, p. 244; my emphasis).[35] In thus betraying his unshakable commitment to the concentric end from the beginning, Babbitt utterly precludes originative and explorative inquiry in scholarship, interpretation, criticism, and teaching in favor of what Pierre Macherey, after Althusser, calls the normative fallacy of confirmation, according to which

> the work should be other than it is; its only reality is its relationship to the model which was the very condition of its elaboration. The work can be corrected and effectively modified by continuous comparison with the model which has an independent, *a priori* existence. . . . Hypothetically, the work is *preceded*. The unfolding of its text is mere fiction. The work can only advance towards an identity already fixed in the model. Whatever the chosen route, it will always be possible to imagine one shorter and better. Any reading, any detour is legitimate. The critical reading is the more direct, and because it is guided by anticipations of the model, it can move faster than the narrative. . . . The literal narrative is irrelevant because it serves only to hide a secret and can be cast aside once this secret is revealed.[36]

The standards of judgment thus precipitated by the establishment of a canon of classics are, of course, archival standards—"rules of discursive formation" as Foucault would call them—which, according to Babbitt, are alone capable of stemming the ("feminine") floodtide of the Rousseauistic dispersion. That is, in establishing the exclusive/inclusive "law of measure in the matters of the mind" (*LAC*, p. 137), the classics inculcate, above all, "sanity and centrality of view" (*LAC*, p. 240)—a standard that both heals spiritual illness and facilitates the recuperation of the "manly" "*assimilative* power of the mind*" (*LAC*, p. 212; my emphasis). A study of this core or canon of classics then assures the reproduction and perpetuation of a circumscribed, inclusive, unified, and hierarchical culture at the apex of which an elite cadre presides. It is not enough, according to Babbitt, to stigmatize American education simply "as 'receptive' . . . 'passive' or 'feminine' " as one German critic does. For this is "to overlook that humane endeavor which it is the special purpose of the college to foster—that effort of reflection, virile above all others, to coordinate the scattered elements of knowledge, and relate them not only to the intellect but to the will and character; that subtle alchemy by which mere learning is transmuted into culture" (*LAC*, p. 101).

Ultimately and predictably, in reaffirming the core of classics and the assimilative powers of the mind it nourishes, Babbitt recuperates the "virile" meta-physical/patriarchal cultural memory, which perceives the differential temporal process of human experience and history (including literary production) from after or above and thus is enabled to *see* or to *supervise* being all at once: "to see life steadily and see it whole!"[37] In other words, Babbitt's "memory" is the masterful—and forgetful— archival or recollective or monumental memory of the dominant culture. Despite the substitutions of one center for another and the insistent interrogation of its authority by "marginal" writers like Euripides (whom Babbitt repeatedly derogates), Rabelais, Cervantes, Sterne, and the Brontës and thinkers like Heraclitus, Rousseau, Kierke- gaard, and Nietzsche, this memory supervises and determines inquiry, poetry, inter- pretation, and pedagogy throughout the history of the West to Babbitt's present—from Plato through Aquinas to More, Descartes, Hegel, and Bentham; from Virgil through Dante to Balzac and T. S. Eliot; from Cicero through Castiglione and Elyot to Newman and Arnold. Finally, it represents be-*ing* and by its violence brings a temporally dis- seminated *presence* to stand in the (still) form of a treasured monument:

> In short, the practical way of promoting humanism is to work for a revival of
> the almost lost art of reading. As a general rule, the humane man will be the
> one who has a memory richly stored with what is best in literature, with the
> sound sense perfectly expressed that is found only in the masters.
> Conversely, the decline of humanism and the growth of Rousseauism has
> been marked by a steady decay in the higher uses of the memory. For the
> Greeks the Muses were not daughters of Inspiration or Genius, as they
> would be for a modern, but the daughters of Memory. (*LAC*, p. 244)[38]

What the monumentalized classics ultimately teach, what the centered "humane en- deavor" they instill in the student reproduces, is the supervisory and forgetful or repressive recollection of metaphysics, variously identified by the postmodern coun- termemory as a *circulus vitiosis* (Heidegger);[39] "a play . . . constituted on the basis of a fundamental immobility and a reassuring certitude, which itself is beyond the reach of play" (Derrida); a paradigm of "Resemblance" (Foucault);[40] a problematic of "expres- sive causality" (Althusser).[41] They reproduce, that is, the panoptic will to power, which, in as-*similating* the "scattered elements of knowledge," coerces, levels, and homogenizes the heterogeneity, the differences, of things-as-they-are (*physis*) into the shape of the *same* (*homo*), the dis-similarities of be-ing into the similarity of Being, multiplicity into the one (the *total simul*), time into *simultaneity* (space); this panoptic will also *simulates* (re-presents and thus falsifies and alienates) the duplicity, the dis- *simulation*, that is, the "essence" of the errant and ludic "truth" of man's and woman's dispersed occasion, the truth not as correspondence but, in Heidegger's term, as *a-letheía*.

This will to power—this "mystery management" in Geoffrey Hartman's apt phrase— informing Babbitt's panoptic assimilative scholarship explains the alienating violence he does to the literature he addresses, not only to those eccentric or deviant texts of

Euripides, Rousseau, Wordsworth, Chateaubriand, or Baudelaire that he would exclude from the canon of humanistic masterpieces, but also to those "centric" and "viant" classics of Plato, Aristotle, Sophocles, Montaigne, Burke, and Goethe that he would reaffirm in behalf of the New Humanism. I mean his reduction of the play of the minute particulars, the disruptive *differance* — the Dionysiac force — of the text to generalized, exemplary doctrine that alienates the being of the text in the degree to which the assimilative power of the "concentric" mind reifies and masters its occasional measure. As R. P. Blackmur puts it, in comparing Babbitt to William James ("a name chosen because it stood for the experimental, the ambiguous, the possible, all of which Babbitt detested"):

> He taught not by sympathy or persuasion or personality, by stretching the student mind, but by force. He limited mind where James stretched it. . . . It was as if he taught music, and taught it magnificently, but only in the written score. . . .
>
> The figure is not as forced as it may sound: for what did he teach — what in all the enormous mass of literature that he read did he praise — but those great dead writers whose works we know precisely only as scores, with an imperfect clue to the notation even there, and which we cannot play at all. These are the writers whose ideas have survived and can be dealt with as formulas, as abstractions of the middle way, but whose poetry, what happened when their ideas got into drama, or got lodged in actuality, we must through ignorance for the most part let go by the board, unless in ourselves, in our own imaginations, in the literature of our own time, we can see the poetry refreshed. Sophocles is nothing without his violence; Antigone a mere mechanical fanatic without her folly; Creon an ineffectual ranting without his stupidity; Ismene a mere vapor without her double charge of fear and love. In short, the whole Greek drama is nothing but exemplary if we do not ourselves supply the violence, the folly, the stupidity, the mixture of fear and love. Babbitt was not only content with the exemplary, he insisted on its dominance at the expense of every other interest. That is why he never seemed inside his examples.[42]

As in the case of Matthew Arnold, though far more overtly and forcefully, this inhumane and alienating will to power, this impulse to discipline beginnings from the panoptic end (outside his examples), is enacted whatever the particular site Babbitt chooses, in his utterly exemplary, exhausted, insistently graceless, tendentious, and judgmental discourse. Its imperialist operation in *Literature and the American College* is not limited to literature, culture, and education; it also extends into the areas of gender and sociopolitics, however marginal these apparently are to his main concern.

One finds this will to power, for example, in Babbitt's peripheral attribution of the historical decline of the authority of classical languages and literatures in college curricula to the emergence of a wide female readership (which he associates with the opening of institutions of higher learning to the utilitarian and opportunistic "multitude") that prefers modern (romantic) novels to Sophocles and Aeschylus or Plato and Aristotle:

> Modern languages . . . have had little to do but succeed. They have benefited by their utilitarian appeal, and in the case of one's mother tongue by their appeal to sentiment. They have benefited by the constantly increasing influence of women in literature and education. As a substitute for Greek and Latin, they have attracted the vast multitude which in its choice of studies follows more or less consciously the line of least resistance. (*LAC*, p. 182)

But it is not so much Babbitt's overtly prejudicial references to "women in literature and education" that betray the patriarchal will to power over being saturating Babbitt's discourse. It is, as in the case of a number of passages already quoted from *Literature and the American College*, the phallocentrism inscribed in yet hidden behind Babbitt's "disinterested" inquiry. I mean the identification, assumed to be natural everywhere in his texts, of the feminine sensibility with the eccentric and expansive impulse (the "Rousseauism") that he believes threatens to overwhelm Western civilization and, conversely, the identification of the masculine or virile principle with the classical spirit, the recuperation of which would save Western civilization.

> [Rousseau's] general readiness to subordinate his ethical self to his sensibility is indubitable. Hence the absence in his personality and writing of the note of masculinity. There is indeed much in his make-up that reminds one less of a man than of a high-strung impressionable woman. Woman, most observers would agree, is more natural in Rousseau's sense, that is, more temperamental, than man. One should indeed always temper these perilous comparisons of the sexes with the remark of La Fontaine that in this matter he knew a great many men who were women. Now to be temperamental is to be extreme, and it is in this sense perhaps that the female of the species may be said to be "fiercer than the male." Rousseau's failure to find "any intermediary term between everything and nothing" would seem to be a feminine rather than a masculine trait. Decorum in the case of women, even more perhaps than in the case of men, tends to be a mere conformity to what is established rather than the immediate perception of a law of measure and proportion that sets bounds to the expansive desires.[43]

As my epigraph for this section from *Rousseau and Romanticism* bears witness, Babbitt's subliminal rhetoric never lets readers forget that the inebriated devotees of Dionysus ("the god of Whirl," who would usurp the authority of "sober" and "virile"

Apollo) were the Bacchae. Indeed, it would not be an exaggeration to say that the phallocentric male/female opposition constitutes the metaphorical configuration that comprehends and includes all the other pairs of his logocentric binary logic.

It should be obvious at this juncture that Babbitt's "virile" — indeed, "virulent" — cultural discourse, however invested by the rhetoric of liberality, betrays, like Arnold's (as well as Bentham's, Locke's, and Mill's) classical liberalism, its affiliation with an essentially reactionary sociopolitics. Like the American college, which in the name of (classical) Man must inculcate the concentric disciplinary measure in its fallen (natural and expansive) students, so the state, governed by the "saving remnant" in the name of the transcendental "best self," must purge the multitude of "natural" and "ordinary" selves of their naturalness and ordinariness. What is only implicit in *Literature and the American College* because of its underdeveloped thematic status becomes explicit in *Democracy and Leadership* (1924), a text written in the aftermath of the Russian Revolution:

> The view that inspired our Constitution [as opposed to the Declaration of
> Independence] . . . has much in common with that of Burke. If the first of
> these political philosophies [that man has certain abstract rights] is properly
> associated with Jefferson, the second has its distinguished representative in
> Washington. The Jeffersonian liberal has his faith in the goodness of the
> natural man, and so tends to overlook the need of a veto power either in the
> individual or in the State. The liberals of whom I have taken Washington to be
> the type are less expansive in their attitude towards the natural man. Just as
> man has a higher self that acts restrictively on his ordinary self, so, they
> hold, the State should have a higher or permanent self, appropriately
> embodied in institutions, that should set bounds to its ordinary self as
> expressed by the popular will at any particular moment. The contrast that I
> am establishing is, of course, that between a constitutional and a direct
> democracy. There is an opposition of first principles between those who
> maintain that the popular will should prevail, but only after it has been
> purified of what is merely impulsive and ephemeral, and those who maintain
> that this will should prevail immediately and unrestrictedly.[44]

Like Arnold, Babbitt invokes Edmund Burke in his apotheosis of the state as the embodiment of the "best self." But unlike Arnold's political discourse, on which Burke's concluding deconstruction of his critique of the French Revolution in "Thoughts on French Affairs" (December 1791) made a powerful and in a sense redemptive impact,[45] Babbitt's, as the rhetoric of purification in this passage and elsewhere in his texts suggests, is so absolutely centered that it cannot allow any disruptive gesture to challenge it. Thus emptied out of temporal content, Babbitt's "virile" or, to anticipate, "Roman" humanistic discourse, for all its justified criticism of the "standardized mediocrity of

American Democracy," becomes in its pursuit of totalization in the face of the Red Scare an absolutely inclusive circle, an instrument—a technology, as it were—of something like totalitarian power:

> The time may come, with the growth of a false liberalism, when a predominant element in our population, having grown more and more impatient of the ballot box and representative government, of constitutional limitations and judicial control, will display a growing eagerness for "direct action." This is the propitious moment for the imperialist leader. Though the triumph of any type of imperialistic leader is a disaster, especially in a country like our own that has known the blessings of liberty under the law, nevertheless there is a choice even here. Circumstances may arise when we may esteem ourselves fortunate if we get the American equivalent of a Mussolini; he may be needed to save us from the American equivalent of a Lenin. Such an emergency is not to be anticipated, however, unless we drift even further than we have thus far from the principles that underlie our unionist tradition. The maintenance of this tradition is indissolubly bound up with maintenance of standards.[46]

Commenting on precisely this passage from *Democracy and Leadership*, R. P. Blackmur writes:

> One reflects how magnificently the notion of humility might have been modified by the notion of the free conscience as a refuge ["from the encroachments of the omnipotent state"], and likewise how the notion of humility (which in Babbitt consists partly in looking up in order to be safe in looking down, and partly in strenuous meditation) could have enriched the function of the free conscience. Instead, Babbitt uses both to strike down the Civil Religion of Rousseau as sentimental and utilitarian and in general a mere vanity of intellect. We can add for him, then, what he did not see, that as he did not possess grace neither did he possess the refuge of a free conscience, whether Christian or its equivalent. It seems almost superfluous to say that had he possessed either he could not have said that "Circumstances may arise when we may esteem ourselves fortunate if we get the American equivalent of a Mussolini; he may be needed to save us from the American equivalent of a Lenin." That the remark was made in 1923 eases its folly but does not reduce either its arrogance, its extravagance, or the failure to understand American history which it implies. Even in 1923 the castor oil cure for political opposition was no more humanistic than it was humanitarian, and castor oil, street fighting, murder and sabotage of spirit, made up the features of fascist decorum.

The point is, that Babbitt was willing to enslave his conscience in fact, to make it a prison rather than a refuge for individual liberty, at the dictation of a merely intellectual order.[47]

In thus exposing Babbitt's reactionary antipathy for democratic politics, Blackmur again bears witness to the exemplary will to power, the "lust for order" that in "contaminating his mind"[48] also contaminated his discourse from one end of the spectrum of being to the other. Unfortunately, though characteristically, Blackmur's purpose is not to interrogate humanism, but to dissociate an authentic (liberal) humanism from Babbitt's "castor oil cure for political opposition," a humanism that, unlike Babbitt's, would be a "refuge from the encroachments of the omnipotent state." Thus despite its exposure of the aggressive antidemocratic politics Babbitt was blind to, Blackmur's critique, insofar as it focuses on Babbitt's private conscience or "proper self," is itself blinded by its enabling problematic to the (semi-)autonomous and hidden power of humanistic discourse at large.

It is not simply that Blackmur's humanism as "refuge from the encroachments of the omnipotent state" leaves the "material interests"[49] free to carry on the business of the world and, in thus isolating the potentially disruptive "free conscience," becomes itself something like a self-imposed prison. However inadvertently, Blackmur's "refuge" is, finally, like Father Mapple's pulpit or Linnaeus's desk or Bildad's Protestant capitalist whaling office in *Moby-Dick*, an "impregnable" and "self-containing strong-hold—a lofty Ehrensbreitstein," immune from the disruptive free play of criticism, a commanding invisible wall behind which a "center elsewhere" does its coercive worldly work.[50] Blackmur's influential critique of Herman Melville, which more than anything else perhaps set the attitude of a whole generation of literary critics toward his "errant art," bears witness to this. For, paradoxically, it is precisely Babbitt's structural model, if not the politics it justifies, that Blackmur brings to bear in his harshly negative judgment of *Moby-Dick* and *Pierre* and the place of their author in the American tradition:

> The dramatic form of a novel *is what holds it together*, makes it move, gives it a center and establishes a direction . . . we may think of different ways in which things go together in a given work, and strangely, the labor of abstraction and violation will seem to deepen our intimacy with the substance of the work and, more valuable, to *heighten our sense of how that substance is controlled*. The sense of control is perhaps the highest form of apprehension; it is understanding without immersion.
>
> The question we have here to ask then is how did Melville go about controlling his two novels, *Moby-Dick* and *Pierre*? The general, strictly true . . . answer would be: *haphazardly*—that is, through an attitude which varied from the arrogance of extreme carelessness to the humility of complete attention. It is not that he attended only to what seriously interested him, *for*

he was as careless of what he thought important as of what he thought trivial, but that apparently *he had no sure rule* as to what required *management* and what would take care of itself. *His rule was vagary*, where consequential necessities did not determine otherwise.[51]

This excursion into the literary criticism of R. P. Blackmur may seem to be a digression, especially if one considers him, as I do, the most open, explorative, and intensely generous, the most postmodern of the New Critics. If, however, it is remembered that my topic is humanism, not Irving Babbitt per se, the significance of my thematization of the blindness of Blackmur's insight will become immediately apparent. It is, I suggest, the characteristic attribution to personal conviction of the reactionary resonances of certain forms of humanism that allows liberal humanists to exclude an Irving Babbitt or a Paul Elmer More from their company without at the same time precipitating self-interrogation of the assumptions inscribed in their own humanistic discourse. (To anticipate a fuller discussion of this characteristic blindness, Blackmur succumbs to what Michel Foucault has called the ruse of "the repressive hypothesis," which, in understanding "truth" as the adversary of [direct] power, distracts the liberal humanist critic from examination of the "regime of truth.") It is also their certain refusal to undertake such an interrogation of the rules of humanistic discursive practice that goes far to explain the perennially, and in the end futilely, recurrent effort to impose the Apollonian measure of restraint — "the inner check," as Babbitt and More call it — in "eras of expansion," in the face of the "disintegrating influence at work in modern life" (*LAC*, p. 239) and of the "eccentric and centrifugal scholarship" spawned and nurtured by elective systems.

This unwillingness to acknowledge the possibility that eras of expansion are manifestations of the contradictions inhering in the discursive practices of disinterested inquiry accounts in large part for the recent effort to rehabilitate Babbitt's reputation.[52] This refusal of self-examination also accounts for the renewed Apollonian project at the present historical conjuncture. I am not referring only to the reactive response of leading conservative and liberal humanist intellectuals of the literary establishment to deconstruction, critical theory, critical genealogy, and the emergence of other hitherto excluded areas of inquiry they misleadingly call "specialism." I am also referring, more broadly, to the studied disregard of the persuasive demystification of "disinterested inquiry" maintained by the authors of the Harvard Core Curriculum Report (and the legion of humanist teachers and administrators they have encouraged). The historical events of the Vietnam decade — above all, the student movement culminating in the events of May '68 — evokes this disregard even more strongly.

IV

Richards entered the hall in Harvard Yard where the large poetry course was to be held, saw the overcrowded room

with undergraduates seated on the floor, heard the fire sirens
shrieking from the Broadway fire station, and pronounced
emphatically (quoting Arnold's Callicles) "Not here, O Apollo,
are haunts fit for thee!" . . . quite aside from the eloquence with
which they were spoken, Richards' first words in that class
surprised in themselves; they were not concerned with class lists
or syllabi; they were addressed to Apollo as though he existed
still (and to Richards, a thoroughgoing believer in Platonic forms,
Apollo was an eternal Being), and they assumed that our
classroom would become (if a fit one could be found) a haunt
of Apollo. I cannot emphasize too much the utter absence
of irony in Richards' quotation.

Helen Vendler, "I. A. Richards at Harvard"

To bring my argument chronologically and genealogically closer to the Harvard
Core Curriculum Report and the educational reform initiative of the 1980s it
activated, and to suggest the insistently supplementary continuity of the Apollonian
ideal of modern humanistic liberal education, one need only recall the educational theory (and practice) of I. A. Richards. For Richards, it will be remembered, was instrumental, with E. M. W. Tillyard, M. D. Forbes, and others, not only in effecting the
"revolution" in English studies at Cambridge in the 1920s. He was also one of the principal influences (one of a committee of twelve) in the shaping of the undergraduate
curriculum at Harvard in the late 1940s. I am referring to the general education program, which was intended to accommodate the knowledge explosion set off by World
War II, and to harness institutions of higher learning in the United States to the cultural
and sociopolitical imperatives of the Cold War.[53] This was the program, according to
the Harvard Core Curriculum Report, which was "eroded" by the "proliferation of
courses" during the 1960s, the period of student protest against American aggression
in Vietnam. However different and more attractive its liberal surface, Richards's interpretation of language and poetics on the one hand, and his analogous idea of the university and pedagogical practice on the other are informed by an updated version of the
panoptic model that determines Arnold's and Babbitt's recuperative humanist
project.[54]

Like Arnold's and Babbitt's, Richards's discourse is an Apollonian discourse, despite
its avowed departure from Arnold's substitution of poetry for the Christian religion as
agency of human salvation in an age of expansion. It is fundamentally motivated by his
anxiety about the "promiscuous" dissemination of knowledge precipitated by a global
conflict. For in exposing millions of Anglo-Americans to alien cultures, the war also put
the cultural agencies of hegemony at risk. These changes made the traditional humanistic problematic vulnerable. As he warns in "The Future of the Humanities in General

Education" (April 1947), exposure to the knowledge explosion constitutes a momentous threat to the balanced and healthy civilization:

> *Minds have become more exposed than ever before*. And this exposure too is
> undergoing explosive increase. Mental and moral communications, within each
> culture and between cultures, have suddenly expanded beyond anyone's power
> to foresee the consequences. The agencies at work—with one exception—
> hardly need more than mention. They are mass education, with its stress on
> verbal or nominal literacy, motion pictures, radio, television, modern
> advertising, and—here is the exception—modern scholarship. These are the
> new forces which already expose every urbanized mind to a range and variety
> and promiscuity of contacts unparalleled in history. . . . There will at least be
> no doubt that this new mental exposure makes immense changes necessary
> in our conceptions of what the humanities have to do and how they can do it.
> (*SI*, pp. 58-59)[55]

Like Arnold and Babbitt, Richards returns nostalgically to Plato's logocentric and hierarchical disciplinary model in *The Republic*. For only such a return to the "origin" of Western education is capable of recuperating the "disinterested" ability to "see life steadily and see it whole" and thus the "healthy"—the ordered and balanced—society from the futility and anarchy precipitated by the dispersal of a common body of traditional knowledge. Richards's "healthy" society, in other words, is the inclusive *polis* impervious to irony and to the free play of criticism, and is thus the sociopolitical analogue of the disinterested and "inclusive" poem he and his New Critical heirs privileged over its interested "exclusive" (positivist) binary opposite:

> There are two ways in which impulses may be organised: by exclusion and by
> inclusion, by synthesis and by elimination. . . .
> The structures of these kinds of experiences are different, and the
> difference is not one of subject but of the relations *inter se* of the several
> impulses active in the experience. A poem of the first group is built out of
> sets of impulses which run parallel, which have the same direction. In a poem
> of the second group the most obvious feature is the extraordinarily [*sic*]
> heterogeneity of the distinguishable impulses. But they are more than
> heterogeneous, they are opposed. They are such that in ordinary, nonpoetic,
> non-imaginative experience, one or other set would be suppressed to give as
> it might appear freer development to the others.
> The difference comes out clearly if we consider how comparatively unstable
> poems of the first kind are. They will not bear an ironical contemplation. . . .
> Irony in this sense consists in the bringing in of the opposite, the
> complementary impulses; that is why poetry which is exposed to it is not of

the highest order, and why irony itself is so constantly a characteristic of poetry which is.[56]

Given the privileged status of the visual metaphorics informing Richards's appropriation of Arnold's remedial prescription, it should come as no surprise that he insistently calls Plato's authorizing structural model a "blueprint" or an "organization chart": an instrument that, as Foucault reminds us, in miniaturizing, locating, and producing positive knowledge of vastness and multiplicity, became essential to the efficient practical operations of the new microphysics of the Enlightenment:

> The first of the great operations of discipline is . . . the constitution of
> "*tableaux vivants*," which transform the confused, useless or dangerous
> multitudes into ordered multiplicities. The drawing up of "tables" was one of
> the great problems of the scientific, political and economic technology of the
> eighteenth century: . . . these [botanical and zoological, economic, military,
> and medical systems of classification and organization] were all twin
> operations in which the two elements — distribution and analysis, supervision
> and intelligibility — are inextricably bound up. In the eighteenth century, the
> table was both a technique of power and a procedure of knowledge. It was a
> question of organizing the multiple, of providing oneself with an instrument to
> cover it and to master it; it was a question of imposing upon it an "order."[57]

Richards's visual/spatial metaphorics betrays the degree to which he understands the educational institution as a technology of knowledge production based on the Benthamite panoptic schema: the disciplinary ideology of supervision. In perceiving an always potentially anarchic, wasteful, and disruptive multiplicity all at once, such a perspective can (mass) *produce* a collectivity of "subjected subjects" or "docile bodies," who ultimately (willingly) exist in order to serve the ends of the state.[58]

Thus in "The Idea of a University," a speech delivered at Harvard in 1953, Richards interprets Plato's *Republic* as an inquiry into " 'What is Justice?'," which "comes down actually to an inquiry into 'What would a just man be?' and 'How could we produce him?' " (*SI*, p. 107). In response to these tautologically related questions (which presuppose each other's answer) vis-à-vis the achievement of the *polis*, *The Republic*, according to Richards,

> lays out *together* an account of the just man ["one with all his or her bits and
> parts and talents and abilities in their right place, doing their work and not
> getting in the way"] and an account of the just society, an organization chart
> for man and for society: on the ground that we can hardly have a truly just
> man without a just society to produce him or a just society without just men
> to guide and guard it. (*SI*, p. 107)

Then, in an interpretive move intended to bring Plato's *polis* "up to date" — into the post-Enlightenment context—Richards amplifies the meaning of the "just man" to include the "sane man":

> It may freshen this up if we use "sane" along with "just." A just man is a sane man—nothing out of order or unbalanced about him. Similarly, a just society is one in which no faction, no pressure group, no self-interested power-seeker, can push the rest of the citizens around. In a just society all serve, not their own aggrandizement, but the commonwealth. (*SI*, pp. 107-8)

In this amplification, Richards's "Platonic" discourse further betrays its affiliation with that strategy archivally inscribed by the Enlightenment, according to Foucault, in order to legitimate the identity and authority of the bourgeois capitalist version of civilized society: its definition of insanity as that which sanity or normality is not; its inclusion by binary exclusion and separation of the mad/unjust man from the sane/just *socius*.[59]

Richards reduces Plato's more complex understanding of men and women to the familiar, simplistic, and thus manageable binary structure which assumes all logocentered thought and practice to be healthful (formative or re-formative and balancing) and all decentered thought and practice to be harmful (deforming and unbalancing) to human being, both in its individual and social capacities. In so doing, the belated son of Matthew Arnold is enabled, like his Harvard predecessor Irving Babbitt, to justify a dynastic and re-formist or recuperative concept of education and political economy on the assumption that, however errant, the human will is correctable (curable). Commending the breakthrough (by way of "Basic English") in the efficiency of teaching illiterates and non-Western peoples to read an alphabetic script, Richards writes in "Responsibilities in the Teaching of English," "if parallel improvements were worked out in the ordering of higher level materials we could then develop what man so urgently needs: a common purpose jointly understood. And this is the only remedy powerful enough to protect him from his suicidal forces—a multiplication of his intelligence and a reformation of his will through an operative knowledge of what he can be and should be" (*SI*, pp. 93-94).[60] It is worth noting the by now familiar, urgent assertion of "the one needful thing"—the identical model as normative standard—in the face of potential social chaos. More important, however, is Richards's concomitant mystification of the metaphysical binary antithesis between order and chaos, culture and anarchy, which, in the rhetoric of his literary and educational discourses, always assumes the psychologistic form of the sanity/insanity opposition.

Such mystification enables him to recuperate from rampant individualism or multiplicity a hierarchical, dynastic, and hegemonic educational model. It is a model grounded in the remedial teacher/disciple relationship and implies a hierarchical and dynastic sociopolitical structure informed by the guardians/guarded (if not precisely the master/slave) relationship, in which the therapeutic (disciplinary) instrument is the norm or standard or measure of sanity/justice. The end of this remedial correctional process, we recall, is the production of the just/sane man or woman, who, in his own words, is "one with all his or her bits and parts and talents and abilities in their right place, doing their work and not getting in the way." What Paul Bové says about Richards's principles and practice of literary criticism vis-à-vis the production of subjects applies as well to his principles and practice of pedagogy at large:

> Richards' "Principles" and "Practice" of criticism not only make man as
> reader available for analysis as a means and object of discipline, but also, by
> pursuing a balanced harmony of experience in perception and communication,
> they normalize individuals through comparison . . . and they do this
> paradoxically by creating different individuals precisely through comparison
> and isolation. That is to say, this technique produces multiple individuals
> among whom discipline allows us to discriminate so that teachers and
> students can struggle for identity in sameness. This identity is produced by
> the practical effect of the authority that judges "sane" and "normal" from
> "insane" and "unselfconscious" responses, but identity—which is like
> "sameness"—is produced even more fundamentally by the praxis that
> incorporates all the individuals within one modality of organization and one set
> of criteria for judgment. . . . Foucault, writing of the classical period's
> educational method for punishing the "shameful class" in French schools,
> offers a comment that I think both adequately represents the nature of
> Richards' achievement and suggests another aspect of his genealogy: "The
> perpetual penalty that traverses all points and supervises every instant in the
> disciplinary institutions compares, differentiates, hierarchizes, homogenizes,
> excludes. In short, it *normalizes*."[61]

It is, of course, "the university"—the repository of the "normative," "the best that has been thought and said in the world," the "tradition" or "core," "the humanistic measure," as it were—which Richards decrees "the supreme organ in such a society for *producing* men and women *able and fit to guard it*: to guard it from foreign enemies (insane states) and still more from its bosom enemies, self-promoting powerseekers" (*SI*, p. 108; my emphasis). (According to the syntactical momentum of Richards's rhetoric, the dissymmetrical analogy conceals another, more fundamental enemy of the state: the deviant.) And the "recipe" the university must follow to achieve this preordained end is predictably the following:

> Take the cream of the school crop, the hand-picked short-list, the most
> talented, liveliest, young men and women, the courageous, untiring learners,
> and give them a long and all-important course. A course in what? Here is the
> course description: "They will take the arts and sciences they have been
> educated in at school and put them into connection, in a comprehensive

synoptic view of their relations with one another and with what truly is."
(*Republic*, 537) (*SI*, p. 108)

This "comprehensive synoptic view," or, as Richards puts it in an essay proffering a more technical definition, this "over-all view," transmitted by an intellectual elite produced and reproduced by the university, is "inescapably normative" (*SI*, p. 124).[62] It conceives of a hermeneutic circle in which being is ontologically prior to temporality, identity to difference, form to process, end to means, the panoptic eye to all the other senses.[63] In so doing, this methodologized version of Arnold's generalization about seeing life steadily and seeing it whole becomes a powerful instrument for effecting what Richards calls, echoing Francis Bacon, "this greatest instauration" (*SI*, p. 94): the "reformation of the [individual] will" and the analogous recuperation of the "healthy," the "sane," the "balanced," and the "just" state: "A Synoptic View therefore—truly Universal Study—would have more than police functions; it should be advisor-general and therapist as well" (*SI*, p. 124).

Everywhere in his discourse on educational theory (as in his discourse on poetics), Richards insistently emphasizes the inculcation of this steadying "comprehensive synoptic view" that simultaneously foresees ends, polices deviance, and cures psychological and social imbalance as the most important functions of the modern university. This, according to Richards (in a rhetoric reminiscent of Arnold's and Babbitt's), is because the belated institutions of higher learning founded on Plato's synoptic model have not, in historical practice, pursued the integrating or assimilating imperatives of such an authoritative center:

> Very likely Plato's Academy (even in his lifetime as its Director) sought almost anything rather than the *synoptic* view. It is arguable that *his* Socrates (of whom we know so little apart from Plato), that model he set up of the ideal University teacher, has in fact only taught people how to trip one another up and catch one another out rather than how to understand one another and use that understanding co-operatively to the common advantage. It is to be feared that the Platonic dialogues and their progeny have spread chiefly the strategy and tactics of intellectual combat. While the original aim may have been to teach people not to fight but to *comprehend*. (*SI*, p. 109)

Richards thus categorically dismisses as inevitably activating intellectual warfare precisely what, in the wake of the demystification of the binary logic of metaphysics, now appears to be the most suggestive possibility in Plato's discourse: an *originative paideia* that takes the form of *antagonistic dialogue*. The oxymoron is Mikhail Bakhtin's. But I am referring to a broader context: that of post-humanism. In this context, knowledge production is grounded in and emerges from the acknowledged uncertainty of human being's decentered situation and thus is always already destructive or genealogical. It is, to adapt Heidegger's hermeneutics to the pedagogical site, a *pai-*

deia characterized by *Auseinandersetzung*: an exchange always unrelenting in its exposure of the repressive center elsewhere (*including the one that initiates its own inquiry*) and at the same time lets the play of difference be. It is a negatively capable *paideia*, the measure of which is not the super-natural and super-visory standard grounded in the seminal Word, but an improvisatory measure grounded in human being's mortal occasion.[64]

Instead, Richards, like Babbitt, restates a regulative methodological theory of interpretation and a correlative educational philosophy based on Matthew Arnold's "best self" and committed to the "comprehensive synoptic view." Analogous to the metaphysical and spatializing poetics of the New Criticism he helped to found as an academic discipline, the "synopticism" of Richards's "best self" assumes truth ("what truly is") to be ultimately integral and transhistorical, and thus capable of being comprehended ("grasped," "taken hold of," colonized) by the distanced synoptic eye.[65] *Paideia*, in Richards's view, is a retrospective or re-collective process that reifies, dedifferentiates, and alienates that which it seeks to know. This alienating consensus is the consequence of Richards's Arnoldian effort to recuperate the authority of the speculative philosopher Plato from the Socrates whom he represents as the dialogic materialist:

> We would have *authority*: an authority which would have behind it *all* that man
> knows in *all* his modes of knowing and *all* that he would will to become
> through *all* his quests for being. It would be an authority which could wholly
> be respected and accepted, because it would represent the whole man, not
> any party or pressure group among his interests. All authority derives from
> the consent of those who acknowledge it. (Any other government rests on
> coercion merely, not authority. The fears are a faction only in our minds.)
> The authority which Plato's *synoptic* view would try to give us could gain our
> complete consent, could be wholly persuasive, because it would unify us.
> (*SI*, p. 112)

Understood in terms of its re-presentational and assimilative imperatives, Richards's "comprehensive synoptic view" becomes another historical supplement of the panoptic perspective privileged in the West since Plato (or more accurately, as I will suggest, Plato's Roman interpreters) posited the memory as the agency of recovering the prelapsarian realm of forms from fallen history, and of imposing the imperial will to power over the historicity of being. As the material extension of this synoptic view, the university Richards envisages for the post-World War II era becomes both a "speculative instrument" for the fulfillment of Western Man's perennial metaphysical (and patriarchal) dream of bringing order into the "chaos" of conflicting historical knowledges and a historically specific strategy to "defend" the common body of Western values against the "threat" of emergent sociopolitical alternatives, not least communism, that rough (Asian) beast slouching toward the West to be born.

In thus referring to Richards's synoptic view as imperial, I want to suggest that its colonialist imperative is not limited to his representation of being and knowledge production but extends into the site of politics. Like the discourses of Matthew Arnold and Irving Babbitt or, say, Sainte-Beuve and Ernest Renan (whom both admired), Richards's rhetoric of assimilation addresses not only the general dissolution of the classical/Christian culture—the "imperial" Virgil/Dante continuum that T. S. Eliot was trying to rehabilitate[66]—but also and simultaneously the historical dissolution, in the decades of World Wars I and II, of Western (essentially British) economic, social, and political hegemony over the worlds of "others." His ontological logocentrism thus manifests itself in an ethnocentricism as well: a methodological Anglo-Americanism that construes other cultures in its own discursive image. Despite appearances to the contrary, Richards's discourse thus augments the Western will to power, which according to Heidegger was bent on the complete "Europeanization of the earth and man."[67] Like Arnold's and Babbitt's dis-engaged and re-presentational optics, Richards's speculative instrument betrays its complicity with that archival Orientalism that, as Edward Said has shown, in naturalizing the historically constructed, textualized, and produced cultural dominance of the West over the East, has authorized the hegemonic cultural/ economic/political purposes of Western knowledge production and political praxis. Referring to Renan's philosophical approach to the Orient, Said writes:

> To be able to sustain a vision that incorporates and holds together life and quasi-living creatures (Indo-European, European culture) as well as quasi-monstrous, parallel inorganic phenomena (Semitic, Oriental culture) is precisely the achievement of the European scientist in the laboratory [read "Panopticon"]. He *constructs*, and the very act of construction is a sign of imperial power over recalcitrant phenomena, as well as a confirmation of the dominating culture and its "naturalization." Indeed, it is not too much to say that Renan's philological laboratory is the actual locale of his European ethnocentrism; but what needs emphasis here is that the philological laboratory has no existence outside the discourse, the writing by which it is constantly produced and experienced. Thus even the culture he calls organic and alive—Europe's—is also a *creature being created* in the laboratory and by philology.[68]

Unlike Renan, Richards lived, studied, and taught for some years in the Orient (in China), but this should not mislead one into concluding that the images of the non-Western cultures he refers to derive from these cultures' *own* actualities. On the contrary, Richards's Oriental discourse no less than Renan's has its point of departure in his anxiety over the fate of the West or Western culture. Like Arnold and Babbitt before him, he attributes the proliferation of knowledges that threaten the measured stability of contemporary Occidental civilization to the invasion of "monstrous" and radically alien cultures, languages, and rhetorics. The familiar (and familial) rhetoric of the "we" in the following representative passage, which does not allow the "they" to speak for themselves in terms of their own historically specific conditions of existence, should not be overlooked:

> Possibly, even probably, the difficulties of reading justly are increasing. Within a well-defined tradition the items and the patterns they enter are fewer and clearer than amid the frothy emulsion of hitherto immiscible cultures in which to-day we live and move and aspire to win some being. Our novel acquaintanceship with the untraditional past and with oddities of thought and feeling from other cultures is unrhythming, it may be, the heart of our mental and moral security. (*SI*, p. 101)

Thus, according to Richards, one of the most urgent tasks of the Western synoptic university is to develop an efficient instrument for teaching the English language. For, like Renan's philology, the sane "clarity" of English will not only neutralize by domesticating the "oddities of thought and feeling [the echo of Arnold is worth noting] from other cultures" that ominously threaten to unrhythm "us"; but, further sanitized by Ogden's and Richards's "Basic English," it will also correct, "normalize," the apparently "monstrous" moral values, the cacophonous or exorbitant measure, in terms of the Western model and thus include them within the Western orbit. Richards's intentions, of course, are insistently ameliorative and "humane"; the achievement of "one world," as the title of a late collection of texts, *So Much Nearer: Essays Toward a World English* (1968), makes clear. But the unexamined rhetoric of his archival discourse, like that of Arnold, Babbitt, Renan, and so many other early and late humanists, betrays its subsuming ethnocentrism:

> Two-thirds of us on this planet are, at the time of writing, analphabetics. Of the 2,200,000,000 people now breathing, some 1,500,000,000 either cannot read at all or read some nonalphabetic script. This is not the time or place in which to argue the merits of the invention of alphabetic writing. Suffice it that if there is to be any truly world-wide communication between peoples within a foreseeable future, it will be in some language which is alphabetic. It could be within our lifetime and through English. (*SI*, p. 93)

A great deal of corrosive history intervenes between the historical conjuncture giving rise to this characteristic statement by I. A. Richards and that of Thomas Babington Macauley's famous "Minute of 1835" arguing for an English education for Indians:

> I have no knowledge of either Sanskrit or Arabic. But I have done what I could to form a correct estimate of their value. I have read translations of the most celebrated Arabic and Sanskrit works. I have conversed, both here and at home, with men distinguished by their proficiency in the Eastern tongues.

I am quite ready to take the oriental learning at the valuation of the orientalists themselves. I have never found one among them who could deny that a single shelf of a good European library was worth the whole native literature of India and Arabia. The intrinsic superiority of the Western literature is indeed fully admitted by those members of the committee who support the oriental plan of education. . . . It is, I believe, no exaggeration to say that all the historical information which has been collected in the Sanskrit language is less valuable than what may be found in the paltry abridgements used at preparatory schools in England. In every branch of physical or moral philosophy, the relative position of the two nations is nearly the same.[69]

Macaulay's Orientalist discourse is articulated "from a position of power where he could translate his opinions into the decision to make an entire subcontinent of natives submit to studying in a language not their own."[70] Richards's takes place in a different context of imperialistic divestment and ethnic emergence and is thus compelled to accommodate its (anthropo)logos to the transformed historical situation. But as his insistence on the remedial power of English makes clear, he does aim at accommodation, a recentering on a different, more discreet register of the Occidental authority decentered by the emergence of ethnic consciousness and the overthrow of overt colonial rule. If "we" cannot govern "them" as colonies, we can at least "influence" them— cultivate, domesticate, and reap their threatening energies—by establishing English as the "auxiliary world language,"[71] by, that is, controlling the informational order. It does not seem to occur to Richards that the emergent Third World nations may not want to work out their fates in and with English; nor does he seem to realize that to a Chinese or an Indian or an Arab, in the middle of the twentieth century, English as a discursive practice is simultaneously an instrument of economic, sociopolitical, and colonialist power:[72] a cultural imperialism.

It is indeed ironic that the distinguished author of the (still) influential *Practical Criticism*, who, in the name of a more "just" mode of reading, insistently exposes the "doctrinal adhesions" and the "stock responses" that contaminate his Cambridge students' protocols, should be so impervious to the panoptic rhetoric and the ethnocentric will to power inscribed in his efficient Benthamite speculative instrument. As the final sentence of the encomium I have quoted as epigraph to this section itself betrays, Richards's Apollonian discourse reveals "just how abstract his grasp of the historical event he is describing is"[73] or, to put it another way, just how trapped this master of irony remains in the philological tradition that the countermemory has exposed as both a socially constituted construct and a coercive disciplinary network:

Having become a dense and consistent historical reality, language forms the locus of tradition, of the unspoken habits of thought, of what lies hidden in a people's mind; it accumulates an ineluctable memory which does not even know itself as memory. Expressing their thoughts in words of which they are not the masters, enclosing them in verbal forms whose historical dimensions they are unaware of, men believe that their speech is their servant and do not realize that they are submitting to its demands. The grammatical arrangements of a language are the *a priori* of what can be expressed in it. The truth of discourse is caught in the trap of philology.[74]

There is, as Foucault and others have reminded us, no more secure prison than the prison house of humanistic language, a prison house assumed by its inmates to be a space of freedom, in which the incarcerated are the unknowingly willing bearers of their own (and others') incarceration.

V

What we have witnessed through the foregoing destruction of the discourses on education of these three exemplary modern poetic humanists — texts spanning the period between the emergence of a proletarian class consciousness in late Victorian England through the globalization of planetary life (reduced to Cold War politics) in the period following World War II — is a continuous, however uneven, allegiance to a paradigm of discreet and subtle coercion informing the alleged disinterestedness of their modes of inquiry, a paradigm capable of accommodating the cultural and sociopolitical dispersions of any particular historical crisis to its centripetal center. For each, of course, this paradigm — the centered circle — which can be traced back through the Renaissance to its origins in the humanism of the Roman Republic and ultimately to Plato (to the late Greeks), is, as it was for their predecessors, the symbolic transcendental structure of perfection — of beauty. But, as I have shown, it is also and simultaneously (as it was somewhat more overtly for their predecessors) the symbolic ideal structure and polyvalent agency of cultural, social, and political domination, positively capable of defusing by circumscribing, disciplining, and subjecting disruptive energy precipitated by historical crisis. No less than the overdetermined panoptic model and its practical apparatuses, which Foucault leads us to believe have their origin in the "objectivity" of post-Enlightenment empirical science, then, the cultural paradigm of these poetic humanists contributes to the reproduction and legitimation of the disciplinary society. In thus disclosing the complicity between the poetic humanism of idealism with the empirical humanism of science, the foregoing genealogy of the modern theoretical discourse of deliverance calls into question the validity of the Two Cultures opposition that has determined the parameters of the debates over educational theory and practice — and effectively disabled criticism — throughout this century.

We will catch a glimpse of this historically continuous affiliation between the symbol of beauty/perfection and power in the West as well as the complicity between poetic and scientific exploitations of it in the material world by retrieving the history of the circular city sketched out in chapter 2. This history, we recall, traces the genealogy of Bentham's Panopticon back beyond the Enlightenment where Michel Foucault locates it to those circular cities envisaged by the humanist utopians of the Renaissance. It shows that these ideal humanist cities modeled on the beautiful and perfect (cosmic) geometry of the divinely ordained circle became inevitably and increasingly, from the Renaissance to the Enlightenment, more than the ideal fortress intended to annul the threat of "enemies" within. However undeveloped, the spatial and spatializing economy of humanist beauty was also intended to achieve a compartmentalized and hierarchized space that, however comely, provided for easy "cultivation" of its inhabitants and thus to guarantee the spiritual health (normalcy) of the *polis* from the threat of sociopolitical "insanity": to effect the disciplinary transformation of potentially disruptive human beings, inhabitants or soldiers, into good—efficient, docile, and dependable—citizens. The circular City Beautiful is intrinsically the City Powerful.

In short, the panoptic disciplinary apparatus that, according to Foucault, suddenly emerged in the period of the Enlightenment was not a historical mutation. It was, rather, a historical *overdetermination* of the power enabled by the rise of scientific inquiry (especially the proliferation of its optical/classificatory procedures), previously underdeveloped but always latent in the figure of the beautiful that has guided artists and philosophers, literary critics, historians—the professors of the "humanities"— ever since Plato, in "correcting" Heraclitus, gave privileged status to meta-physical thinking. Understood in terms of this genealogy, the "Greek" imperative to "see life steadily and see it whole" in the poetic humanism of Arnold, Babbitt, Richards, and their contemporary progeny is ultimately continuous with the Newtonian optics informing Benthamite panopticism and the modern disciplinary society to which it contributed its efficient microtechnology of power. However effaced in and by their rhetoric of "deliverance"—and their oppositional stance toward an educational institution that privileges a scientific/technological curriculum—this relationship between the idealized circle and practical power, reconstituted and sanctioned by the *studia humanitatis* in the Renaissance, remained the unacknowledged basis of Arnold's, Babbitt's, and Richards's educational projects. For all their appeal to the "liberal arts," it was this hidden ideological agenda—this complicity between the panoptic view afforded by the circle whose center is both inside and outside with disciplinary practice—that lay under and enabled Arnold's advocacy of "culture," Babbitt's advocacy of the "classical measure," and Richards's advocacy of "the synoptic university" in the face of the discursive explosions that threatened the sociopolitical stability of their particular historical conjuncture. As much as the pedagogy of science they were contesting, their efforts to reclaim "our" disrupted "classical heritage" were efforts to recuperate and reinform the threatened hegemony of the dominant sociopolitical order: the disciplinary *polis*.

To extend the trope of the centered circle informing these recuperative efforts, far from retrieving the originative, differential, and errant thinking of the classical Greeks they invariably invoke as authority, the pedagogical discourses of the representative modern humanists I have been interrogating in this chapter in fact recuperate the thinking of *Homo romanus*. I am referring to the secondary and derivative, calculative, and masterful thinking that, according to Heidegger, has its belated institutional origins in the strategic reduction and domestication of the Greek *a-letheía* (truth as unconcealment) to *veritas* (truth as *adequaetio intellectus et rei*) by the Romans in behalf of an end-oriented pedagogical problematic that would both secure and extend the cultural and sociopolitical hegemony of their *metropolis* — the rule of empire — over the other "barbarian" worlds.

VI

> Whoever has emerged victorious participates to this day in the triumphal procession in which the present rulers step over those who are lying prostrate. According to traditional practice, the spoils are carried along in the procession. They are called cultural treasures, and a historical materialist views them with cautious detachment. For without exception the cultural treasures he surveys have an origin which he cannot contemplate without horror. They owe their existence not only to the efforts of the great minds and talents who have created them, but also to the anonymous toil of their contemporaries. There is no document of Civilization which is not at the same time a document of barbarism. And just as such a document is not free of barbarism, barbarism taints also the manner in which it was transmitted from one owner to another. A historical materialist therefore dissociates himself from it as far as possible. He regards it as his task to brush history against the grain.
>
> Walter Benjamin, "Theses on the Philosophy of History"

In undertaking a destructive genealogy of the enabling educational ideals of Arnold, Babbitt, and Richards, my purpose has not been essentially negative. It has also been intended to provide a context for retrieving the projective possibilities closed off by the structuring of being in terms of the binary logic that privileges the archic over the anarchic measure. I will develop the positive possibilities repressed by this representation more fully in later chapters. Here, I want to bring into focus a crucial motif of the discourse of humanism that has until now remained marginal in my text: its perennial appeal to Greek antiquity. It is the genealogy of this insistent invocation of classical Greece that will suggest most clearly the destructive/projective and errant itinerary of the (multicultural) educational narrative *precluded* by the humanist representation of the cultural history of the Occident.

Nietzsche's suggestion in *The Birth of Tragedy* and elsewhere of a "classical Greek culture" quite *different* from Arnold's influential late Victorian English version that polarized Apollo against Dionysus comes readily to hand for this project. To "repeat" the preceding critique of Arnold's, Babbitt's, and Richards's humanism, the disclosure that their disinterested discourse is a panopticism also implies that their classical ideal—the polyvalent circle—they ostensibly appropriate from the Greeks is not primary but secondary and derivative: a construction. It is a conceptualization of a more primordial experience *of thinking*: a structural model grounded in a fixed idea about Man—an anthropo-logy. It is legitimized tautologically by a tendentious selection of particulars from the prolific and contradictory disclosures of originative Greek thinking that both substantiates the preconceived end and makes it the norm and method of inquiry and educational practice, a measure, a standard, and a rule. According to Heidegger's interrogation of the ontotheological tradition in *Being and Time*, such a calculative thinking becomes increasingly normative for the Occident: In the tenacious search for certitude and mastery of the earth, the temporality of being hardens into Being (the *summum ens*), words turn into the Word of reason, and *a-letheía* (un-concealment) becomes *veritas*: the correspondence of mind and thing.[75]

The crucial point is this: the classical *paideia* of Arnold, Babbitt, and Richards, and actually of humanism at large, *is not Greek at all* insofar as it valorizes a derivative and circular mode of thinking as primary, a "manly model" to be imitated against the apparent "female disorder" of lived experience. Rather, as Heidegger, following Nietzsche, has shown, *this classical paideia is essentially Roman*. Because this point is highly significant for the arguments I am making in this book, the following passage from his "Letter on Humanism" (1947) deserves extended quotation:

> *Humanitas*, explicitly so called, was first considered and striven for in the age of the Roman Republic. *Homo humanus* was opposed to *homo barbarus*. *Homo humanus* here means the Romans, who exalted and honored Roman *virtus* through the "embodiment" of the *paideia* [education] taken over from the Greeks. These were the Greeks of the Hellenistic age, whose culture was acquired in the schools of philosophy. It was concerned with *eruditio et institutio in bonas artes* [scholarship and training in good conduct]. *Paideia* thus understood was translated as *humanitas*. The genuine *romanitas* of a *homo romanus* consisted in such *humanitas*. We encounter the first humanism in Rome: it therefore remains in essence a specifically Roman phenomenon which emerges from the encounter of Roman civilization with the culture of late Greek civilization. The so-called Renaissance of the fourteenth and fifteenth centuries in Italy is a *renascentia romanitatis*. Because *romanitas* is what matters, it is concerned with *humanitas* and therefore with Greek *paideia*. But Greek civilization is always seen in its later form and this itself is seen from a Roman point of view. The *homo romanus* of the Renaissance also

stands in opposition to *homo barbarus*. But now the in-humane is the supposed barbarism of gothic Scholasticism in the Middle Ages. Therefore a *studium humanitatis*, which in a certain way reaches back to the ancients and thus also becomes a revival of Greek civilization, always adheres to historically understood humanism. For Germans this is apparent in the humanism of the eighteenth century supported by Winckelmann, Goethe, and Schiller. On the other hand, Hölderlin [the English language equivalent would, perhaps, be Blake and Keats and, more recently, William Carlos Williams, Charles Olson and, more radically, Thomas Pynchon] does not belong to "humanism" precisely because he thought the destiny of man's essence in a more original way than "humanism" could.[76]

Heidegger's summary of Nietzsche's genealogy of the origins of the humanistic *paideia* is determined by his ontological concerns about the ontotheological tradition at large. However, his emphasis on the ontological question in his destruction of modern humanism does not preclude implicating the sociopolitical order in the imperialism of (Roman) humanist truth and pedagogy. This is made remarkably clear in his neglected lectures on the *Parmenides* (winter semester 1942/43), where what is only implicit in the distinction he makes between the Greek *a-letheía* and the Roman *veritas* in "Letter on Humanism" becomes explicit, however problematic it is rendered by their historically specific context. In these lectures, Heidegger's destruction of modern humanism—specifically his disclosure of the Roman/imperial origins of its concept of "the false" (*falsum*, the opposite of *veritas*)—constitutes a remarkable anticipation of Michel Foucault's insistent but overlooked emphasis on the enabling role played by the Roman model in the production of culture and sociopolitical formations in the age of the Enlightenment. I am referring to "the Roman reference" that informs Foucault's disclosure of the complicity between the panoptic gaze, the disciplinary educational practice, and the imperial project of the post-Enlightenment.[77] As Heidegger says in these lectures:

> The essential domain that prevails for the deployment of the Roman *falsum* is that of the *imperium* and of the imperial. *Imperium* means "command" [*Befehl*]. . . . The *imperium* is the command in the sense of the disposing order. To commanding, as the essential foundation of sovereignty, belongs "being above" [*Obensein*]. That is only possible through constant surmounting [*Überhöhung*] in relation to others, who are thus the inferiors [*Unterer*]. In the surmounting, in turn, resides the constant ability to oversee [super-vise and dominate: *Übersehen-können*]. We say "to oversee something," which means "to master it." To this commanding view, which carries with it surmounting, belongs the "always-being-on-the-lookout." That is the form of all action that oversees [dominates from the gaze], but that holds itself, in

Roman the *actio* of the *actus*. The commanding overseeing is the dominating vision expressed in the often cited phrase of Caesar's: *veni, vedi, vici*—I came, I *oversaw* [*übersah*], I conquered. Victory is already nothing but the consequence of the Caesarian gaze that dominates [*Übersehens*] and the seeing [*Sehens*] which has the character of *actio*. . . . The imperial *actio* of the constant surmounting over others implies that the others . . . are fallen [*gefalltwerden*]—in Roman: *fallere* (participle: *falsum*). The "bringing-to-fall" [*Das Zu-Fall-bringen*] belongs necessarily to the domain of the imperial.[78]

Even more important, Heidegger's genealogy of what is represented as "the false" in the discourse and practice of humanist modernity also anticipates Foucault's related genealogy of the repressive hypothesis (as well as Louis Althusser's genealogy of the interpellated subject of late capitalism): the representation of truth/power relations that has transformed the aggressive colonialism of nineteenth-century imperial states into the "benign" neocolonialism of twentieth-century liberal capitalist nations:

The "bringing-to-fall" can be accomplished in a "direct" assault [*Ansturm*] and an overthrowing [*Niederwerfen*: literally, "throwing down"]. But the other can also be brought to fall by being outflanked [*Um-gehen*] and tripped up from behind. The bringing-to-fall is now the way of deceptive circumvention [*Hintergehen*]. Considered from the outside, going behind the back, is a complicated, uncircumstantial and thus mediate "bringing-to-fall" as opposed to an immediate overthrowing [*Niederwerfen*]. In this way, what is brought to fall does not thereby become annihilated, but in a certain manner redressed within the boundaries staked out by the dominators. This "staking out" is called in Roman: *pango*, whence the word *pax*, peace. . . . In truth, the bringing-to-fall in the sense of deception [*Hintergehens*] and outflanking [*Umgehens*] is not the mediate and derived imperial *actio* but the imperial *actio* proper. It is not war, but in the *fallere* of deceptive outflanking [*hintergehenden Umgehens*] and its appropriation to the service of dominion that the proper and "great" trait of the imperial reveals itself.[79]

The humanist *paideia* that Arnold, Babbitt, and Richards would recuperate in the face of the knowledge explosions they confronted does not instigate the errant but originative thinking of the Greeks (truth as *a-letheía*), which was willing to risk its prejudices in dialogic engagement with time and history. In calling for the imitation of a model designed to inculcate *virtus*, "the best self," "the centripetal measure," "the blueprint" or "organization chart") it is, rather, intended to inscribe the representational or calculative thinking of the Romans (truth as *adequatio intellectus et rei*) filtered through the eyes of the Enlightenment, a thinking intended to achieve certainty about and dominion over what it surveys.[80] It is a *paideia* filtered through the eyes of the Enlightenment, one based on an authorized and authoritative abstraction of the original

Greek experience of time/space (being) that annuls the dread (*Angst*) it provokes and, by comprehending its errancy, renders it docile and useful. By interpreting temporality's differential force negatively, this re-presentational education, which specifically privileges the *genetic model*, justifies and instrumentally enables its *cultivation/colonization*. It is designed to guide the immature and wayward ephebe from the dark wood of adolescent desire into the enlightened maturity (and reason) of civilized (that is, correct) conduct and filial duty to a higher patriarchal authority, from feminine weakness into manly power (*virtus*), and from *Homo barbarus* into *Homo romanus*. "In the effort to turn his son against Greek culture," we recall from Plutarch's *Lives*, "[Cato the Elder] allowed himself an utterance which was absurdly rash for an old man: he pronounced with all the solemnity of a prophet that if ever the Romans became infected with the literature of Greece, they would lose their empire."[81] As *eruditio et institutio in bonas artes*, the end envisioned by the modern humanist *paideia*, like that of the Romans, is the reproduction of a responsible and reliable citizenry for the hegemonic empire.

To put this reciprocal relationship between citizen and empire in a way that recalls I. A. Richards's speculative educational discourse, the self-present subject as citizen thus produced becomes the structural model of the human *polis*: just as the humanistic *anthropologos* justifies the domestication by means of cultivation of the differential energies of immature youth, so the self-present metropolis or capital justifies the colonization of the "barbarous" energies of those extraterritorial peoples who "threaten" its "civilized" space. Understood in the forgotten or repressed context of this Roman origin, the principle of disinterested inquiry prized by the modern liberal humanist problematic betrays a center enabling and empowering a relay of circumscription, cultivation, and colonization that saturates the indissolable continuum that affiliates the subject, civil society, the political order, and the international world.

It is no accident that the English words "culture," "cultivate," "acculturation" (the privileged Latinate names that have figured forth the ideal end of education in the cultural discourses of Arnold, Babbitt, Richards, and more recently Walter Jackson Bate, Allan Bloom, and E. D. Hirsch) are cognates of *colonize* (from the Latin *colonus*, "tiller," "cultivator," "planter," "settler,") and *colere* ("cultivate," "plant": colonies, for example, were called "plantations" by the English settlers in the New World). All these have their origin, not in ancient Greek words referring to such agents and acts, but in the Roman appropriation of the Greek word κύκλος, "cycle," or Κιρκος, "ring," "circle," the spatial image symbolizing beauty and perfection.

The Roman reduction of the originative thinking of the Greeks to "scholarship and training in good conduct" did more than enable the theory and practice of the Roman Empire. In appropriating and harnessing Greek thought and pedagogy to the production of loyal and dependable citizens devoted to the preservation and extension of the metropolis's cultural and sociopolitical heritage, it also provided the structural model for the various manifestations of the Holy Roman Empire, the imperial project of Great

Britain, and, more discreetly and indirectly, as Sacvan Bercovitch has suggested, the theory and practice of American Manifest Destiny from the Puritans' "errand in the wilderness"—building their City on the Hill—through the founding of the Republic to the establishment of the New World order in the post-Cold War period.[82]

Modern poetic humanists may object that the ontological genealogy of the *paideia* I have discovered is remote from the actual texts that are invariably invoked as its origins. Traditional professors of English would, for example, invoke Homer's art as the obvious origin of the Western literary tradition and its formal impulse, as the spirit that has, despite periods of deviation such as the neoclassical, guided its *poiesis* up until the recent past, when the nihilistic postmodern impulse gained prominence. It is true that modern humanists, especially since the German Romantics' reevaluation of Greek literature in the late eighteenth and early nineteenth centuries, have apotheosized Homer's Odysseus as the origin of that tradition. Despite their protestation on this point, however, it is Virgil's Aeneas, the relic-bearer of the shattered city and the paragon of responsibility (*pietas*) to the higher cause, whom modern humanists in the name of the saving remnant have affirmed and continue to privilege as the "standard," the "model," and the "measure" for Western Man and for the itinerary of narrative construction: personal, cultural, and sociopolitical. Or to be more accurate: these origins lie in the *Odyssey*—and Greek literature in general—*filtered through the corrective eye of Virgil*, who reduced Homer's errant art to a disciplined and rigorously structured art of truth in behalf of the legitimation of imperial power.[83]

Consider the exemplary and inordinately influential instance of Matthew Arnold's appeal to the Greek classics in his effort to promote a disinterested pedagogy of Hellenic "sweetness and light" against the emergent threat of anarchy. In his inaugural lecture as professor of poetry at Oxford University Arnold calls for the reclamation of the legacy of "classical Greek literature." In the process, he deliberately displaces Sainte-Beuve's Virgil as the classic poet of the Western tradition in favor of what, following the classical scholarship of late eighteenth- and early nineteenth-century German idealists, he calls the "seriously cheerful" poets of Periclean Athens, especially Sophocles.[84] But his displacement does not constitute a rejection or even modification of the prophecy/fulfillment (teleological) narrative structure of Virgil's *Aeneid*. Nor does it abandon, as Nietzsche was to do fifteen years later in *The Birth of Tragedy*, the German idealist representation of the classic as the organic figuration of a comprehensive, mature, and adequate *vision*—a vision that "sees life steadily and sees it whole"—capable of making a complex expansive age threatened by intellectual and sociopolitical anarchy intelligible, graspable, and appropriatable. These inclusivist characteristics, which Sainte-Beuve[85] and T. S. Eliot singled out as the defining terms of Virgil's redemptive art—an art, in Eliot's words from another but related context, that could give a "shape and significance to the immense panorama of futility and anarchy which is contemporary history"[86]—are precisely those that, according to Arnold, make Greek literature (and "the small remnant" professing it) the necessary measure for those committed to the "deliverance" of modern man from the disruptive partiality, "the incompleteness" of a provincial perspective. We are compelled to repeat the passage from "The Modern Element in Modern Literature" quoted earlier in this chapter to recall in the present context how deeply the ideology of the supervisory center elsewhere is inscribed in Arnold's "disinterested" cultural criticism and also how Virgilian it is in its comprehensive resonance; how much, that is, his humanist discourse is written by the Roman code:

> I propose, in this my first occasion of speaking here [at Oxford], to attempt . . . a general survey of ancient classical literature and history as may afford us the conviction—in presence of the doubts so often expressed of the profitableness, in the present day, of our study of this literature . . . that, even admitting to their fullest extent the legitimate demands of our age, the literature of ancient Greece is, even for modern times, a mighty agent of intellectual deliverance . . .
>
> But first let us ask ourselves why the demand for an intellectual deliverance arises in such an age as the present, and in what deliverance itself consists? The demand arises, because our present age has around it a copious and complex past; it arises, because the present age exhibits to the individual man who contemplates it the spectacle of a vast multitude of facts awaiting and inviting his comprehension of this present and past. It begins when our mind begins to enter into possession of the general ideas which are the law of this vast multitude of facts. It is perfect when we have acquired [as the Greeks did] that harmonious acquiescence of mind which we feel in contemplating a grand spectacle that is intelligible to us; when we have lost that impatient irritation of mind which we feel in presence of an immense, moving, confused spectacle which, while it perpetually excites our curiosity, perpetually baffles our comprehension.
>
> This, then, is what distinguished certain epochs in the history of the human race [especially the age of Pericles] . . . : on the one hand, the presence of a significant spectacle to contemplate; on the other hand, the desire to find the true point of view from which to contemplate this spectacle. He who has found that point of view, he who adequately comprehends this spectacle, has risen to the comprehension of his age.

Arnold's displacement of Sainte-Beuve's Virgil, in short, does not abandon the comprehensive panoptic eye—"the true point of view from which to contemplate this spectacle"—that oversees Virgil's providential world. Nor, to invoke its artistic and sociopolitical allotrope, does it reject the abiding center or capital. It simply relocates the ontological, cultural, and sociopolitical center/capital from Rome to (a British version of) Athens. As such a metropolis, the classic retains the authority and power that enables it to annul by cultivating and domesticating the "provincialism"—the "doing as one likes"—which for him as for Sainte-Beuve (as well as for the exponents of the British Empire), constitutes the most ominous contemporary threat to the law and order of literature, literary history, and the (imperial) state.[87] This, if we thematize its political implications, is the conclusion that Frank Kermode draws about Arnold's "Greek" project in *The Classic*:

> Hellenism, rather than a renewed relation with metropolitan Rome, was the English Arnold's cure for "provincialism." He assumed, like the Latin imperialists, that the classic belongs to a privileged order of time and history. But whereas for Sainte-Beuve [and T. S. Eliot] this order is continuous, almost genetic, because Latin, and, because French, institutionalized—a quality the Englishman rather envied—for Arnold it is a Victorian version of fifth-century Athens. What the two critics share are a belief in the modernity of the true classic, and the notion of provincialism, which implies a metropolis.[88]

For all of Matthew Arnold's appeal to the "sweetness and light" of the "seriously cheerful" Greeks he admired, the culture that "sees life steadily and sees it whole" and the Academy that preserves and transmits its monuments had their origins less in, say, Sophocles' profoundly ambivalent *Antigone* than in Horace's *"Dulce et decorum est"* (*Odes*, III: ii), and had its pedagogical end in the inscription of a blind ethnocentric code that, like the code of the English public school system, reduced the energies of youth to the sacrificial service of the imperial state. This is the genealogical testimony of the multitude of young victims living and dying at the historically specific moment in British history that brought the Victorian era to its cataclysmic end. It is the testimony of Wilfred Owen in a poem—not so filled with "sweetness and light"—written from the trenches in France in 1918, not long before he was killed in action at the "immature" age of twenty-four. It is no accident that Owen addresses his poem to the "mature" contemporary institutional custodians of the classical legacy bequeathed to them by Dr. Thomas Arnold, the headmaster of Rugby and founder of the English public school system, and his filial school-inspector son: those who, like Arnold's "Greeks," have found "the true point of view from which to contemplate" and "adequately comprehend" "this ['significant'] spectacle" and have thus "risen to the comprehension of [their] age":

> Bent double, like old beggars under sacks,
> Knock-kneed, coughing like hags, we cursed through sludge,
> Till on the haunting flares we turned our backs
> And towards our distant rest began to trudge.
> Men marched asleep. Many had lost their boots
> But limped on, blood-shod. All went lame; all blind;
> Drunk with fatigue; deaf even to the hoots
> Of tired, outstripped Five-Nines that dropped behind.

Gas! Gas! Quick, boys!—An ecstasy of fumbling,
Fitting the clumsy helmets just in time;
But someone still was yelling out and stumbling
And flound'ring like a man in fire or lime . . .
Dim, through the misty panes and thick green light.
As under a green sea, I saw him drowning.

In all my dreams, before my helpless sight,
He plunges at me, guttering, choking, drowning.

If in some smothering dreams you too could pace
Behind the wagon that we flung him in,
And watch the white eyes writhing in his face,
His hanging face, like a devil's sick of sin;
If you could hear, at every jolt, the blood
Come gargling from the froth-corrupted lungs,
Obscene as cancer, bitter as the cud
Of vile, incurable sores on innocent tongues, —
My friend, you would not tell with such high zest
To children ardent for some desperate glory,
The old Lie: Dulce et decorum est
Pro patria mori.[89]

The "Roman" metaphorical chain (circle/culture/colony) and the relay of binary oppositions it enabled (identity/difference, citizen/deviant, civilization/barbarism) is implicit in Arnold, Babbitt, and Richards. It is, however, openly thematized in the "mature" cultural criticism of T. S. Eliot, one clearly of their company, as his appropriation of the same constellation of terms suggests, however critical he was of the geographical, ideological, and temporal "provincialism" of their anthropological humanism.[90] As a consequence of the rigorous pursuit of the logic of this historically constituted humanism, Eliot came to know all too well that it was not the culturally immature and erratic Greeks who could redeem a disintegrating Europe. Nor was it the Europeans of the Renaissance, whose Roman heritage had become Romance: a vulgarized and provincial Romanism. Rather, it was *Homo romanus*: the classical Augustan Roman, whose world was for Eliot preferable to the world of Homer because it was "a more civilized world of dignity, reason and order";[91] because, that is, it was characterized by greater "maturity":

Maturity of mind: this needs history, and the consciousness of history.
Consciousness of history cannot be fully awake, except where there is other
history than the history of the poet's own people: we need this in order to
see our own place in history. There must be the knowledge of the history of

at least one other highly civilized people, and of a people whose civilization is sufficiently cognate to have influenced and entered into our own. This is the consciousness which the Romans had, and which the Greeks, however much more highly we may estimate their achievement—and indeed, we may respect it all the more on this account—could not possess.[92]

The model for such an adult world was, of course, Virgil, who possessed a "historical consciousness" and "maturity of mind" that, like Arnold's "Sophocles," made it possible to transcend the provincial immediacy of his Greek predecessors. More precisely, Virgil's consciousness of history enabled him to perceive the presence of the *logos* informing the differences that temporal history disseminates, which the Greeks only glimpsed through a glass darkly; prefiguratively, as it were. Unlike his Greek precursors' immature historical sense, in short, Virgil's mature and comprehensive historical consciousness empowered him not simply "to see life steadily and see it whole," but to *foresee* and *comprehend*, indeed to prophesy, the future and end of European art and history: "In Homer," Eliot observes, "the conflict between the Greeks and the Trojans is hardly larger in scope than a feud between one Greek city-state and a coalition of other city-states: behind the story of Aeneas is the consciousness of a more radical distinction, a distinction which is at the same time a statement of *relatedness* between two great cultures and finally, of their reconciliation under an all-embracing destiny" ("WC," p. 62).

Behind Eliot's version of Western literary history, in which Virgil is privileged over Homer yet is continuous with him, lies a very sophisticated theoretical apparatus: the typological interpretation of the Patristic Fathers, which understands the events prior to the coming of the theologos into history as a prefiguration of that coming.[93] But this should not obscure the continuity between his providential understanding of the distinction that is at the same time a "relatedness between two great cultures" and Matthew Arnold's less theoretical distinction, which is also a relatedness, between the Homeric and Periclean cultures:

> Aeschylus and Sophocles represent an age as interesting as themselves; the names, indeed, in their dramas are the names of the old heroic world, from which they were far separated; but these names are taken, because the use of them permits to the poet that free and ideal treatment of his characters which the highest tragedy demands; and into these figures of the old world is poured all the fullness of life and of thought which the new world has accumulated. This new world in its maturity of reason resembles our own; and the advantages over Homer in the greater significance for us, which Aeschylus and Sophocles gain by belonging to this new world, more than compensates for their poetic inferiority to him.[94]

Both Eliot's and Arnold's representation of their respective histories has its condition of possibility in the ontological priority of identity over difference.

To put this binary distinction in terms of the relay of metaphorics that subsumes Eliot's genetic model, the paradigm of the adult world he prefers is not "blind Homer"; it is the *visionary* (panoptic) Virgil. For the prophecy/fulfillment structure in *The Aeneid* and the fourth *Eclogue*—and the "comprehensiveness" and "maturity" ("WC," pp. 55, 67) of the logocentric ontology enabling it—rectified the "adolescent" errancy of Homer.[95] By apotheosizing the idea of historical destiny (*fatum*) in terms of the pre-figurative model, it justified the *Pax Romana*, which is to say, the inexorable dynastic claims of the Augustan Empire—the *"imperium romanum,"* as Eliot calls it ("VCW," pp. 126, 129)[96]—on the rest of the scattered world. This is why, according to Eliot, Virgil's *Aeneid* has acquired the "centrality of the unique classic," why it constitutes the "criterion," the "classical standard," the "classical measure" for Europe as a whole, especially "in its progressive mutilation and disfigurement [in the modern period]":

> And of all the great poets of Greece and Rome, I think that it is to Virgil that we owe the most for our standard of the classic. . . . His comprehensiveness, his peculiar kind of comprehensiveness, is due to the unique position in our history of the Roman Empire and the Latin language: a position which may be said to conform to its *destiny*. This sense of destiny comes to consciousness in the *Aeneid*. Aeneas is himself, from first to last, a "man in fate," a man who is neither an adventurer nor a schemer, neither a vagabond nor a careerist [note the colonized allusions to Homer's Odysseus], a man fulfilling his destiny, not under compulsion or arbitrary decree, and certainly from no stimulus to glory, but by surrendering his will to a higher power behind the gods who would thwart or direct him. He would have preferred to stop in Troy, but he becomes an exile, and something greater and more significant than any exile; he is exiled for a purpose greater than he can know, but which he recognizes; and he is not, in a human sense, a happy or successful man. But he is the symbol of Rome; and, as Aeneas is to Rome, so is ancient Rome to Europe. Thus Virgil acquires the centrality of the unique classic; he is at the centre of European civilization, in a position which no other poet can share or usurp. The Roman Empire and the Latin language were not any empire and any language, but an empire and a language with a unique destiny in relation to ourselves; and the poet in whom that Empire and that language came to consciousness and expression is a poet of unique destiny. ("WC," pp. 67-68)[97]

As the figure of centeredness, Virgil becomes for Eliot what Sophocles was for Matthew Arnold: the unsurpassable because definitive *model* to be imitated by contemporary poets, transmitted by contemporary literary critics and teachers, and studied in the schools by contemporary students. This image of Virgil may enable the future resolution of a prodigal narrative of literary and cultural history gone increasingly astray since the abandonment of the Virgilian "imperial measure" in favor of the provincial temporal standards that confound "the contingent with the essential, the ephemeral with the permanent," and, in privileging the immediate present over the past, make the world "the property solely of the living, a property in which the dead hold no share" ("WC," p. 69). To shift the horizontal focus to another site on the continuum of Eliot's discourse, Virgil's text, as classic, becomes the authoritative model for the recuperation of the "common heritage of thought and feeling" ("WC," p. 70) and of the historical peace shattered by the intellectual warfare precipitated by the "dissociation of sensibility"—and the proliferation of knowledge it occasioned—in the seventeenth century.

The parallel with the humanist educational project of Matthew Arnold (and with Babbitt and Richards) should now be quite obvious. The names are different, but the beginning, agency, and end are fundamentally the same: the *logos*, cultural production, and the hegemony of Western civilization; or, to put this in terms of the post-Enlightenment: the comprehensive (panoptic) eye, disciplinary circumscription of the other, and the containment, pacification, and utilization of its force. The humanist *paideia*—its representation of the truth of being as such, of culture, of human beings' relation to the world—has always been complicitous, however unevenly in any specific historical instance, with the imperial project.

What, then, are the theoretical and practical pedagogical imperatives of this genealogical displacement of the origins of humanism from Greece to Rome? To think this difficult question will be the burden of the last two chapters of this book. Here, it will suffice to say that such thinking must take its point of departure precisely in the crisis precipitated by this genealogy. It must, that is, explore the positive possibilities of the relay of forces, which the binary—"Roman"—logic of the humanist anthropologos has denied a history and has perennially colonized and exploited.

FOUR

THE VIOLENCE OF DISINTERESTEDNESS

A GENEALOGY OF THE EDUCATIONAL "REFORM" INITIATIVE IN THE 1980S

> This concert [of ideological state apparatuses: political system, cultural institutions, communications media, religion, the family, etc.] is dominated by a single score, occasionally disturbed by contradictions (those of the remnants of former ruling classes, those of the proletarians and their organizations): the score of the Ideology of the current ruling class which integrates into its music the great themes of the Humanism of the Great Forefathers, who produced the Greek Miracle even before Christianity, and afterwards the Glory of Rome, the Eternal City, and themes of Interest, particular and general, etc., nationalism, moralism and economism. Nevertheless, in this concert, one ideological State apparatus certainly has the dominant role, although hardly anyone lends an ear to its music: it is so silent! This is the School.
>
> Louis Althusser, "Ideology and Ideological State Apparatuses"

> This summer I hear the drumming
> Four dead in Ohio.
>
> Neil Young, "Ohio"

I

The destructive reading of the exemplary discourses of Matthew Arnold, Irving Babbitt, and I. A. Richards in the foregoing chapter has discovered the history of modern humanistic educational theory that these three writers exemplify to be a history that has naturalized and covered up its ideological origins. This history is characterized not by disinterested inquiry but by a recurrent call for the recuperation of a logocentric pedagogy in the face of historical ruptures that betrayed the complicity of humanistic discourse with an essentially reactionary bourgeois ideology and its discreetly repressive capitalist state apparatuses, which have dominated the vision and practices of liberal Western industrial societies, especially in North America. In undertaking this reading, I want to emphasize, it was not my intention simply to focus on past instances of this complicity with the practices of domination. I am not writing a history of modern education. I am, rather, engaged in genealogy. My purpose, in Walter Benjamin's terms, is to brush the historical narrative implied by the reforms presently being enacted in institutions of higher learning against the grain. I want to call into question the massive contemporary effort to recuperate the core curriculum in the name of the disinterested inquiry, rationality, and civilization that have allegedly been undermined by the "madness," "barbarism," and "immature" or "provincial" interest of a generation of youth abetted by "a collective loss of nerve and faith on the part of both faculty and academic administrators during the late 1960s and early 1970s."[1]

My purpose is to give back historical materiality to these strategic abstractions, which rarefy and misrepresent the disruption of the university by students, black and other racial minorities, and women, in the decade of the Vietnam War. For the history the reform movement tells is, as I have shown, not simply a history that, in Foucault's words, assumes a suprahistorical perspective, that "always encourages subjective recognitions and attributes a form of reconciliation to all the displacements of the past; a history whose perspective on all that precedes it implies the end of time, a completed development." It is also a form of "recollection" that overlooks and forgets or represses history for the sake of relegitimating the dominant educational establishment and "our national heritage" in the face of the emergence of voices the dominant cultural and sociopolitical order must subjugate or reform in order to legitimate, reproduce, and extend its hegemony.

In this chapter, I want to examine North American education in terms of the reform movements undertaken by the institutions of higher learning (especially by Harvard University, since its reform initiatives have been historically enabling) in this century: those that occurred during and immediately after World War I, World War II, and the Vietnam War. I want to focus on the first two in order to provide the historically specific ideological context that the third and most recent has strategically overlooked and left unsaid. This most recent reform movement is that initiated by the Harvard Core Curriculum Report in 1978, which has culminated in the massive representation of contemporary theory and the multicultural studies it has in part enabled as a discourse and practice of "political correctness." These historically specific institutional reform movements not only repeat in practice the theoretical strategies of the leading intellectuals I have discussed, but do so in ways that make visible how crucial the institutions of higher learning are to the reproduction of the dominant sociopolitical order. They have become, in an age of extraordinary expansion (of knowledge), perhaps the most important agency of the disciplinary state.

II

The complicity I am pointing to between the liberal university and the disciplinary society has at no time been more evident than in the historical instances of institutional educational reform in the United States during and after World War I (the period represented in the narrative of the cultural memory first as the menace of "the Hun" and then of "the Red Bolshevik") and again after World War II (the period of the Cold War). In both instances we witness not simply the reaffirmation of a core curriculum—the monumental tradition threatened by a discursive explosion—but to a reaffirmation which made visible the center elsewhere of the "disinterested" inquiry that allegedly gave it its shape. In both, that is, we witness the will to power inhering in the benign discursive practices of the Occidental humanist institution as an ideological cultural apparatus serving the hegemonic purposes of a repressive sociopolitical order.

We first encounter this materialized will to power during and after World War I, when the American colleges and universities, administrators and faculty alike, harnessed some version of the Great Books or Great Ideas courses to the teaching of "Americanism," a massive project which obfuscated questions about Western imperialism precipitated by the war with Germany and about economic and sociopolitical oppression in Western nation-states activated by the October Revolution. In response to this crisis moment, the administrations and faculties of most American institutions of higher learning read the historical disclosure of capitalist violence (hitherto justified by representing it as the *mission civilatrice* of Western nations) in the framework of the narrative of the "Great Crusade" (Woodrow Wilson's slogan) against "German barbarism." Immediately after the war, the Bolshevik Revolution and the emergence of a working-class consciousness were similarly read, in the framework of the narrative of the Red Scare. The university dealt with the threat to the national consensus these new knowledges posed by measuring their "deviations" from the "humane" values informing the idealized philosophical and literary monuments—the master narrative—of the Western heritage.

As Carol Gruber observes in a book about the political uses to which higher education was put in the United States during World War I (a book published in 1975, no doubt as a reminder to the post-Vietnam university of the susceptibility of its humanistic discourse to ethnocentrism and complicity with state power): "After the war was over the themes of absolute good versus absolute evil characterizing the state-mandated War Issues Course introduced into the curriculum along with the Students' Army Training Corps (SATC) was retained by simply putting the Bolshevik in the place of the Hun as the menace to Western democracy everywhere."[2] As evidence of this easy transition, Gruber cites from the still-extant summary of the representative War Issues lectures given at the University of Michigan (1918) by professors Clark H. Van Tyne, Edward L. Turner, and William A. Frayer:

Tyne notified the students that the struggle against Bolshevism was more important even than the military struggle that had just been won and urged them to throw their influence "on the side which is most likely to maintain . . . [the better] forces, so that chaos, which had already ruined Russia, may not come to us." Frayer advised them to study "the wild excesses of the revolutionists," remarking that "a surprising number" of them were Jews. The Russian Jew was particularly dangerous, he said, because centuries of suffering at the hands of the government had made him a bitter man. The students were warned that Bolshevik friends and sympathizers "are everywhere — in Germany, in France, in Italy, in England, in the United States — they are on the campus of the University of Michigan." The great task of social reformation facing the world, they were told, must not be given to men whose sense of honor, right and justice is utterly perverted.[3]

The astonishing self-righteous arrogance that manifests itself as a virulent and racist ethnocentrism needs no comment. What does need to be made explicit, however, is that these universal intellectuals were professors of the humanities. As Gruber's history makes clear, they were not isolated individuals whose lectures could easily be discounted as perversions of the liberal spirit of humanism in general, but rather representative of what humanists were saying in college classrooms everywhere in the United States during this historical crisis that had precipitated a symptomatic discursive explosion threatening the hegemony of the "American way of life." Under the pressure of this discursive explosion their discourse makes explicit the latent violence inherent in the binary logic informing the "disinterestedness" of humanist inquiry and the "apolitical" structure of the institution to which it gave shape. Enabled by the anthropologos, this circular logic privileges and empowers the first term to represent the second as a negative that will legitimate its authority. Thus, in this historically specific context of crisis, the "disinterestedness" of Western humanism becomes, first, the "better force" and then, even more narrowly, American (capitalist) democracy, whereas the practice of the emergent subject positions activated by the explosion of new knowledges is represented as the "wild excesses" of Russian Jews/Bolshevik friends and sympathizers who "are everywhere . . . [even] on the campus of the University of Michigan."

Contrary to the universalist representation of the amnesiac cultural memory, general education or the core curriculum as we have come to know it had its genealogical origins, in fact, in the historically specific crisis moment in which the invisible center elsewhere was compelled by the irruption of "alien" knowledges to become visible and material — to manifest its power in the public sphere. As Gruber makes clear, it was the state-mandated and universally compulsory War Issues Course that generated the General Honors (Great Books) and Contemporary Civilization courses at Columbia University in 1919:

The introduction of the required course in contemporary civilization at Columbia illustrates clearly the relationship between the War Issues Course and curricular reform. While the course was in progress, Dean Woodbridge, who was its director and had been chiefly responsible for preparing its syllabus, indicated that the course was beginning to be viewed as a prospective basis of "a liberal education for the youth of today." In the face of the confusion of ideas and standards left by the demise of classical education, he said, the War Issues Course seemed to afford the "opportunity to introduce into our education a liberalizing force which will give to the generations to come a common background of ideas and commonly understood standards of judgment." . . . A required course in contemporary civilization, offered by members of the departments of history, economics, government, and philosophy was introduced at Columbia in the fall of 1919. Its purpose was to survey the historical background of Western civilization and to acquaint the students with current world problems. Its promotion as a bulwark against radicalism betrayed its origins in the patriotic War Issues Course. Dean Herbert E. Hawkes, one of the founders of the contemporary civilization course, described it as being intended to silence the "destructive elements in our society" by preparing students to "meet the arguments of the opponents of decency and sound government" and thus to make the college student a "citizen, who shall be safe for democracy."[4]

These Columbia survey courses, it should be emphasized, did not remain peculiar to Columbia. They immediately became two of the most influential and widely imitated general education courses in the history of modern higher education in the United States. As the similarity between the rhetoric of the Columbia reformers and that of the reformers of the 1980s suggests—their invoking of crisis and their consequent appeal to the ideals that would allay it—they elaborated the essential structure that was to inform American undergraduate education until the Vietnam decade. The prefigurative educational reform instituted by Columbia University in the aftermath of the Russian Revolution tells us overtly that the original end of general education was not simply an intellectual matter of accommodating new knowledge that rendered "classical education" obsolete to a wider framework. This perennially humanist educational imperative was simultaneously a sociopolitical matter of establishing a cultural apparatus capable of silencing the "destructive elements in our society," of making the college student for generations to come a "citizen, who shall be safe for democracy." By surveying, not history as such, but the *monuments* of Western history, students would recover standards of judgment that would give certainty and direction to their intellectual pursuits and their sociopolitical practice, standards an "ominously" antidemocratic social philosophy in the "East" and "radicalism" at home were threatening to undermine.

The vicious circularity of the logic of this pedagogic project should not be over-looked. Education in this view from above is not a process of generating critical consciousness but of gaining confirmation, of reaffirming at the end the (Western/American) standards of judgment that determine the pedagogical process from the beginning. The "liberalizing force" that the War Issues Course made it possible to introduce in the Columbia curriculum was thus, in fact, like Arnold's "mighty agency of deliverance," a discreet force of intellectual, cultural, and sociopolitical constraint. This, then, is the genealogy that the amnesiac cultural memory will insistently forget or repress in its unexamined commitment to "a common body of knowledge"; not least, as we shall see, at Harvard University in the aftermath of World War II and again in the wake of the turbulent Vietnam decade, in the process of restoring the general education program.

This overt institutional practice of the will to power, latent in the discourse of humanism, is also visible in *General Education in a Free Society*—the proposed curricular reforms of which were adopted by Harvard University after World War II (in the historically specific context of the Cold War with the Soviet Union). As its letter of transmittal suggests, its authors' recommendations were not simply addressing curricular problems at Harvard precipitated by President Charles Eliot's elective system. Relying on Harvard's cultural authority, they hoped that these reforms would be enacted by institutions of learning, lower and higher, throughout the United States:

> In short, we were directed not so much to make recommendations for
> general education in Harvard College as to venture into the vast field of
> American educational experience in quest of a concept of general education
> that would have validity for a free society which we cherish. This concept if
> found would be a true basis upon which to build such special contribution as
> education in Harvard College could make to American Democracy.[5]

This influential text, which came to be called the Harvard Redbook, was mandated by the politically active president of Harvard University, James Bryant Conant, and was written by a committee of twelve prestigious Harvard administrators and faculty, I. A. Richards among them (all white males), appointed by Conant.[6] It is the general education Program articulated by this select committee that, in the view of the committee authorizing the Harvard Core Curriculum Report of 1978, was "eroded by the proliferation of courses" or, to retrieve the history this rhetoric obfuscates, was shattered by the student, feminist, and black protest movement during the decade of the Vietnam War.

The rhetorical focus of the Redbook's justification for curricular reform was on "a centrifugal culture in extreme need of unifying forces" or, alternatively, on the "staggering expansion of knowledge" precipitated by the present historical conjuncture (*GEFS*, p. 5). (These phrases recall the encoded metaphorics of the centered circle that Matthew Arnold, Irving Babbitt, and I. A. Richards insistently use to characterize the crises of culture they respectively address.) But it is also clear that the Redbook's call for "education in a common heritage and toward a common citizenship" (*GEFS*, p. 5) had much to do with the uncoordinated expansion of educational opportunities in this century and the molding of a national consensus in the face of the "threat" of the Soviet Union and, more importantly, the internal dissidence activated by the neoimperialist tendencies of American Cold War policy.

In his institutional history of the profession of English in America, Gerald Graff misleadingly implies that the essential goal of the Harvard committee was the reconciliation of specialism (the Redbook's alleged source of cultural fragmentation) and " 'preparation for life in the broad sense of a human being.' "[7] There is, according to Graff (following the lead of Daniel Bell's critique of the humanities course at Columbia in the early 1960s),[8] "a curious discrepancy . . . between the urgency of the committee's appeal to a unified cultural heritage" and its proposal for achieving it by dehistoricizing the "great works," by means of reading them New Critically: as decontextualized or autonomous texts (*PL*, pp. 170-71). For this would render the study of the humanities, as according to Graff it did, an "irrelevant" formalist activity.

This interpretation, however, obscures the intended ideological function of the Redbook's general education program: the neutralization of internal cultural and sociopolitical divisions precipitated by the questions about democracy released by American Cold War politics. By restricting the Redbook's generalized scope to its implications for literature departments and concluding that their appropriation of a decontextualized close reading was symptomatic of "the chronic inability of general education programs to compel faculty support" (*PL*, p. 173), Graff's interpretation also obscures the conservative (and disciplinary) cultural and sociopolitical implications — and consequences — of "practical criticism," of reading the "great works" from a formalist or end-of-ideology perspective. For, as I. A. Richards (who, as Graff rightly observes, was responsible for the New Critical emphasis), was in large degree aware, such a close reading of the canonical texts recuperates the "common heritage" in a far more subtle way. (This is contrary to Graff's insistently reiterated assumption that the great books represent "an inherently refractory and ideologically conflict-filled . . . cultural setting" [*PL*, p. 173].) In assuming that the great work is characterized by its harmonious unity — its accomplished reconciliation and integration of discordant (individual) elements into a "stable," "balanced," and "inclusive" whole "impervious to irony" — this Richardsian reading (and pedagogical) procedure would reinscribe the centered circle — the privileged diagram of beauty and power which has been fundamental to the recuperative theory and practice of the humanistic/liberal democratic tradition — as a fundamental structure of educated consciousness.

As such subjects, those educated under the aegis of this "objective" close reading (and pedagogy) would be enabled to understand the centrifugal knowledge precipitated by the expansive events of World War II as cultural and sociopolitical tendencies that were menacing the consensus necessary for the "defense" or "survival"[9] of the "free—Western (American)—world" in the conflict with communism. By recontextualizing this polyvalent diagram to contemporary pedagogical uses—by putting it to the uses envisaged by the authors of the Redbook—the general education program would also fulfill the Benthamite imperatives of the disciplinary society. What Paul Bové says in his Foucauldian critique of Richards's disciplinary pedagogy of practical criticism, at the heart of which "lies the figure of the leading intellectual," applies as well to the teaching of the "great works" sponsored by *General Education in a Free Society*:

> Richards [through the "protocol" approach] enacts the position of the sublime master teacher, of the leading humanistic intellectual, in his practical and theoretical extension of disciplinary power in which the students and others become "readers" who are the subjugated objects of study. Practical criticism creates "readers" as such an object for critical investigation and critical training. The entire project of creating a sane and balanced world resting on the theory of contextualism [which "requires a theory of signs that can be derived only from a study of others"] depends on the critic's assuming the role of scientific investigator of "reading" and "readers" in order to systematize and correct the practice. In addition, of course, this extension of discipline has important social effects of individuation, normalization, and exclusion. At the heart of the project, however, lies the arrogant figure of the leading intellectual whose authority, interacting with that of the institutions and discourses in which he practices, legitimates the disciplinary extension of humanism in an essentially antidemocratic process of subjugating people within categories of social being constituted by the discursive and nondiscursive practices of humanism.
>
> In the process of training teachers and readers, Richards proposes the extension of discipline not to "repress" difference, which seems, to him, unfortunately prevalent in the postwar world of a failed liberal and imperialistic "consensus." We must remember that Richards's immediate "modest" aim was simply to train the newly emergent groups who would be assuming power and responsibility.[10]

By interpreting the Redbook's emphasis on practical criticism as a disabling contradiction in its appeal for the recuperation of "the common heritage," Graff obscures the underlying ideological function of its general education program: the inscription of a *diversified loyalty* to the nation; that is, the transformation of an inefficient, because atomistic, individualism into a more socially oriented individualism. The purposes informing Richards's course in practical criticism are, in fact, those articulated by the

Redbook in broader terms (reminiscent of Matthew Arnold's and Babbitt's identification of the "best self" with the state) in its justification of the general education program at large:

> Just as it is wrong to split the individual person into separate parts, so would it be wrong to split the individual from society. We must resist the prevalent tendency . . . to interpret the good life purely in terms of atomic individuals engaged in fulfilling their own potentialities. Individualism is often confused with the life of private and selfish interest. The mandate of this committee is to concern itself with "the objectives of education in a free society." It is important to realize that the ideal of a free society involves a two-fold value, the value of freedom and that of society. Democracy is a *community* of free men. We are apt sometimes to see freedom—the power of individual choice and the right to think for oneself—without taking sufficient account of the obligation to cooperate with our fellow men; democracy must represent an adjustment between the values of freedom and social living. (*GEFS*, pp. 76-77)

Understood in the light of Heidegger's destruction of the metaphysical tradition and Foucault's genealogy of the disciplinary society, the benign oxymoron "community of free men" discloses another, darker agenda: the production of "subjected subjects"—of individuals who are not only subordinated to the identity of the state, but who also work actively to enhance its hegemony—on the basis of the enabling metaphysical fiction that identity is the condition for the possibility of difference and not the other way around. In more historically specific terms, to read the Richardsian literary component of the general education program envisaged by the Harvard Redbook against the grain, as it were, discovers its hidden agenda to be the establishment of a Cold War politics of national consensus.[11]

This dark underside of "general education in a free society"—this ideologically motivated "diversified loyalty"—is not simply the hidden goal of the literary component; it is the end of the total educational apparatus envisaged by the authors of the Harvard Redbook. Thus, for example, they also propose in the area of the adjacent social sciences that "all students should take a course which might be called "Western Thought and Institutions," a course which, though it "would not parallel with any exactitude the proposed course on great texts which we suggest for the areas of the humanities," would nevertheless provide "rewarding opportunities for cross-reference and for comparison in the two courses" (*GEFS*, p. 216). Initially they considered the possibility of calling such a course "The Evolution of Free Society," but because it carried "implications of indoctrination which would be unacceptable to many" (*GEFS*, p. 214), they rejected it:

> For while we agree that Harvard College should assume "a full and a

conscientious responsibility for training men in the nature of the heritage which they possess, and in the responsibilities which they must assume as free men for its enlargement and perpetuation," we do not believe that the course should be one which would attempt to convince students of the eternal perfection of existing ideas and institutions. The central objective of the course would be an examination of the institutional and theoretical aspect of the Western heritage. (*GEFS*, p. 214)

On the surface, this passage appears to be a caution against the dangers of ideological indoctrination. What the liberal rhetoric obscures, however, as the failure to question the crucial terms of Conant's agenda—the "enlargement and perpetuation" of our heritage—is its origins in the restricted economy of discipline developed in the post-monarchical age of the Enlightenment: the principle that visible power (indoctrination) is intrinsically open to resistance ("would be unacceptable to many") or, conversely, that power must be invisible, internalized and distributed throughout the student body. This duplicity becomes remarkably manifest in the committee's exemplary selection from the "immense body of philosophical literature available for use in a course of this kind": "Aquinas, Machiavelli, Luther, Bodin, Locke, Montesquieu, Rousseau, Adam Smith, Bentham, and Mill." It is not simply that this suggested list consists exclusively of Eurocentric white males and culminates in an overwhelming emphasis on the Anglo-American empirical, bourgeois capitalist, utilitarian, and disciplinary tradition. What is especially telling is the remarkable "oversight" of the immensely significant writings of Karl Marx, not to say of women and black thinkers.

It is no accident, then, that in the end, the authors of the Redbook inform the reader that what they had in mind from the beginning in making such a required course proposal was the Columbia model (without reference to its genealogy as the War Issues Course): "The course is not unlike the very successful introductory course 'Contemporary Civilization,' which has been given at Columbia during the past twenty-six years" (*GEFS*, p. 217). It is no accident, in other words, that the articulation and adoption of the general education program by Harvard at the time of the origins of the Cold War repeats the pattern of educational reform in the United States largely precipitated by the Russian Revolution and the emergence of a subaltern consciousness.

As I previously suggested, the end sought by the Roman *studium humanitatis* in reducing the Greek *paideia*—the instigation of originative thinking—to *erudito et institutio in bonus artes* (scholarship and training in good conduct) was the cultivation of a disciplined, loyal, and predictable citizenry (*Homo humanus*) to secure the stability of the metropolis and extend its hegemony over *Homo barbarus* and "barbarian" lands. However more benign the hegemonic rhetoric of "freedom" and "defense" makes the Redbook's project seem, this too, as that of the Columbia survey course in contemporary civilization after World War I, is finally the end of general education enabled, if not exactly envisioned, by its liberal humanist authors.

The Redbook's justification of President Conant's educational agenda—the "enlarge-ment and perpetuation of the heritage which [students] possess"—is not finally an au-thentic caution against totalitarian indoctrination. It is rather an effort to conceal the slippage in Conant's rhetoric that gives visibility to power. It is, in other words, a rec-ognition that Conant's "Roman"—and ultimately imperial—project can be more effi-ciently achieved by a hegemonic educational apparatus that internalizes power, that renders students willing and unquestioning exponents of the "heritage" they possess.

That the molding of a loyal and disciplined postwar citizenry against a now-powerful communism was indeed the essential intention of the general education program for-mulated by the Harvard committee at the close of World War II is strongly confirmed by President Conant in *Education in a Divided World* (1949), his own more overt ideo-logical contribution to curricular reform, in which he stresses more forcefully than the Redbook the role of the emergent secondary schools, where the potential for class divisions was greater, in the production of cultural and sociopolitical consensus:

A set of common beliefs is essential for the health and vigor of a free society. And it is through education that these beliefs are developed in the young and carried forward in later life. This is the social aspect of general education, one might say. The future citizens we desire to educate should have strong loyalties and high civic courage. These loyalties ought to be to the type of society we are encouraging and to the United States as the home of this society. Such emotional attitudes are in part the product of a common knowledge and a common set of values . . .

The war has underlined the fact that the most effective loyalties are often to small groups of men bound together by a common experience and a unity of immediate purpose. A unifying faith is in most instances not a matter of words or intellectual concepts but of a direct relationship between men. What we mean by democracy may be illustrated for some people better by action than by words.[12]

Like his appointed committee of twelve earlier, Conant puts his liberal humanist case against those "who worry about radicalism in our schools and colleges"—"reaction-aries" or "defeatists"—in terms of the dialogue of free individuals.

The first group are consciously or unconsciously aiming at a transformation of this society, perhaps initially not as revolutionary or violent as that which the Soviet agents envisage, but one eventually equally divergent from our historic goals. The others are unduly timid about the outcome of a battle of *ideas*; they lack confidence in our own intellectual armament. (I mean literally the battle of ideas, not espionage or sabotage by secret agents.) They often fail to recognize that diversity of opinion within the framework of loyalty to our free society is not only basic to a university but the entire nation. For in a

THE VIOLENCE OF DISINTERESTEDNESS

democracy with our tradition only those reasoned convictions which emerge from diversity of opinion can lead to that unity and natural solidarity so essential for the welfare of our country. (*EDW*, p. 178)

But it is also clear, as the phrase "diversity of opinion within the framework of loyalty to our free society" suggests, that the play of difference he would defend against "reactionaries" (he is obviously referring to the emergent McCarthyism) must be inexorably tethered to "the emotional attitudes" or, more specifically, to the "strong loyalties and high civic courage" that are "the product of a common knowledge and a common set of values": to the ideology that it is "the social aspect of general education" to inculcate in the students. One should not overlook Conant's identification of the ends of education with the bonding experience of *men* at war nor the remarkable similarity between his stress on the necessity of generating emotional commitment to the nation and the Victorian J. C. Collins's insistence in *The Study of English Literature* (quoted in chapter 2) that the people "need to be impressed sentimentally" by the teachers of English literature about the grandeur of the English way of life. Indeed, if the imperatives of this social aspect of the general education curriculum are to be properly fulfilled, the educational institution must inculcate "these [centralized, unifying, and directive] loyalties" in the form of an "intellectual armament" homologous with the state's build-up of "defensive" weaponry. For only such a centering center or ground or principle of identity will be able to disarm the disruptive threat of cultural and sociopolitical difference. As Conant puts this implicit appeal to Roman *virtus* in justifying his liberal humanist call for the "general education of *all* American youth (instead of merely one small segment of young men)" (*EDW*, p. 88), to "defeat the high hopes of the believers in the Communist doctrine," educational institutions in America must annul the "explosive force inherent in a stratified society"—the force these alien believers rely on—by "prevent[ing] such stratification" (*EDW*, p. 15).

That this symptomatic reading is not a distortion of the restricted economy of Conant's liberal humanism becomes evident elsewhere in his text, where he ostensibly makes a plea for the toleration of differing discourses in the institutions of learning:

How are we to answer the thoughtful and troubled citizen who wonders if our universities are being used as centers for fifth column activities? By emphasizing again the central position in this country of tolerance of diversity of opinion and by expressing confidence that *our* philosophy is superior to all alien importations. After all, this is but one version of the far wider problem which we encounter at the outset: How are we to win the ideological conflict if it continues on a non-shooting basis? Clearly not by destroying our basic ideas but by strengthening them; clearly not by retreating in fear from Communist doctrine but by going out vigorously to meet it. Studying a philosophy does not mean endorsing it, much less proclaiming it. We study cancer in order to learn how to defeat it. We must study the Soviet philosophy in our universities for exactly the same reason. No one must be afraid to tackle that explosive subject before a class. If an avowed supporter of the Marx-Lenin-Stalin line can be found, force him into the open and tear his arguments to pieces with counter-arguments. . . . Doctrines that are not combated in the classroom but treated merely with silence may be appealing to the immature. (*EDW*, p. 173)

In the process of this astonishingly crude argument, the "diversity of opinion" to be tolerated is systematically reduced by Conant's binary logic, first to "all alien importations," then to "Communist doctrine," then to "Soviet philosophy," and finally to the "Marx-Lenin-Stalin line" (all of which are defined in terms of the analogy with cancer) and the role of open-minded educators to one, not of response to the questions about capitalist democracy Marxist thought raises, but of combating its appeal to "immature" students from the "mature" position of absolute certainty that "*our* philosophy is superior." Written from a liberal humanist perspective, Conant's discourse conveys the general impression that "our philosophy" is that combination of Jeffersonian and Jacksonian democracy (also invoked by the authors of the Redbook), that is grounded in free and disinterested inquiry. However, his reduction of the dialogic imperatives of the educational process to the binary structure of Cold War (and male) rhetoric betrays another meaning: "our philosophy" becomes "corporate capitalism." That is to say, the (not so) hidden agenda informing Conant's rhetoric of deliverance is the calculated harnessing of knowledge production to power or, more specifically, of the means of education to the purposes of the corporate capitalist state: the annulling of potential internal resistance ("perpetuation") and the expansion of its hegemony ("enlargement"). Indeed, in thematizing the positive productivity of knowledge, it constitutes a classic example of the knowledge/power relationship that Michel Foucault has found to be the enabling agency of the disciplinary society:

> Statesmanship [in a divided world] will be required not only in affairs of state but in other vital areas; two in particular are of prime importance: industry and education. As to the first, almost every reader will agree; and the significance of the second is the thesis of this book. Their close connection, however, is not always realized—nor the need for solving problems in both areas by a cooperative approach. . . .
>
> The future prosperity of America depends on the capacity of its economy to remain dynamic while providing satisfying employment in industry as may best forward the interests of the nation. . .
>
> The methods of certain of the social sciences have already been developed to a point where studies of society by competent scholars can provide basic information to assist the leaders of the nation. The scholars in these

disciplines can help train not only public officials but those who carry responsibilities for resolving the many human problems in our complex industrial economy. We must expect no miracles, of course, but certain types of work in sociology, anthropology, and social psychology seem full of promise. If basic research is as adequately supported in these fields as in physics and chemistry, in a few decades we should be in possession of much social knowledge. (*EDW*, 35-36)

The "cooperation" between the institutions of knowledge production and industry that Conant's and Harvard's liberal humanist educational reforms were intended to achieve materialized in the next decade, far more rapidly than Conant envisaged, when American educational institutions became what Clark Kerr, president of the University of California at Berkeley, called in 1963 "the knowledge industry,"[13] an industry on which the military-industrial complex relied heavily in its execution of the war in Vietnam; an industry that, as the protest movements on college campuses everywhere in the United States attest,[14] finally betrayed the contradictions inherent in the discourse of liberal humanism.

What Conant's text confirms, in fact, is Althusser's Gramscian analysis of the liberal humanist educational institution in the capitalist West as ideological state apparatus. In contradistinction to the state apparatus itself (government, the administration, the army, the police, courts, the prisons, etc.), which "functions massively and predominantly by repression," the ideological state apparatus (religion, educational institutions, the family, the legal system, the political system, the trade union, communication, including press, radio, television, etc.), according to Althusser, "functions massively and predominantly by ideology":[15] *"a 'Representation' of the Imaginary Relationship of Individuals to Their Real Conditions of Existence"* ("IISA," p. 162). As such this apparatus is always, despite its benign and private appearance, in complicity with ideology and with the "ruling class" that controls it:

If the ISAs "function" massively and predominantly by ideology, what unifies their diversity is precisely this functioning, insofar as the ideology by which they function is always in fact unified, despite its diversity and its contradictions, *beneath the ruling ideology*, which is the ideology of the "ruling class." Given the fact that the "ruling class" in principle holds State power (openly or more often by means of alliances between classes or class fractions), and therefore has at its disposal the (Repressive) State Apparatus, we can accept the fact that this same ruling class is active in the Ideological State Apparatus insofar as it is ultimately the ruling ideology which is realized in the Ideological State Apparatuses, precisely in its contradictions. ("IISA," p. 146)

In calling for a more cooperative and efficient relationship between economic production and knowledge production as an imperative of the "divided world," Conant's text also betrays the growing awareness by the dominant economic and sociopolitical order of the emergent overdetermination of the cultural site, or, as Althusser puts it, of the historically specific reality that *"no class can hold State power over a long period without at the same time exercising its hegemony over and in the State Ideological Apparatuses"* ("IISA," p. 146).

If, then, we read the widely imitated Harvard general education program articulated by the humanist authors of the Redbook alongside Conant's more historically specific discourse, it becomes quite clear that the play of difference it would defend against "reactionaries" is, on the ontological level at which Derrida sites his critique of humanistic discourse, "a play based on a fundamental ground and a reassuring certitude, which itself is beyond the reach of play." To put it in Foucault's more sociopolitical terms, the society of free individuals that the general education program envisaged is a society of "subjected subjects": a disciplinary society. Far from thinking the new knowledge occasioned by the disruption of a decade of world war, far from engaging the various emergent voices attempting to articulate and practice this new knowledge, the reformation of the curriculum in the United States in the aftermath of World War II was, in fact, a deliberate strategy of accommodation and containment in the name of an anthropology brought up to date: American (capitalist) democracy. One wonders, then, despite assertions to the contrary, about the degree of Harvard's real complicity in the violence of McCarthyism in the 1950s.

III

My purpose in invoking the practices of general education in the aftermaths of World War I and World War II has not been simply to criticize them. As genealogy, it has also and more importantly been to *remember* in the present what the essentially amnesiac cultural memory of humanist anthropology necessarily forgets in its naturalized effort to recuperate its authority in the face of e-mergent knowledge.[16] As we have seen in each of these historical occasions of crisis, the forgetting intrinsic to the recollective humanist memory manifests itself in varying degrees in the form of overt repression: as institutional "Egyptianism." In each instance, the humanist problematic *itself* betrays its alleged naturalness; it shows itself to be an ideological agency in complicity with the dominant sociopolitical order, an ideological state apparatus. My purpose, in other words, has been to retrieve the contradictory history that the renewed and increasingly pervasive and strident educational reform initiative in our present (post-Vietnam) historical conjuncture has largely, in some cases strategically, ignored or repressed in its staging of the crisis of higher education. More specifically, it has been to provide a genealogical context that will expose the reactionary ideology hidden behind the initiative to restore the general education program, the core curriculum, or "cultural literacy" and to "save" disinterested inquiry, its agencies of knowledge production and transmission, and "our cultural heritage" first from the "barbarism" of the youth movement of the 1960s, then from the "nihilism" of poststructuralist theory in the 1970s, and finally from the "left-inspired" "political correctness" of the emergent multicultural practices in the 1980s and early 1990s. In short, my purpose has been to prepare us to understand the appeal of the post-Vietnam reform initiative to "free" and "disinterested" inquiry as, in fact, a concerted effort to *reestablish* a discourse of "political correctness": a strategy intended to recuperate not only the university's shaken authority but also the hegemony of the dominant sociopolitical order; that is, the disciplinary society.

As the theoretical and institutional history I have recalled suggests, it is no accident that the massive institutional reform initiative in the aftermath of the Vietnam War had its immediate origins at Harvard University. In 1974, at the behest of President Derek Bok, administrative officials and faculty began deliberating a program of undergraduate educational reform with the intention of restoring the general education program which, in the misleading euphemisms of Dean Henry Rosovsky, the appointed chairman of the committee, had been "eroded" by the "proliferation of courses" in the previous decade. As in the case of Conant's mandate to the Harvard committee in the 1940s, Bok's mandate to his administrators and faculty was to develop a program of general education appropriate not only for undergraduate education at Harvard University but, in its generality, for undergraduate education in the United States at large. The result of these deliberations was the Harvard Core Curriculum Report, published in February 1978 and adopted by the Harvard faculty in May of that year. Following its publication, the report was widely discussed in, and by and large enthusiastically endorsed by, the media. This attention coupled with Harvard University's prestige generated a momentum that has resulted in the widespread adoption of some version of that core curriculum in colleges and universities throughout the United States, and also in widespread and highly vocal calls for analogous reforms in the lower levels of schooling—from preschool and kindergarten through high school—and on the graduate level, especially in those disciplines where postmodern theory has made inroads.

Read against the grain—in the theoretical and historical context discovered by the preceding genealogy of modern general education, the context left unsaid by its authors—the Harvard Core Curriculum Report is disclosed as little more than a replication—thinned out by the consensual imperatives of "democratic" academic politics—of I. A. Richards's synoptic idea of the university, and of the general education program of the Cold War period that he was instrumental in developing. In fact, Barry O'Connell makes this point in his ironically entitled essay, "Where Does Harvard Lead Us?," one of the working papers of the conference "Towards the Restoration of the Liberal Arts Curriculum" sponsored by the Rockefeller Foundation in September 1978. "The curriculum recently adopted in Cambridge is neither original nor particularly distinguished. The Harvard 'Core' is, at best, a watered-down version of the experiments in general education at Columbia in the 1920s, at Hutchins' Chicago in the 1930s, and at Harvard itself in the late 1940s."[17] Although O'Connell's essay—the only one of the working papers of the Rockefeller Foundation that calls into question the educational value of the Harvard Core Curriculum Report—constitutes a critique of the report's failure to review graduate along with undergraduate education and to interrogate the specialization and the departmental hegemony it perpetuates, the essay does point broadly to the elitist implications of the report and its tendency to legitimate the existing sociopolitical power structure; that is, its strategic tendency to contain and neutralize dissent and to produce disciplinary knowledge. For example, O'Connell writes:

> A dispassionate observer might conclude that Harvard has shaped the ideal curriculum for a corporate future. Its mode of design and its form of operation provide a model of bureaucracy. Like all effective bureaucracies, this one seems likely to specialize in persuading its clients that everything it does is in their best interest, while using the appearances of responsiveness to dilute and to hinder clear thinking about the ends of the institution. ("WDHL," p. 61)

And again, more tellingly:

> Harvard has attracted notice for its prestige, of course, but also because its new curriculum so easily can be taken as the nostrum for what ails us [the malaise precipitated by "the proliferation of knowledge"]. Yet much more is at issue than has been acknowledged. An examination which clearly formulated the deeper problems in higher education would raise the questions neither the universities nor much of the society is prepared to face. I suspect it is for this reason that the media and many faculties have produced such superficial analyses and reforms. ("WDHL," p. 63)

Despite the implications of complicity with sociopolitical power structures, however, O'Connell's equation of the Harvard core curriculum and the old general education program does not generate an adequate critique of the former. For, finally, he implies that the qualitative limitations of the core curriculum have their source in its quantitative rather than in theoretical limitations: "The reforms Harvard has adopted are not in themselves wrong. They are too little and too late" ("WDHL," pp. 68-69); in other words, its failure is a failure of redistribution of existing pedagogic agents, rather than a failure to interrogate their informing ontology and its ideological consequences. To put this differently, he fails to read the report in its historical context: as a conservative gesture to recuperate the onto-sociopolitical center that was decentered by the protest movement during the decade of the Vietnam War. His text, that is, betrays a failure of the genealogical historical sense.

It is not possible in this limited space to demonstrate the relationship between the conservative panoptic impulse informing the Harvard core curriculum and that which, beginning with Irving Babbitt's classicist opposition to Charles W. Eliot's reforms, culminates in I. A. Richards's traditional "synoptic view" and the general education program articulated in the Harvard Redbook. Nor is it especially necessary or desirable to demonstrate it. For it is not so much the curriculum as such—the quantitative distribution of core course requirements in the areas that represent the "five important modes of understanding": letters and arts (3 half courses); history (2); social and philosophical analysis (2); sciences and mathematics (2); and foreign language and culture (1)—that bears investigation.[18] What demands questioning, rather, is the apparently innocent but nevertheless determining rhetoric of the report and, above all, *what it insistently leaves unstated* in the process of articulating its rationale; what it does not say about its historical origins and its relation to the pervasive postmodern critique of the archival language and figures (the semiotic system) of the humanistic *epistème*. Such a destructive reading, I suggest, discloses that, despite its avowed intentions to accommodate higher education to the "needs of the late twentieth century" (RCC, o.v., p. 2), the report, in emphasizing the imperative to return to a core curriculum, constitutes in reality an act of nostalgia for a lost origin and covertly sponsors and legitimates a subsuming theory of disciplinary power. Like Arnold's and, in a more immediately filial context, like Irving Babbitt's and I. A. Richards's humanistic educational theories (and Harvard's Cold War pedagogical practices) it comes to be understood not only as an effort to recuperate an idea of the university based on the model of the panoptic centered circle that the rupturing of the old (metaphysical) habits of thought in this century have called into question. It also comes to be seen as an attempt to nullify the symptomatic educational and sociopolitical manifestations of this rupturing, especially in the United States and France, during the almost revolutionary 1960s, to which the report insistently and thus, one is compelled to conclude, deliberately—ideologically—omits reference.

As in the case of Richards's and his predecessors' discourses, the rhetoric of the report justifies the restoration of a core curriculum by insistent reference to the increasing dispersal of knowledge in our time. In the original report to the Harvard faculty (February 15, 1978), this justification for containment is put in terms of the "overwhelming endorsement" of the principle of non-concentration course requirements "based on the wide [faculty] agreement that the proliferation of courses had eroded the purpose of the existing General Education Program" (p. 1). But what the report means by the "proliferation of courses" turns out to be, in fact, the increasing cultural dispersion that threatens the alleged harmony and stability of the world— which is to say, that threatens to discredit the humanistic representation of being and its accumulated archive.

This is made clear in the introduction to the edited version of the report published by the Rockefeller Foundation, which comments, by way of background, on the old program's inability to contain and domesticate (familiarize) the knowledge explosion:

> At mid-century, breadth was provided by requiring courses that surveyed the
> three main divisions of knowledge (humanities, social sciences, and natural

sciences), and offered a grounding in the traditions and cultures of Western civilization. But in the last decade or more [the 1960s] this curriculum pattern has seemed inadequate or inappropriate. Colleges now serve an extraordinarily diverse body of students; knowledge has proliferated immensely and familiar lines of demarcation have broken down; there is a growing interest in the history and problems of non-Western countries and peoples. These currents have made it increasingly difficult to agree upon a body of knowledge that could be considered essential to the education of undergraduates, and they have called into question the structure of the traditional liberal arts curriculum. (RCC, r.v., p. 37)

Nor should the disarming reference to the emergence of the disturbingly problematic Third World as "a growing interest in its history and problems" invalidate this interpretation. For the rhetorical momentum generated by the first two of the series of currents destabilizing the definition of the educated ("just") man and the educated ("just") society insists that the third, which ostensibly breaks the syntactic/semantic thrust, be interpreted in a more ideologically loaded way. It demands that it be read as a proposition that betrays an anxiety similar to Babbitt's response to the Romantics' historical method, which "proved so powerful a solvent of both Christian and classical dogma" and to Richards's response to the "centrifugal" dynamics of modern life precipitated by the "frothy emulsion of hitherto immiscible cultures." Procedurally, the Harvard faculty arrives, at the *beginning* of its inquiry, at a standard of the educated person "that meets the needs of the late twentieth century" or, as the report puts it with remarkable self-assurance and complacent (ritualist) authority, at an answer to the question, "What does our faculty and our university mean when we welcome a student at graduation 'to the company of educated men and women'?" (RCC, o.v., p. 2). And it is a standard (and answer) that constitutes nothing newer than a reaffirmation of the already questionable logocentric and elitist ideal of humanistic education; the ideal, in fact, that has oriented discussion of undergraduate education at Harvard at least since the beginning of the twentieth century, when Irving Babbitt attempted to introduce a (more disciplinary) version of Matthew Arnold's classical humanism to the "Rousseauistic" ("feminine"), "barbaric" scene of American education:

In his Annual Report for 1975-1976, Dean Rosovsky attempted to state what it means to be an educated person in the latter part of the twentieth century. The standard that he outlined provided the context for the review of undergraduate education at Harvard, including the development of the Core Curriculum. The elements of this standard, which broadly outline the educational goals of the college, were as follows:

1. An educated person must be able to think and write clearly and effectively.

2. An educated person should have achieved depth in some field of knowledge. Cumulative learning is an effective way to develop a student's powers of reasoning and analysis, and for our undergraduates this is the principal role of concentrations.

3. An educated person should have an integral appreciation of the ways in which we gain and apply knowledge and understanding of the universe, of society and of ourselves. Specifically, he or she should have an informed acquaintance with the aesthetic and intellectual experiences of literature and the arts; with history as a mode of understanding present problems and the processes of human affairs; with the concepts and analytical techniques of modern social science; and with the mathematical and experimental methods of the physical and technological sciences.

4. An educated person is expected to have some understanding of, and experiences in thinking about moral and ethical problems. It may well be that the most significant quality in educated persons is the informed judgment which enables them to make discriminating moral choices.

5. Finally, an educated American, in the last third of the century, cannot be provincial in the sense of being ignorant of other cultures and other times. It is no longer possible to conduct our lives without reference to the wider world within which we live. A crucial difference between the educated and the uneducated is the extent to which one's life experience is viewed in wider contexts. (RCC, r.v., pp. 39-40)

Despite the assertions that "the standard" Dean Rosovsky outlined in his annual report for 1975-76 "provided the context for the review of undergraduate education at Harvard," the fact is that the definition of the educated person that begins the Harvard faculty's inquiry is identical with the definition bringing it to a close. This circularity implies, of course, that Dean Rosovsky's initial statement of the standard or center or norm is an archival point of departure, that it panoptically determined and limited the horizon of inquiry; the questions, that is, that the reviewers could ask and also the possible range of answers they could deliver. In Derrida's rhetoric, the "methodology" governing this "disinterested" inquiry was characterized by "a free play . . . instituted upon a fundamental immobility and a reassuring certitude which is itself beyond the reach of free play."[19] In this sense, the procedural structure of the re-view itself constitutes an exemplary instance of that vicious circularity that Heidegger discovers to be historically endemic to the metaphysical, logocentric, and panoptic mode of inquiry. Far from openly addressing the pedagogical questions precipitated by the critical historical context in which "knowledge has proliferated immensely and familiar lines of demarcation have broken down," Rosovsky reappropriates the center informing the general education program in the Redbook—the center that generated the crisis in the first place. In accommodating these questions to the comprehensive and mastering panoptic perspective this center affords, he precludes the possibility of an authentic free play of ideas grounded in the actual historical realities of the late twentieth century.

Read as an autonomous text, superficially and in isolation, as it is intended to be, the sedimented rhetoric of this rationale for the core curriculum is disarming in its apparent free play. It is written, clearly, to achieve a consensus among specialists (the agents responsible for the proliferation of knowledge) in behalf of a generalist approach to undergraduate education. Read, however, in the context of the postmodern critique of the metaphysical tradition and its archival procedures, and of the crisis of culture to which this critique is a response—the historical context, to repeat, which the Harvard faculty incredibly overlooks—the rhetoric of the report suggests that the idea of the university concealed in its omissions and its essentially quantitative terms is not simply, as Barry O'Connell observes, "anachronistic" in its failure to appreciate the centrality of new modes of understanding to our present lives ("WDHL," p. 64). It is essentially reactionary in its willful effort to recuperate the waning authority of the old re-collective or spatializing habits of a metaphysical mindset. For despite the report's initial acknowledgement that the knowledge explosion has not only "made it increasingly difficult to agree upon a body of knowledge that could be considered essential to the education of undergraduates" but has also "called into question the structure of the traditional liberal arts curriculum,"[20] the standard the report posits and the accompanying commentary fail to confront the persuasive postmodern challenge to the validity of received logocentric or metaphysical epistemological assumptions. The report fails to consider the possibility, retrieved by this destructive critique, that temporality and the differences it disseminates is ontologically prior to Being (or Form) in the circular act of hermeneutic understanding and inquiry. Instead, in the archival rhetoric of executive authority ("must," "should," "is expected") and in the careless clichés of executive authority and the habitual methodology of logocentric inquiry, the report calls for a renewed inculcation of "the knowledge, skills, and habits of thought that the faculty considers to be of general and lasting intellectual significance" (RCC, r.v., p. 41). Predictably, what is considered significant is the ability "to think and write clearly and effectively," the power of "reasoning and analysis," of "discrimination," of "judgment" that renders one capable of grasping or comprehending; capable of mastering or appropriating being. The report calls, in other words, for the reinstitution of the disciplinary apparatuses.

This hidden agenda is nowhere more visible than in the first of these recuperative pedagogical imperatives, which in a fundamental way subsumes all the others: the inculcation of the ability "to think and write clearly and effectively." Although the report reasonably emphasizes the need to restore the writing requirement to the undergraduate curriculum, the language of this repeated emphasis is consistently the same as that quoted above. For example, the expository writing requirement is intended "to improve the ability of the student to write effectively, concisely, clearly" (RCC, o.v., p. 31); and again, "the first goal, that our students learn to communicate with precision, cogency and force, is addressed by the requirement in Expository Writing and rein-forced throughout the curriculum" (RCC, r.v., p. 40). The report would reinstitute a writing requirement that understands language as it was understood in the academy prior to the crisis that precipitated its abolition. It fails to indicate even the slightest awareness that the old humanist ideals of "clarity" and "effectiveness" and "con-ciseness"—the ideals which as early as the mid-nineteenth century Dickens demysti-fied as "Gradgrindianism" in *Hard Times* and Dostoevsky as the "straightforward language of the straightforward gentlemen" who built the Crystal Palace in *Notes from the Underground*—have been called radically into question both directly, by such Amer-ican critics of academic writing programs as Richard Lanham, James Berlin,[21] and, above all, Richard Ohmann,[22] and indirectly, though more radically, by postmodern the-orists of language and discourse.[23]

Despite these interrogations, the report continues to understand language use in terms of the narrative model produced by the Enlightenment. Grounded on the logo-centric assumption that signifier and signified are identical, language is inherently able to comprehend and master the mystery of being. To thematize the enabling meta-phorics of this representation, it is naturally endowed with the power to bring the "truth" out of darkness into permanent and inescapable light ("clarity") by way of the force of a systematic executive method ("effectiveness") that gets rapidly to the es-sence of apparent difference ("conciseness") without digression and thus the costly waste of time. To put its amnesiac recommendation concerning the writing require-ment in sociopolitical terms, the Harvard Report continues to base its understanding of writing on a discredited problem-solving (rigorously end-oriented) epistemological model, a model that (as Richard Ohmann has devastatingly shown in his analysis of the "memoranda" of "the Harvard- and Yale-trained statesmen" that occupy the discursive space of *The Pentagon Papers*) rendered the freshman composition course one of the enabling technological agencies for the production of the appallingly dehumanized dis-course of the bureaucrats and technicians who were responsible for the planning and execution of the Vietnam War:

> English 101 has helped, willy nilly, to teach the rhetoric of the bureaucrats
> and technicians. Its architects would doubtless prefer Roosevelts to Rostows,
> but the constraints upon English from the rest of the university and especially
> from outside it are strong. Though the writers of the textbooks [that Ohmann
> analyzes] and the planners of courses may be generalists and humanists by
> intent, they can hardly imagine what passes for intellectual currency in that
> part of the world where vital decisions are made or what kind of composition
> succeeds in the terms of that part of the world. Problem formulation and
> problem solving, distancing of people, abstraction away from historical
> circumstance, disappearance of the writer as a being with social attributes,
> and denial of politics: these are threads that run through both the textbooks

for English 101 and the examples [from *The Pentagon Papers*] of successful writing I have considered. Perhaps the similarity goes some way towards explaining the usefulness of our subject, English, to America.[24]

It is, of course, true that the Harvard faculty alleges commitment to a "Core Curriculum based not on some theoretical division or hierarchical ordering of knowledge, but rather on 'distinctive ways of thinking that are identifiable and important' " (RCC, r.v., pp. 38-39). As in the case of Richards and his humanistic forebears (and of the Harvard Redbook that institutionalized his "synoptic university" in the form of the general education program), however, the report's definition of the educated person is informed by the unquestioned assumption that a single and abiding rational norm or *télos* subsumes all the "basic modes of understanding": those intrinsic to the study of literature and the arts, history, the social sciences, the physical and biological sciences, and foreign cultures. In the face of apparent diversity, such a synoptic view re-presents Being as homogenous. In Edward Said's phrase, it is inscribed by the "textual attitude" that accommodates not only the differences within each mode but the differences between them. Despite its liberal exterior, this view authorizes an essentially disciplinary pedagogy based on the privileged status of the "civilized" professor and the errant tendencies of the "uncivilized" student. When (and if) it is mastered, it becomes for the user an *efficient* "speculative instrument" of knowledge production and power ("justice") over the devious and duplicitous "object of inquiry."

In other words, the knowledge explosion in the Vietnam decade serves the Harvard faculty simply as a point of departure to justify the recuperation of a lost absolute origin and its binary logic, thus to restore a disciplinary panoptic model of higher education in which the center or core (a rational, sane, healthy, standard) corrects or re-forms the ec-centric, the err-atic, the ex-orbitant, the ab-normal, or de-generate (fallen) impulse to de-viate: to stray from the right (normative) way. In thus enacting this recollective strategy, the Harvard faculty, like its predecessors after World War I and World War II, predictably repeats the theoretical move made by Arnold, Babbitt, and Richards in the face of the "threat" of intellectual and sociopolitical anarchy precipitated by earlier proliferations of knowledge. Indeed, it repeats the recuperative move made by most Western humanist reformers of educational curricula ever since the supernatural narrative of the fall into time—the diaspora of the *Logos*, as it were—was naturalized in the discourse of Man.

This nostalgic metanarrative which, according to Foucault, represents the "lofty origin" as "always preceding the fall" and always coming "before the body . . . the world and time" and whose "story is always sung as a theogony," informs the Harvard Core Curriculum Report at large, however muted the older sonorities by its monochromatic administrative style. But for the sake of brevity I will consider the goals of and rationale for the core requirements in literature and the arts as a synecdoche for the whole. Such a procedure is justified because, despite protestations to the contrary, the report is inscribed by the Two Cultures opposition. It clearly assumes that the study of these areas (especially literature) is intrinsically more capable of "humanizing" students in an age dominated by classical scientific thinking and the new technology to which it has given rise. Thus, for example, the report states:

> The common aim of these courses is to foster a *critical understanding* of how man gives artistic expression to his experience of the world. Through the examination of *selected major works*, students will be expected to *develop and refine skills of reading, seeing, and hearing*; to apprehend the possibilities and limitations of the artist's chosen medium and the means available for expression; to understand the complex interplay between individual talent, artistic tradition, and historical context. In the requirements for this area, the written word takes precedence over other forms of artistic expression to the extent that the study of literature is required of all students, while a choice is offered between music and fine arts. (RCC, r.v., p. 43. My emphasis.)

This statement obscures the original version, which asserts that "two further guiding principles are employed in formulating the course requirement; that the written word should take precedence over other forms of artistic expression in the sense that the study of literature is required of all students while a choice is offered between music and the fine arts, *and that not all arts and art forms in literature, music, and the visual arts are appropriate for the Core Curriculum*" (RCC, o.v., p. 15; my emphasis).

This significant omission of the italicized clause in the edited version quoted above makes explicit the Harvard faculty's deliberately conservative exclusion not only of what might be called the "eccentric" forms of traditional artistic media, but also of the new and undisciplined, essentially musical and visual media, such as cinema, rock and roll, video; "low" forms that, however symptomatically, nevertheless have emerged from and address themselves to the crisis of contemporary culture in order to challenge the privileged status of "high" literary expression. As Barry O'Connell ironically observes, "Visual [he could have added "popular musical"] literacy, arguably essential in a culture dominated by the visual media, is . . . unattended. . . . Harvard's conception of the essentials of a good education in 1978 is limited to subjects most scholars in 1900 would have regarded as the core" ("WDHL," p. 64). Indeed, this doctrinaire devaluation of the new popular visual and musical arts in favor of the traditional written word is reminiscent not only of Babbitt's willfully arrogant antimodernism, but also of Richards's exclusive anxiety over (if not contempt for) "motion pictures, radio, television," which, along with mass education and modern advertising, "expose every urbanized mind to a range and variety and promiscuity of contacts unparalleled in history."[25] As such, the report not only repeats the reaction against novelty that has perennially characterized the authoritarian response of the ancients to the experimental impulse of modernism. It also repeats the reaction against the popular, the contemporaneous, the open-ended, the playful and parodically disruptive artistic impulse, which according to Mikhail Bakhtin has perennially characterized the response of the custodians of official culture in the name of "high seriousness." All artistic expressions of those "lowly" sociopolitical groups marginalized by the dominant sociopolitical order are overlooked. In that oversight, the Harvard faculty conceals its literary and socio-political elitism.

More specifically, vis-à-vis the privileged literary requirements, the report goes further:

> We assume that in dealing with such questions [intrinsic to literary studies] students will be exposed to a variety of critical approaches, but the primary purpose of the Core Literature courses is to show how great authors have contrived distinctive statements about timeless and universal aspects of human experience. (CCR, r.v., p. 44)

As in the other core areas, which will also focus on the study of "selected major texts," this understanding of literary study presupposes, not simply a continuity in the history of Western literature, but an authoritative tradition based on a dynastic model, a tradition in which, as the allusion to T. S. Eliot's "Tradition and the Individual Talent" makes clear, "the whole of the literature of Europe from Homer and within it the whole of the literature of [a Western writer's] own country has a simultaneous existence and composes a simultaneous order."[26] More important, the assertion that the "great authors" are those who make "distinctive statements about timeless and universal aspects of human experience" assumes that the "major texts" in this tradition are "contrived" microcosms mirroring an ultimately suprahistorical and ordered—a metaphysical—universe, despite their historical specificity. The distinctiveness of the "major text," that is, has its condition of possibility in the principle of identity and not the other way around. In thus conceiving the "major text" to be a spatialized image, the report assumes that its essential function is to distance the reader aesthetically from his ambiguous existential experience, to purge the reader (as Aristotle initially put it) of the dislocating pity and terror, the anxiety, that immediate being-in-the-world activates. As in Arnold, Babbitt, and Richards, the report insists that the masterpieces of the tradition constitute resolved internalizations of worldly crisis or historically specific conflict (in this case the contestatory sociopolitical context precipitated by the events of the Vietnam decade). In sum, they function, like the texts monumentalized by Arnold, Babbitt, and Richards, to reproduce politically quiescent subjects.

The texts that do not obviously conform to the received spatialized decorum of the masterpiece are defused in two related ways. As in the case of powerful anticanonical novels written in the past, they are coerced into the spatial mold and the geometric curve of its history (and their disruptive force neutralized) by overlooking or excusing the formal eccentricities they enact. They are, that is, *accommodated* to the canonical

tradition. This has been the fate of such essentially marginal, open-ended, and dislocating works as Cervantes's *Don Quixote*, the narrative errancy of which disrupts the
interwoven shape of the circuitous journey of the questing knight of medieval romance
and the inclusive "reality" this Golden Age journey would recuperate even by rational-
izing discontinuity in the last resort figure of the enchanter; of Laurence Sterne's *Tristram Shandy*, the infinitely regressive movement of which disrupts the authoritative
dynastic plot of Fielding's *Tom Jones* and the monolithic Deistic macrocosm informing
its utterly determined "accidents"; and of Herman Melville's *Moby-Dick*, the devious
narrative of which precipitates an orphaning that disrupts the assured patriarchal
Adamic structure of American Renaissance literature to disclose the absence at the
heart of the centered circle informing the gravely pantheistic "central man" of New England transcendentalism, thus calling into question the monomaniacal will to power
over being this Ahabian anthropomorphism authorizes. Or, as in the case of postmodern American novels that disrupt both traditional and Modernist closure (and the received self-representation of American culture), they are, in essence, whatever the
degree of tolerance elsewhere in the academy, excluded from the core curriculum. Just
as the madman becomes the measure of sanity in the civilized Enlightenment, according to Foucault, postmodern texts such as Thomas Pynchon's *V* or *Gravity's Rainbow*,
John Barth's *Lost in the Funhouse*, Robert Coover's *Public Burning*, E. L. Doctorow's
Book of Daniel, Donald Barthelme's *The Dead Father*, Ishmael Reed's *Mumbo Jumbo*,
or Kathy Acker's *Don Quixote*, and poems such as William Carlos Williams's *Paterson*,
Charles Olson's *Maximus Poems*, Robert Creeley's *A Day Book*, or Edward Dorn's
Gunslinger become instances of what the New Critics called "the fallacy of imitative
form." They are, that is, implicitly represented as a kind of writing that the Western
masterpiece is not, because they fail to master their recalcitrant material. Nothing in
the report would suggest that this powerful and disconcerting literature of the countermemory is worthy of serious study by Harvard undergraduates.

Like Matthew Arnold's and Irving Babbitt's disciplinary uneasiness about including
contemporary literature in the liberal arts curriculum, or like Lionel Trilling's celebrated reservations about teaching such disturbing moderns as Dostoevsky, Kafka,
Mann, Nietzsche, and Freud to innocent Columbia undergraduates,[27] the report's con-
spicuous silence in the face of a literature intended to retrieve the integrity of difference from the assimilative subject represents a failure of nerve, a refusal to confront
what Derrida might call these works' disorienting force and Foucault, their discordant
monstrosity. Either this failure of nerve in the face of otherness or, more likely, the
certainty of its authors about the accommodational operations of the anthropological
center lies behind the report's failure to engage the mounting critique of the patriarchal, racist, and ethnocentric implications of the traditional literary curriculum and this
critique's demand for a program of literary studies including disruptive texts of women,
blacks, and other minorities hitherto excluded from the Anglo-American canon.[28]

The Harvard Report does emphasize "interdisciplinary study" (RCC, o. v., p. 17) to counteract the prevailing disciplinary character of specialized literary and artistic education. But this does not constitute a recognition of and commitment to the cultural differences that postmodern cultural criticism insists on exploring, whatever the risks. Its rationale for interdisciplinary courses in the arts, including those that "will [also] encourage enterprise on the part of faculty members, some of whom may wish to join together in a single offering" (RCC, o.v., p. 17) rests upon the mystified synoptic model of the assimilative anthropological imagination. Rather than engagement with radical "conflict, competition, contradiction"—with the diversity that, according to Henry Adams, animates the mind—the goal of interdisciplinary study envisaged by the Harvard Core Curriculum Report is, as it was for Adams's generation, insistently the comprehension of normative sameness. Adams's postmodern heir, Thomas Pynchon, illuminates this obsessive and unrelenting rational pursuit that ends in leveling of differential being, and in the inertia of in-difference.

> She [Oedipa Maas] had heard all about excluded middles; they were bad shit,
> to be avoided; and how had it ever happened here [in San Narciso, i.e.,
> America], with the chances once so good for diversity. For it was now like
> walking among matrices of a great digital computer, the zeros and ones
> twinned above, hanging like balanced mobiles right and left, ahead, thick,
> maybe endless.[29]

In its effort to recuperate the tradition, in sum, the Harvard faculty's archival understanding of the function and goal of undergraduate study of literature and the arts does not overlook only the discursive explosion of the Vietnam decade. It also ignores the disclosures of postmodern literature and the de-structive or de-constructive theory to which the discursive explosion of the 1960s in part gave rise: their radical interrogation of the privileged concept of "the central man" (so fundamental, since Emerson, to the Harvard tradition); of the subject; of the language and signs of signification; of authorship; of endings in thinking about beginnings; of logocentric or teleological forms; of dynastic models of history; of the archival network of tropes—metaphors, figures, myths—and syntactic constructions that legitimate these principles of the tradition. In so doing, the Harvard core curriculum betrays its complicity with the late-capitalist economy that exploits these mystified cultural paradigms for its hegemonic ends.

The one aspect of the Harvard Core Curriculum Report that suggests a real departure from the Redbook's general education program and the old logocentric pedagogical model—a departure that appears to call into question the privileged status of the encompassing Western epistemological sociopolitical perspective—is the addition of "foreign cultures" to the three main divisions of knowledge of the traditional liberal arts core curriculum. Even this inclusion, ostensibly intended to acknowledge the emergence "in the last decade or more" of the insistent (desiring) voices of Third World peoples, does not make a radical break with the synoptic view of I. A. Richards and the Harvard general education program of the Cold War era:

> A Foreign Languages and Cultures requirement in the proposed core is specifically designed to expand the student's range of cultural experience and to provide fresh perspectives on his or her own cultural assumptions and traditions. . . . The intention here is not merely to avoid an exclusive focus on Western tradition, but to expose students to the essential and distinctive features of major alien cultures, whether Western or non-Western. (RCC, o.v., p. 4; see also pp. 27-28.)

Framed by a justification that reduces the anti-imperialistic praxis of postcolonial peoples to "a growing interest in [their] history and problems," this rationale is hardly adequate to meet the demands of the postmodern (or postimperialist) age for understanding cultures that have assumed momentous global economic, political, and social importance because of their concerted action against perennial Western colonialist exploitation. The report's perspective is not open to the radical questioning of Western archival discourse about non-Western cultures by such writers as Frantz Fanon, Jean-Paul Sartre, C. L. R. James, Regis Debray, Paolo Freire, Gayatri Spivak, Malek Al-loula, Chinua Achébé, Edward Said, and others. Not only is the one-semester course required by the core curriculum, as Barry O'Connell observes, "simply insufficient" ("WDHL," p. 65) and symptomatic of a lack of commitment to activating a dialogue with non-Western cultures. It is also unable to provide a context acknowledging that the traditional discourse of the West concerning the Third World—whether about the peoples of Africa, the Orient, or Latin America—has been a self-perpetuating representational discourse based on the panoptic ethnocentric perspective of Western archival knowledge of the Third World. As Edward Said has persuasively shown in his analysis of "Orientalism," the Western discourse about the Orient, this productive archival cultural discourse has done more than contribute to the West's cultural domination of the Orient. As in the overdetermined case of Napoleon's Egyptian expedition (a project not incidentally modeled on the imperial practice of Augustan Rome), it has also contributed to the West's political domination of this "other" world:

> My idea is that European and then American interest in the Orient was political according to some of the obvious historical accounts of it. . . . but that it was the culture that created that interest, that acted dynamically along with brute political, economic, and military rationales to make the Orient the varied and complicated place that it obviously was in the field that I call Orientalism. . . . Orientalism is not a mere political subject matter or field that is reflected passively by culture, scholarship, or institutions; nor is it a large and diffuse collection of texts about the Orient; nor is it representative and expressive of some nefarious "Western" imperialist plot to hold down the

"Oriental" world. It is rather a *distribution* of geopolitical awareness into aesthetic, scholarly, economic, sociological, historical, and philosophical texts; it is an *elaboration* not only of a basic geographical distinction (the world is made up of two unequal halves, Orient and Occident) but also of a whole series of "interests" which, by such means as scholarly discovery, philological reconstruction, psychological analysis, landscape and sociological description, it not only creates but also maintains; it *is*, rather than expresses, a certain *will* or *intention* to understand, in some cases to control, manipulate, even to incorporate, what is a manifestly different (or alternative and novel) world; it is, above all, a discourse that is by no means in direct, corresponding relationship with political power in the raw, but rather is produced and exists in an uneven exchange with various kinds of power, shaped to a degree by the exchange with power political (as with a colonial or imperial establishment), power intellectual (as with reigning sciences like comparative linguistics or anatomy, or any of the modern policy sciences), power cultural (as with orthodoxies and canons of taste, texts, values), power moral (as with ideas about what "we" do and what "they" cannot do or understand as "we" do). Indeed my real argument is that Orientalism is—and does not simply represent—a considerable dimension of modern political-intellectual culture, and as such has less to do with the Orient than it does with "our" world.[30]

The failure of the Harvard Report to provide a historical context and to acknowledge the perennial affiliation of humanistic archival education with Western political and economic exploitation of the non-Western world strongly suggests that, at best, the inclusion of the study of foreign cultures is little more than a token accommodation—a concession, in fact—forced by the decentering imperatives of the resistance by Third World peoples to overt and visible manifestations of power. At worst, the inclusion of a foreign cultures requirement is a gesture of productive accommodation in the context of Vietnam, Latin America, and the Middle East, similar to the recentering hegemonic strategy that, according to Said, informs the "re-visionary" research discourse of such academically and politically influential postimperialistic Orientalists as Sylvain Lévi, Louis Massignon, and Sir Hamilton Gibb.

What Said says of the early modern humanistic reformulations of Western educational attitudes toward the Orient by Silvain Lévi (professor of Sanskrit at the Collège de France and president of the Société Asiatique between 1928 and 1935) parallels in a remarkably revealing way the recentering and co-optive goal behind the Harvard faculty's introduction of "foreign" or "non-Western cultures" to the undergraduate core curriculum. This passage from *Orientalism*, which includes Lévi's illuminating (and prophetic) confrontation of the emergent "East-West problem," deserves extended quotation for the way it undermines and refocuses in terms of hegemony the apparent departure from the ethnocentrism of earlier versions of humanistic educational theory at Harvard, such as those of Irving Babbitt and I. A. Richards:

> In the period between the wars, as we can easily judge from, say, Malraux's novels, the relations between East and West assumed a currency that was both widespread and anxious. . . . The Orient now appeared to constitute a challenge, not just to the West in general, but to the West's spirit, knowledge, and imperium. . . . Such issues forced reconsideration of Western knowledge of the Orient. No less a personage than Sylvain Lévi . . . reflected seriously in 1925 on the urgency of the East-West problem:
>
> > . . . If because of laziness or incomprehension Europe does not make the effort that its interests alone require from it, *then the Asiatic drama will approach the crisis point.*
> >
> > It is here that that science which is a form of life and an instrument of policy—that is, wherever our interests are at stake—owes it to itself to penetrate native civilization and life in their intimacy in order to discover their fundamental values and durable characteristics rather than to smother native life with the incoherent threat of European civilizational imports. We must offer ourselves to these civilizations as we do our other products, that is, on the local exchange market. . . .
>
> Lévi has no difficulty in connecting Orientalism with politics, for the long—or rather, the prolonged—Western intervention in the East cannot be denied either in its consequences for knowledge or in its effect upon the hapless native; together the two add up to what could be a menacing future. For all his expressed humanism, his admirable concern for fellow creatures, Lévi conceives the present juncture in unpleasantly constricted terms. The Oriental is imagined to feel his world threatened by a superior civilization; yet his motives are impelled, not by some positive desire for freedom, political independence, a cultural achievement *on their own terms,* but instead by rancor, a jealous malice. The panacea offered for this potentially ugly turn of affairs is that the Orient be marketed for a Western consumer, be put before him as one among numerous wares beseeching his attention. By a single stroke you will defuse the Orient (by letting it think itself to be an "equal" quantity on the Occidental marketplace of ideas), and you will appease Western fears of an Oriental tidal wave. At bottom, of course, Lévi's principal point—and his most telling confession—is that unless something is done about the Orient, "the Asiatic drama will approach the crisis point."[31]

Given the core curriculum's inordinate emphasis on the transmission of humanistic culture and its related failure to engage the increasing interrogation of humanist ethnocentrism, we may justifiably conclude that the common purpose of the core courses in the foreign cultures area—to provide "fresh perspectives on the student's own cultural assumptions and traditions"—replicates, in fact, the accommodational synoptic perspective and goals of I. A. Richards's pedagogical project vis-à-vis the "immiscible" and "unrhythming" knowledge of non-Western cultures precipitated by World War II: "Two-thirds of us on this planet are, at the time of writing, analphabetics. Of the 2,200,000,000 people now breathing, some 1,500,000,000 either cannot read at all or read some non-alphabetic script. If there is to be any truly worldwide communication between peoples within a foreseeable future, it will be in some language which is alphabetic. It could be within our lifetime and through English."[32] Like Richards during the Cold War—and, it should not be forgotten, the Harvard brain trust that was largely responsible for American foreign policy in Southeast Asia (President John F. Kennedy's "New Frontier") in the 1960s—the authors of the Core Curriculum Report in the aftermath of the Vietnam War continue to perceive non-Western societies as ultimately "immiscible" and "unrhythming" cultures, which must now be seduced, if not forcefully incorporated, into the cultural orbit of the Western (late capitalist) logos. Like Richards, they also continue to understand the goal of cross-cultural education as making the instrument of knowledge production more flexible or "expansive": less overtly, but equally, coercive as the more visibly violent instruments of the imperialistic era. In short, this mode of producing knowledge about foreign cultures becomes an exemplary instance of the power/knowledge relation that, according to posthumanists from Gramsci to Foucault, identifies the "disciplinary" or the "hegemonic" society.[33]

The fourth element of the Harvard faculty's definition of an "educated person," and the most important, has to do with morality and ethics:

> An educated person is expected to have some understanding of, and about,
> experience in thinking about moral and ethical problems. It may well be that
> the most significant quality in educated persons is the informed judgment
> which enables them to make discriminating moral choices.[34]

This way of putting it appears to be innocuous. Understood in the context of the invisible logocentrism that informs virtually every explicit course proposal of the Harvard Core Curriculum Report, however, the disarmingly familiar humanistic rhetoric discloses a different imperative. In reducing the question of ethics, which is essentially ontological—a question concerning *ethos* (abode) grounded in and emerging from the "ontological difference"[35]—to "an understanding of, and about" philosophical problems, the core curriculum does not call for the activation of a moral or ethical consciousness. It calls rather for the inculcation of a discriminatory, publically authorized, moral norm derived from the student's assimilation of canonical texts. Despite the humanistic claim to disinterested inquiry, such a norm is, like the guardian in Bentham's Panopticon, out of reach of criticism. It becomes a privileged deontologized standard that levels moral and ethical complexities to conceptual and socially manageable status.

As Heidegger says in recalling the fate of thought in late antiquity, it becomes an archival imperative that negates thinking: "Along with 'logic' and 'physics,' 'ethics' appeared for the first time in the school of Plato. These disciplines arose at a time when thinking was becoming 'philosophy,' philosophy, *epistème* (science), and science itself a matter for schools and academic pursuits. In the course of a philosophy so understood, science waxed and thinking (*Denken*) waned. Thinkers prior to this period knew neither a 'logic' nor an 'ethics' nor a 'physics.' Yet their thinking was neither illogical nor immoral. But they did think *physis* in a depth and breadth that no subsequent 'physics' was ever again to attain. The tragedies of Sophocles — provided such a comparison is at all permissable — preserve the *ethos* in their sagas more primordially than Aristotle's lectures on 'ethics.' "[36] Despite its explicit sponsorship of a curriculum that envisions the development of a liberal ethical consciousness, what the core curriculum calls for, finally, is the renewed standardization of the anthropocentric idea of Man as measure; that is, of measure as anthropological will to power.

Far from providing a philosophy of education and a curriculum capable of preparing students (including perennially excluded minorities and the increasing number of middle-aged and older students seeking reeducation) to encounter the complex realities of the late twentieth century — the differential knowledge precipitated by the decentering of the anthropologos in the 1960s and after — the Harvard faculty reinscribes a pedagogy designed to prepare men and women for a world that the events of history have fundamentally transformed. Like the humanistic alternative to classical science and technology of Arnold, Babbitt, and Richards, as well as that of F. R. Leavis and Lionel Trilling,[37] it finally posits a *paideia* that, in the name of "full self-development" (CCR, o.v. 6) and tolerance, reproduces, extends, and enforces the power of the very dehumanizing disciplinary agencies of Modernity it ostensibly seeks to humanize.

Like Plato's synoptic view, Bentham's panopticism, Arnold's culture, Babbitt's classical measure, Richards's speculative instrument, the *paideia* the authors of the Harvard Core Curriculum Report would recuperate in the face of its crisis of legitimation constitutes and interested effort to render students docile, willing, and useful agents of a leveling abstract power that governs America and insistently seeks hegemony over the entire planet in the name of the humanistic *logos*. Ontologically, it is implicated in the perennial metaphysical effort of Western Man to impose his will to power over being in all its indissolubly related manifestations. To appropriate Nietzsche's metaphorics by way of Heidegger's understanding of the always renewing "strife between world and earth,"[38] it derives from and perpetuates the all-encompassing (imperial) Apollonian impulse to bring the obscurity of being to light — to "world the earth" and thus to obliterate the "rift" between them that always makes a difference. Politically, as I have tried to suggest, in tracing its historically specific genealogy back through the Harvard Redbook (and its origins in the Cold War) to the Columbia Western civilization course (and its origins in the period of the Red Scare), this humanist *paideia* is implicated with precisely those economic and sociopolitical agencies that throughout this century have been bent on establishing an American hegemony—its metropolitan status, as it were—both at home and abroad in the name of the "free world," regardless of the glaring contradictions of that project.

It is this dark underside of the Harvard Core Curriculum Report—this disciplinary imperial sociopolitical agenda which is also and simultaneously a teleological/panoptic ontological and epistemological agenda—that is betrayed by its free-floating universalist rhetoric of deliverance, by its putting the case for the restoration of the liberal arts in terms that omit reference to the Vietnam War and to the multiple and varied oppositional energies it paradoxically but significantly provoked to speak out.

IV

It may be objected that my reading of this document constitutes a strategic deconstructive operation that willfully distorts the actual context and the motives of the Harvard faculty on behalf of an interested (and exclusive) left perspective. That such a historical contextualization of the Harvard Core Curriculum Report is not a misleading imposition is shown by Phyllis Keller in *Getting at the Core*, a historical account of the events leading to the adoption of the core curriculum published by Harvard University Press in 1982, four years after the publication and distribution of the report. In her representation of these events Keller provides the historically specific occasion from which the report emerged. In so doing, her narrative reveals more overtly than the report the ontological/sociopolitical ideology that informs its representational discourse.

In the Preface to her history, Keller insists that "this book is not in any sense an official or 'authorized' account of what happened at Harvard before, during, or after the 1970s. I have tried to make this record of the Core controversies as full and objective as possible and to give a fair and accurate representation of opposing views [by which she means those of the faculty and administrative participants]."[39] Keller's predictable claim to disinterested inquiry should not obscure important facts. The author, a historian trained in American history, "came to Harvard as an assistant dean in the summer of 1973, two weeks after Henry Rosovsky, who led the campaign [in behalf of the restoration of a core curriculum], took office as dean of the Faculty of Arts and Sciences." She "worked closely with him on the planning and coordination of the effort," and served on "several key committees," (*GC*, p. x) and her book was published by Harvard University Press. This illogical logic of the putatively detached humanist characterizes Keller's narrative generally. For the sake of economy I will focus on two central passages:

1. The Breakdown of Order
In the late 1960s, student rebellions occurred in Western European countries and Japan as well as in the United States—countries where the youth cohort was uniquely large, emancipated, and accustomed to the benefits of peace

and prosperity. Universities, always gathering places of the privileged and articulate young and almost always (in democratic nations) hospitable to dissident views, provided a natural base for political activists. What seemed incomprehensible at the time was that the universities themselves were the prime object of attack. Students' demands varied in specifics, but everywhere they asserted their right to a new and influential role in university governance and decision making.

The situation was complicated in the United States by military conscription for the unpopular Vietnam war, which gave a special (and personal) justification to rebellion. Political and cultural radicals alike saw the universities as the mainstay and symbol of the status quo. But their ideologies were less potent weapons of mutiny than their militant style and rhetoric: indiscriminate, narcissistic, populist, and morally self-righteous. Malcontents of all ages were drawn to the crusade against constraints and self-disciplines that limit individual action. What better place to test those limits than in a university committed to free expression and individual autonomy? (*GC*, pp. 29-30)

2. The Search for a Mandate
When Derek Bok, former dean of the Harvard Law School, assumed Harvard's presidency in 1971, many advisers urged him to turn his attention to undergraduate education. In his first annual report, Bok observed:

It would be difficult to point to many substantial innovations in teaching or education that were introduced within the recent past. Changes were made, it is true, but almost all took the form of relaxing old requirements rather than implementing new programs . . . for the most part, the changes are very much the product of a period that has been critical of old traditions and ancient requirements yet largely devoid of new visions for educational reform.

He also noted changes in university governance that limited the capacity of the president to take on the problem directly:

. . . The president's influence will remain more *indirect*, centering on his power to appoint deans of the different schools and to participate in the appointments process to insure that faculty selections have been made with the necessary thoroughness and care . . .

But the obligation of presidential influence persisted. Returning to questions of educational policy in his 1972 report, Bok dared to raise potentially divisive curriculum issues in a community still nursing the wounds of uncivil strife. What troubled him was that there seemed to be no "general understanding of what young men and women should expect to gain from a liberal arts education." . . .

In 1973 Bok appointed Henry Rosovsky, professor of economics, as dean of the Faculty of Arts and Sciences. . . .

Rosovsky [who had taught at the University of California at Berkeley since 1958] left Berkeley in 1965, joining the small stream of "White Berkeleyans" who emigrated eastward after the campus confrontations of the Free Speech Movement. At Harvard in the late 1960s he was chairman of the Economics Department and presided over the faculty committee whose recommendations for an academically traditional Program of Afro-American Studies were at first accepted, and then, within a few months, rejected. Disillusioned once again by the politicization and disruptions of university life, Rosovsky steered clear of the faculty caucuses—"liberal" and "conservative"—that negotiated the issues raised in 1969. This lack of identification with any faction made his appointment as dean of faculty politically acceptable.

Towards the end of his first year in office, Rosovsky assembled half a dozen senior faculty and administrators to get their views on the problems of undergraduate education in Harvard College. (*GC*, pp. 34-36)

What is most remarkable about the discursive practice of these passages of liberal humanist historiography is its blindness to the self-destruction of its binary logic. In naively assuming the privileged status of the sovereign subject—the principle of "free expression and individual autonomy" that the protesting students "incomprehensibly" violated—it exposes its refusal to let the other history speak for itself; it also betrays its willful imposition of a familiar family of demonized names on the agents of resistance that work to contract the expansive and disruptive—centrifugal—force of history into comprehensible and manageable form within the enclosure of the dominant sociopolitical formation. Keller, in other words, interprets and represents the *real* voices of dissent—the difference that could make a difference in the world—in light of a humanistic commitment to the inviolable (because ontologically prior) boundaries of order. In the process, she utterly levels, subdues, and co-opts them.

The most objectionable of the multiple reductions of this "full," "objective," "fair," and "accurate" representation of what happened at Harvard are those that represent 1) the American protest movement as subsidiary to a larger and more amorphously oriented international student movement, thus obscuring the importance of the students' historically specific identification of the university with the United States' war effort in Vietnam; 2) the students who protested against the war as either dupes of outside agitators or as self-serving draft dodgers; 3) the university as apolitical and innocent of complicity with the conduct of the war; 4) and the institutionally sponsored curricular reform at Harvard as the spontaneous and disinterested expression of right reason against uncivil strife. In thus assuming a suprahistorical and panoptic perspective *sub specie aeternitatis*, Keller's humanistic memory predictably becomes amnesia, and her "disinterested" historiography a *hermeneutic* "Egyptianism"—"a history whose function is to compose the finally reduced diversity of time into a totality fully closed upon itself; a history that always encourages subjective recognitions and attributes a form of reconciliation to all the displacements of the past; a history whose perspective on all that precedes it implies the end of time, a completed development."[40] As her invocation and defense of the university as an intellectual space committed to the full development of the sovereign individual suggests, her history also becomes a legitimation of a *sociopolitical* "Egyptianism" brought up to date: the disciplinary society. As Foucault reminds us,

> [Humanism] is the totality of discourse through which Western man is told: "Even though you don't exercise power, you can still be a ruler. Better yet, the more you deny yourself the exercise of power, the more you submit to those in power, then the more this increases your sovereignty." Humanism invented a whole series of subjected sovereignties: the soul (ruling the body, but subjected to God), consciousness (sovereign in a context of judgment, but subjected to the necessities of truth), the individual (a titular control of personal rights subjected to the laws of nature and society), basic freedom (sovereign within, but accepting the demands of an outside world and "aligned with destiny"). In short, humanism is everything in Western civilization that restricts *the desire for power*: it prohibits the desire for power and excludes the possibility of power being seized. The theory of the subject (in the double sense of the word) is at the heart of humanism and this is why our culture has tenaciously rejected anything that could weaken its hold upon us.[41]

Keller's "objective" discursive practice unwittingly discloses the complicity of the humanistic center and the historical narrative it authorizes with institutional and state power. Despite her protestations to the contrary, this strategic blindness of the Apollonian gaze renders the story that *Getting at the Core* tells to be an "official or 'authorized' account of what happened at Harvard before, during, or after the 1970s." In reading her recollective history, one is reminded of Nietzsche's account of monumentalized history as a self-parodic "masquerade."[42] Just as the monumental historian diminishes the life-enhancing forces of the differential present by representing the diminisher as the hero of an inflated universal narrative, so Keller's narrative represents the events leading up to and through the adoption of the core curriculum at Harvard as a heroic romance in which the "troubled" but "daring" President Bok (who calls the new "old" and the old "new": "visionary") imagines a new educational dispensation that is realized by his appointed dean of arts and sciences, the intransigent idealist Henry Rosovsky (who "left Berkeley in 1965, joining the small stream of 'white Berkeleyans' [who] emigrated eastward after the campus confrontations of the Free Speech Movement").

In thus pushing the logic of her recuperative history to its carnivalesque limits, Keller's text, like that of Nietzsche's monumental historian, self-destructs or, in Foucault's version, "unrealizes" itself. The representational excess to which she puts the same binary logic that determined the historiography of earlier reformers makes explicit the hegemonic—and anachronistic—subtext of the curricular reform initiative at Harvard and the institutional reform initiatives throughout this century. As Edward Said has insistently reminded us, the historical emergence of non-Western cultures and societies or nonmetaphysical social, political, and aesthetic orders has foregrounded the paradoxical provincialism of the Western university's hegemonic perspective, has disclosed its humanist discourse to be inadequate to the task of thinking that the prolific present age demands:

> We are now, I think, in a period of world history when for the first time the compensatory affiliative relationships interpreted during the academic course of study in the Western university actually exclude more than they include. I mean quite simply that, for the first time in modern history, the whole imposing edifice of humanistic knowledge resting on the classics of European letters, and with it the scholarly discipline inculcated formally into students in Western universities through the forms familiar to us all, represents only a fraction of the real human relationships and interactions now taking place in the world. Certainly Auerbach was among the last great representatives of those [such as Arnold, Babbitt, and Richards] who believed that European culture could be viewed coherently and importantly as unquestionably central to human history. There are abundant reasons for Auerbach's view being no longer tenable, not the least of which is the diminishing acquiescence and deference accorded to what has been called the Natopolitan world long dominating peripheral regions like Africa, Asia, and Latin America. New cultures, new societies, and emerging visions of social, political, and aesthetic order now lay claim to the humanist's attention, with an insistence that cannot long be denied.
>
> But for perfectly understandable reasons [basically, those related to "our" culture's investments in "humanistic" education: the classical texts that are assured to "embody, express, represent what is best in our, that is, the only tradition"] they are denied.[43]

Keller's text, in short, constitutes a telling example of the massive revisionary representational campaign of the post-Vietnam custodians of American culture to trash the 1960s, and also to deny—indeed, to repress—the multiple knowledges emerging from this critical historical moment. As an authorized narrative that colonizes the real history of education at Harvard (and elsewhere in North America) since the beginning of the 1960s, it betrays both its nostalgic affiliation with the earlier Apollonianism of Matthew Arnold, Irving Babbitt, and I. A. Richards and, more important, the extraordinary parochialism of the hegemonic educational policies of the prestigious institution it represents: a blindness, whether willed or unwilled, to the historical decentering of the "Occident" and a failure or unwillingness to think the opening of the educational/cultural horizon. Keller's text, in other words, betrays its own and her university's complicity with the cultural and sociopolitical colonialism that continues to characterize the domestic and foreign policies of the United States; indeed, of the Western postindustrial nations at large.

Far from reflecting a transformation of educational goals that would "meet the [real] needs of the late twentieth century," the "curricular reforms at Harvard" that Keller's text celebrates repeats the Cold War project of *General Education in a Free Society*. It reflects, that is, an amnesiac strategy designed to shore up the hegemonic authority of the "metropolitic" institution—and the minority dominant culture it represents—that the proliferation of knowledge since the beginning of the Vietnam War threatens to undermine. As such, the educational reforms initiated at Harvard University epitomize the essentially narrow, self-serving, and finally politically reactionary focus of the "liberal" contemporary Western university at large to which Edward Said has insistently drawn our attention. To put this in a way that enables positive resistance, the institutional legislation of the core curriculum in the face of new knowledges that its logic can no longer contain or accommodate discloses the contradictions inhering in the discourse and practice of "free inquiry." In thus fulfilling the educational imperatives inhering in the anthropologos, the humanist university comes to its "end." It discloses its discourse of deliverance to be, in Heidegger's term, "a broken instrument" that demands rethinking from the ground up.[44]

V

The continuity of the historical narrative of the cultural memory in this century should not obscure the difference between the ruptures it attempted to suture in the aftermaths of World War I and World War II and the rupture precipitated by the events of the Vietnam decade. The cultural and sociopolitical crisis characterizing the present historical occasion is perhaps the most critical one in the history of modernity. The global upheaval provoked by the United States' intervention in Vietnam and its ruthless conduct of its war against the Vietnamese people in the name of the "free world" that a decadent European power was too enervated to "defend"—not least the exposure of the contradiction between the liberal discourse of humanism (epitomized by James Bryant Conant and Clark Kerr) and the massive complicity of the institutions of knowledge production with the military/industrial/legal complex—suggest something like an epistemic break in the totalizing representational narrative of Occidental civilization, to which the reformers insistently appeal. Our time has witnessed the proliferation not simply of new knowledge—about the self, language, gender and race relations, cultural institutions, information media, and economic, social, and political formations — but of new knowledge articulated by those hitherto spoken for by the dominant humanistic culture now theorized by the various postmodern or posthumanist discourses. Given the threat this knowledge poses for a hegemonic discourse whose problematic is necessarily blind to the relay of questions concerning being precipitated by such knowledge, it is no accident, as Said observed earlier on, that our time is also witnessing a concerted effort to deny the claims of "new cultures, new societies, and emerging visions of social, political, and aesthetic orders on the humanists' attention."

But to put this concerted humanist effort of denial in such generalized terms is disablingly to obscure its specificity: that it manifests itself in two ways which, on the surface, seem to have little relationship to one another. I mean the sociopolitical denial that takes the form of *accommodating* the various emergent others to the national identity and the reactionary denial that takes the form of *repression*. The present conjuncture has witnessed not simply a concerted effort both in theory and institutional practice to incorporate this emergent knowledge within the monologic pluralism of the discourse of liberal humanism, as in the case of Wayne Booth's *Critical Understanding* (1979), E. D. Hirsch's *Cultural Literacy* (1987), Gerald Graff's *Professing Literature* (1987),[45] and Harvard University's adoption of the Core Curriculum Report. It has also witnessed a powerful and, thanks to the mainstream media, highly visible campaign to discredit this new knowledge on the part of an increasing number of influential theoretical and institutional custodians of "our humanistic heritage" — custodians who fictionalize the embattled predicament of traditional humanists as "relic- or seed-bearers" of a shattered civilization. This reaction does not take the form of knowledgeable debate with the discourses of its adversaries (which are seldom read), but (as Paul de Man, Jacques Derrida, Stanley Fish, Paul Bové, Joseph Buttigieg, and others have pointed out)[46] of an increasingly strident call for a policing action by university administrators, leading intellectuals (Walter Jackson Bate, Allan Bloom, Roger Kimball, David Lehman, Dinesh D'Souza, the spokesmen of the NAS), and governmental agencies (William Bennett and Lynne Cheney). Thus, for example, Bennett's use of his privileged political status, first as a director of the National Endowment for the Humanities and subsequently as secretary of education, to recuperate the humanist curriculum — and the "cultural legacy" it passes on — which was "shattered" as a consequence of what he has called a "collective loss of nerve and faith on the part of both faculty and academic administrators during the late 1960s and early 1970s."[47] Thus, also, Walter Jackson Bates's use of his prestigious position at Harvard to launch an appeal to university administrators (and alumni), calling on them to enforce the *litterae humaniores* against the incursion of postmodern theory.[48] Thus, not least, Allan Bloom's use of his affiliation with the Committee on Social Thought at the University of Chicago to excoriate the disruption of the university in the 1960s by a "barbarous rabble" of the young, blacks, and women, aided and abetted by professors characterized by their "servility, vanity, and lack of conviction."[49]

If in the years of the Reagan administration this reactionary discourse and practice was defensive in character, in the years of the Bush administration it has assumed the offensive against posthumanist theory and the emancipatory practices of those hitherto marginalized or excluded constituencies of the university it has encouraged. In the early 1980s, the reactionary discourses and practices were aligned with a massive ideological project intended to suppress by *forgetting* the complicity of the American university with the state's brutal conduct of the Vietnam War: it was called "healing the wound" inflicted on America's cultural identity by the exposure of the dark side of America's cultural self-representation. In the early 1990s, however, this reactionary discourse and practice has been empowered, by a series of radically ambiguous historical events, to mount a massive counteroffensive against contemporary theory and practice. I am referring, of course, to the opportunity afforded to the custodians of the American cultural identity (1) by the "revolutions" in the Soviet bloc to represent these far-from-confirming events as the triumph of American democracy over communism in the Cold War; (2) by the revelations of the Nazi affiliations of Paul de Man and Martin Heidegger to represent deconstruction or poststructuralism as ethically enervating, if not fascist in its implications; and, finally, (3) by the United States' victory against Saddam Hussein (at a cost of few American deaths) to represent the healthy self-doubts of a large segment of the American public precipitated by the contradictions in the discourse of freedom exposed by the Vietnam War as "the Vietnam Syndrome," which the war supposedly cured, ushering in George Bush's "New World Order."

As a consequence, what were initially isolated calls for a policing action have become a pervasive attack, within and outside the university, against the theory of multicultural education and the minimal gains it has achieved in the university. It is an attack that represents resistance to racism, colonialism, patriarchy, homophobia, etc., as a totalitarianism of the Left, which, in its resort to "intimidation," threatens not only "the best that has been thought and said in the world," but also "free inquiry": the very foundations of the "visionary greatness" of American civilization and the "great global hopes" of the "new world order." Here, for example, is a representative assessment of the present scene of American higher education posited by the powerful director of the National Endowment for the Humanities, Lynne Cheney, in a nationally televised interview:

> Well, I think that education, not just in our schools, but in our colleges and universities, is the shadow on what might otherwise be a sunny prediction for the next century and America's role in it. If you look at culture from a global perspective, there is every reason to be optimistic. The events of Eastern Europe and the Soviet Union of the past year or so have, in many ways, been affirmations of American culture, not just of our political system and our economic system, but people have read our books and they've seen our films and they've listened to our music and they've liked what they've read, seen,

and heard. . . . I think perhaps the most serious symptom [that casts its shadow across the sunny future of the world and America's role in it] is this idea of political correctness, that there are some thoughts that it is now proper to express and some thoughts that it is improper to express. Perhaps the most worrisome aspect of political correctness to me is one that you [the politically conservative syndicated columnist, George Will] hit on a little bit in the earlier conversation. Somehow, Western civilization, that whole long story of human failure and triumph and thought and achievement, has become politically incorrect in many places. It's become regarded as oppressive and indeed, it is the wellspring of those many, many attributes that we have as a country that people throughout the rest of the world envy. We saw students in Tiananmen Square, we saw students in Prague and in Budapest and Warsaw who know John Locke better than our students do because we don't teach John Locke as much as we used to, if we teach him at all.[50]

In these remarks, the director of the National Endowment for the Humanities represents the American state as the natural and organic end of disinterested or free inquiry, and the discourse of contemporary theory and the minimally emancipatory practice it has enabled as unnatural: an ideologically motivated, indeed totalitarian, threat to the new world order that the naturally derived American state is, by simply being, bringing into being. Addressed from the limited (vestigially disciplinary) perspective of any one of the many discourses that collectively constitute contemporary theory, the cultural and sociopolitical American environment that facilitates the transmission and distribution of this kind of grotesquely simplified representation of the present pedagogical occasion (not to say its attribution of the student uprisings in Eastern Europe and China to the reading of John Locke) does indeed bode a dire future for the theory and practice of multiculturalism in the American university. Seen from the genealogical perspective that understands the humanist representation of being as an indissoluble relay of representations encompassing being as such ("nature") and the subject through culture, gender, and race to sociopolitics, however, this reactionary discursive practice, which makes explicit the relay between cultural production and the state, is not, paradoxically, entirely negative in effect.

Perhaps I can explain this paradox by recalling the hierarchical distinction Antonio Gramsci makes in his analysis of the function of the intellectual between " 'civil society,' that is, the ensemble of organisms commonly called 'private' [including educational institutions] and 'political society' or 'the state,' " and by thematizing a dimension of this distinction that he and those recent North American critics his writing has influenced fail to perceive. "These two levels," according to Gramsci, "correspond on the one hand to the function of 'hegemony' which the dominant group exercises throughout society and on the other to that of 'direct domination' or command exercised through the State and 'juridical' government," and, he emphasizes, "are organizational and connective," that is, hierarchical and complicitous. In this context, he goes on,

> Intellectuals are the dominant group's "deputies," exercising the subaltern functions of social hegemony and political government. These comprise:
>
> 1. The "spontaneous" consent given by the great masses of the population to the general direction imposed on social life by the dominant fundamental group; this consent is "historically" caused by the prestige (and consequent confidence) which the dominant group enjoys because of its position and function in the world of production.
>
> 2. The apparatus of state power which "legally" enforces discipline on those groups who do not "consent" either actively or passively. This apparatus is, however, constituted for the whole of society in anticipation of moments of crisis of command and direction when spontaneous consent has failed.[51]

This hierarchized distinction is, of course, the source of Althusser's distinction between ideological state apparatuses and (repressive) state apparatuses and, perhaps, of Foucault's distinction between invisible and visible power, and it reflects the posthumanist rejection of what Foucault calls the "repressive hypothesis," the shift of the focus of radical critique from direct and overt manifestations of domination to the site of culture, where power disguises itself as liberation. What I want to foreground, however, is Gramsci's analysis of the function of the apparatus of state coercive power: it is not simply a matter of enforcing discipline in the public sphere. It is an apparatus that is "constituted for the whole of society"—private and public, civil and political—"in anticipation of moments of crisis of command and direction when spontaneous consent has failed." Power wielded by the dominant group, through the discourse of culture, takes the invisible form of consent in times of stability. It becomes overt and direct— and takes the form of policing action—in times of crisis, when, that is, the discourse of hegemony is ruptured and the spontaneous consent it is intended to accomplish is withdrawn. One might say, then, without violating the thrust of Gramsci's argument, that the center elsewhere, the will to power informing the cultural discourse of deliverance, becomes visible, discloses itself as a contradiction, when the logical imperatives of this discourse have been fulfilled. Its naturalness comes to be seen as a socially constituted fiction, its disinterestedness as vested interest, and its "reformist" altruism as a discreet and insidious strategy of containment and repression. In Foucault's phrase, the end of the discourse of disinterestedness is "the regime of Truth."

Gramsci's discourse was determined by a revolutionary sociopolitical context and thus discriminates between intellectuals as cultural and political functionaries of the dominant group. But this does not preclude the application of his insight into the operations of power in bourgeois capitalist societies to the North American context, where the distinction to which Gramsci is pointing manifests itself primarily and necessarily (given the specific sociopolitical circumstances that obtain here) *within* civil society, specifically the educational institution.[52] For what we have witnessed within the sphere of culture by way of this genealogy of the ideal of general education is not only the "organizational and connective" functions of the hegemonic apparatus vis-à-vis the apparatus of "direct domination." In seeing leading humanist intellectuals repeatedly identifying their educational discourses with the state or appealing to the state to intervene at historical moments of crisis—when spontaneous consent threatens to fail—we also see the *overt* manifestation of the power hidden *but always ready to be activated* within the "benign" cultural discourse of hegemony.

This repeated historical pattern, I submit, explains the paradoxical positivity I see in the monolithic and reactionary humanist discourse that has become increasingly strident and visible since the fall of Saigon. In becoming an overt call for repression in the texts of these reactionary humanists, the Apollonian discourse of humanism testifies to the loss of its ability to command spontaneous consent from those intellectuals—students as well as teachers—it must rely on to maintain its hegemony. To put it in terms of the contradiction inhering in the spatial metaphorics humanism has perennially privileged in the name of "truth," this call for a "police action" in response to the knowledge explosion and the e-mergence of a multiplicity of differential voices precipitated by the Vietnam War has exposed the "center elsewhere" informing the "disinterested," the "value-free" discourse of deliverance. In thus making visible the anthropologos and the secular power it enables, which in the context of spontaneous consent is invisible—"beyond the reach of free play"—these reactionary texts have also been compelled to *situate* the discourse of humanism, to expose it to the free play of worldly criticism. Indeed, it is this self-destruction, this self-exposure of its contradictions, that has in large part precipitated at the site of culture the multiple posthumanist critical discourses that humanists have pejoratively called "theory" and "P.C."

Like Heidegger in his interrogation of the planetary technology of modernity, this latest phase of Western metaphysical thought that he aptly calls "the age of the world picture," I am suggesting, finally, that the humanist *paideia* is coming to its end. In fulfilling the inclusive and comprehensive implications of its restricted anthropological economy, in showing itself to be a "regime of Truth," this allegedly life-affirming perspective has, in Nietzsche's term, betrayed itself as a reactive discursive practice of *ressentiment*—and thus as a life-denying nihilism that must be overcome. In coming to its end, to put it "projectively," the humanist discourse of deliverance has dis-closed the others that its supervisory and amnesiac memory must necessarily exclude or forcefully accommodate (colonize) in order to maintain the hegemony of its project of consensus. "The forgotten mystery of Dasein," Heidegger says, "is not eliminated by the forgottenness; rather, the forgottenness bestows on the apparent disappearance of what is forgotten [by the ontotheological tradition] a peculiar presence."[53] It is the thought of this peculiar forgotten presence—if it is understood not only as the onto-logical difference, as Heidegger tends to do, but also as historically specific psychic, linguistic, sexual, cultural, social, and political difference—that the end of the human-istic *paideia* has enabled. It is also this peculiar presence—or rather, this proliferation of absented presences—that postmodern or posthumanist intellectuals now have the responsibility not only to think but to practice.

FIVE

THE UNIVERSITY IN THE VIETNAM DECADE

THE "CRISIS OF COMMAND" AND THE "REFUSAL OF SPONTANEOUS CONSENT"

> The [educational] system is telling you in effect: "if you wish to understand and perceive events in the present, you can only do so through the past, through an understanding—carefully derived from the past—which was specifically developed to clarify the present." We have employed a wide range of categories—truth, man, culture, writing, etc.—to dispel the shock of daily occurrences, to dissolve the event.
>
> Michel Foucault, "Revolutionary Action: 'Until Now' "

> To be certain, American universities, particularly Harvard, do not contain the systematic and coordinated terror and regimentation of military barracks, concentration camps, or industrial factories. Universities are, most of them, "liberal institutions." . . . Universities do indeed function as forums of intellectual debate, dissent, and critical thinking. To equate this latter set of facts with "the University," however, is to confuse a part with the whole—the whole which students are educated to be blind to. For *one* of the central functions of the forum-dialogue-criticism aspect of the university is to weave a democratic veil which enshrouds a concentrated, highly organized, and undemocratic system of wealth and power. From the point of view of the university as a structure of power and control, debate, dissent, and criticism are healthy and productive only so long as they leave the power structure intact. This is a system of dual power in which one side has no power. It is the truth of the phrase "the marketplace of ideas," in which ideas and men of ideas are transformed into commodities.
>
> *How Harvard Rules*, a critique compiled by the African Research Group in Cambridge, Mass., and the *Old Mole*, a radical newspaper, 1969

I

Throughout this book, I have tried to convey a sense of the crisis of education in the contemporary Western world, particularly in North America, by thematizing the contradictory will to power inscribed in the humanistic rhetoric of deliverance and the institutions of learning this rhetoric has legitimized. My reasons for this largely critical opposition are not restricted to disclosing the complicity of these institutions with the ideology of the various privileged hierarchical oppositions—identity/difference, subject/object, space/time, male/female, black/white, culture/anarchy, high culture/low culture, maturity/youth, and so on—intended to guarantee the hegemony of the dominant sociopolitical order. Indeed, my destructive discourse (as the etymology suggests) has been intended as an affirmative praxis. I have attempted to articulate what the problematic determining the discourse of humanism has left unsaid, to disclose and liberate by hermeneutic violence the futural possibilities that the privileged and sedimented closure of structure has concealed and repressed throughout the indissoluble field of forces that constitute being. To recall Heidegger, "if the question of Being is to achieve clarity regarding its own history," then it is necessary to loosen the sclerotic tradition and dissolve its concealments. Unlike the deconstructive critics, whose commitment to an undecidable textuality precludes asking the *Seinsfrage*, I understand the task of postmodern thinking in general and pedagogy in particular "as the destruction (*De-struction*) of the traditional content of ancient ontology which is to be carried out along the guidelines of the question of Being," and is based "upon the original experiences in which the first and subsequent guiding determinations of Being were gained." The ultimate purpose of "destruction" is not to negate the tradition or to reduce it to an indeterminate textuality, but to retrieve (*Wiederholen*) its primal context from the oblivion of a naturalized supernatural discursive practice: "The destruction does not wish to bury the past in nullity; it has a positive intent. Its negative function remains tacit and implicit."[1] If such a retrieval includes the original provenance of modern representations of the subject, cultural production, gender relations, and sociopolitical formations as well as of being as such (to which Heidegger more or less delimited his project), the destruction of the discourse of humanism discloses the *projective* possibilities at all these sites closed off and forgotten by the humanistic memory in naturalizing a derivative or structuralist mode of inquiry.

My destruction of the discursive practices of humanism, in other words, compels the retrieval, from the Apollonian thinking privileged by North American institutions of higher learning, of an educational theory and practice grounded in originative thinking rooted in history, in the occasion of human being. A crucial qualification is necessary, however. The "leap" into the hermeneutic circle "primordially and wholly"[2] is not merely a matter of reversing the binary opposition between a derived space (identity) and a primal time (difference), that is, of releasing a primordial Dionysiac force circumscribed and contained by the Apollonian principle. To think simply that was the case is to disregard one of the fundamental disclosures of the postmodern countermemory: that a discourse or cultural formation or sociopolitical order is always sociopolitically constituted. Rather, "destruction" releases the *awareness* that every discourse, cultural formation, or sociopolitical order is positional and arbitrary, manifested in exclusions or assimilations, and therefore *historical* and subject to transformation. In Adorno's phrase, this awareness is "the infinitismal freedom"[3] — the possibility, however limited, of human agency — that, according to some critics, both sympathetic and adversarial, is annulled by the postmodern interrogation of the subject; above all, by Heidegger's account of being (in his post-*kehre* discourse), Gramsci's account of hegemony, Foucault's account of disciplinary power, and Althusser's account of the functioning of ideological state apparatuses.[4] At the critical site of traditional pedagogy, where the most comprehensive and least visible binary opposition, that between age (maturity) and youth, does its silent disciplinary work in "speaking for" a multiplicity of "others," the "agency" enabled by destructive criticism manifests itself in various emancipations: for example, in Heidegger the discourse of "difference" from metaphysical identity; in Derrida "writing" from speech; in Foucault the discourses of social "deviation" in general ("madness," "sickness," "criminality," "youth," etc.) from the disciplinary society; in Kristeva the discourse of women (as well as other categories of being relegated to the imaginary by the law of the Father) from the patriarchal symbolic order; in Said the discourse of the "oriental" and, by extension, of other third worlds from the practice of "Orientalism"; in Bakhtin the discourse of "low" or "sub-" cultures from canonical or official literary genres; in Fanon the discourse of "blacks" and other racial "minorities" from white hegemony.

To repeat differently, "destruction" opens up spaces of learning to the possibility of a discourse that might be called "critical theory" — *provided it is understood as an oxymoron*. It should not be forgotten that the term "theory" was given its institutional currency by traditional humanists who wanted to assign pejorative connotations to the new theoretical discourses: the aura of abstraction and remoteness from the objects of its inquiry. The term "theory" (from the Greek *theoria* — contemplation, speculation, sight) has its source in the metaphorics of vision and light (and the centered circle) invented by the post-Heraclitan Greek philosophers and institutionalized by Roman pedagogy to privilege metaphysical knowledge: a mode of inquiry that was intended to spatialize time and the difference it disseminates. *Theoría* itself derives from *theorós* (spectator) and, farther back, from *théa* (sight) and *théasthaí* (to look upon), all of which have their ultimate origin in *theós* (the Latin *deus*), the omniscient (panoptic), omnipresent, transcendent, but always hidden deity beyond the temporal realm of conflict, of crisis or criticism who looks down uncritically, which is to say indifferently, from an aesthetic distance on the totality of things-as-they-are.[5]

In stressing the oxymoronic character of "critical theory," I want to suggest that the destruction opens up the possibility of a theory that is simultaneously a praxis, a material intervention in the constituted microworld of the university. This is how I read

Heidegger's insistent distinction between originative and derivative thinking. Whereas the "disinterested" humanist subject thinks the temporal process *metá-tá-physicá* and thus subjects it to a vicious circularity, the interested destructive "subject," aware of its constitutedness, enters the circle of be-ing "wholly and primordially" and thus thinks being as "repetition" (*Wiederholen*), as an always already ontic-ontological and thus open-ended dialogical process:

> The resoluteness which comes back to itself and hands itself down, then becomes the *repetition* of a posssibility of existence that has come down to us. *Repeating is handing down explicitly*—that is to say, going back into the possibilities of the Dasein that has-been-there. The authentic repetition of a possibility of existence that has been . . . is grounded existentially in anticipatory resoluteness. . . . The repeating of that which is possible does not bring again (*Wiederbringen*) something that is "past," nor does it bind the "present" back to that which has already been "outstripped." Arising as it does, from a resolute projection of oneself, repetition does not let itself be persuaded of something by what is "past," just in order that this, as something which was formerly actual, may recur. Rather, the repetition makes a *reciprocal rejoinder* [*Widerruf*] to the possibility of that existence which has-been-there. But when such a rejoinder is made to this possibility in a resolution, it is made *in a moment of vision: and as such* it is at the same time a *disavowal* of that which in the "today," is working itself out as the "past." Repetition does not abandon itself to that which is past, nor does it aim at progress. In the moment of vision authentic existence is indifferent to both these alternatives.[6]

The humanist subject assumes itself to be natural, present to itself, universal, and free, but is in fact determined by a derivative thinking of mastery; the destructive subject is *both* secondary *and* primary, both inscribed and temporal and thus *enabled*, that is, capable of critical theory. In this, not incidentally, it is also different from the deconstructive "subject" which, assuming its "irreducible secondarity,"[7] tends to privilege a universality in reverse, a universality, that is, of the *aporia*, which thus dis-ables its thinking, renders it always already "theoretical," a spectator at the "scene of writing in general."

II

The historically specific events of the Vietnam decade—which the contemporary humanist reformers forget or repress (the authors of the Harvard Core Curriculum Report, Walter Jackson Bate, E. D. Hirsch, and Wayne Booth) or willfully reduce to a negative abstraction (William Bennett, Allan Bloom, Roger Kimball, Dinesh

D'Souza)—bore witness to what I have elsewhere called an "ontological invasion."[8] In harnessing the Occidental representation of ontology, gender, culture, race, education, law, economics, politics, and so on—the ideological state apparatuses—to the project of extending its hegemony in Southeast Asia, the United States, as self-appointed custodian of the liberal/democratic ethos, gave general visibility to the "center elsewhere" of the "disinterestedness" of this ethos. It disclosed, that is, the will to power latent in the "disinterested" discourse of deliverance and the "democratic" sociopolitical practices this discourse legitimates. In terms of Antonio Gramsci's analysis of the power relations binding civil and political society—hegemony and direct domination—this self-exposure of the power hidden behind the rhetoric of liberal democracy precipitated, in turn, a knowledge explosion all through the field of forces constituting being. It was an explosion that reflected not only the crisis of command instigated by the refusal of spontaneous consent by the general American public to the discourse of "the free world," but the emancipation of a multiplicity of voices hitherto spoken for—contained and pacified—by the dominant discourse of hegemony. Within the specific space of knowledge production, the Vietnam decade bore witness not only to the complicity of the American institutions of higher learning—latent in their evolution into a "knowledge industry," as Clark Kerr put it immediately before the war—with the military-industrial complex and the legal and policing agencies, but to its complicity with sexual and racial discrimination, as the well-documented and exemplary case of Columbia University's Morningside gymnasium project testified.[9]

This is the historically specific genealogy of the spontaneous protest movement that turned American college and university campuses into ideological battlegrounds in the late 1960s. It was not, as Bennett and Bloom would have it, "a collective loss of nerve and faith" or "the casuistry of weakness and ideology" on the part of faculty and academic administrators[10] that activated the students' spontaneous demands for the breaking of institutional ties with the military-industrial complex and state information retrieval agencies, for the end of racial and sexual discrimination, for the right to participate in the governance of the university, and for a pedagogy of relevance. It was, rather, the disclosure implicating the discourse and practice of higher education with political and cultural colonialism, above all at the sites of race and gender, which hitherto were generally understood as problems separate from and external to the value-free space of the university. It was also this historically specific knowledge that precipitated the productive, if essentially unthought, *opening* of the closed general education curriculum: what the reformers insistently and pejoratively refer to as "the shattering of the humanities" (William Bennett), "the proliferation of courses" (Harvard Core Curriculum Report), "the over-optioned curriculum" (Gerald Grant), and lament as abetting "cultural illiteracy" (E. D. Hirsch).

In reading the student protest movement as an opening of the circumscribed space of the university, I do not want to suggest that the transformation it accomplished was adequate to the imperatives of the knowledge disclosed by the real history of the Vietnam decade. However promising the democratic horizon opened up by its decentering of the university's center, the protest movement failed both theoretically and practically to fulfill the possibilities of this opening.

On the positive side, the massive student demonstrations at Berkeley, Columbia, Harvard, Cornell, Kent State, and elsewhere throughout the United States focalized as never before the contradictions inhering in the benign liberal image of higher education. In engaging the complicity of the modern university as knowledge industry with the repressive state apparatuses (the military/industrial/legal/administrative complex) and also with other ideological state apparatuses (the nuclear family, the church, the media, etc.) that made whiteness and maleness the condition of intelligibility of racial minorities and the female sex, the student protest movement foreclosed an adequate rationalization of the university's political neutrality, its independence from state power. Further, in demanding a pedagogy of relevance in the face of a curriculum oriented to a monumentalized past, it also foregrounded the indifference of the transhistorical humanities to sociopolitical history, if not their complicity with the authority of the state. However indirectly, that is, the protest movement enabled *critical theory*. Or, at any rate, it opened a space in the educational institutions of North America for the reception of radical continental thought, primarily the antihumanist or decentered thought of French poststructuralism (itself largely the consequence of the events of May '68).

On the negative side, the protest movement failed to effect productive changes in the university commensurate with the knowledge explosion precipitated by the events of the Vietnam War. This is because it refused or failed adequately to theorize its spontaneous dissatisfactions with the discourse and practice of the institutions of higher education, especially the complicity of the core curriculum with the scientific/technological disciplines: those overdetermined sites of the university that were more overtly implicated with the state's execution of the Vietnam War.

Blinded by their resistance to theory at large, the rank-and-file activists and the intellectuals of the protest movement—Tom Hayden is exemplary in this respect[11]—failed to perceive clearly that the human sciences were in fact, if at a deeper and more hidden structural level, as much agencies of the repressive state apparatuses as the more visible physical and applied sciences and university management. In short, the activists failed to theorize *hegemony*: the affiliation between cultural and material production and their relations to state power; between the ideology of "disinterested" humanistic discourse and the ideology of "objective" scientific discourse.[12]

The student protest movement's resistance to theory resulted in two very broad untheorized oppositional orientations: existential and Marxist, both of which were intrinsically limited in their ability to interpret the complicity between the institutions of learning and the economic and sociopolitical order waging the war in Vietnam and thus to effect radical and lasting changes in the structure of the existing university and, insofar as education reproduces civil society, the dominant sociopolitical order.

On the one hand, the existential orientation, especially the commitment to "authenticity," resulted in three kinds of praxis based on a privileged self-identity: that of the liberal individual whose resistance took the limited active form of challenging the "bad faith" of the university that had betrayed its truly democratic essence and mission in "selling out" to the worldly interests outside; that of the "beat" individual, whose "resistance" took the equally limited form of "dropping out" and/or drug-induced consciousness expansion; and that of the communard, who repeated the pioneer myth of the American Adam (Leatherstocking, Daniel Boone, Thoreau, etc.) in rejecting a decadent technological civilization in favor of nature. All three forms minimized the possibility of collective action within and among subaltern constituencies. In failing to interrogate the idea of the sovereign subject privileged and transmitted by the university itself—especially by the humanities—they also inadvertently fulfilled in their spontaneous action the divisive and pacifying ends of the microphysics of power that the disciplinary society, especially its educational institutions, had developed to defuse collective action against the dominant sociopolitical order. This existential thrust of the protest movement definitely exposed the complicity of the university—as historically specific institution—with the state apparatuses, but it left one of the most important agencies of hegemonic subjection utterly intact: the self-identical subject, which, to recall Foucault's insistent thematics, it is the essential function of the humanities to inscribe and transmit.

The "radical" Marxist or "New Left" orientation, on the other hand, was more aware of the genealogy of the sovereign subject of bourgeois capitalist society. Unlike the existential orientation, that of groups like the Students for a Democratic Society was able to generate an active sense of collectivity. But they engaged the university at those overdetermined sites—the scientific disciplines and, above all, the administrative agencies—that had transformed it into a "knowledge *industry*." They thus failed to achieve an effective affiliative solidarity with those differential and marginalized constituencies—racial minorities, women, workers, gays, conscripted soldiers, etc.—precipitated by exposure of the linguistic, sexual, and racial—that is, cultural—limits of the discourse and practice of the humanist university, as well as its economic limits. The Marxist orientation, in other words, was based, however vaguely, on what Althusser calls the economism of traditional Marxism: on the base/superstructure model inherited by the modern Left from the nineteenth-century context that provoked Marx's and Engels's revolutionary discourse, the anachronistic model that always understands the historically specific and thus differential superstructural sites (for instance, the space of culture) as essentially determined by class-oriented modes of production and thus as epiphenomenal. This model, for example, informs the following passage, which must be quoted at length, from the so-called Columbia Statement, one of the most visible and representative documents of the New Left, written by Paul Rockwell and adopted by the Columbia SDS on September 12, 1968, following the events of April 23-30:

There is no group—neither Trustees, nor their School of International Affairs, no NROTC, nor SDS—that does not use the University for political ends. Columbia is *already* a world-wide institution involved in a world-wide struggle. Columbia would be an active political force regardless of SDS. Its Institute of Defense Analysis, for instance, devoted to counter-insurgency and riot control, serves the political ends of the rulers of America; it quells the uprisings of the Blacks and pre-empts revolutions abroad. Hence SDS, among many other groups, demanded an end to IDA. The gym affair also transcended the issue of local student power. For Columbia's seizure of Morningside represented a case of absentee control of Harlem's land. True, the question is not whether we use the University—for who does *not* use it?—but for what ends and whose interests the University should be used. . . . The Trustees say that they will not allow the University to become an "agent of revolt." What that signifies is that the University will continue to be an agent of Imperialism. For it is clear that, without a sustained struggle in the University, it will not change its present role. At Columbia, we [SDS] measure the scope of our activity by the scope of Columbia's repressive operations. We believe that we cannot be free until the general exploitation of our society is overcome. Our present struggle transcends local bounds, not because we are subversives, not because we are missionaries, but because the unified system of Empire can be overcome in no other way than massive, international struggle. . . . The Trustees are giants of corporate enterprise. Their businesses—from Allied Chemical to Socony Mobil—envelop more than half of the world. Radicals who refuse to be parochial are subversive to the Trustees because, while the Trustees can manipulate local struggles (playing one off against the other), a mass struggle, welding many strata of society, threatens the very fabric of their privilege.

The Trustees are shrewd. They induce students to dissent only in a local way; while they, giants of Empire, transform the University into a bastion of Imperialism. "Our Colleges and Universities," said John A. Hannah, President of Michigan State University in 1961, "must be regarded as bastions of our defense, as essential to the preservation of our country and our way of life as supersonic bombers, nuclear-powered submarines, and intercontinental ballistic missiles." The "bastions of defense"—Michigan State, Columbia, MIT, Pennsylvania, Stanford, among many others—are not financed by local groups, any more than Saigon is run by the people of Saigon. The class that turns Universities into bastions of defense is not rooted in any single city, nor any single country—so ubiquitous is its wealth, property, and power.[13]

This document is a perceptive disclosure of the general racism underlying the Columbia administration's benign "pluralism" and of the repressive global political agenda hidden behind its strategy to disarm criticism and divide resistance by localizing the "Columbia problem." However perceptive its analysis of the tactics of disarming collective resistance, the Columbia Statement nevertheless reinscribes the very model of power it would delegitimize. The statement interprets the University's racist practices (the unilateral decision to build a new gymnasium in Morningside Park, which also involved the buying up of property adjacent to Columbia University and eviction of the mostly black tenants) in essentially economistic terms: "the class that turns the University into bastions of defense is not rooted in any single city, nor any single country—so ubiquitous is its wealth, property, and power." It therefore reduces the historical specificity of black oppression to a rarified abstraction defined by an essentially white economistic discourse. The disaffiliation of the black student constituency (Student Afro-American Society) from the white one during the entire period of the disturbances and especially at the time of the occupation of Hamilton Hall—a disaffiliation repeated virtually everywhere on college and university campuses and elsewhere throughout that time—bears sad witness to this failure of understanding. At the caucus of the full steering committee of both blacks and whites occupying Hamilton Hall, blacks declared that the commitment of whites to the enterprise of confronting the university was "inadequate" and asked them to leave the building. The theoretical naiveté of the SDS position is painfully suggested by their response to this disaffiliating gesture: "Regardless of their ability to accept black separatism in a theoretical context, the whites were shocked by their expulsion from the building. Mark Rudd, who announced the black students' decision, was visibly shaken, yet he advocated compliance and others either agreed or felt that no real choice existed. The white students withdrew from Hamilton Hall about 5:30 A.M. [Wednesday, April 23], after occupying the building for 16 hours" (CC, 107-8).

Similarly, the Columbia Statement interprets the university's complicity with state apparatuses prosecuting the war in Vietnam—its sponsorship of the Institute for Defense Analysis,[14] its secret contracts with the Central Intelligence Agency, and so on—in essentially economistic terms: aiding and abetting the hegemonic ends of multinational capitalism. However justified this indictment, it abstracted the complex materiality of the university into simply an "agency of Imperialism" and obscured the cultural ethnocentrism informing both those overdetermined agencies of the university that gave it the image of an industry serving the capitalist state and those underdeveloped but no less active agencies such as literature, philosophy, history, and art departments; in privileging and canonizing Anglo-American or Western culture as "the best that has been thought and said in the world," these agencies secretly (however unintentionally on the part of many educators) legitimize and extend the hegemony of the dominant economic-sociopolitical order. In short, the Marxist base/superstructure model on which SDS grounded its resistance was precisely the model invalidated by the symptomatic disclosure during the Vietnam War of the significant degree to which the production of information—discourse, education, culture—was an agency as repressive, if far less visibly, as material production.

Despite the symptomatic exposure of humanistic education as an ideological state apparatus, however, the Vietnam War did not significantly dislocate the economism of the New Left intellectuals.[15] As the events of the Modern Language Association meetings of 1968 attest, it is true that academics in the humanities, especially literary studies, began to focus increasingly on the implication of their disciplines in the conduct of the war. But as their discourses at that time make clear, the leading spokesmen of the so-called Movement—literary intellectuals such as Louis Kampf, Richard Ohmann, Paul Lauter, Florence Howe, and others—interpreted this complicity in terms of the *institutional structure* rather than the cultural content of their discipline. Even as late as the mid-1970s, when radical critics of the university began to theorize the ideological affiliation between the humanistic disciplines and the state, it was still in terms of a general economism—the university at large as scientific/technological instrument of bourgeois capitalism—that this complicity was articulated.

The failure to perceive the ideological affiliation between cultural and material production is epitomized by Richard Ohmann's otherwise persuasive critique of literature departments in *English in America* (1976). This is because he tends to reduce the multiple and unevenly developed functions of the post–World War II English department to essentially that of teaching freshman composition; specifically, a writing pedagogy that privileged instrumental reason. Ohmann's critique of English 101 is powerful and compelling in its disclosure that this universally mandated "service" course reproduced the technobureaucratic liberal elite responsible for the appallingly dehumanized execution of the war against Vietnam. But in representing the English Department *at large* as an agency of instrumental reason reflecting the scientific, technological, capitalist bias of the university, he also exculpates those other, humanistic functions of English departments from such complicity. However more radical than that of the liberal humanists, his discourse remains locked within the parameters of the Two Cultures debate or, what is the same thing from a Marxist perspective, of the base/superstructure problematic:

> It seems to me that the special responsibility of literary intellectuals and scholars has to do with precisely the center of their vocation: literature itself. Academic humanists often speak of themselves, a little grandly, as the preservers and transmitters of literary culture *and I have no quarrel with that design*. What should be questioned is the *means* of preservation and transmission.
>
> It might be to the point here to mention that the literature we are to preserve includes works by Milton, Voltaire, Rousseau, Swift, Goethe, Byron, Blake, Shelley, Carlyle, Shaw, and others of that rebellious ilk. Beyond that, I think it is accurate to say that *every good poem, play, or*

novel, properly read, is revolutionary, in that it strikes through well-grooved habits of seeing and understanding, thus modifying some part of consciousness. Though one force of literature is to affirm the value of tradition and the continuity of culture, another, equally powerful, is to criticize that which is customary and so attack complacency. . . .

How have we preserved and transmitted it? A distinction is necessary. The critical force of literary culture must have played some role in the personal-political lives of literature professors this past decade. I admire the many teachers of literature who, like many poets, spoke out early against our government's conduct in Vietnam, and I would like to think that their humanistic training and practice helped them see and oppose injustice. *But in our institutional efforts to preserve and transmit culture,* I see only a denial of the critical spirit. Our computerized bibliographies, our fragmented "fields," our hundreds of literary journals and 30,000 books and articles, our systems of information storage and retrieval, our survey courses and historical pigeonholes, our scramble for light loads and graduate students, our 67 sections and 67 seminars, our emphasis on technique and procedure, our hierarchy of scholarly achievement, our jealous pursuit of social neutrality and political vacuity—in all this I see retreat from criticism and a movement into more comfortable ways of life.

John McDermott has argued persuasively that technology, rather than being the neutral and willing servant we like to think it is, is fundamentally "systems of rationalized control over large groups of men, events, and machines by small groups of technically skilled men operating through organizational hierarchy." If this is true, how might we curtail its capacity to limit our freedom—not to mention to destroy the biosphere and the like? A hopeful answer is that culture would serve its critical function and do something to retrieve civilization from the hole that capitalist technology has dug. This is why it is no small matter to find that the largest organization devoted to the furtherance of literary culture has acted as if its aim were to imitate technology, rather than control it.[16]

What Ohmann says about the *functioning* of English departments in the decade of the Vietnam War is true. They organized humanistic work according to the rules of discursive formation established by the science/technology/capitalist production nexus. But it is a truth that all too characteristically and innocently overlooks the *content* of literary studies itself in favor of its institutional mechanisms, as if there were little or no genetic relationship between the two, as if, that is, the literature as such and the in-stitutional agencies of its transmission constituted a contradiction. In identifying En-glish studies in terms of the technological *means* of preserving and transmitting culture, Ohmann identifies them more or less exclusively with technology and the capitalist institutional organization endemic to it. In other words, he understands "English literature" as a superstructure of the capitalist base. According to Ohmann, it was not "English literature" (and criticism) per se that contributed to the power of the dominant sociopolitical order that in turn initiated and conducted the war in Vietnam. It was rather the *organization* and *administration* of its transmission in terms of the machinery of capitalism. Indeed, were literary culture to free itself from the disabling constraints of an institution modeled on capitalist principles to fulfill its intrinsic revolutionary imperatives, it would generate a kind of critical consciousness capable of transforming the university and the dominant capitalist sociopolitical order it legitimates and reproduces in favor of a more truly democratic society. Ohmann fails to perceive the hidden logocentrism, ethnocentrism, racism, patriarchy informing the literary texts (and the humanistic discourses of literary criticism to which they gave rise) that are privileged, monumentalized, and canonized by Western culture to legitimize its authority. Like the radical students of the 1960s, in short, Ohmann in the 1970s fails to theorize *hegemony*: the cultural discourse, increasingly relied on by the state since the Enlightenment, which enables the spontaneous assent of those it dominates by producing symbolic representations that naturalize the constituted values and power of the dominant sociopolitical order.

On the other hand, Ohmann's invocation of "works by Milton, Voltaire, Rousseau, Swift, Goethe, Byron, Shelley, Carlyle, Shaw and others of that rebellious ilk" as examples of the "critical force of literary culture" fails to interrogate the interpretive/critical/pedagogic means by which these "oppositional" works have achieved their paradoxical canonical status. In this omission, he also fails to perceive the logocentric, ethnocentric, racist, and patriarchal ideology informing the critical discourses — including his own — produced by and, in turn, reproducing that predominant literature whose purpose, he observes, is "to affirm the value of tradition and the continuity of culture"; the critical discourses that domesticate and pacify the oppositional force of revolutionary texts too visible to be simply excluded by assimilating their differential voices to the mainstream of literary culture. Ohmann's text discloses the degree to which it continues to be inscribed by the vulgar Marxist model, which renders literary culture an epiphenomenal superstructure to a managerial/economistic base. Despite the overt evidence of the complicity of the liberal arts with the state's material projects in the aftermaths of World War I, World War II, and during the Vietnam War, his "radical" text also betrays the degree to which it continues to be inscribed and determined by the anthropological problematic: its emancipatory Marxist discourse remains complicitous with the discourses and practices of the positive sciences and technology, those academic disciplines, according to Ohmann, that English departments, in contradiction to their intrinsic critical purposes, have appropriated, thus lending themselves inadvertently to the violent purposes of the capitalist state.

It may be true that a small minority of literature professors spoke out early against the United States government's conduct in Vietnam. It is extremely doubtful, however much Ohmann "would like to think" it, "that their humanistic training and practice helped them to see and oppose injustice." What motivated the large majority of the small minority had little to do with their humanistic training and practice. It is, unfortunately, much more likely that they were responding, as good liberal humanists, to the sudden and shocking display of explicit and direct power by the government of a "liberal democratic state"; that they were shaken by a latent capitalist fascism that was *contradictorily* threatening the foundations of American democracy. Humanities professors motivated by their training were of two affiliated kinds. On the one hand, they were those like George Kennan, who, despite the flagrant "Egyptianism" of the American government, as he put it, and their "misgivings" about "national policy" which they "shared" with their students,[17] put their efforts into maintaining the natural "neutrality" of the university in the name of the transcendental *logos* against the "radical" students' misguided immersion in the momentous historically specific events, (characteristically referred to as "the affairs of this passing world") and their immature and improper attempts to politicize it:

> There is an ideal that has long been basic to the learning process as we have known it, one that stands at the very center of our modern institutions of higher education and that had its origin, I suppose, in the clerical and monastic character of the medieval university. It is the ideal of the association of the process of learning with a certain remoteness from the contemporary scene—a certain detachment and seclusion, a certain voluntary withdrawal and renunciation of participation in contemporary life in the interests of the achievement of a better perspective on that life when the period of withdrawal is over. It is an ideal that does not predicate any total conflict between thought and action, but recognized that there is a time for each. . . .
>
> There is a dreadful incongruity between this vision and the state of mind—and behavior—of the radical left on the American campus today. In place of a calm science, "recluse, ascetic, like a nun," not knowing or caring that the world passes "if the truth but come in answer to her prayer," we have people utterly absorbed in the affairs of the passing world. And instead of these affairs being discussed with knowledge and without passion, we find them treated with transports of passion and with a minimum, I fear, of knowledge. In place of slowness to take excitement, we have readiness to react emotionally, and at once, to a great variety of issues. In place of self-possession, we have screaming tantrums and brawling in the streets. In place of the "thorough way of talk" that [Woodrow] Wilson envisaged, we have banners and epithets and obscenities and virtually meaningless slogans. And in place of bright eyes "looking to heaven for the confirmation of their hope," we have eyes glazed with anger and passion, too often dimmed as well by artificial abuse of the psychic structure that lies behind them, and looking

almost everywhere else but to heaven for the satisfaction of their aspirations.[18]

Then there were those humanists, such as Allan Bloom, equally indifferent or oblivious to the "passing world," who construed themselves as relic-bearers of a shattered civilization and, in the name of and from the transcendental perspective of the scriptural authority and sanity of the Platonic anthropologos, condemned the professors who reversed their essential pedagogical role when they capitulated to the Dionysian barbarism of the students. Bloom identifies these students—the white, black, and female "rabble"—with the Nazi youth movement in the 1930s:

> The professors [at Cornell University], the repositories of our best traditions and highest intellectual aspirations, were fawning over what was nothing better than a rabble; publicly confessing their guilt and apologizing for not having understood the most important moral issues, the proper response to which they were learning from the mob; expressing their willingness to change the university's goals and the content of what they taught. As I surveyed this spectacle, Marx's overused dictum kept coming to my mind against my will: History always repeats itself, the first time as tragedy, the second as farce. The American university in the sixties was experiencing the same dismantling of the structure of rational inquiry as had the German university in the thirties. No longer believing in their higher vocation, both gave way to a highly ideological student populace [note the Arnoldian term]. And the content of the ideology was the same—value commitment. The University had abandoned all claim to study or inform about value— undermining the sense of the value of what it taught, while turning over the *decision* about values to the folk, the *Zeitgeist*, the relevant.[19]

Reminiscent of Matthew Arnold's reaction to the Hyde Park demonstrations, these relic-bearers such as Bloom called for the intervention of the state's policing agents to forcefully repress the student uprising:

> Obvious questions were no longer obvious: Why could not a black student be expelled as a white student would be if he failed his courses or disobeyed the rules that make university community possible? Why could the president [of Cornell University] not call the police if order was threatened? Any man of weight would have fired the professor who threatened the life of the student. The issue was not complicated. Only the casuistry of weakness and ideology made it so. Ordinary decency dictated the proper response. No one who knew or cared about what a university is would have acquiesced in this travesty. It was no surprise that a few weeks later—immediately after the faculty had voted overwhelmingly under the gun to capitulate to outrageous

demands that it had a few days earlier rejected—the leading members of the administration and many well-known faculty members rushed over to congratulate the gathered students and tried to win their approval. I saw exposed before all the world what had long been known, and it was at last possible without impropriety to tell these pseudo-universitarians precisely what one thought of them.[20]

The humanist discourses of the Kennans and Blooms insistently advocated different institutional responses to the campus situation they addressed. The one is a liberal discourse that acknowledges the worldly concerns of the students but proposes a Platonic distance from the event to allow the processes of rationality to mediate educational and sociopolitical "change." The other is a reactionary discourse that, in the name of absolute certainty, contemptuously bypasses the question of the validity of the students' worldly concerns in favor of reasserting the authority of the received idea of the university and thus its right—indeed, its responsibility—to repress the sociopolitically motivated deviance of the students (and faculty) from its scriptural norms. However, both discourses are entirely determined by the same sedimented and reductive ideological terms: the relay of binary oppositions constituted by the Western ontotheological tradition and increasingly rendered "natural" since the Enlightenment by its modern anthropological allotrope: the humanist/bourgeois or capitalist/disciplinary society. As the typical passages from Kennan and Bloom make remarkably manifest, both discourses unquestioningly privilege identity over difference, thus enabling a relay of affiliated oppositions in which the first, *always specular*, term determines the meaning or colonizes the temporal experience to which the second "refers": center/periphery, absolute past/contemporaneity, the universal/the ephemeral, perspective/immediacy, detachment/engagement, reason/passion (madness), self-present subject/mob or rabble, male/female, high/low, age/youth, light/darkness, wisdom/ignorance, teacher/student, propriety/impropriety (bad manners), civility/barbarism, democracy/mob rule (fascism). Each, that is, demonizes the force that threatens its hegemony, thus justifying a policing action intended to re-form its deforming energy. Furthermore, both discourses are inscribed by the myth of the saving remnant. In a distortion of the actual relations of cultural and sociopolitical power, their enunciations (like Arnold's and Babbitt's, like those of most humanist reformers before them) assign themselves a subject-position that makes them appear Isaiahs or Aeneases (or both), the relic- or seed-bearers of a transcendentally sanctioned body politic torn apart by its demonic enemies.

There is, however, a significant difference—one recalling Gramsci's distinction between power relations in "private" (civil) and "public" (political) spheres—between these two related discourses that should be remarked. The reactionary discourse of humanists like Bloom *makes explicit* the power that is only latent or held in reserve in the liberal discourse of humanists like Kennan. It is not simply, as Foucault insistently observes, that the difference between the "reformers" who exert power overtly on the basis of a certain authority and the "reformers" who wish "to change the institution without touching the ideological system that legitimates it"[21] is only an apparent one; it is also that the latter is more economical and effective than the former because it obscures power in the name of disinterested truth.

To return to Ohmann's text, the "humanistic training and practice" it tends to privilege as agency of critique and transformation of a university and sociopolitical order organized in terms of capitalist economy and technology did not, I submit, help professors of English to "see and oppose injustice." Rather, it blinded them to the essentially microphysical nature of power in the disciplinary society—to the essential role played by the literary tradition in extending the hegemony of the repressive state. By thus obscuring the complicity between the humanities and capitalism, it misled them as to the object of their criticism. More pervasively perhaps, it inscribed or confirmed their belief in the sanctity of the anthropologos, the cultural tradition it has produced, and the bourgeois capitalist sociopolitical order that relies on this monumentalized heritage to legitimate and enhance its hegemony. The professors of English literature who fulfilled the cultural and sociopolitical imperatives of the English graduate programs in place during the Vietnam decade were not so much those whom Ohmann admires for their resistance to the accommodation of freshman English (composition) to the requirements of a capitalist economy and "acted against the injustices of American foreign policy." It was rather those rank-and-file members of the Modern Language Association represented by the letters Ohmann cites in his account of the events at the MLA convention in December 1968, which brought a radical, Louis Kampf, *momentarily* to the second vice-presidency of this professional organization. These letters hide the ideological complicity between the anthropologos and Americanism behind an elitist rhetoric justifying rightful authority in terms of the quantity and distinction of scholarship:

> I am curious to know whether, considering the infinitesimally small [*sic*] members-come-lately of the MLA who nominated you for the second vice-presidency of the MLA, you would really undertake to serve as president, assuming the unlikely possibility of two more such fluke elections as the last one. If so, I suggest you have a look at the list of distinguished scholars who have been presidents of the Association. . . . If you do, I should think the membership should be given a list of your scholarly attainment. (*EA*, p. 36)[22]

Or, like Allan Bloom's text, they overtly assert the affiliation between the profession of English and Americanism as a fundamental responsibility of the professor of English:

> Whenever any American cannot exercise his right to travel and be secure in his person because of the threats of violence and disruption by any other group of "Americans" such as your "New University Conference" then I

believe it is necessary to request the Federal government's aid. Therefore, all the information from MLA on violence and the threat of violence—along with your statements and those of the President and the Executive Secretary of MLA—have been sent to the House Committee on Un-American Activities and the U.S. Justice Department. (*EA*, p. 47)[23]

What I am suggesting is that Ohmann's account of the profession of English in America is disabled as a vehicle of educational change, as was the Columbia statement of the SDS, by the Marxist base/superstructure model, which determines his "radical version" of the profession, though he is more cognizant than the writers of the statement of the complicity of cultural apparatuses with the war effort, and his history is more concrete and dense than theirs. For, as I have shown, his broadly economistic insight blinds him to the repressive ideology of the centered circle that informs the aesthetics, the literature, the interpretive and critical practices, the literary history, and, not least, the pedagogy[24] privileged by English departments at the time of the events he is interpreting. For all his insistence on the historicity and sociopolitical impact of literary discourse, Ohmann's text thus reinscribes itself into the misleading "debate" between literature (the humanities) and science. Like the SDS's discourse and practice vis-à-vis the black minority during the Columbia University disturbances, it also misses the opportunity to theorize the affiliation between the various unevenly developed cultural knowledges—knowledges pertaining to race, ethnicity, gender, age, language, interpretation, etc.—precipitated by the events of the Vietnam War and the economic, scientific, technological, military and sociopolitical knowledge overdetermined during that historically specific occasion.

Resistant to the theorization of its felt dissatisfactions with the system, the protest movement by and large reinscribed itself inside the liberal problematic of humanism, which was in some fundamental way complicitous with, if not ultimately responsible for, the dominant economic-sociopolitical order. In Althusser's terms, in failing to interrogate the disinterested inquiry privileged by the discourse of humanism the protest movement and the academic intellectuals who were sympathetic with the students failed to perceive that the dominant economic-sociopolitical order was as reliant on the ontological determination of cultural phenomena as on the more obvious military-industrial-political complex in waging the war in Vietnam, that the humanistic discourse of the general education program was not an offspring of nature, but, like the overdetermined sciences (the university as knowledge industry), a construction of the dominant order, an agency of discipline, repression, and consensus: that is, a hegemony.[25]

In the failed discursive practices of the protest movement during and immediately after the Vietnam War, in other words, we find a telling instance of the way adherence to what Foucault has called the "repressive hypothesis" obfuscates the power that has been reconstituted and redistributed in terms of the knowledge (truth)/power nexus in the so-called liberal democracies. Power in the *ancièn régime* was direct or overtly repressive — *visible*. It was thus economically and politically inefficient: subject to random and wasteful abuse and, above all, to resistance. The post-Enlightenment humanists harnessed the knowledges hitherto arbitrarily repressed and forbidden for "positive" purposes, thus giving the covert disciplinary apparatuses, including the agencies of cultural production, a benign appearance capable of commanding spontaneous assent and loyalty from the very objects of its repression. This strategic conjoining of productive knowledge and power, according to Foucault, was the greatest achievement of post-Enlightenment humanism not simply because it internalized power, and concealed its operations from sight. In spreading power throughout the social body, it limited the possibilities of emancipatory practices to the appealing fiction that truth and power are binary opposites; that, on the one hand, power is always visible/repressive and distorts truth and, on the other, that truth is external to and the adversary of power. "The repressive hypothesis," as Dreyfuss and Rabinow put it, "is anchored in a tradition which sees power only as constraint, negativity, and coercion. As a systematic refusal to accept reality, as a repressive instrument, as a ban on truth, the forces of power prevent or at least distort the formation of knowledge. Power does this by suppressing desire, fostering false consciousness, promoting ignorance, and using a host of other dodges. Since it fears the truth, power must suppress it. It follows that power as repression is best opposed by the truth of discourse. When truth is spoken, when the transgressive voice of liberation is raised, then, supposedly, repressive power is challenged."[26]

This deceptive version of the relation between truth and power — the ruse of the repressive hypothesis — lies behind the insistent effort of many "reasonable" liberal humanists during the period of the campus disturbances to justify the *idea* of the university in the face of the militant students' indictment of and action against it, or to localize its culpability to those specific areas where the abuse of power was most visible, direct — and reformable. To cite one of many possible examples, this strategy is epitomized by Charles Frankel's *Education and the Barricades* (1968), a widely read and much-discussed book published in the immediate aftermath of the events at Columbia University to justify the idea of the liberal university as an ideal space devoted to the pursuit of reasonable truth (and to criticize the "violent" excesses of the student militants) while at the same time questioning the wisdom of Columbia University — the specific institution — for pursuing its ill-conceived Morningside gymnasium project, and for its sponsorship of the Institute for Defense Analysis, and for other specific manifestations of its abuse of power. I quote at length from the central chapter entitled "The Moral Right to Impose on Others," to suggest the remarkable symmetry between Frankel's representation of power relations in a liberal democratic society and Foucault's analysis of the ruse of the repressive hypothesis of the disciplinary society:

> These gradations in the nature of force [between socially necessary coercion and culpable violence] are . . . the decisive consideration with regard to the

argument [of the militant students at Columbia and the intellectuals who supported them] that our existing society relies on force and violence, and that everyone employs these methods or acquiesces in them, and that no one, therefore, is in a position to point the finger of blame at anyone else. It is true that in American society, as in all societies, democratic or not, almost everyone is coerced in some respects. People pay bills or obey traffic laws at least sometimes because they fear the application of force against them. It is true, too, that in American society many gross injustices are maintained through unfair laws that are backed by force, or through the connivance of the authorities with illegality, and, sometimes, as in the case of the murdered civil rights workers in Mississippi, through outright violence. But to say that this society, taken as a whole, relies on force and violence, and that all decent law-abiding citizens share the guilt for this state of affairs, is to ignore distinctions that have fundamental import for everyday human experience, and for the quality of human relations, human feelings, and human conduct.

Force that is merely latent has a different social and psychological significance from force that is actively employed. Force that is employed subject to strict legal restrictions is not the same genre with force that does not recognize such bounds. To utter broadside denunciations of the force and violence on which society depends while ignoring such facts is to imply that there is no significant difference between the conditions of a man who pays his taxes because he does not want to go to jail and that of a man who is afraid to vote because his house may be bombed. It overlooks the difference — and it is not an abstract difference but something as palpable as a knife in one's side — between living under the law and living under terror. . . .

So we return to the four propositions on which the rationale for the methods used by the student activists depends. . . .

Begin with the first proposition: that exceptional methods were in order because the evils being combatted — Vietnam and race-cum-poverty . . . — were extreme. But there are places closer than a university campus to these evils, where they can be combatted more directly. The university campus is merely convenient, safer, and more vulnerable because force is so alien to its habits and so lethal to it. Would anyone accept the contamination of public beaches or the invasion of hospitals as a legitimate means of protest against the war? Why, then, the university?

The answer that is given, of course, is that universities are in the service of the war machine and racism. But this is not a proposition that can be defended without significant qualifications. If it is true at all, it is true only in part. The universities of the United States have been principal centers of protest against the war in Vietnam and against racist practices. Only in certain of their activities can a connection be drawn between them and these wrongs. If complaint is justified, therefore, it has to be a specific complaint. If there is to be an issue, a concrete issue has to be found, based on a definite and particular connection between the university and the wrongs under attack. And the fact is that, at Columbia, this is what was attempted. Some sort of ostensible connection had to be established between the university and the great evils which, in theory, justified disruptive action. The *specific* issues being fought on the Columbia campus were not Vietnam and race-cum-poverty; they were a relationship to the Institute for Defense Analysis, a gymnasium project, and a maldistribution, real or alleged, of power in the university. . . .

If we accept the description of events at Columbia and at other institutions that has been offered by the most ardent defenders of the student activists, there has been no issue of fundamental student rights (e.g., the right to dissent), no issue of academic freedom, no issue of forced collaboration with either racism or the Vietnam War. These, conceivably, might qualify as issues justifying a forceful defense of basic principles.[27]

In succumbing to the essentially liberal humanist ruse of the repressive hypothesis, oppositional activists—students and faculty, blacks, women, and other "minorities," radical Marxists and New Left liberals—directed virtually their entire attention and energy to the sites where power was being compelled by the historical situation to manifest itself overtly. It read the economic-political complicity of the institutions of higher learning with the repressive agencies of the state as a *betrayal* of their essentially critical and cultural mission. Though this focus on the visible manifestations of power exposed the university's abuse of scientific knowledge production, it left the "center elsewhere" that affiliates the liberal arts and the physical sciences, the *litterae human-iores* and technological training, and renders them a continuous and totalizing agency of hegemony, intact. In other words, this focus of resistance, both existential and Marxist, on the university as simply "the knowledge industry"—a superstructural agency of the capitalist base—reinscribed the discourse and practice of liberation into the dialectics of the centered circle and, in so doing, *overlooked* the disciplinary ideology that gave rise to the ruse of the "repressive hypothesis": to the transformation of the *ancien régime* into a "regime of truth."[28]

III

The protest movement obviously generated significant, if highly amorphous, positive transformations in the general structure of consciousness of the university community, as the editors of *Social Text* observe in their important retrospective reaffirmation of its revolutionary ethos in the face of the "trashing [of] the 60s," which "has become a strategic feature of the current struggle for hegemony."[29] These transformations included: "the emergence of new historical subjects, or at least groups that constituted themselves as subjects on the basis, for instance, of sex and race"; "a profound transformation in cultural relations: deformalization of the dress code in public places, introduction of Anglo-Saxon expletives into ordinary middle-class speech"; "the appropriation and rearticulation" by way of rock and roll of "the urban music of the black migration after World War II," and other popular forms, "many of which originated in Africa and rural American environments: blues, syncopated rhythms, riffs of early-20th-century jazz," all of which contributed to the delegitimation of "high culture"; the contribution of a popular base "to the ecological movement and, equally important, a cadre for conducting political wars against certain forms of capital accumulation"; and, for the first time in this century, the permeation of public discourse by "new global perceptions" about imperialism, the domination of capital, "the forces, as well as the relations of production," "the prevailing sexual division of labor," and "discrimination based on circumstances of birth (such as race)." These emergent freedom movements "were limited to the world underclass in a complex way which put into question not only the glaring fact of economic exploitation but also the whole system of cultural domination."[30] Further, under the pressure of student resistance, the university disaffiliated itself from state agencies such as the CIA, ROTC, IDA, and so on. The racist admissions policies of colleges and universities were in some degree altered to accommodate the demand of minorities (especially blacks and Hispanics) for access to a college education. The patriarchal hiring mechanisms in higher education were modified to open departments to women. The paradigm that determined administrative/student relations was readjusted to allow students greater personal freedom and greater participation in the governance of the institutions of higher learning. The dominant core curriculum gave way to a more open, relevant, and sometimes idiosyncratic body of course offerings. And, not least, the universally required freshman composition course was, if not entirely abandoned, reconstituted as an elective. It was not by chance, as Richard Ohmann shows, that this course produced the "problem-solving" discourse that "routinized war" (*EA*, p. 199), the specular discourse of the " 'futurists,' the planners and think-tank forecasters and technological prophets who try to make forecasting of the future scientific and thus useful to governments and corporations," of the liberal writers on United States foreign policy, "who write theory but in a context of developing events they try to explain," of the "powerful men" in governmental administrative positions "who make decisions of consequence" (*EA*, p. 173), those whose memoranda make up *The Pentagon Papers*, for example:

> To put the obvious label on this paradigm [which informs *The Pentagon Papers*,] it is a model for *problem solving* in the same way that of the Foreign Affairs article was *problem formulation*. Any model reduces complexity— exchanges faithfulness to reality for finiteness. If you have to decide something tomorrow or next week, it is helpful, maybe necessary, to sort

reality out on a familiar grid that connects reality to a desired future by one or more acts. To do that it must pick out those elements from reality that have the most salient ties to the desired future. This is, of course, an abstraction of elements from the present in a way that reflects one's own needs and interests. It is worth looking at some consequences of this intellectual strategy, honored by freshman rhetorics in theory, and more rigidly by the Pentagon memos in practice — as indeed it is to some degree in each complex technological society. (*EA*, pp. 196-97)

The symmetry between Ohmann's analysis of the reductive, utilitarian, and violent agenda of freshman composition and Foucault's account of the role of the panoptic table in the production of discipline is too obvious for further comment.

Although the protest movement of the Vietnam decade shook the foundations of the university, the actual changes it effected were unfortunately superficial in a disabling way. Again, this was not only because these ineffectual changes were by and large the consequence of a spontaneous practice that was resistant to theory. As in the case of SDS and the Left in general, which did attempt to theorize resistance, it was also because that theory was grounded in an oversimplified and reductive base/superstructure model that, despite recognition of the complicity of cultural institutions with state power, nevertheless interpreted the former in economistic terms, as simply agencies of the capitalist state waging a neocolonial war. This disabling theoretical blindness, for example, can also be seen in the passage on freshman composition from Richard Ohmann's *English in America* quoted above, in which he demonstrates the complicity between rhetoric textbooks (and pedagogy) and the worldly discourse of the futurists, sociopolitical theorists, and state administrators involved in the planning and conduct of the war in Vietnam. What he leaves unsaid is that the common and consequential specular problem-solving paradigm informing worldly discourse was not the inscribed determinant only of scientific/technological thinking and writing, but also of the thinking and production of writing about literature and the other arts privileged by the humanistic disciplines of higher education.

As a consequence of this double failure of theory, the changes effected by the protest movement were asymmetrical to and incommensurate with the actual knowledge/power relations that obtained in higher education. Some transformations, such as the affirmative action programs involving blacks and women, that were instituted as a result of the vocal demands of "new historical subjects" were effectively neutralized, with the tacit consent of those they affected, by their accommodation to the existing structure of the university. As one African-American oppositional critic recently puts it:

The main proposal here is that the calls made in the 1960s and 1970s for new areas/programs of studies, were, although nonconsciously so at the time, calls which re-enacted in the context of our times a parallel counter-exertion, a parallel Jester's heresy to that of the *Studia*'s [at the time of the Renaissance]. But because of our non-consciousness of the real dimensions of what we were about, we asked at first only to be incorporated into the normative order of the present organization of knowledge as add-ons, so to speak. We became entrapped, as a result, in Bantustan enclaves labelled "ethnic" and "gender" and/or "minority studies." These enclaves then functioned, as David Bradley notes, *inter alia*, to exempt English Departments from having to alter their existing definition of American literature. Even more, these enclaves functioned to exempt the callers for the new studies from taking cognizance of the anomaly that confronted us, with respect to a definition of American literature which lawlikely functioned to exclude not only Blacks, but all the other groups whose "diverse modalities of protest" (Detienne, 1979) in the 1960s and 1970s had fuelled the call for new studies.[31]

In the case of newly instituted affirmative action programs for black students "unprepared" for college study (like the so-called Educational Opportunity Program at the State University of New York at Binghamton), the immediate and essential purpose was to teach them to speak and write standard English. Such "liberal" programs, in other words, were finally intended to annul as much as possible the linguistic difference endemic to the life of African-Americans, Hispanics, and other ethnic minorities in the ghettos (their historically specific occasion), and thus to induce them to take their *proper* place in the dominant culture and sociopolitical order—the white world. Encoded in this gesture of deliverance, though inadequately thought by both black and white activists in the 1960s, is the pernicious binary opposition between standard (read *identical*) and nonstandard (*different*) linguistic usage that identifies the users as racially superior or inferior; as socially acceptable or socially deficient; and, ultimately, if we recall black praxis during the Vietnam decade, as sociopolitically safe or sociopolitically threatening.

Most of the specific institutional changes were in due course interpreted by the humanist custodians of higher education as the ominous manifestation of the impending disintegration of the university. Unencumbered by a critical theory that exposed the complicity with the state of an assumed self-evident subject position, these traditionalists easily read the disintegration of the core curriculum and the abolition of freshman composition in the negative narrative terms enabled by the untouched binarism of their humanistic discourse: as "the shattering of the humanities" (William Bennett) or the "erosion of the general education program" (Harvard Committee) or the "decomposition of the University" (Allan Bloom) or "the decline of cultural literacy" (E. D. Hirsch) precipitated by the irresponsible immaturity of a "rabble" of youth (Bloom) and the "indiscriminate, narcissistic, populist, and morally self-righteous" militant style and rhetoric of "malcontents of all ages" (Phyllis Keller), aided and abetted by "a collective loss of nerve and faith" (Bennett) or a studied neglect of the "American cultural memory" (Lynne V. Cheney) on the part of both faculty and academic administrators and by the "nihilism" (Walter Jackson Bate, M. H. Abrams, Wayne Booth, Dennis Donoghue, Gerald Graff, and others) of deconstruction—that is, the "suppression of reason and the denial of the possibility of truth in the name of philosophy" (Bloom). Most recently, in the wake of the revolutions in Eastern Europe and the victory of the "United Nations" in its "just war" against Iraq, this defensive representation of the symptomatic knowledge explosion precipitated by the Vietnam War has taken a militantly positive form. It identifies the demands of the new historical subjects for a diversified curriculum as a "new McCarthyism of the Left" sponsored by the "tenured radicals" of the 1960s, as a practice of "political correctness" that threatens the "free speech" that constitutes the greatness of the American University (Roger Kimball, David Lehman, Dinesh D'Souza, the National Association of Scholars).

It was the failure of the various transgressive marginal and differential voices of the protest movement to adequately interpret the origins and the cultural and sociopolitical implications of the contradictions in the discourse and practice of deliverance that has allowed the humanist institution represented by the Harvard Core Curriculum Committee, Bennett, Bate, Bloom, Cheney, Hirsch, and so on to reinstitute the core in the face of what it calls the "proliferation of courses" or the "over-optioned curriculum," to recenter its panoptic disciplinary diagram, the hegemony of the anthropologos and its cultural heritage. Although these contradictions were *symptomatic* manifestations of an educational tradition—that is, an anthropological *paideia*—coming to its end, to its fulfillment and demise, the protest movement simply did not have a theoretical vocabulary adequate to perceive these contradictions as the return of the repressed Dionysian force at the moment of its final ontological, linguistic, and cultural suppression by the Apollonian *principium individuationis*. The largely spontaneous irruption of all-too-random acts of transgression against the structure of the university all across the indissoluble field of forces constituting being thus was itself *symptomatic* of a world historical process and, as such, subject to practical, if not in the end theoretically and historically justifiable, reconstitution and recontainment.

It was this pathos of the failure of the protest movement in North America, in France, Germany, and indeed everywhere in the West, that (by way of the reappropriation of Nietzsche and Heidegger, Marx and Freud, who, in one way or another, all proclaimed the "end" of the anthropological tradition in terms of the return of the repressed) precipitated the belated transgressive discourse of postmodern or posthumanist "theory," the interrogation of Man (the patriarchal white bourgeois capitalist subject), of Derrida, Foucault, Deleuze and Guattari, Althusser, Lyotard, Lacan, Cixous, and Kristeva in France. It was also this conjuncture that provided a matrix, however problematic the disciplinary machinery in place renders it, for the reception of this antihumanist discourse in at least some quarters of the North American university. To achieve what the protesters of the 1960s failed to achieve—to fulfill the educational imperatives disclosed by their extraordinarily suggestive but finally practically incon-sequential spontaneous efforts—it will be necessary for oppositional intellectuals to think and act these symptoms in the context of their locus—the transdisciplinary site of the educational institution—and in terms of the perspective on them afforded by posthumanist theory in general.

For up to now, it seems to me, postmodern theory has in some crucial ways disabled oppositional intellectuals in the task they have inherited from the generation of the 1960s. Despite its demystification of the anthropologos and the institutional compart-mentalization (into what is called *disciplines*) of the indissoluble field of forces (that is, the field of *knowledge*), it has remained in practice *essentially* humanist and disciplinary. Using the insights of posthumanist theory understood not as a series of discreet and antagonistic discourses, but as a discourse the parts of which, however unevenly, are in dialogic relationship, I will articulate in the last chapter in a provisional way the un-thought and unsaid of the protest movement. I will thematize the affirmative theoretical/practical implications for higher education symptomatically disclosed by the university's self-destruction: its "crisis of command" and the ensuing "refusal of spon-taneous consent" to its discursive practices during and immediately after the Vietnam War.

SIX

THE INTELLECTUAL AND THE POSTHUMANIST OCCASION

TOWARD A DECENTERED *PAIDEIA*

Expect poison from standing water.

William Blake, *The Marriage of Heaven and Hell*

That an education with this goal and this result ["the cultivation
of the 'history sense' which produces the historical-aesthetic
cultural philistine . . . the man who appreciates everything, the
insatiable stomach which nonetheless does not know what honest
hunger and thirst are"] is an anti-natural one is apprehensible
only to one who has not yet been fully processed by it; it is
apprehensible only to the instinct of youth, for youth still
possesses that instinct of nature which remains intact until
artificially and forcibly shattered by this education. He who
wants, on the contrary, to shatter this education has to help
youth to speak out, he has to light the path their unconscious
resistance has hitherto taken with the radiance of concepts and
transform it to a conscious and loudly vocal awareness.

Friedrich Nietzsche, *On the Uses and Disadvantages of History
for Life*

The oppositional discourse and practice of the protest movement during the decade of
the Vietnam War were symptomatic gestures and, as such, were both productive in
revealing the contradictions of the idea of the humanistic university and futile in their
failure to enable a praxis commensurable with their symbolic function. What, then, are
the educational imperatives disclosed by the irruption of repressed or accommodated
historical subjects in the late 1960s and early 1970s? Despite the self-destruction of
humanistic practice and the postmodern theoretical demystification of the discourse of
deliverance, the vast majority of professors of the humanities and the custodians of the
culture industry continue to believe in the ultimate legitimacy of this discourse and to
assume the truthfulness of the fiction of the saving remnant. Indeed, this belief has
been visibly enforced by the events of 1989 in Eastern and Central Europe and of 1991
in the Middle East (and by the revelation of Paul de Man's early collaborationist jour-

nalism and of Heidegger's extended association with German National Socialism). Given the inertia of the university, it would be quixotic to proffer a comprehensive program of institutional transformation detailing changes in curricula, institutional organization, and pedagogy grounded in the adversarial perspective of posthumanist theory. Such a program would be self-contradictory, moreover, since it would entail a reappropriation of the machinery of authority that posthumanist theory has attempted to de-authorize in behalf of the principle of contestatory dialogue.

Instead, it will be more useful to suggest in general what the decentering of the anthropologos and the making visible of the relay of binary oppositions it has constituted demand of the adversarial intellectual—both as research scholar and as teacher of college and university students—in an institution that continues to resist recognizing the contradictions in its cultural agenda being exposed by the emergence of otherness all across the continuum of being.

To justify these imperatives, however, it will be necessary to recall the argument for reconciling the ontological critique of the ontotheological tradition at large with the historically specific critique of the modern disciplinary society: destruction and genealogy. For, as I have suggested, to focus a critique of higher education in terms exclusively of destruction or of genealogy is to reinscribe the crisis of the university within the false (disciplinary) terms of the "two cultures." The one becomes a rarified theoretical exercise that leaves the historically overdetermined economic-sociopolitical domain elaborated by positive science and technology more or less intact. The other becomes a praxis that leaves the traditionally understood cultural domain elaborated by the ontology of metaphysics—the discourse of poetic Humanism—more or less intact: it tends, that is, to exculpate the cultural agencies—philosophy, literature, art, and the criticism and commentary that legitimate and reproduce them—of complicity with the disciplinary society. To put it another way, the latter tends to blind its practitioners to the degree to which this agenda of culture, especially its commitment to the "sovereign subject," has become in our century the privileged means of hegemony. By naturalizing the anthropologos, high academic culture generates spontaneous and universal consent, in the subaltern classes, to the imperial values of the dominant sociopolitical order. This is the lesson precipitated by the massive representation of the revolutions in the Soviet Bloc by the cultural apparatuses of the West as the triumph of the principle of individual freedom over the socialist collectivity.

In thematizing the affiliative relationship between the specular/circular metaphysical thinking of the ontotheological tradition at large and the panoptic discourse and practices of the post-Enlightenment, I am suggesting that the two cultures—and the "individual" disciplines within each—are, however diverse on the surface, ultimately one: they work according to a self-confirming recollective problematic that determines the meaning of difference in the enlightening light of the privileged Apollonian principle of identity. I am also suggesting that this critical disclosure is itself the consequence of a mode of inquiry that has its condition of possibility in difference; it understands structures of identity not as naturally given but as derivative—that is, as socially constituted and thus available to differential transformations.

However diverse the manifestations of posthumanist theory—Heidegger's destruction, Derrida's deconstruction, Lacan's psychoanalysis, Kristeva's semiotics, Foucault's genealogy, Althusser's neo-Marxism—this diversity is essentially a matter of the specific sites of knowledge chosen as the focus of engagement: ontology, textuality, the psyche, gender relations, history, material production. Taking a cue from the disclosures of the contradictions exposed by the fulfillment (the coming to its end) of the discursive practice of anthropology in this "age of the world picture," each writer ultimately proceeds according to a circular mode of inquiry that, by way of putting the forestructure—the constituted self or center—at risk (in crisis), always already discovers or repeats difference at the "end" of the process of inquiry. What Heidegger says theoretically about the hermeneutical circle vis-à-vis being (ontology)—*if "the most primordial kind of knowing" he refers to is understood as an originative thinking that retrieves the differential temporality of being from the spatialized or reified Being of anthropology*—applies as well, despite theoretical disagreements, to the critical practice of Derrida, Lacan, Kristeva, Foucault, Althusser, and a number of other posthumanist theorists: to the deconstructive reading of a text, to the Lacanian reading of the subject, to the semiotic reading of sexual identity, to the genealogical reading of the history of the disciplinary society, and to the neo-Marxist reading of advanced capitalism:

> *But if we see this circle as a vicious one and look out for ways of avoiding it* [as the objective or disinterested anthropologist does], *then the act of understanding has been misunderstood from the ground up.* . . . . If the basic conditions which make interpretation possible are to be fulfilled, this must rather be done by not failing to reorganize beforehand the essential conditions under which it can be performed. What is decisive is not to get out of the circle but to come into it in the right way. This circle of understanding is not an orbit in which any random kind of knowledge may move; it is the expression of the existential *fore-structure* of Dasein itself. It is not to be reduced to the level of a vicious circle, or even of a circle which is merely tolerated. In this circle is hidden a positive possibility of the most primordial kind of knowing. To be sure, we genuinely take hold of this possibility only when, in our interpretation, we have understood that our first, last, and constant task is never to allow our fore-having, fore-sight, and fore-conception to be presented to us by fancies, and popular conceptions, but rather to make the scientific theme secure by working out these fore-structures in terms of the things themselves.[1]

Impelled by the existential care or interest of being-in-the-world, each of these modes of inquiry pursues the "commonsense" logic of the alleged natural structure it engages to the point where this structure disintegrates. Each, that is, discloses the *aporia*—the absence of presence (or center)—this second-order humanist logic (problematic) would conceal or, alternatively, the temporally disseminated difference it would exclude or colonize; the difference, in other words, which is in fact the condition of the possibility of structure.

In short, each mode forces the "center elsewhere" of the ontotheological narrative into visibility (discloses it as a construct) and thus enables the critical play of the difference it had hitherto repressed. What I want to add to Heidegger's all-too-disciplinary epistemological project is a realization that the difference thus decolonized is not limited to an ontological category. It is, we recall, a relay of worldly differences: temporality, the non-identical self, the feminine, "low" or "popular" culture, the an-*archic* cultural object, racial minorities, the working class, peoples of the Third World, and all those "others" that have in some degree emerged in and by means of the discursive practice of the posthumanist occasion.

If the decentering of the anthropologos (partially) theorized by this broadly de-structive mode of inquiry is understood as a decentering that occurs simultaneously, if unevenly, throughout the indissoluble field of forces constituting being-in-the-world, then the essential implication of the symptomatic explosion of a multiplicity of cultural and sociopolitical resistances in the late 1960s and early 1970s, especially on college and university campuses, becomes remarkably clear for oppositional intellectuals. To put it provisionally, they must focus their critical energies on dismantling the disciplinary structure of knowledge, *both horizontally and vertically*. Horizontally, because the traditional classification and compartmentalization of knowledge hides the hegemonic function of knowledge production and transmission, hides the affiliation between the discourse and practice of the human sciences and that of the physical sciences and their complicity with the repressive state apparatuses; at the same time, this compartmentalization renders differential (disciplinary) learning a matter not of direct repression, but of knowledge produced on behalf of normalization and consensus: the extension of the power of those who already have power. Vertically, because a merely horizontal dismantling—the retrieval of interdisciplinariness—does not, as such traditional liberal projects as the so-called humanities courses of the late 1940s and 1950s make clear, affect the transcendentally ordained hierarchical structure that privileges high culture against low culture. I am referring to the archive of literary, philosophical, artistic, and musical texts canonized by the anthropological discourse of the dominant culture that subordinates the massified texts produced by the "culture industry" of late capitalism as well as those carnivalesque texts (including the postmodern theoretical discourses celebrating play and/or *jouissance*), produced by "the people," women, racial minorities, the Third World, etc., which symptomatically or deliberately exist to undermine the *télos* of the official genres.

However decisive their demystification of the binary logic of logocentric thinking, the various practitioners of postmodern theory have failed to break out of the established disciplinary parameters. They tend in practice, despite their interrogation of boundaries, to limit critical inquiry to more or less specific sites, with only minimal (though quite suggestive) gestures of crossover into others. It is this general failure to fulfill the radical *transdisciplinary*[2] imperatives of the decentering of the anthropologos that accounts for the easy accommodation of a number of these discourses to the established curriculum; not the least, deconstruction and the new historicism. To put it another way, the tendency—this must be emphasized—of the various postmodernist theoretical discourses to work inside the university's disciplinary structure has, as the now highly visible example of the conflict between deconstructionist and Left social and neo-Marxist critics suggests, rendered these practitioners more like adversaries of each other's discourse—adversaries, furthermore, in the nonconflictual, rarified arena of institutional economy, where what is at stake is celebrity, professional advancement, and rate of consumption—than adversaries of the discourse and practice of the dominant culture at large.[3] As such they inadvertently tend to fulfill the productive and hegemonic ends of the disciplinary logic of division and mastery, the logic, that is, which constituted the sovereign subject and the sovereign disciplines. The theoretical recognition of the polyglossic necessity of a nonfoundational mode of inquiry to always already reexamine its own discourse is what distinguishes posthumanist thinking in general from the monoglossic "pluralist" discursive practices of "disinterested" humanist inquiry. In some sense the debates internal to "theory" are symptomatic evidence of this openness to self-criticism. But the failure to theorize the positive possibilities of this absolute imperative of a mode of inquiry professing the decentered center as point of departure is disabling. The particular difference retrieved by a particular discourse must, of course, be understood in its own historically specific terms. As Gayatri Spivak has shown, a critic, whether Western or non-Western, who undertakes a critique of patriarchal structures of modern India from a Western subject position without self-examination does violence rather than contributes to the project of decolonization.[4] But in focusing *too* exclusively on a chosen disciplinary site, the practitioner of a particular postmodern discourse is too often blinded by his or her particular insight to the nonfoundational point of departure of practitioners at other sites and thus to the relay of differences—the constituencies or blocs of repressed—that affiliates their discourses in a common adversarial enterprise against the dominant culture. Such a practitioner will only repeat the situation that, for example, disabled the student uprising at Columbia: the mutual alienation of the black students and the white SDS.[5]

An example of this tendency of postmodern theory is the set of mutually exclusive discourses that divide and affiliate Heideggerian destructionists and Foucauldian genealogists. In pursuit of the retrieval of the ontological difference on the one hand, and of the "singular event" on the other, these two discourses have been blinded to the relationship between metaphysics (re-presentation/oversight) and the disciplinary society (panopticism/super-vision) and thus to the relationship between the differences these reduce to identity: respectively, the difference temporality disseminates, and sociopolitical deviation. Such a critique can, in varying degrees, be extended to include most postmodern discursive practices. It can be applied to deconstruction, which in focusing its critical intervention on writing overlooks the historicity of discourse and sociopolitical differences (the working class, sociopolitical deviants, the Third World, etc.); to neo-Marxism, which in focusing on the means of production as determinant "in the last instance" minimizes the relationship between the proletariat and ontological, sexual, political, and even cultural differences; to new historicism, which in intervening at the site of historiography minimizes the sociopolitical configurations of the historicity it retrieves from History; to Lacanian psychoanalysis, which in focusing on the textualized subject minimizes the affiliation of the imaginative differences with the economic, social, and political differences contained in the symbolic order. It can also be applied to feminism—though in its poststructuralist version it is, of all the recent theoretical discourses, least susceptible to this critique—which, in focusing on gender, minimizes the relationship between the feminine difference (*jouissance*) and ontological difference (the play of difference) and sociopolitical differences (polyglossia).

This is, of course, a reductive and misleading account of these particular postmodern discourses. For each is characterized by significant crossovers into adjacent sites. For example, feminist criticism transgresses disciplinary boundaries by entering into the domain of textuality as understood by Derrida, psychoanalysis as understood by Lacan, and in some cases sociopolitics as understood by Marxists. Neo-Marxist criticism moves into the domain of culture and information. Heideggerian criticism crosses into the domain of technology and the "Europeanized" world picture. Since these crossovers are incompletely realized, however, they are symptomatic manifestations rather than deliberately articulated, fully theoretical understandings of the transdisciplinary critical imperatives of decentering the center/Capital.

This point can be further amplified and refined by reference to Edward Said's essay "Secular Criticism." In his brilliant genealogy of the contemporary Western intellectual class, Said proposes that the responsibility of the oppositional critic is to study "affiliation," the compensatory order constituted and elaborated in the late nineteenth and early twentieth centuries to recuperate the cultural and sociopolitical power delegitimated by the disintegration of natural filiation—"the generative impulse that justified the dynastic model of sociopolitical relations":

> In a certain sense, what I have been trying to show is that, as it has
> developed through the art and critical theories produced in complex ways by
> modernism, filiation gives birth to affiliation. Affiliation becomes a form of
> representing the filiative processes to be found in nature, although affiliation
> takes validated nonbiological social and cultural forms. Two alternatives
> propose themselves for the contemporary critic. One is organic complicity

with the pattern I have described. The critic enables, indeed transacts, the transfer of legitimacy from filiation to affiliation; literally, a midwife, the critic encourages reverence for the humanities and for the dominant culture served by those humanities. This keeps relationships within the narrow circle of what is natural, appropriate, and valid for "us," and thereafter excludes the non-literary, the non-European, and above all the political dimension in which all literature, all texts, can be found. It also gives rise to a critical system or theory whose temptation for the critic is that it resolves all the problems that culture gives rise to. . . .

The second alternative is for the critic to recognize the difference between instinctual filiation and social affiliation, and to show how affiliation sometimes reproduces filiation, sometimes makes its own forms. Immediately, then, most of the political and social world becomes available for critical and secular scrutiny. . . . This secular critical consciousness can also examine those forms of writing affiliated with literature but excluded from consideration with literature as a result of the ideological capture of the literary text within the humanistic curriculum as it now stands.[6]

In insisting that the function of the oppositional critic is to demystify the naturalness of cultural production, or as he puts it elsewhere, to "recreate the affiliative network," "to make visible, to give materiality back to, the strands holding the text to society, author and culture,"[7] Said is proposing a variation on my recommendation that the adversarial intellectual must recognize the indissoluble ideological continuum hidden behind the discrete sites of disinterested knowledge and make visible the complicity between this ideological relay and the dominant sociopolitical order. But in restricting oppositional criticism to the critical interrogation of the affiliative order, in limiting criticism to negation, Said fails to perceive (or refuses) the possibilities for collective praxis disclosed by the decentering of the anthropologos. Indeed, he betrays a vestigial and finally disabling commitment to the humanistic subject. Thus, no doubt against the grain of his project, to "study affiliation" should not simply be a matter of forcing the invisible relay of arbitrary power that runs from the texts privileged by the dominant culture through the sociopolitical order into the arena of the free play of criticism, but should also be, in accordance with the projective possibilities disclosed by destructive criticism or genealogy, a matter of recognizing and exploring the educational possibilities inhering in the relay of affiliated disaffiliations, the alienated organic "classes" decolonized by a critique of the affiliative order.

What the related decenterings demand of the oppositional intellectual is the recognition of the affiliative bonds between the specific sites of repressed and alienated knowledge, and thus a *collaborative* practice among the various species of posthumanist inquiry that thwarts the division of intellectual labor invented by the disciplinary society, which annuls collective intellectual practice and, by producing knowledge/power, extends and deepens the sway of hegemony. This is not to say, however, that the task of the posthumanist intellectual is to reduce the historically specific ontological, psychological, sexual, cultural, economic, legal, and sociopolitical differences to an identical totality. Such a project would simply reinscribe the totalizing and transhistorical model it would undermine. It would fall into the trap that Said has called "traveling theory." An interested discursive practice ought rather to engage the discursive practice of the dominant culture at the immediate site of *crisis*, the site that precipitated that particular interest. As Said puts it:

> Theory . . . can never be complete, just as one's interest in everyday life is never exhausted by simulacra, models, or theoretical abstracts of it. . . . I am arguing . . . that we distinguish theory from critical consciousness [by which he means the consciousness activated by the sudden irruption of a historically specific contradiction that betrays the totalizing "reality" to be a repressive fiction] by saying that the latter is a sort of spatial sense, a sort of measuring faculty for locating or situating theory, and this means that theory has to be grasped in the place and the time out of which it emerges as a part of that time, working in and for it, responding to it; then, consequently, that first place can be measured against subsequent places where the theory turns up for use. The critical consciousness is awareness of the differences between situations, awareness too of the fact that no system or theory exhausts the situation out of which it emerges or to which it is transported. And, above all, critical consciousness is awareness of the resistances to theory, reactions to it elicited by those concrete experiences or interpretations with which it is in conflict. Indeed, I would go as far as saying that it is the critic's job to provide resistances to theory, to open it up toward historical reality, toward society, toward human needs and interests, to point up those concrete instances drawn from everyday reality that lie outside or just beyond the interpretive area necessarily designated in advance and thereafter circumscribed by every theory.[8]

Nor do I not want to imply that collaborative practice would mean a recuperation, in the face of the delegitimation by Gramsci, Deleuze, Foucault, and others, of the traditional intellectual, the intellectual, in Deleuze's term, as "representing and representative consciousness," who from a panoptic subject position speaks the truth *for* those diverse sociopolitically oppressed groups "who [have] yet to see it."[9] The intellectual I am projecting is, if we interpret the struggle against "a system of power" in terms of a *relay* of local and regional struggles, akin to the one Foucault, no doubt with Gramsci in mind, characterizes (in a way that seems to be contradicted in his later work by his tendency to abstract the operation of power/knowledge) in the wake of the "events of May 1968":

In the most recent upheaval, the intellectual discovered that the masses no longer need him to gain knowledge: they *know* perfectly well, without illusion; they know far better than he and they are certainly capable of expressing themselves. But there exists a system of power which blocks, prohibits, and invalidates this discourse and this knowledge, a power not only found in the manifest authority of censorship, but one that profoundly and subtly penetrates an entire societal network. Intellectuals are themselves agents of this system of power—the idea of their responsibility for "consciousness" and discourse forms part of the system. The intellectual's role is no longer to place himself "somewhat ahead and to the side" in order to express the stifled truth of the collectivity; rather, it is to struggle against the forms of power that transform him into its object and instrument in the sphere of "knowledge," "truth," "consciousness," and "discourse."

In this sense theory does not express, translate, or serve to apply practice; it is practice. But it is local and regional . . . and not totalizing. This is a struggle against power, a struggle aimed at revealing and undermining power where it is most invisible and insidious. It is not to "awaken consciousness" that we struggle . . . but to sap power, to take power; it is an activity conducted alongside those who struggle for power, and not illumination from a safe distance. A "theory" is the regional system of their struggle. ("IP," p. 208)

In other words, the essential task of oppositional intellectuals is to free themselves from the institutional role tradition has assigned them, the role, in Paul Bové's resonant phrase, of "leading intellectual"[10] that renders them—even traditional radicals like Richard Ohmann—agents of the "regime of truth," of a "system of power" that, in the name of "universal truth," "blocks, prohibits, and invalidates" the knowledge and discourse of the oppressed fraction and more immediately, by way of annulling its specific occasion, the knowledge and discourse of the intellectual class. To conflate Said's understanding of the oppositional intellectual as "critical consciousness"—the consciousness that emerges in and from the immediate context of crisis—with Foucault's " 'specific' intellectual"[11] in terms of a version of Gramsci appropriate to the cultural and sociopolitical occasion obtaining in North America, they should become "organic intellectuals."[12] They should recognize themselves and the institutional context in which they labor as but one site, however crucial, in a relay of unevenly developed and asymmetrical sites of repression. Their "theoretical" activity, therefore, must be seen as a local and regional praxis, but one at the same time conducted alongside those other blocs that struggle for power.

The affiliative relay of disaffiliated constituencies disclosed by leaping into the hermeneutic circle primordially and wholly—*interestedly*—calls into question the oppositional project of the totalizing ("universal") intellectual: the traditional Marxist, for example.

Yet it justifies the collaborative project of intellectuals in different local and regional disciplines just as it links intellectuals as a class with those particular blocs—workers, women, gays, blacks, ethnic minorities, and youth—whose struggle is activated by their own organic occasion, their own specific interest. If the operation of power he wishes to focalize is itself informed and enabled by the panoptic/circular principle that identity is the condition for the possibility of difference, this is what Foucault says in his critique of the Marxist identification of power with economic exploitation in the following passage:

> As soon as we struggle against exploitation, the proletariat not only leads the struggle but also defines its targets, its methods, and the places and instruments for confrontation; and to ally oneself with the proletariat is to accept its positions, its ideology, and its motives for combat. This means total identification. But if the fight is directed against power, then all those on whom power is exercised to their detriment, all who find it intolerable, can begin the struggle on their own terrain and on the basis of their proper activity (or passivity). In engaging in a struggle that concerns their own interests, whose objective they clearly understand and whose methods only they can determine, they enter into a revolutionary process. They naturally enter as allies of the proletariat, because power is exercised the way it is in order to maintain capitalist exploitation. They genuinely sense the cause of the proletariat by fighting in those places where they find themselves oppressed. Women, prisoners, conscripted soldiers, hospital patients, or homosexuals have now begun a specific struggle against the particularized power, the constraints and controls, that are exerted over them. . . . And their movements are linked to the revolutionary movement of the proletariat to the extent that they fight against the controls and constraints which serve the same system of power. ("IP," p. 216)

II

In insisting that the theoretical practice of oppositional intellectuals ought to be a local and regional struggle aimed at revealing and undermining power, Foucault, like the critical theorists of the Frankfurt School before him (Horkheimer, Adorno, and Marcuse) locates this struggle at the site of culture in general, where by means of the discursive practices that constitute it, power is "most invisible and insidious." I want to suggest, by way of a specifying qualification based on a curious but telling historical oversight on the part of critical theorists of the post-Vietnam decade (who shifted the focus of critique from the economy of material production to the hegemonic economy of culture), that this struggle should be waged at the site of the educational institution in general and the university in particular. As I have suggested in focusing on the student revolt in the United States, in France, in Germany, and elsewhere in the West (and Japan) in the late 1960s, it is in the operations of education more than any other cultural apparatus elaborated by modern liberal bourgeois capitalist Western societies — more than in family, church, political system, information and entertainment media — that power is "most invisible and insidious." It is the school, in other words, that employs what I have been calling the "hegemonic discourse of deliverance" most effectively in disciplining the young and reproducing the dominant sociopolitical order. While other ideological cultural apparatuses are situated in the material world and, as in the case of the media's coverage of the revolutions in Eastern Europe or the American response to Iraq's invasion of Kuwait, partake more or less visibly in its productive operations, the school is represented fundamentally as a separate and value-free space in which the pursuit of knowledge is undertaken for the benefit of all "mankind," if not for knowledge's own sake.

The only European theoretician who, in the aftermath of the events of May 1968, recognized the fundamental importance of the schools in reproducing the dominant sociopolitical order was Louis Althusser:

> [It] is by an apprenticeship in a variety of know-how wrapped up in the massive inculcation of the ideology of the ruling class that the *relations of production* in a capitalist social formation, i.e. the relations of exploited to exploiters and exploiters to exploited, are largely reproduced. The mechanisms which produce this vital result for the capitalist regime are naturally covered up and concealed by a universally reigning ideology of the School, universally reigning because it is one of the essential forms of the ruling bourgeois ideology: an ideology which represents the School as a neutral environment purged of ideology (because it is . . . lay), where teachers respectful of the "conscience" and "freedom" of the children who are entrusted to them (in complete confidence) by their "parents" (who are free, too, i.e. the owners of their children) open up for them the path to the freedom, morality and responsibility of adults by their own example, by knowledge, literature and their "liberating" virtues.[13]

In theorizing the disclosure of the symptomatic events of May 1968 in terms of "the School" in general, however, Althusser overlooked the historically specific focus of the struggle. He minimized the critical role the university plays in the transmission of the ideology of the ruling class and the reproduction of the power relations of late capitalist societies. Characteristic of his "scientific" Marxist discourse, in other words, Althusser derived his totalizing conclusions about the primacy of the educational apparatus more from his theory of history than from history itself. In overlooking the fact that the events of May 1968 in France were precipitated by *university students*, he, like most postmodern critics of the dominant social order — including those affiliated with the "critical pedagogy" movement, who have revised Althusser's "scientism"—also failed to perceive what the student's refusal of spontaneous consent to the dominant discourse had symptomatically disclosed: that "youth"—by which I mean that transitional or, what is the same thing, *critical* stage between adolescence and adulthood—was not simply one more second (minority) term in the relay of binary oppositions that characterizes the logic of anthropology and empowers the dominant sociopolitical order, but one that, however asymmetrically, *includes* all the others.[14]

Postmodern theory—neo-Marxist, deconstruction, genealogy, new historicism, critical theory—has not adequately thought the relationship between the student revolt in the late 1960s and the simultaneous precipitation of what has been called the generation gap: the emergence for the first time in Western history of a youth culture, a symptomatic consciousness on the part of the young of their "oppression" by an institution of learning (and its pedagogical apparatuses) representing a sociopolitical order perennially validated, empowered, and reproduced by the privileged status it gives to adulthood in the name of the prolific metaphysically derived opposition between maturity and immaturity. For all its demystifications of the various empowering binary oppositions enabled by the center elsewhere of anthropological discursive practices—identity/difference, speech/writing, reason/madness, truth/error, male/female, white/black, west/east, and civilization/barbarism—postmodern theory has failed to perceive (in a way that conservative or liberal humanists like Bloom, Bennett, Bate, and Hirsch have not) that these oppositions constitute a massively reinforced relay that gives identity to the university. As a result, it has also failed to see that it is the essential function of the university more than any other cultural apparatus (situated as such a microcosm of the sociopolitical macrocosm at the intersection between the world of adolescence and the world of adulthood) to inscribe this relay of oppositions in the young in order to reproduce the dominant sociopolitical order. Despite their common critique of what is variously called the "representative," the "general," the "universal," the "traditional," the "leading" or the "sublime" intellectual—the intellectual who, having achieved "maturity," is authorized to speak for all the others who have not (and their common insistence that these "others" should be allowed to speak for themselves)—there is remarkably little evidence in postmodern oppositional discourses to suggest awareness of the implications of this critique for pedagogy. Not even Jacques Derrida's otherwise immensely suggestive essay, "The Principle of Reason: The University in the Eyes of Its Pupils," fully addresses the most crucial because most inclusive emergent historical subject: the university student.[15]

The theorization of the student protest movement and the irruption of the "generation gap" during the Vietnam decade suggest imperatives of opposition that modify without annulling Foucault's insistence that the struggle of intellectuals should be local and regional. If the university as a locus of struggle is understood as a microcosmic, ideological state apparatus, intellectuals—both as scholars and as teachers—must come to understand that the local struggle involves a paradoxically global dimension that is simultaneously local: the systematic demystification and disempowerment of the relay of ideological binary oppositions informing the maturity/immaturity opposition. They must realize that it is this inclusive opposition on which the traditional university, in the name of culture but in behalf of sociopolitical colonization, fundamentally relies to inscribe the relay of "mature" identities—psychological, sexual, cultural, social, political, and international—in the student body, both undergraduate and graduate.

This means, above all, that there is need for a demystification of one of the most basic myths of the oppressor ideology: what Paolo Freire calls "the absolutizing of ignorance."[16] It means a decentering of the traditional relationship between the scholar-teacher and the student, which in order to facilitate "deliverance" from the bondage of uncultivated passion puts the former in a privileged (supervisory) position over the latter. The essential—because "naturally" given—assumption informing the raison d'être of the traditional humanist university, the repository of the mature fruits of civilization, is that it constitutes a site offering the uncultivated or "ignorant" individual student an "opportunity" for "self-fulfillment." As a consequence of this assumption, students—especially minority students hitherto denied the opportunity of higher education—are expected to feel grateful to the liberal society that in its knowing largesse offers them such an opportunity to achieve fruition (and they largely do). The student protest movement during the Vietnam War demystified this assumption. In precipitating a resistant youth culture, it disclosed students at large, however heterogeneous, to be a body of subjected subjects; a class of oppressed, as it were, insofar as the end of such a liberal education came to be seen as the colonization and pacification of youth's youthfulness. I mean that revolutionary energy—so important to Nietzsche's critique of modern European culture—which in the name of maturity the binarist discourse of a humanist such as Allan Bloom reduces and demonizes by representing it as "Dionysiac," "barbarous," "uncivilized," "ignorant," "errant," "prodigal," and so on. As such a class, youth takes its "proper" place, in an affiliative relationship to the relay of classes—workers, racial and ethnic minorities, women, gays, etc.—disaffiliated by the dominant sociopolitical order. One of the essential tasks demanded of adversarial intellectuals, a task largely ignored both in theory and practice, is to think their relationship to students in terms of this disclosure.

To reduce the student body in the liberal society to such a general and homogeneous local class or bloc is, however, to obscure (as Nietzsche does) its crucially resonant heterogeneity, the fact that it consists of elements representing a cross-section of all the constituencies in the visibly productive world that the dominant sociopolitical order assimilates and exploits for their use value. Students are also females, blacks, working-class, ethnics, gays, Third World, and so on. In so far as the youth culture that emerged in the 1960s was constituted of such diverse groups, it exposed not only the prejudice of the liberal university against youth in general but also against these specific but interrelated constituencies of the young. It exposed traditional liberal education to be a practice of repressive accommodation: the colonization and domestication of the revolutionary energy of the young and of their class consciousness (femininity, black-ness, ethnicity, gayness, etc.) in the name of normalization. It revealed the self-under-standing of the university's progressive inclusion of these errant "minorities" within its "liberal" framework as developmental—as the gradualist fulfillment of the romance of the *litterae humaniores*—to be, in fact, a strategy designed to transform young women into "men," blacks into "whites," Hispanics into "Americans," gays into "straights," and so on, in behalf of an imperial economy. It is worth recalling the example cited earlier in a different context of the mounting critique by black intellectuals of the "whiteness" of the newly "democratized" post-Vietnam university: the Euroamerican-ness of the expanded core curriculum and equally the standard Englishness of the tran-sitional year writing programs increasingly appended to the university structure to provide educational "opportunities" for ghetto blacks:

> Blacks would be allowed on the campus as a group, admitted to have even a culture, as long as this "culture" and its related enclave studies could be made to function as the extra-cultural space, in relation, no longer to a Wasp, but now more inclusively to a White American, normatively Euroamerican intra-cultural space; as the mode of Chaos imperative to the latter's new self-ordering. (The re-adapted Western culture Core Curriculum is the non-conscious expression of this more "democratizing" shift from Wasp to Euro.) Indeed once this marginalization had been effected, the order of value recycled in different terms, with the category homeostasis returning to its "built-in normalcy," the abuse and bomb threats ceased. Order and Chaos were once more in their relational interdefining places, stably expressing the bio-ontological principle of Sameness and Difference of the present order, as the rule-governed discourse of Galileo's doctors of philosophy functioned to verify the physico-ontological mode of Sameness and Difference on which the Christian medieval order rested before the *Studia* [*Humanitatis*] and Copernicus, before the Jester's heresy of the figures of rogue/clown/fool, had pulled the "high seriousness" of its self-justifying self-representation down to earth.[17]

Given this revealed yet obscured context, it should be evident that oppositional in-tellectuals in their capacity as scholars and teachers must struggle against their tradi-tional roles as leading or representative intellectuals, who "place [themselves] 'somewhat ahead and to the side'" of students "in order to express the stifled truth of the collectivity." They must resist the arrogance or condescension accompanying this role in behalf of establishing a dialogic space in which both teachers and students un-derstand themselves as organic intellectuals: as mutually, if differently, oppressed by the central and centering discursive practices of the liberal humanist institution. The achievement of such a dialogic environment is no easy task. Oppositional teachers are propelled in their research and pedagogical practice by the momentum of institutional centeredness and the rules of discursive formation to which it gives rise. This is especially evident in the tendency of the various proponents of theory to teach in competition with one another rather than pose the hitherto unasked questions concerning education that their discourses have disclosed. As a result, theory becomes academically cultist, the proponent of a particular theoretical approach a priestly authority and his/her students acolytes: "Heideggerians," "Derridians," "de Manians," "Lacanians," "Althusserians," "Kristevans," "Habermasians," and so on.

This unfortunate consequence of the failure to transform pedagogy according to the imperatives of decentering is nowhere more forcefully evident than in the predictable unitary response of de Manians — especially his former students — to the recent disclosure of his early journalistic criticism for a prominent collaborationist Belgian newspaper, which suggests de Man's political complicity with German National Socialism.[18] In virtually every case their responses have been defenses of de Man that rationalize the revelations of this period by interpreting his early writing retrospectively in terms of his later philosophy of deconstruction. In other words, either the early writing was a youthful mistake, the guilt over which precipitated a radically textual theory of deconstruction ultimately intended to reveal that his initial commitment to decidability and the possibility of sociopolitical praxis originally led him to espouse such illiberal Eurocentric political views (Christopher Norris and Geoffrey Hartman for example);[19] or his later deconstruction was the theoretical fulfillment of the latent or indirect antifascism implicit in his early exposure of the complicity between the German aestheticization of philosophy and political totalitarianism (Cynthia Chase).[20] In the first instance, the defense circumvents the very question that, according to politically left postmodern theorists, de Man's version of deconstruction refuses to engage: the question of the politics of deconstruction. In the second instance, the defense minimizes, if it does not entirely bypass, the concrete evidence of what de Man actually wrote in this early period.

My point is not to take a negative stand on the issue of de Man's ethics (though I am troubled by his, as well as Heidegger's, sustained silence in the face of his ever greater influence in the Academy). Nor do I want to focus on the question of the politics of his version of deconstruction (although I have argued elsewhere — and long ago — that, *insofar* as it pursues the logic of textuality to its extreme, it repeats in reverse the apolitical political ethics of the New Criticism).[21] Indeed, I would "defend" de Man's deconstructive discourse (as I have elsewhere Heidegger's), despite his early practice, as essentially emancipatory against those humanists who have crudely appropriated these revelations to discredit his later texts and to recuperate the diminished authority of the anthropological discourse. My point, instead, is to show the degree to which an oppositional intellectual who does not heed the dialogic imperatives of decenteredness repeats the power relations within pedagogy that his or her discourse in fact undermines.

Students, on the other hand, have inherited the general legacy of the 1960s, especially the thematization of pedagogical relevance, which has rendered the traditional hierarchical structure of the teacher/student relationship more problematic and the classroom a more uneasy space. But because this legacy continues to remain unthought, it has been all too easily co-opted in the devious name of pluralism. This, however, is not necessarily a purely negative and disabling situation. For such an unsettled activity in the ideological apparatuses of the university calls attention to the temptation on the part of the adversarial teacher to reinscribe an alternative authoritarian "overview" and on the part of the student to remain a passive receptor of its monologic discourse in favor of a context of mutual questioning.

The pedagogical project of committed (interested) teachers in this decentered context thus begins with *respect* for the students they encounter in (and out of) the classroom, a respect that has its origin in the acknowledgment of the decentered occasion and the students' *interest*. Such respect begins with the recognition that the teacher's experience of repression is not the students' experience of repression, however affiliated these are. It inhibits the teacher's inscribed impulse to interpret the students' experience for them, instigating instead what Freire aptly calls "a generative thematic" context[22] that would allow them, both as an organic collective of youth and as particular and differential instances of this collective, to think and speak their experiences themselves. In thus dismantling the pyramidal structure concealed behind the pluralism of traditional liberal pedagogical practice, such a context enables a reciprocal deconstructive learning process, one in which the oppositional teacher becomes a student and the interested student a teacher.

Paolo Freire's revolutionary "problem-posing" pedagogy has its occasion in the plight of the Latin American peasant; the effects of oppression on these students are more obvious than those of the "benign" oppression of affluent students of developed Western nations. But his refusal to romanticize their consciousness of this oppression—to minimize their uncritical adhesion to the dominant bourgeois capitalist ideology— suggests itself by analogy as a fundamental structure of oppositional pedagogy in the modern North American university. I quote from *Pedagogy of the Oppressed* at length to suggest, in the face of its unwarranted neglect by oppositional intellectuals (probably because of its "limited" focus on the site of education or its radical historicity), the significant contribution it makes to the postmodern interrogation of the imperial discursive practices of cultural hegemony and to the exploration of the positive (and revolutionary) cultural and sociopolitical possibilities this interrogation has disclosed:

> Liberating education consists in acts of cognition, not transferals of
> information. It is a learning situation in which the cognizable object (far from
> being the end of the cognitive act) intermediates the cognitive actors—
> teacher on the one hand and students on the other. Accordingly, the practice
> of problem-posing education entails at the outset that the teacher-student

contradiction be resolved. Dialogic relations—indispensable to the capacity of cognitive actors to cooperate in perceiving the same cognizable object—are otherwise impossible. Indeed, problem-posing education, which breaks with the vertical patterns characteristic of banking education [as "an act of depositing, in which the students are the depositories and the teachers the depositors"], can fulfill its function as the practice of freedom only if it can overcome the above contradiction. Through dialogue, the teacher-of-the-students and the students-of-the-teacher cease to exist and a new term emerges: teacher-student with students-teachers. The teacher is no longer merely the one-who-teaches, but one who is himself taught in dialogue with the students, who in return while being taught also teach. They become partly responsible for a process in which all grow. In this process, arguments based on "authority" are no longer valid; in order to function, authority must be *on the side of* freedom, not *against* it. Here, no one teaches another, nor is anyone self-taught. Men teach each other, mediated by the world, by the cognizable objects which in banking education are "owned" by the teacher. . . .

The problem-posing method does not dichotomize the activity of the teacher-student; he is not "cognitive" at one point [in his/her study] and "narrative" at another [in the classroom]. He is always "cognitive," whether preparing a project or engaging in dialogue with the students. He does not regard cognizable objects as his private property, but as the object of reflection by himself and the students. In this way, the problem-posing educator constantly re-forms his reflection in the reflections of the students. The students—no longer docile listeners—are now critical co-investigators in dialogue with the teacher. The teacher presents the material to the students for their consideration, and re-considers his earlier considerations as the students express their own. The role of the problem-posing educator is to create, together with the students, the conditions under which knowledge at the level of *doxa* is superseded by true knowledge at the level of the *logos*.

Whereas banking education anesthetizes and inhibits creative power, problem-posing education involves a constant unveiling of reality. The former attempts to maintain the *submersion* of consciousness; the latter strives for the *emergence* of consciousness and *critical intervention* in reality. (*PO*, pp. 67-68)[23]

In thus "breaking with the vertical patterns" characteristic of traditional humanistic pedagogy, oppositional pedagogy becomes problematic and existential. The teacher descends into the arena of differential history, where difference, because it is ontologically prior to identity, really makes a difference. In such an arena of crisis, the teacher becomes an *active* intellectual, and the student becomes an *intellectual* activist. In the agora, the theory of the Olympian teacher becomes praxis and the practice of the stu-

dent becomes theoretical. As such, pedagogy becomes reciprocally re-visionary (originative) and the knowledge that emerges from dialogue is not the universal and eternal
knowledge of a lofty *doxa* but the temporal and differential knowledge of *logoi*: always
already revolutionary.

On the one hand, the "mature" teacher relearns existentially from the "immature"
student what the restricted institutional economy of maturation has submerged and repressed: what it *feels* like to be reduced to an object of the "matured" disciplinary gaze.
This renewed knowledge, in turn, always already deconstructs the inscribed temptation to *theorize*—to totalize, universalize, and rarify—theory in favor of addressing the
historical specificity of the pedagogical occasion. On the other hand, the "immature"
student learns from the "mature" teacher what it *means* to be reduced to such an object of the panoptic disciplinary eye. This knowledge, in turn, not only instigates the
student's *e-mergent* consciousness, but also enlarges this awareness to encompass
awareness of his or her affiliation with other specific emergent consciousnesses.

What Freire means in the above passage by the "creative power" that a dialogic
problem-posing pedagogy would liberate, it should be emphasized, is not what it is represented to mean in the humanistic tradition: self-fulfillment. As his insistence on the
causal relationship between "emergence" from "submergence" and "critical intervention" suggests, it means rather a critical consciousness (Freire calls it *conscientização*),[24] a consciousness that is simultaneously critical and productive. Through the act
of dialogue both teacher and student partake in a *"constant* unveiling of reality" (my
emphasis) not simply the critical demystification or decoding of the oppressive "universe of themes" that characterizes the socially constituted "reality" of bourgeois capitalist culture, but also and simultaneously the release and exploration of the *"untested
feasibility"* which "those who are served by" the dominant discourse "regard as threatening" and thus act "to disallow its materialization" (*PO*, p. 92). In the terms of my
text, "creative power" means *de-structive* consciousness, that is, a consciousness simultaneously destructive and projective: e-mergent. The "constant unveiling of reality" achieved by the dialogue between teacher and student is at once a delegitimation of
the oppressive hegemonic discourse of the dominant cultural order and the liberation,
the decolonization, of the knowledge this discourse represses and conceals by sub-
merging or colonizing it. In the context of the North American university, Freire's "untested feasibility" is, to appropriate Derrida's Nietzschean terms, the "force" of youth
and the "force" of the multiplicity of otherness all along the lateral continuum of being
that this category of being-in-the-world embodies and which it is the ultimate purpose
of hegemony to colonize and pacify: by inculcating identities that take their *proper*
places in the imperial whole.

The dialogic space opened up by the historical decentering of the center and the
consequent breaking with the traditional vertical patterns of knowledge transmission
demand a pedagogical practice of repetition rather than recollection: one that, beginning in the midst (*interesse*), retrieves in the destructive circular process the *youthful-*

ness of youth and the differential energies it embodies. Analogous to the traditional interpretation of a text, entering the pedagogical circle with the end (*télos*) already inscribed generates a derivative, calculating, and erosive thinking, a thinking of colonized and docile bodies in the service of the dominant sociopolitical order whether conceived as disciplinary society or imperial state. Entering it wholly and primordially enables a dialogic thinking simultaneously *theoria* and *praxis* (ek-sistent in-sistence). In other words, it enables a thinking that is at once fully aware of the coerciveness of the comprehensive (narrative) structure repeatedly reconstituted and imposed on historically specific knowledge by the Western suprahistorical consciousness—by the panoptic cultural memory epitomized in modernity by the theoretical discourses of Arnold, Babbitt, Richards, Bloom, and Hirsch, and the institutional practices of Columbia University in the aftermath of World War I, and by Harvard University in the aftermaths of World War II and the Vietnam War, and negatively capable of always acting futurally. To enter the pedagogical circle dialogically provides the occasion, not for *training* in good citizenship, *eruditio et institutio in bonas artes*, but for the activation of critical consciousness on behalf of the perpetual renewal of a truly diversified culture and the perpetual revolution of a truly diversified (democratic) *polis*.

This is what Nietzsche means in his historical reversal of the symbolic binary opposition between Apollo and Dionysus that has determined the official modern understanding of Greek culture: of the ideal of textual interpretation, of the ideal *paideia*, of the ideal *polis*—and its representation of the forces, not least the force of youth, that threaten it. It is also this insight, instigated by his perception of the emergent knowledge contradictorily exposed by the "maturation"—the coming to its end—of Western culture, that drives Nietzsche's ironical invoking of the "universal [suprahistorically determined] history" so basic to Hegel's discourse and that of his "grey-haired" humanist offspring as the pedagogical agent of retrieving the "unhistorical culture" of the Greeks from its codified, sedimented, and enfeebled old age:

> For the origin of historical culture—its quite radical conflict with the spirit of any "new age," any "modern awareness"—this origin *must* itself be known historically, history *must* itself resolve the problem of history, knowledge *must* turn its sting against itself—this threefold *must* is the imperative of the "new age." . . . Or is it actually the case that we . . . must always be no more than "heirs" in all the higher affairs of culture, because that is all we *can* ever be; a proposition once memorably expressed by Wilhelm Wackernagel. . . . And even if we Germans were really no more than heirs [of "the world of antiquity"]—to be able to look upon such a culture as *that* as our rightful inheritance would make the appellation "heirs" the greatest and proudest possible: yet we would nonetheless be obliged to ask whether it really was our eternal destiny to be *pupils of declining antiquity*: at some time or other we might be permitted gradually to set our goal higher and more distant,

some time or other we ought to be allowed to claim credit for having developed the spirit of Alexandrian-Roman culture so nobly and fruitfully—among other means through our universal history—that we might now as a reward be permitted to set ourselves the even mightier task of striving to get behind and beyond this Alexandrian world and boldly seek our models in the original ancient Greek world of greatness, naturalness and humanity. *But there we also discover the reality of an essentially unhistorical culture and one which is nonetheless, or rather on that account, an inexpressibly richer and more vital culture.* Even if we Germans were in fact nothing but successors—we could not be anything greater or prouder than successors if we appropriated such a culture and were the heirs and successors of that.

What I mean by this—and it is all I mean—is that the thought of being epigones, which can often be painful enough, is also capable of evoking great effects and grand hopes for the future in both an individual and in a nation provided we regard ourselves as the heirs and successors of the astonishing powers of antiquity and see in this our honour and our spur. What I do not mean, therefore, is that we should live as pale and stunted late descendants of strong races coldly prolonging their life as antiquarians and gravediggers.[25]

The reductive effects of a *paideia* determined by a suprahistorical perspective, according to Nietzsche in the passage that stands as the epigraph for this chapter, "is apprehensible only to the instinct of youth, for youth still possesses that instinct of nature which remains intact until artificially and forcefully shattered by this education. He who wants, on the contrary, to shatter this education has to help youth to speak out, he has to light the path their unconscious resistance has hitherto taken with the radiance of concepts and transform it to a conscious and loudly vocal awareness."[26]

It was in large part the failure of radical intellectuals during the decade of the Vietnam conflict to light the students' path of institutional resistance "with radiant concepts"—to think the positive pedagogical imperatives of spontaneous disturbances on American campuses in terms of the implications for a "new age" of a culture that has come to its enfeebled, if not dead, Apollonian end—that rendered the changes these youthful disturbances effected in the idea of the university, the curriculum, and institutional governance random and ephemeral. More specifically, the failure to establish a pedagogical context consonant with the decentered center—the kind of dialogic space articulated above—inhibited an adequate perception of this resonant affiliation and interplay between youth and maturity, energy and reflection, practice and theory. It thus made it all too easy for "antiquarian" custodians of the American university to interpret the disturbances retrospectively as the irrational action of youthful Dionysiac mobs and to reaffirm the "reformist" Apollonian/Roman principle when the sociopolitical crisis had subsided. Despite the momentous demystification of the disinterested discourse of deliverance by postmodern theory at large, this failure of intellectuals to theorize the end of the humanist *paideia* continues to disable oppositional pedagogy in the present.[27]

III

In focusing on the question of the teacher/student relationship, I do not want to imply that the decentered occasion renders it prior to the question of content, of what texts get taught in the curriculum. I have emphasized this relationship simply because it suggests the degree to which even sophisticated theorists continue to be implicated in the hegemonic discourse of the dominant culture. However, theory taken to its analytical limits has disclosed the indissolubly continuous affiliation between the question of pedagogy and the curriculum. The decentering of the center has shown that the binary logic of humanism produces a pedagogical educational structure in which the professor is the privileged bearer of the anthropologos; it has also shown that this binary logic produces the pyramidal structure of the traditional humanist curriculum. As certified bearer of the Word, the professor, like the Biblical exegete in the age of the theologos, becomes both the custodian of the sacred books that legitimate the dominant culture and the authorized transmitter of the "common [canonical] knowledge" they contain. As such, and despite the imperative of objectivity, the professor's ultimate function is not only to teach the canonical texts in a way that is consonant with the ruling ideology that produced them. It is also to guard against "misreading" them; and, to recall M. H. Abrams's representative humanist manifesto, it is to delegitimize texts or classes of texts that are "too inadequately human to engage our continuing interest, or which require our consent to positions so illiberal or eccentric or perverse that they invite counterbeliefs which inhibit the ungrudging 'yes' that we grant to masterpieces."

To be more specific, the decentering of the anthropologos has also shown that the ultimate function of the institutionally certified professor is, consciously or unconsciously, to exclude or marginalize texts or classes of texts the historical specificity and differential play of which would subvert the authority and power of the universalized canon: for example, the parodic or travestying arts of the people (not least, at the present, the rock music of contemporary working-class or underprivileged or disaffiliated middle-class youth), texts that articulate the immediate sociopolitical perspective of women, of blacks, of gays, of ethnic minorities, and of Third World peoples, and texts that deviate from the norms of "common experience, common sense, and common moral consciousness." This exclusion or marginalization is accomplished not so much (any longer) by censorship as by hierarchical evaluation or by accommodation to the canon: by overlooking the deviant elements or representing them as explicable developments of the generative and evolutionary center/entelechy of the Occidental tradition. Indeed, it is essentially by means of the curriculum thus understood as the core of a commonly shared body of knowledge that the certified professor, and the institution such a figure represents, is empowered to *cultivate* the fallow ground of youth in general in terms of the principle of *maturity*, and to inscribe the particular (though overlapping) blocs of young people — women, blacks, gays, working class, ethnic — with the affiliated sexual, racial, cultural, sociopolitical, and international identities that, combined, reproduce the dominant late capitalist sociopolitical order and extend its hegemony.

Thus the breaking of the vertical pattern determining the hierarchical relations between teacher and student must also be accompanied by an oppositional pedagogy that breaks the pyramidal structure of the core curriculum and liberates the differential forces it cultivates and colonizes. This, however, does not entail the deliberate repetition of the curricular model precipitated more or less accidentally by the radical students and faculty activists in the 1960s: the randomizing of the curriculum, the proliferation of a multitude of discrete and autonomous course offerings, which has justified the postwar educational reformers to reaffirm and reinstitutionalize the core curriculum.[28] As in the case of the teacher/student relation, it means rather the dislocation of the canon from its transcendental heights into the arena of the free play of criticism; or, more specifically, the genealogical critique or de-struction of the narrative history that produced the canon. To recall Nietzsche's "Uses and Disadvantages of History," rather than the abandonment of this cultural history (as if that were possible), the breaking of the pyramidal structure of the canon calls *for using this history against itself*, for deliberately and rigorously pursuing its binary logic from its "origin" to its promised "end," to that final moment in this history — the Vietnam War — which discloses its contradictions: the differences all along the continuum of being it has violently repressed in the name of deliverance and culture to reproduce and extend its power and authority. If, as Walter Benjamin suggests, "there is no document of civilization which is not at the same time a document of barbarism" and "barbarism taints also the manner in which [such a document] was transmitted from one owner to another," then the oppositional teacher, like Benjamin's "historical materialist," must "disassociate himself as far as possible from it," not by obliterating it or forgetting its existence, but by engaging it from the demystified and estranged perspective (in the midst) of its genealogical origin. The oppositional intellectual must "regard it as his task to brush" the monuments of this monumentalized history "against the grain."

What, then, are the practical curricular imperatives demanded by the decentering of the humanist center? Given the prevailing institutional conditions, it would be quixotic to articulate a systematic alternative to the traditional general education program. In the real context of the inordinately uneven distribution of power in the political economy of the university, such an alternative program would not be viable, despite the inevitable disclaimers of the conservative and liberal humanists who dominate its "democratic" space. The unnegotiability of an alternative curriculum, therefore, makes it necessary to put the question in terms of struggle: What are the practical responsibilities in relation to the curriculum of an adversarial pedagogy that would brush history against the grain?

All too obviously, perhaps, the primary responsibility of oppositional intellectuals, teachers and students, is to resist the false alternative—made available in the humanities by I. A. Richards, T. S. Eliot and the New Critics, and in a more sophisticated way by F. R. Leavis and Lionel Trilling—to dehistoricize history by way of aestheticizing the texts it has produced.[29] As the complicity of the literary component of the curriculum envisaged in *Education in a Free Society* in the aftermath of World War II with the Cold War project suggests, this kind of compensatory internalization of historical conflict constitutes a reinscription of the historically specific ideology of the dominant culture in a more discreet way than a curriculum justified in terms of an overt affirmation of "our heritage." Oppositional intellectuals must rather engage in the task of *opening up* the traditional curriculum: to introduce, and to work politically for the introduction of, texts and courses that reflect the (historically specific) knowledge that the canon and the genetic narrative informing it have hitherto excluded or marginalized in the name of "the best that has been thought and said in the world" or, what is finally the same thing, the "mind of Europe."[30] To put this responsibility merely in terms of supplementation, however, is grossly inadequate to the resonant disclosures about the operations of ideological subtexts accompanying the decentering of the center, since it does not forestall their accommodation to and domestication by the institution in the name of pluralism. Indeed, under the pressure of various oppositional blocs, the institutions of higher learning, especially in North America—from their administrations down to the faculties of departments—have in the past decade given way to precisely the oversimplified demand for greater "diversification" of the curriculum (as well as of faculty and student body) only to recuperate their reductive and repressive authority in less visible because more apparently ameliorative terms.

This is increasingly happening in the sensitive area of the general humanities, in required undergraduate core courses, for example, which are now being opened up to include texts formerly excluded from the canonical syllabus ostensibly for their failure to rise to the artistic or intellectual standards of the masterpiece, but in fact excluded because they "represent" the experiences of women, blacks, and other minorities in terms of their marginalization by the hegemonic ideology informing the canon. We witness this accommodational operation in the highly publicized instance of the revised Western civilization course at Stanford, which culminated in the televised debate between William Bennett and Donald Kennedy, the president of that university:

PRESIDENT KENNEDY: Now the outcome [of the Stanford curriculum debate] is not [as Secretary Bennett alleges] to junk Western culture. The tracks in the course now called "Culture, Ideas, Values" will still consist of most of the same materials. But there will be added to it significant works from other cultures and from other kinds of authors. I don't think anything has been thrown overboard. I think what we have has been enriched. . . .

SECRETARY BENNETT: Again, I think, the means inhere in the end. Right from the beginning there was an assault on Western culture and Western civilization. And if you look at the Stanford newspaper and editorials and other things, you will see that, over this time, there were many editorials saying Western culture is sexist, racist, imperialistic, and so on: all sorts of things written out of ignorance, which demonstrated the need for students to study Western culture so that they would understand that it was Western culture that taught the rest of the world to overcome many of these things. But the process, of course, was therefore a problem. But so was the end. This was no trifling change. There were fifteen books in the original course. . . . The so-called modest change dropped nine of those books and that's pretty substantial. Dropping Homer and dropping Dante, and dropping Freud, and dropping Darwin, and Luther and Thomas More, I think, is pretty significant. . . . Let me make it plain. I think that students at Stanford should study non-Western culture. In fact, when I was chairman of the National Endowment for the Humanities, I gave Stanford University a grant to develop a course in non-Western culture. But you don't make the case for studying non-Western culture by trashing Western culture, and you don't know non-Western culture any better by knowing Western culture less.

KENNEDY: I want to promise everybody that we didn't trash Western Culture. . . .

BENNETT: Check the record.

KENNEDY: . . . that Secretary Bennett's grant was and is very much appreciated, and that the enrichment of this course retains ninety percent of what was there. . . . It is correct that we cut the core list a bit more than in half. That is the absolutely required list that must be included in all the so-called tracks. There's a whole additional list of strongly recommended works that our faculty has always drawn on, including now the ones that were deleted from the absolutely required list. The faculty teaching that course actually asked for a marginal measure in flexibility because, for example, philosophers interested in studying the relations exposing the history of the relationship between state and citizen wanted a little more freedom to assign Locke and Hobbes and Rousseau, which were not on the original absolutely required list. So this was the Stanford faculty deciding how it best could teach. . . . I don't think that there's any reason for us to "trash" Western culture and that's why we haven't. That buzz word doesn't make a case. All it does is to reflect the Secretary's annoyance at an outcome that I think is actually much less of a change than he has perceived it to be. But let there be no doubt about it. We do believe that the study of even Western culture considered by itself will be more valuable by the introduction of some of these other strands, more meaningful to our students, and that it will make this kind of study more exciting and spread it more broadly.[31]

This accommodational and recuperative process, in which the liberal humanist's response to the reactionary humanistic charges of cultural betrayal obscures their fundamental agreement, can be found most visibly in English departments, where representatives of "minority" blocs are now teaching courses hitherto off-limits in areas of their interest: feminists, who teach women's writing; blacks, who teach black writing; Marxists, who teach Marxist writing; poststructuralists, who teach poststructuralist writing; new historicists, who teach new historicist writing; and so on. These courses constitute symbolic evidence of the contradictions inhering in the traditional core curriculum. They thus represent a welcomed interruption of its traditional monoglossic discursive practices. But as symptomatic signs, they do not adequately interrogate the anthropologic center nor do they respond to the imperatives of collective praxis that such an interrogation demands. They by and large repeat in practice the disabling situation that obtains for intellectuals in general. It is not simply that all too many of the professors who teach these courses interpret the hitherto marginalized texts they introduce from the "theoretical" vantage point that marginalizes them in the first place.[32] Nor is it simply, as Sylvia Wynter has observed, that they fail to resist the disciplinary institutional machinery that splits them off from the department as a whole in the name of pluralism. Pursuing their specialty in a monologic vacuum, these professors isolate themselves from adversarial colleagues in other fields or disciplines whose particular subject matters constitute different but allied bodies of hitherto marginalized knowledge.

Each tends, therefore, to attract specific homogeneous categories of the student body whose interest their subject matter naturally engages at the expense of a pedagogical context that might instigate a broader sense of their disaffiliation. Feminist-inclined students gravitate toward courses in feminist writing, blacks toward black writing, political radicals toward new left writing, each with its separate enclave. Such courses indeed activate a deeper awareness, for specific student constituencies, of the ideological origins and consequences of their marginality. But because they are too often taught in terms of the disciplinary machinery in place, these students are deprived of the opportunity to become aware not only of their marginality as youth in general but also of the affiliation of their particular marginality with other marginalized groups. This disabling situation is the consequence of the pervasive failure of specific oppositional intellectuals to perceive marginality in terms of the curriculum as an institutional whole. It follows from an obedient if also vestigial adherence to the disciplinary compartmentalization of knowledge that is the divisive mechanism par excellence of the disciplinary university, and that analogous to the subjected subject, works to defuse the threat of collective resistance by harnessing intellectual energy to the hegemonic project.

As important as the task of opening up the curriculum is in the oppositional intellectual's struggle to achieve the truly democratic sociopolitical potentialities of the decentering of the anthropologos, it is not enough. To brush history against the grain, to utilize history to overcome history, imposes on intellectuals the responsibility of *knowing this "history,"* which is to say, having a "command" or "overview" of the history that constituted the traditional curriculum. I do not, of course, mean this in the panoptic institutional sense of mastery, which is how the imperative "to have a command of the tradition" is usually practiced and transmitted to students by universal intellectuals. I mean, along with Nietzsche, to know it in its demystified sense: as a tradition and curriculum historically invented by the dominant sociopolitical order to legitimate its hegemony. Intellectuals as historical agents who have rejected the fiction that knowledge production is neutral must bring the archival interpretation of this tradition and its curriculum into the classroom—whatever the course offering—as a *forestructure* in the "circular" interpretive/pedagogical process: not as transcendental standard, which is always—and erosively—self-confirming in the encounter with specific texts, but as a "beginning" of critical inquiry to be always interrogated, that is, put at risk before the assaults of the disruptive *historicality* of history.

This "interested" strategy, which "locates" the teacher both inside and outside the onto-theo-logical tradition (and the "common" body of texts it has monumentalized), which gives him or her a command that is not a command of it—which is dis-locating— should be the fundamental pedagogical strategy of the "specific" oppositional intellectual. It should operate not only in the survey or period courses required by the traditional curriculum but also in courses devoted to the study of bodies of knowledge hitherto excluded but now increasingly accommodated to the traditional core curriculum. As the destructive/genealogical argument of my text has shown, it is this strategy that is best suited not only to disclose to students the differential knowledges that the logocentric tradition (and its core curriculum) has necessarily forgotten or accommodated to the "truth" of its knowledge, but to facilitate the activation of the critical consciousness of the student body in general and to instigate the sense, not of identity, but of affiliative solidarity among that student body's differential parts. This strategy, in short, provides a transdisciplinary, global, and dialogical context for undermining the "regime of truth." Given the asymmetrical configuration of power relations in our historical conjuncture, this "interested" pedagogy is also best suited to facilitate (without taking over) the decolonizing or liberating task of the differential subaltern groups whose particular energies the dominant sociopolitical order has colonized in the name of the truth of the knowledge informing our "cultural heritage."

Some will object that such a destructive strategy compels an oppositional pedagogy to be always determined by the terms of the dominant discourse: a repetition compulsion in which the minor oppositional impulse is inevitably subordinated to the major structure it opposes. This is, of course, the dilemma of the oppositional intellectual who would utilize the traditional curriculum against itself. It is, however, a dilemma that, given the historically specific configuration of power relations in the West and especially in North America, must be faced and overcome. To explore marginal and differential bodies of knowledge in a context that ignores this situation can only result in precisely what it seeks to avoid: the compartmentalization of these knowledges, the division of the labor that produced them, and thus their easy institutionalization and subjection to the "liberal consensus" (the "toleration" of minority opposition that confirms the dominant discourse it would oppose).

In response to the above objection, two points can be made:

1. By an "oppositional pedagogy," I do not mean a pedagogy of persuasion, but a pedagogy of *resistance* or *struggle*. It is of crucial importance that the intellectual who would undermine the authority of the core curriculum by pursuing its logic to its contradictory end avoid the ruse of the "repressive hypothesis": the temptation to think institutional change in terms of a revised curriculum intended to provide a context for the negotiation of "conflicts of interpretation," which is to say, the reduction of conflict to *cognitive* give and take.[33] This, despite protestations to the contrary, is the temptation to which, for example, Gerald Graff succumbs in his advocacy of the "institutionalization of theory," a project that would bring to visibility, for the purpose of debate, the multiple ideological conflicts that, according to Graff, brought the disciplinary structure of the university at large, and of each of its divisions, into being, but which, because of the randomness of the process of accretion, have been forgotten by teachers and students:

> Falling into the creases as they do, interdisciplinary [ideological] conflicts go unperceived by students, who naturally see each discipline as a frozen body of knowledge to be absorbed rather than as social products with a history that they might have a personal and critical stake in.
>
> At issue in the teaching of literature, then, and in the formation of a literature curriculum, are how much of the "cultural text" students must presuppose in order to make sense of works of literature, and how this cultural text can become the context of teaching. That there is no agreement over how the cultural text should be understood, or whether it should come into play at all in the teaching of literature, seems to me an argument for rather than against a more explicitly historicized and cultural kind of literary study that would make such disagreements part of what is studied. The important thing, in any case, is to shift the question from "Whose overview gets to be the big umbrella?" in which form it becomes unanswerable, to "How do we institutionalize the conflict of interpretations and overviews itself?" To emphasize conflict over consensus is not to turn conflict into a value, nor certainly is it to reject consensus where we can get it — as would the silly recent argument that identifies consensus with repressive politics. It is simply to take our point of departure from a state of affairs that already exists.[34]

This proposal by an "oppositional" intellectual is, on the surface, enticing in its commitment to providing an interdisciplinary pedagogical context that would foreground ideological conflicts forgotten or concealed by the insularity of disciplinary studies. It would make the critical text a "cultural" or "social" text. But its reductiveness is betrayed by the questionable premise (one also shared, though differently understood, by conservative humanists) that the university is in disarray, that the divisions (the disciplinary structure) of the university as a whole and within (departments) are for all practical purposes autonomous, isolated, and functional or instrumental, and therefore that resistance to change is essentially a pragmatic matter of structural inertia: "The most formidable obstacle to change is structural rather than ideological. The great advantage of the present system of patterned isolation over any system that tried to pair courses and bring different viewpoints into relation and contrast is that in the short run it is easier to administer" (PL, p. 262). In assigning the cause of this fragmentation to random accretion—to taking the practical path of least resistance—Graff fails or refuses to perceive the possibility that what *appears* to be disarray, a structure of "patterned isolation," is, as I have tried to show by way of Foucault's genealogy of modern disciplinary institutions, the systematic effect of the panoptic schema and ultimately of the metaphysical principle of discipline par excellence: that identity is the condition for the possibility of difference or, in Graff's terminology, consensus is the condition for the possibility of individual institutional disciplines.

As his mocking dismissal of the "recent argument that identifies consensus with repression" as simply "silly" makes quite clear, Graff either fails to understand or refuses to take seriously the analysis of the discourse and practice of hegemony fundamental to the intellectual labor of Antonio Gramsci, Theodor Adorno, Walter Benjamin, Raymond Williams, Louis Althusser, Jacques Derrida, Jacques Lacan, Michel Foucault, Edward Said, Fredric Jameson, and Julia Kristeva, to name only the most prominent of those otherwise diverse voices who have addressed themselves to the question of power in "liberal" Western societies. That is, he refuses to entertain the possibility that the resistance to "theory" he laments follows from the serious threat it poses to the university's ruling ideology and thus to the authority of its dominant constituents.

In thus interpreting the disciplinary space of the contemporary university as a structural rather than ideological problem, Graff succumbs to the lure of humanist pluralism. "The point," he says elsewhere, "is not to destroy pluralism, but to transform it into a pluralism defined by a community of debate rather than a pluralism of incommensurable positions."[35] In disregarding the uneven balance of power that obtains in the university, he compromises his oppositional stance by putting his discourse in terms that naively assume its negotiability, the gesture of a loyal opposition.[36] In arguing in behalf of the institutionalization of the conflicts of interpretation in these accommodational terms, he also reduces, as *Professing Literature* at large does, the force of theory—it becomes a neutral instrument for generating a free-floating and conflict-free debate of ideas. Graff's commitment to a theoretically informed pedagogy would lead students to see each discipline, not "as a frozen body of knowledge to be absorbed," but "as social products with a history that they might have a personal and critical stake in." In his practice, however, theory becomes a pluralist agency of negotiation and, as such, of hegemony. This is, in fact, what Graff's understanding of contemporary theory must come down to, given his precautionary efforts to annul the element of struggle in opposition:

> As I use the term here, "literary theory" is a discourse concerned with the legitimating principles, assumptions, and premises of literature and literary criticism. . . . It is at least as legitimate, and more in line with normal usage, to think of literary theory not as a set of systematic principles, necessarily, or a founding philosophy, but simply as an inquiry into assumptions, premises, and legitimating principles and concepts.
>
> Thus, another way of describing literary theory is as a discourse that treats literature as in some respects a problem and seeks to formulate that problem in general terms. Theory is what is generated when some aspect of literature, its nature, its history, its place in society, its conditions of production and reception, its meaning in general, or the meanings of particular works, ceases to be given and becomes a question to be argued in a generalized way. Theory is what inevitably arises when literary conventions and critical definitions once taken for granted have become objects of generalized discussion and dispute. (*PL*, p. 252)

Despite his intentions, Graff's advocacy of theory in the classroom amounts in the end to an enlightened liberal humanist's appeal to his conservative colleagues to abandon a reactionary discourse—one that, in making the center of power visible, goes far to verify the antihumanist charges that the discursive practices of humanism are a colonialism—in favor of a discourse of consensus that can accomplish the disciplinary end of humanism in a far more efficient and politically economical way. It is as if Graff has learned—and would transmit—the lesson of the debate between William Bennett and Donald Kennedy:

> Such [traditional] educators are saying, in effect, that it is more important to protect the integrity of the great tradition than to relate that tradition to the cultural controversies of its time. This seems a mistake from a tactical point of view, if no other, for it is doubtful that the traditional canon profits from being insulated against challenges. It seems finally to be in the interest of the traditionalists to help create a situation in which their quarrel with their enemy would be dramatized. For one thing, their traditionalism would suddenly begin to *stand for* something in the eyes of the students, as it does not so long as teachers representing opposing positions are structurally isolated by the field-coverage system. For another, if the traditionalists persist in keeping things institutionally as they are, they are certain to lose their

battle by attrition or default, as earlier conservative factions in the history of literary studies always have. Of course these traditionalists will be able to console themselves, as their predecessors have always done, by constructing stories of cultural and educational decline that will rationalize their defeat, but such consolation may no longer afford the pleasure it once did. (*PL*, p. 261)

In not recognizing the "fragmentation" of the university to be the strategic and disciplinary classification and *individuation* of knowledge, whose condition of possibility, like that of the subjected subject, resides in the anthropo-logo-centric principle of identity, Graff, despite his advocacy of the "cultural text," reduces the potential praxis of his oppositional discourse to a free-floating *verbalism*. As Freire observes, "There is no true word that is not at the same time a praxis. . . . An inauthentic word, one which is unable to transform reality, results when dichotomy is imposed upon its constitutive elements. When a word is deprived of its dimension of action, reflection automatically suffers as well; and the word is changed into idle chatter, into *verbalism*, into an alienated and alienating blah" (*PO*, pp. 75–76). To recognize the monologic power concealed behind the pluralistic structure of higher education implies an entirely different kind of opposition. In a context that makes visible the highly uneven distribution of power informing present university space, the opposition of the oppositional intellectual cannot be a matter of negotiation. It has to involve praxis: the use of language not to precipitate verbal debate but to instigate *real conflict* in behalf of transforming the world.

Understood as struggle, however, an oppositional pedagogy that always refers to "the simultaneous order" of the tradition and the canon of "classics" it legitimates does not necessarily result in the subordination of its terms to those which it opposes. I am not simply suggesting negatively that the present institutional circumstance—the uneven configuration of power relations that obtain in the university—compels struggle against the canon. I am also suggesting that such a struggle has paradoxically positive consequences, especially at this historical conjuncture, vis-à-vis the overcoming of the dominant discourse. For this historical moment—especially the period of the Vietnam War and its aftermath—has borne witness to a fissuring of the set of structures that have traditionally legitimated the disproportionate distribution of power in the university and has thereby rendered its dominant constituency vulnerable. As I have shown, the symbolic refusal of spontaneous consent to the traditional curriculum by a large and differential body of students and faculty during the Vietnam decade or, conversely, the highly visible "Egyptianism" of the reaction of traditional conservative humanists such as Walter Jackson Bate, William Bennett, Allan Bloom, Lynne Cheney, Dinesh D'Souza, and others to this fissuring has gone far to disclose the contradictions inhering in the disinterested discourse of liberal humanism. To invoke the metaphor that symbolizes the anthropological cultural tradition, the disruptions of the Vietnam era have compelled the invisible center elsewhere of the liberal curriculum into the arena of the free play of criticism. As a consequence of this fall into visibility, oppositional intellectuals are increasingly becoming aware of the complicity between liberal and conservative humanists—that the debates between them, as in the case of President Donald Kennedy and William Bennett, are obfuscatingly familial. Because the canon the former would recuperate in behalf of liberal culture is *essentially* the same canon the latter would reaffirm in behalf of "our ['western' or 'national'] heritage," the complicity of the discursive practice of humanist cultural production and the dominant sociopolitical order is also becoming apparent. However intact the old balance of power remains, the fact is that the humanist university is in crisis.

Given that crisis condition, this is not the time for an oppositional pedagogy that would negotiate an alternative curriculum nor for one that refuses the encounter with the dominant curriculum and its affiliated discourses because it fears that it would be determined by them. Focused by the global events of 1989, which have called into question the traditional critical problematic of the Left, it is the time for a sustained and intellectually rigorous offensive against the logo-phallo-ethnocentric assumptions informing a curriculum that, despite their symbolic exposure, continues to masquerade as the triumphant end of natural, disinterested, and free inquiry. The struggle of oppositional intellectuals against the curriculum in place involves, then, a pedagogical praxis that would facilitate the process of demystification precipitated by the historical events of the last twenty years. It involves, in sum, the critical theorizing of the student protest movement's demand for a "relevant" curriculum and of the recuperative reaction of the humanist university to the "proliferation" of courses that "eroded" the general education program, to, that is, the students' symptomatic refusal of their spontaneous consent to the hegemony of the core curriculum in the decade of the Vietnam War.

This is not to say, as Gerald Graff supposes, that the struggle of oppositional intellectuals necessarily demands an interpretation of the curriculum grounded in an alternative center, "a *system* or *foundational discourse* that aims to 'govern' critical practice from some outside metaphysical standpoint" (*PL*, p. 252). Although this may be a tendency in some versions, the oppositional theory I am espousing vis-à-vis the curriculum has its genealogical origins in the recognition of the foundational and (however obscured) systematic nature of the discourse of humanism. To put this positively, oppositional theory begins with the acknowledgment of the decentered center and of indeterminacy, and thus in the affirmation, not of a dialectical but of a dialogic approach to the teaching of the curriculum.[37] It would neither replace one authority with another nor produce a pedagogic context in which anything goes. It seeks to create a space that is *always already* interested yet free, contestatory yet open-ended.

2. In thus defining the struggle of oppositional intellectuals as a theoretical praxis that works to conceptualize youth's unconscious resistance to the core curriculum, we are prepared to meet the objection that an oppositional pedagogy that always keeps the tradition "in view" dooms itself to a repetition compulsion. De-struction, we recall,

does not simply entail a negative critique of the canonical tradition: "In the circle is hidden a positive possibility of the most primordial kind of knowing."[38] It simultaneously involves a "projective" phase: the exploration of differential energies, voices, and constituencies liberated by the decolonization of the imperial domain of this dominant high cultural apparatus. This project is not simply a matter of retrieving for study the "forgotten" or excluded texts of marginal groups—of the "people," women, blacks, and other "eccentrics." Such a retrieval of, for example, the "Carmina Burana" or Bob Dylan, Jimi Hendrix, and the Doors, of Kate Chopin, Zora Neale Hurston, or Kathy Acker, of Muddy Waters or Amiri Baraka and Bob Kaufmann, of the *Coeni Cyprianus* or Charles Bukowski would render these additions to the curriculum vulnerable to what I have called accommodation: vulnerable to a process of recolonization analogous to the neocolonialism of late capitalism that strategically superseded the ruthless imperial project of the Western nations in the nineteenth century. This process is epitomized by the example of the most recent Norton anthologies, which have broadened the scope of selections for the purpose of "enriching" rather than interrogating the tradition. If the decentering of the anthropologos informing Occidental cultural practices points to the priority of difference over identity rather than the other way around, then the projective phase of a destructive pedagogy also requires a pedagogical comportment toward the curriculum that reverses the binary terms of the principle of identity that has historically determined canon formation and knowledge production (what it is permissible to publish); this should address not simply its earlier arbitrary exclusions but also its more recent disciplinary accommodational practices. It must begin, that is, by acknowledging that the cultural production of "minorities" is the condition for the possibility of the identity of Occidental cultural production *and not the other way around.*

Such a reversal—which is not at the same time a binary opposition—would dislocate the body of canonical texts, disclosing it to be in fact dependent on the marginalized texts of the various "others" for its commanding identity. It would also *free* previously marginalized texts (and scholarly commentary about them) from the domination of the core curriculum and the hegemonic apparatuses (university presses, scholarly and critical journals, professional organizations, etc.) that serve it. In a way analogous to the symptomatic credo that "black is beautiful," such a reversal would enable texts hitherto spoken for or represented by the dominant discourse to "speak for" or "represent" themselves in a truly democratic dialogue—not with the tradition *as such*, but with the texts displaced and de-authorized by the decentering of the core of the core curriculum.

I have put quotations around "speak for" and "represent" to disarm the obvious objection that such a pedagogical comportment toward the curriculum would simply reinscribe in reverse the chain of authorities—from center through the "proper self" to the cultural and sociopolitical identities now at work in the curriculum and thus would precipitate a chaos of arbitrary and fixed identities. Understood in terms of the imperatives of the decentered center, however, the cultural productions of minority constituencies are no less socially constituted than those of the dominant culture. The difference is that whereas the traditional intellectual assumes the canon he or she professes is the natural and evolving fruit of free inquiry, the posthumanist specific or organic intellectual is acutely aware that *all* cultural production is finally without transcendental justification. This means that the pedagogical space activated by the oppositional intellectual who would enable hitherto marginalized texts to speak for and represent themselves is a space of *crisis*, even though that space is dominated by the hegemonic ideology of the canon. It is a space in which the center determining the self-representation of the various minority texts is, no less than the (hitherto invisible) center determining the canonical texts of the dominant culture, open to the free play of criticism. In this cultural space, intellectual labor begins in *interest*—by commitment to a position—in behalf of the liberation and articulation of the voices of marginalized texts against the canon, *yet* it is also, as traditional pedagogy is not, always already open to transformation in its encounter with its monologic adversaries. The "end" of such an oppositional approach to the curriculum is thus not simply the retrieval of differential texts hitherto excluded from or represented by the traditional curriculum. It is also to provide a context that would enable both teachers and students to think the internal and external chain of indissolubly affiliated "identities" that are not identical—psychic, sexual, linguistic, cultural, ethnic, social, and political—that, by means of the ruse of the "sovereign subject," the traditional core curriculum dedifferentiates and normalizes within the omnivorous circle of anthropological identity.

Identities that are not identical: Contrary to Gerald Graff (and the humanists whose anxieties he would appease by reducing oppositional conflict to negotiation), the alternative approach to the curriculum demanded by posthumanist theory at large does not involve the substitution of one foundational discourse or self-identical and totalizing (panoptic) overview for another, nor the indoctrination of students with an identity (or series of discrete identities) that perceives itself in a binary opposition to the identity in place. *It does not, in short, demand a practice of "political correctness."* In rejecting the self-identity of the anthropological center (and the ruse of the sovereign subject to which it gives rise), posthumanist theory implies a view of the curriculum that would compel both teacher and student into the *dialogic* arena of crisis, of historicity, the disruptive force of which discloses their identities to be fictions, the *effects* of difference. These identities are necessary for praxis in a world dominated by the anthropological/ disciplinary overview, but they are always subject to radical change.

This response to the objection that liberating the identities of hitherto marginalized texts only reinscribes the authority of an overview might be interpreted as undermining my larger argument: that, in facilitating the e-mergence of differential texts that speak for or represent themselves, an oppositional approach demanding a commanding view of the canonical tradition would overcome the repetition compulsion that leaves the hierarchical structure in place. On the contrary, forcing pedagogical praxis into the

arena of crisis not only de-authorizes the canonical texts; it also reveals the commanding identity of the core curriculum to be *dependent* for its definition and authority on the
texts it marginalizes, just as the identity of the discourse and practice of eighteenth-
century bourgeois rationality was, according to Foucault, dependent for its definition
and authority on the experiences of "madness."[39] An oppositional pedagogical practice
that takes place in the arena of crisis where power is unevenly distributed theoretically
makes students aware of the latent force of these subaltern texts—of their mastery of
the Master, as it were—without falling into the trap of reinscribing them into the structure of a commanding center. In thus rejecting the authority of a Transcendental Signified, such a contestatory dialogic (and transdisciplinary) space escapes the charge of
political correctness. It also constitutes a strong argument against those oppositional
discourses that advocate the abandonment of the canon entirely in favor of studying the
marginalized texts in and for themselves. Whereas the latter strategy would in the end
precipitate a futile separatism, a decentered pedagogy that facilitated emergence—the
liberation of the *force* and a *theoretical understanding* of the force of the marginalized
texts—would enable a truly multicultural democracy, a democracy in which the differential voices always already risk their identities in dialogue and, in so doing, always
already preclude the closing of the circle.

IV

What I have said about the disciplines, the teacher-student relationship, and the curriculum by no means constitutes an exhaustive theorizing of the positive possibilities
latent in the protest movement on college and university campuses during the decade
of the Vietnam War and by the reaction of the custodians of "our heritage" in its aftermath. One could say much more about the complicity of the economy of architectural
space, of the politics of departments, of hiring procedures, of graduate assistant and
adjunct labor, of publication, of professional associations, of the writing requirement
(including the recently instituted "writing across the curriculum" program) with the
state apparatuses. One could also say much more about the revisionary orientation to
these economies that oppositional intellectuals ought to explore. I have not intended
my effort to turn the contradictions inhering in the liberal practices of the humanist
university to positive uses to be systematic and inclusive. Rather, I have intended my
analysis to be provisional but disruptive. What matters now is not so much the articulation of a comprehensive alternative program; what is needed is for oppositional intellectuals to disassociate themselves as far as is possible from the anthropological
problematic of humanism, and for them to think the questions that, in the blindness of
its insight, this problematic cannot (afford to) ask. What matters, to put this ontological
imperative more specifically, is to get outside of the circular/specular frame of the dominant culture and to rethink the relay of minority terms that its imperial binary logic has
systematically demonized and colonized in the name of disinterested inquiry.

Indeed, in looking back over what I have written, it occurs to me with considerable ironic force that, despite my willed effort to resist the enticements of the panoptic gaze, I have been more systematic than the decentering of the anthropologos warrants. It occurs to me not only how difficult it is *within the uneven distribution of power relations obtaining in the academy* for the oppositional intellectual to articulate an alternative pedagogy that does not resort to a totalized and totalizing theory, but also how necessary it is that he or she always think this inhibiting predicament. In other words, I do not present the projections of this last chapter as definitive and affirmative statement. I offer them, rather, as an "interested" *forestructure* that I put at risk in the face of the historicity of the present institutional and cultural moment. I offer these remarks to both teacher/scholars and students who, in response to the increasingly overt force with which the cultural apparatus exercises power, have become aware of the complicity of an assimilative pedagogy with sociopolitical domination. I offer them on behalf of the difference that these oppositional energies might make in the "new world order."

1. HUMANISTIC UNDERSTANDING AND THE ONTO-THEO-LOGICAL TRADITION: THE IDEOLOGY OF VISION

1. Henry Rosovsky, Report on the Core Curriculum (Cambridge, Mass.: Faculty of Arts and Sciences of Harvard University, February 15, 1978), 1. Hereafter cited as RCC.
2. Walter Jackson Bate, "The Crisis in English Studies," *Harvard Magazine*, vol. 85 (September-October, 1982), 53.
3. William J. Bennett, "To Reclaim a Legacy: Report on Humanities in Education," *The Chronicle of Higher Education* (November 28, 1984), 16.
4. Ibid., 19. Since Bennett's report, a number of other humanist "reformers" have justified their calls for educational reform by explicitly locating the cause of disarray in higher education in the politically motivated excesses of the student protest movement and the pusilanimity of the faculty in the decade of the Vietnam War, most notably — and stridently — Allan Bloom in *The Closing of the American Mind: How Higher Education Has Failed Democracy and Impoverished the Souls of Today's Students* (New York: Simon and Schuster, 1987); Roger Kimball, *Tenured Radicals: How Politics Has Corrupted Our Higher Education* (New York: Harper and Row, 1990); David Lehman, *Signs of the Times: Deconstruction and the Fall of de Man* (New York: Poseidon Press, 1991); and Dinesh D'Souza, *Illiberal Education: The Politics of Race and Sex on Campus* (New York: The Free Press, 1991). See also Phyllis Keller, *Getting at the Core: Curricular Reform at Harvard* (Cambridge, Mass.: Harvard University Press, 1982).
5. William J. Bennett, "The Shattered Humanities," *Wall Street Journal* (December 31, 1982). In his report in behalf of the National Endowment for the Humanities, "To Reclaim a Legacy," Bennett appeals to the authority of Walter Jackson Bate, quoting "The Crisis in English Studies," in which the latter "warned that 'the humanities . . . are plunging into their worst state of crisis since the modern university was formed a century ago' " and called on the executive branch of the university to reserve tenure appointments to those professing "the world's great literature" (by which he really means the "unrivalled" Anglo-American canon). In a characteristic sleight of hand, Bennett rewrites Bate's addressees, substituting "graduate humanities departments" for Bate's university administrators.

For a similar anxiety over "our cultural heritage," see Lynne V. Cheney, *American Memory: A Report on the Humanities in the Nation's Public Schools* (Washington, D.C.: National Endowment for the Humanities, 1988): "A system of education that fails to nurture memory of the past denies its students a great deal: the satisfactions of mature thought, an attachment to abiding concerns, a perspective on human existence. As adversary group member Linda Miller observed, 'We take a tremendous risk of national character by failing to ground our students in history and literature.' Indeed, we put our sense of nationhood at risk by failing to familiarize our young people with the story of how the society in which they live came to be. Knowledge of the ideas that have molded us and the ideals that have mattered to us functions as a kind of civic glue. Our history and literature give us symbols to share; they help us all, no matter how diverse our backgrounds, feel part of a common undertaking" (p. 7). See also E. D. Hirsch, Jr., *Cultural Literacy: What Every American Needs to Know* (Boston: Houghton Mifflin, 1987).

6. Jacques Derrida, "Structure, Sign and Play in the Discourse of the Human Sciences," *Writing and Difference*, trans. Alan Bass (Chicago: University of Chicago Press, 1978), p. 280. See also Michel Foucault, "Nietzsche, Genealogy, History," *Language, Counter-Memory, Practice: Selected Essays and Interviews*, ed. Donald Bouchard (Oxford: Basil Blackwell, 1977), pp. 138-64.

7. Martin Heidegger, *Being and Time*, trans. John Macquarrie and Edward Robinson (New York: Harper and Row, 1962), p. 44. I have quoted from Joan Stambaugh's translation of the "Introduction" to *Being and Time* in Martin Heidegger, *Basic Writings*, ed. David Farrell Krell (New York: Harper and Row, 1977), pp. 67-68.

8. Friedrich Nietzsche, "On the Uses and Disadvantages of History for Life," *Untimely Meditations*, trans. R. J. Hollingdale (Cambridge: Cambridge University Press, 1983), pp. 57-123.

9. See, for example, my essays "Heidegger, Kierkegaard, and the Hermeneutic Circle: Toward a Postmodern Theory of Interpretation as Disclosure," in *Martin Heidegger and the Question of Literature*, ed. William V. Spanos (Bloomington: Indiana University Press, 1979), pp. 115-48; and "Postmodern Literature and the Hermeneutic Crisis," *Union Seminary Quarterly Review*, vol. 24, 2 (Winter 1979), 119-31. The first of these originally appeared in *boundary 2*, vol. 4, 2 (Winter 1979), 455-88.

10. Martin Heidegger, "Who Is Nietzsche's Zarathustra?" *The New Nietzsche: Contemporary Styles of Interpretation*, ed. David B. Allison (New York: Dell, 1977), p. 73.

11. Martin Heidegger, "The Question Concerning Technology," *The Question Concerning Technology and Other Essays*, trans. William Lovitt (New York: Harper and Row, 1977), pp. 3-35.

12. Martin Heidegger, *Being and Time*, p. 55.

13. According to Heidegger, speech (*Rede*) is equiprimordial with Dasein's original and inescapable being-in-the-world as thrown (*Befindlichkeit*) and understanding (*Verstehen*) as possibility-for-being. In this sense speech is fundamentally temporal in nature. This, of course, is an interpretation of the ontology of speech different from that of Jacques Derrida, who posits the privileging of *parole* as the source of the essentially metaphysical or, in his term, "logocentric" orientation of Western thought.

14. Jacques Derrida, "Differance," *Speech and Phenomena and Other Essays on Husserl's Theory of Signs*, trans. with introduction by David B. Allison (Evanston, Ill.: Northwestern University Press, 1973): "The verb 'to differ' [*différer*] seems to differ from itself. On the one hand, it indicates difference as distinction, inequality, or discernibility; on the other, it expresses the interposition of delay, the interval of a *spacing* and *temporalizing* that puts off until 'later' what is presently denied, the possible that is presently impossible. Sometimes, the *different* and sometimes the *deferred* correspond [in French] to the verb 'to differ.' This correlation, however, is not simply one between act and object, cause and effect, or primordial and derived. In the one case 'to differ' signifies nonidentity; in the other case it signifies the order of the same. Yet there must be a common although entirely different [*différente*], root within the sphere that relates the two movements of differing to one another. We provisionally give the name *differance* to this *sameness* which is not *identical*: by the silence of its *a*, it has the desired advantage of referring to differing *both* as spacing/temporalizing and as the movement that structures every dissociation" (pp. 129-30). What distinguishes my appropriation of Derrida's "nonconcept," *differance*, from that of most deconstructive critics'—and, as will be seen, it is a crucial distinction—is its emphasis on *temporality*. Whereas the latter understand *differance* as an essentially textual phenomenon, I read it as equiprimordially ontological and textual. Such a reading, closer to Heidegger's understanding of the ontological difference, allows a discourse on and of difference to traverse textuality to other worldly sites that difference *as* textuality inhibits.

15. This formulation is medieval in origin, but according to W. B. Macomber in *The Anatomy of Disillusion: Martin Heidegger's Notion of Truth* (Evanston, Ill.: Northwestern University Press, 1969), "in his numerous historical studies Heidegger attempts to show that Greek thinking, especially since Plato, prepared the way for such a conception, and that modern thought—even in Kant, Hegel, and Nietzsche—reflects a series of covert variations on the same theme. The two essential characteristics which Heidegger attributes to this notion of truth are (1) that truth is primarily in the mind and (2) that it consists in the correspondence of a judgment with its object, the judgment

combining subject and predicate in the same way a thing and its property are combined in nature" (p. 13).

16. Heidegger, *Being and Time*, p. 389.
17. Ibid., pp. 64, 413.
18. Michel Foucault, *The Archaeology of Knowledge*, trans. A. M. Sheridan Smith (London: Tavistock Publications, 1972), pp. 126-61. See also Edward Said's application of Foucault's definition of the archive as "the first law of what can be said, the system [of discursivity] that governs the appearance of statements as unique events" (*Archaeology*, p. 129), in *Orientalism* (New York: Random House, 1979), especially chapter 2, "Orientalist Structures and Restructures," pp. 111-97.
19. Martin Heidegger, *An Introduction to Metaphysics*, trans. Ralph Mannheim (Garden City, N.Y.: Anchor Books, 1961), p. 161.
20. Jacques Derrida, "Structure, Sign and Play," p. 279.
21. Martin Heidegger, "What is Metaphysics?" trans. R. F. C. Hull and Alan Crick, in *Existence and Being*, ed. Werner Brock (Chicago: Henry Regnery, 1949), p. 344. See also Thomas Langan, *The Meaning of Heidegger: A Critical Study of an Existential Phenomenology* (New York: Columbia University Press, 1961), pp. 11-12.
22. Martin Heidegger, *Introduction to Metaphysics*, p. 161.
23. Michel Foucault, *Discipline and Punish: The Birth of the Prison*, trans. Alan Sheridan (New York: Pantheon Books, 1977), p. 148.
24. Søren Kierkegaard, *Johannes Climacus or De Omnibus Dubitandum Est and A Sermon*, trans. T. H. Croxale (Stanford: Stanford University Press, 1958), pp. 151-52: "Reflection is the possibility of relationship. This can also be stated thus: Reflection is disinterested. Consciousness is relationship, and it brings with it interest or concern; a duality which is perfectly expressed with pregnant double meaning by the word 'interest' (Latin *interesse*, meaning (i) 'to be between,' (ii) 'to be a matter of concern')."
25. Charles Olson, "Letter 27," *The Maximus Poems* (New York: Jargon/Corinth Books, 1960), p. 100. See my essay "Charles Olson and Negative Capability: A De-structive Interpretation," *Repetitions: The Postmodern Occasion in Literature and Culture* (Baton Rouge: Louisiana State University Press, 1987), pp. 107-47.
26. Jacques Derrida, "Structure, Sign and Play," p. 279.
27. Plato, *Phaedrus and the Seventh and Eighth Letters*, trans. Walter Hamilton (Hammondsworth, England: Penguin Books, 1973), pp. 55-57.
28. See especially M. H. Abrams, "The Deconstructive Angel," *Critical Inquiry*, vol. 3 (Spring 1977), 425-27.
29. M. H. Abrams, *Natural Supernaturalism: Tradition and Revolution in Romantic Literature* (New York: W.W. Norton, 1973), pp. 234-35. The emphases are mine and are intended to anticipate further discussion of the recollective memory as agency of humanistic inquiry. It is worth noting at this point, however, that Abrams, strategically (?), makes no reference to Søren Kierkegaard's fundamental and insistent critique of Hegel's notion of recollection as, in fact, a forgetting, a critique repeated in Martin Heidegger, Jacques Derrida, and Louis Althusser. See especially " 'On the Young Marx,' " in Althusser's *For Marx*, trans. Ben Brewster (London: Verso Editions, 1979), pp. 49-86. In this, Abrams, like Hegel, epitomizes precisely the recollective interpretive process that my text is interrogating.

For an even more recent—and more monolithic, nostalgic, and elitist—reaffirmation of the circular educational journey, see Allan Bloom, *The Closing of the American Mind*. As his acknowledgment that "Plato's *Republic* is for me *the* book on education" (p. 380) suggests, this Platonic paradigm of fall and return permeates Bloom's book. But I will restrict citation to its extraordinary conclusion: "Men may live more truly and fully in reading Plato and Shakespeare than at any other time, because then they are participating in essential being and are forgetting their accidental lives. The fact that this kind of humanity exists or existed, and that we can somehow still touch it with the tips of our outstretched fingers, makes our imperfect humanity, which we can no longer bear, tolerable. The books in their objective beauty are still there, and we must help protect and cultivate the delicate tendrils reaching out toward them through the unfriendly soil of students' souls.

Human nature, it seems, remains the same in our very altered circumstances because we still face the same problems, if in different guises, and have the distinctively human need to solve them, even though our awareness and forces have become enfeebled" (p. 380).

30. Martin Heidegger, "The Age of the World Picture," *The Question Concerning Technology and Other Essays*, trans. William Lovitt (New York: Harper and Row, 1977), pp. 126-27.

31. This recuperative movement explains the inordinate importance of Virgil in the cultural history of Western civilization, not only for Christians from Augustine through Dante to T. S. Eliot and C. S. Lewis, but for humanists from Sir Philip Sidney to Sainte-Beuve and Erich Auerbach as well. Virgil, it has too easily been forgotten, "corrected" Homer's *Odyssey* by transforming its explorative and errant form into a prophecy/fulfillment construct, in which the origin (Troy) is recovered in the form of Rome, in order to establish a *logos* upon which he could justify Augustan imperialism. As I will suggest in chapter 4, the appeal of Virgil's teleological interpretation of history (above all, the itinerary of the "saving remnant" in the *Aeneid*) was not restricted to future Christian exegetes: to the Patristic Fathers, who made his *Pax Romana* a *figura* of the New Jerusalem in their effort to justify providential history (and the Holy Roman Empire); to the New England Puritans (above all, Cotton Mather), who, for reasons antithetical to those of the Roman Church, read the journey of Aeneas—the "relic-bearer"—from Troy to Latium as a prefiguration of their founding (and territorial extensions) of the City on the Hill (see Sacvan Bercovitch, *The American Jeremiad* [Madison: University of Wisconsin Press, 1978], especially p. 78; and my essay "De-struction and the Critique of Ideology," *Repetitions*, pp. 282-84); and to T. S. Eliot: "Thus Virgil acquires the centrality of the unique classic; he is the center of European civilization. . . . The Roman Empire and the Latin language were not any empire and any language, but an empire and a language with a unique destiny in relation to ourselves; and the poet in whom that Empire and that language came to consciousness and expression is a poet of unique destiny" ("What Is a Classic?" *On Poetry and Poets* [London: Faber and Faber, 1952], p. 68). Virgil's teleological historical model also explicitly informs the writing of humanists such as Sainte-Beuve, who, as Frank Kermode observes, "appropriates the old legend [and the typological interpretive practice] to his own use, and makes the Advent a stage in the development of Latin civilization" (*The Classic* [Cambridge, Mass.: Harvard University Press, 1983], p. 17). See also Sainte-Beuve, *Etude sur Virgile, suivre d'une étude sur Quintus de Smyrne* (Paris: Garnier fréres, 1857) and, far more liberally, but no less fundamentally and nostalgically, Erich Auerbach, who Hegelianizes Christian figural history in his effort to reaffirm the continuity of the Western humanistic tradition in the face of the catastrophe of World War II. This, of course, is no place to argue this view. I submit, however, that it will be verified by a reading of the structural development of *Mimesis*, trans. Willard R. Trask, from the original German edition published in 1946 (Princeton: Princeton University Press, 1968), which ends in a poignant hope at the site of exile from the homeland that his book "may contribute to bringing together again those whose love for our western history has serenely persevered" (p. 557), in the light of the concluding paragraphs of his essay " 'Figura,' " *Scenes from the Drama of European Literature: Six Essays*, trans. from the original German text published in Istanbul in 1944 (New York: Meridian Books, 1959): "For what has been said here of Cato and Virgil applies to the *Comedy* as a whole. It is wholly based on a figural conception. In my study of Dante as a poet of the earthly world (1929) I attempted to show that in the *Comedy* Dante undertook 'to conceive the whole earthly historical world . . . as already subjected to God's final judgment and thus put in its proper place as decreed by the divine judgment, to represent it as a world already judged. . . . In so doing, he does not destroy or weaken the earthly nature of his characters, but captures the fullest intensity of their individual earthly-historical being and identifies it with the ultimate state of things. . . . At that time I lacked a solid historical grounding for this view, which is already to be found in Hegel and which is the basis of my interpretation of *The Divine Comedy*. It is suggested rather than formulated in the introductory chapters of the book. I believe that I have now found this historical grounding; it is precisely the figural interpretation of reality" (pp. 71-72).

32. Michel Foucault, *Discipline and Punish*, especially the chapter entitled "Panopticism," pp. 195-228.

33. Jacques Derrida, "Force and Signification," *Writing and Difference*, pp. 26-27. Heidegger, following Kierkegaard's critique of Hegelian recollection, calls the forgetting of being by modern Western man *die Seinsvergessenheit*. As he says in the first sentence of *Being and Time*—that momentous enabling act of the postmodern countermemory—it is in response to this forgetting of the question of being, or rather of what it means to be (*die Seinsfrage*), that he undertakes to retrieve (*Wiederholen*) a "fundamental ontology": "1. *The Necessity for Explicitly Restating the Question of Being.* This question has today been forgotten. Even though in our time we deem it progressive to give our approval to 'metaphysics' again, it is held that we have been exempted from exertions of a newly rekindled γιγαμτομαχία περί τῆς οὐσίας [gigantic struggle over the being-question]. Yet the question we are touching upon is not just any question. It is one which provided a stimulus for the researches of Plato and Aristotle, only to subside from then on *as a theme for actual investigation*. What these two men achieved was to persist through many alterations and 'retouchings' down to the 'logic' of Hegel. And what they wrested with the utmost intellectual effort from the phenomena, fragmentary and incipient though it was, has long since become trivialized" (p. 2).

34. Henceforth I will spell "being" in lower case to remind the reader of the transitive element I am thematizing by this tautological phrase in opposition to the capitalized—and nominalized—"Being" of traditional usage.

35. Søren Kierkegaard, *The Concept of Irony, with Constant Reference to Socrates*, trans. with introduction by Lee M. Capel (London: Collins, 1964), pp. 238ff.

36. Paul de Man, *Blindness and Insight: Essays in the Rhetoric of Contemporary Criticism* (New York: Oxford University Press, 1971).

37. In Nietzsche's discourse, this metaphysical eye that spatializes time belongs to the "monumental" and the "antiquarian" historian. See Friedrich Nietzsche, "On the Uses and Disadvantages of History for Life," and Michel Foucault, "Nietzsche, Genealogy, History," pp. 138-64.

38. Jacques Derrida, "Force and Signification," pp. 20-21.

39. Martin Heidegger, "A Dialogue on Language," *On the Way to Language*, trans. Peter D. Hertz (New York: Harper and Row, 1971), p. 15.

40. Edward Said, *Orientalism*, pp. 21-22.

41. Friedrich Nietzsche, *Thus Spoke Zarathustra*, trans. R. J. Hollingdale (Baltimore: Penguin Books, 1974), p. 162.

42. Martin Heidegger, "The Question Concerning Technology": "When man investigating, observing, ensnares nature as an area of his own conceiving, he has already been claimed by a way of revealing that challenges him to approach nature as an object of research, until even this object disappears into the objectlessness of standing-reserve" (p. 19). This "challenging claim which gathers man thither to order the self-revealing as standing-reserve" is what Heidegger appropriately called "enframing" (*Ge-stell*), p. 19. It is important to point out that Heidegger's account of enframing is not a conventional humanistic attack on technology as such. As a "challenging claim," it is a summons to human being from being. But neither is it a defense of technology. It is, rather, an appeal to *let* being reveal itself through technology. More specifically, it expresses Heidegger's recognition that technology and its cybernetic rhetoric, as the fulfillment of the amnesiac ontotheological tradition, has become being's agency of revealing "itself" to modern man. In thus concealing (or alienating) being in something like a final way by transforming *physis* into "standing reserve," it can paradoxically reveal the meaning of what it means to be more clearly than any other time in Western history has been able to do. Another way of putting this is that, in bringing the ontotheological tradition to its end, technology undermines the hegemony in the human subject of metaphysical discourse, allowing men and women for the first time to stand outside it in some degree; to call it into question.

43. In defining the sociopolitical formation of the post-Enlightenment (modern) *epistème* as the "disciplinary society," Foucault intends to subsume more traditional and ideologically restricted names such as the age of the bourgeoisie, capitalism, or positivistic science under it. Henceforth, when I use this term, it is to be understood in Foucault's sense.

44. Hans-Georg Gadamer, *Truth and Method* (New York: Seabury Press, 1975).

45. See my essay "Theory in the Undergraduate Curriculum: Towards an Interested Pedagogy," *boundary 2*, vol. 16, 2, 3 (Winter/Spring, 1989), 41-70.

46. Joseph Frank, "Spatial Form in Modern Literature," *Sewanee Review*, vol. 53 (Spring, Summer, Autumn, 1945), 229-30; rpr. in *The Widening Gyre: Crisis and Mastery in Modern Literature* (New Brunswick, N.J.: Rutgers University Press, 1963). The unstated—and misleading—assumption behind this inordinately influential passage is that temporality exists only in the sequential mode: as causality. (It is an assumption that pervades the binary thinking of the "poetic" humanists.) In thus limiting his interpretation of temporality to that provided by scientific humanism, Frank overlooks another, more originary understanding of temporality: the disclosive or open-ing existential time—the time that disseminates difference—which it is the purpose of Heidegger and other posthumanist thinkers to make explicit in their interrogation of the concept of time—both positivistic (chronometric) and idealistic (mythic)—of the ontotheological tradition. Understood in the context of the destruction of metaphysics, Frank's characteristic distinction between sequential humanistic time and the spatialized time of antihumanist moderns conceals their essential similarity: that, in assuming the ontological priority of the end over temporal process, both are (circular) forms of logocentric thought and exist as technological agents of the humanistic will to power over being.

47. Henri Bergson, *Time and Free Will: An Essay on the Immediate Data of Consciousness*, trans. F. L. Pogson (New York: Macmillan, 1910), p. 226. Frank also overlooks T. E. Hulme's similar account of the scientific intelligence in his explication of Bergson's distinction between intuition and the scientific intelligence in *Humanism and the Philosophy of Art*, ed. Herbert Read (New York: Harcourt, Brace, 1924): "Explanation [the essential characteristic of scientific intelligence] means *ex plane*, that is to say, the opening out of things on a plane surface. . . . The process of explanation is always a process of unfolding. A tangled mass is unfolded flat so that you can see all its parts separated out and any tangle which can be separated out in this way must be of course an extensive manifold. It seems then that the [scientific] intellect distorts reality . . . because it persists in unfolding things out in space. It is not satisfied unless it can see every part. It wants to form a picture" (pp. 178-79). In his defense against his critics, "Spatial Form: Thirty Years After," *Spatial Form in Narrative*, ed. Jeffrey R. Smitten and Ann Daghistany (Ithaca: Cornell University Press, 1981), Frank acknowledges Bergson's use of the term, now to broaden the concept of spatial form to accommodate the discourse of structuralism. In so doing, he annuls the crucial distinction he made in the early essays between Modernism and traditional literature (realism); that is, between the aesthetic or formalist imagination and the scientific intelligence. But he refuses to confront Bergson's critique of the spatialization of time (its reification of duration in the name of utility) and that poststructuralist extension of Bergson's critique that thematizes its repressiveness.

48. Louis Althusser, " 'On the Young Marx' ": "To discomfit those who set up against Marx his own youth, the *opposite position* is resolutely taken up: Marx is reconciled with his youth—*Capital* is no longer read as *On the Jewish Question, On the Jewish Question* is read as *Capital*; the shadow of the young Marx is no longer projected on to Marx, but that of Marx on to the young Marx; and a pseudo-theory of the history of philosophy in the '*future anterior*' is erected to justify this counter-position, without realizing that this pseudo-theory is quite simply Hegelian" (p. 54). Althusser's critique of the Hegelian and Hegelian Marxist concept of time as "history . . . in the 'future anterior' " is his version of what I take in this book to be the fundamental point of departure of the discourse of posthumanist theory at large: its demystification of metaphysics and metaphysically determined linguistic, cultural, and sociopolitical systems as temporality interpreted from after or above its differential process: from the end (in both senses of the word) or spatially (from the perspective of a determining transcendental eye). It is this critique, deriving, no doubt, from Kierkegaard's critique of Hegel's sublating *Er-Innerung* (recollection), that precipitates or is consonant with a constellation of terms in the vocabularies of posthumanist theory that relate the metaphorics of *completion* (teleology, totalization, presence, representation, etc.) with the metaphorics of *(omni-)vision* (the panoptic gaze, structuralism, prefiguration, providence, preformationism, enframement, the centered circle, etc.), *reification and grasping* (comprehension, concept [German *Begriff*], perception, etc.), and *peace* (satisfaction, promise/fulfillment, etc.). This explains the affiliations I find between the otherwise diverse discourses of postmodern theory: Heidegger's de-

struction of the ontotheological tradition, Derrida's and de Man's deconstruction of logocentrism, Foucault's genealogy of the panoptic gaze of the disciplinary society, Lacan's critique of the mirroring of the symbolic order, Irigaray's feminist critique of the specular discourse of the patriarchal society, Barthes's demystification of bourgeois realism as a discourse constituted in and by the preterite mode, to suggest but a few of the discourses that in one way or another play around this constellation of enabling metaphors.

49. T. S. Eliot, "*Ulysses*, Order, and Myth," *Dial* (1923), rpr. in William Van O'Connor (ed.), *Forms of Modern Fiction* (Bloomington: Indiana University Press, 1929), p. 113.

50. Claude Lévi-Strauss, *The Savage Mind* (New York: Harper and Row, 1966), pp. 23-24. See also Lévi-Strauss's discussion of the analogy between music and myth in *The Raw and the Cooked: Introduction to a Science of Mythology: I*, trans. John and Doreen Weightman (New York: Harper and Row, 1969): "It is as if music and mythology needed time only in order to deny it. Both, indeed, are instruments for the obliteration of time. . . . Mythology makes demands primarily on the neuromental aspects because of the length of the narration, the recurrence of certain parallel themes, and the other forms of back references and parallels which can only be *correctly grasped* if the listener's mind *surveys*, as it were, the whole range of the story as it is unfolded. All this applies, too, in the case of music" (p. 16; my emphasis). The parallel with Joseph Frank and the mediation of Proust between the two should not be overlooked.

51. Michel Foucault, "Nietzsche, Genealogy, History," p. 143. The passages from Nietzsche are quoted from *The Wanderer and His Shadow* and *The Dawn*.

52. I use the term "problematic" in Althusser's sense. See especially "'On the Young Marx,'" pp. 66-70; and "From *Capital* to Marx's Philosophy," *Reading Capital* (London: Verso, 1970), pp. 19-38. The problematic is the theoretical framework that determines the questions an inquirer can ask about the object of inquiry *and* the answers at which he/she arrives. Anything outside the problematic is simply not a question for the inquirer. Or to put it in terms of the visual metaphorics informing my text, the insight of the inquirer blinds him or her to the questions that would be posed if it were possible to step outside the given problematic. Since it is normally assumed to be unproblematic — a natural rather than a socially constituted point of departure — the problematic is, therefore, the hidden ideology informing a mode of inquiry. Althusser's understanding of the problematic is thus a crucial aspect of postmodern interpretive practice. For it calls for a reading of the disinterested discourse of humanism against the grain, one that takes into account *what is left unsaid* as much as what actually gets said in a text. As Ben Brewster observes in his glossary to Althusser's *For Marx*, the problematic "can . . . only be reached by a symptomatic reading (*lecture symptomale* . . .) on the model of the Freudian analyst's reading of his patient's utterance" (p. 254).

2. HUMANISTIC INQUIRY AND THE POLITICS OF THE GAZE

1. For an amplification of this argument, see the chapter entitled "The Indifference of *Différance*: Retrieving Heidegger's Destruction," *Martin Heidegger and Criticism: Retrieving the Cultural Politics of Destruction*, forthcoming, University of Minnesota Press.

2. Michel Foucault, *The History of Sexuality, Vol. I: An Introduction*, trans. Robert Hurley (New York: Pantheon Books, 1978), p. 17.

3. See Barry Smart, "On the Limits and Limitations of Marxism," *Foucault, Marxism and Critique* (London: Routledge and Kegan Paul, 1983), pp. 4-31. Smart traces the origins of the European crisis of Marxism to "a series of events which took place in 1968," namely, the events of May '68 in France and the Prague Spring in Czechoslovakia. These events precipitated a general awareness among Western Marxists that Marx's and Engels's adversary discourse was essentially determined by the dominant liberal bourgeois capitalist discourse, i.e., the nineteenth-century *epistèmé*, and thus is subject to the same limitation as the latter.

4. See Louis Althusser, "Contradiction and Overdetermination," *For Marx*, trans. Ben Brewster (London: Verso Editions, 1979), pp. 111-12.

5. Raymond Williams, *Marxism and Literature* (Oxford: Oxford University Press, 1977), pp. 77-78.

6. Ibid., pp. 80-81.

7. Martin Heidegger, *Being and Time*, trans. John Macquarrie and Edward Robinson (New York: Harper and Row, 1962), p. 170. For his analysis of these indissoluble structures of being-in-the-world, see especially sections 28-38, pp. 169-224. For an extended analysis of my interpretation of the relationship between Heidegger's philosophical discourse and his National Socialist practice see my essay "Heidegger, Nazism, and the Repressive Hypothesis: The American Appropriation of the Question" *boundary 2*, vol. 17, 1 (Summer 1990), 199-228; reprinted in *Heidegger and Criticism*.

8. Martin Heidegger, "Letter on Humanism," trans. Frank A. Capuzzi in *Basic Writings*, ed. David Farrell Krell (New York: Harper and Row, 1977), pp. 219-20.

9. Edward Said, "Reflections on Recent American 'Left' Criticism," *boundary 2*, 8 (Fall, 1979), 27; rpr. in William V. Spanos, Paul Bové, and Daniel O'Hara (eds.), *The Question of Textuality: Strategies of Reading in Contemporary American Criticism* (Bloomington: Indiana University Press, 1982), pp. 1-30, and in Said, *The World, the Text, the Critic* (Cambridge, Mass.: Harvard University Press, 1983), pp. 158-77.

10. Report on the Core Curriculum, (original version, published on Feb. 15, 1978, by Dean Henry Rosovsky for distribution to members of the Faculty of Arts and Sciences and other members of Harvard University), p. 2.

11. The term "synoptic," which bears a significant resemblance to Jeremy Bentham's Panopticon, the point of departure of Foucault's critique of the disciplinary society, pervades the discourse of humanism in this century, especially after World War II.

12. Michel Foucault, "Final Interview," *Raritan*, vol. 5, 1 (Summer 1985), 8-9; originally published in *Les Nouvelles* (June 28, 1985). The essay to which Foucault refers is "Nietzsche, Genealogy, History," in which his focus (on historiography) is most clearly on the ontological critique of the metaphysical tradition, i.e., most clearly Heideggerian. See also Paul Rabinow, Introduction, *A Foucault Reader* (New York: Pantheon Books, 1984): "Foucault has often mistakenly been seen as a philosopher of discontinuity. The fault is partially his own; works such as *The Archaeology of Knowledge* and *The Order of Things* certainly do emphasize abrupt changes in the structures of discourse of the human sciences. But Foucault has also stressed, in other contexts, the long-range continuities in cultural practices. The stray lines of discursive discontinuity in the human sciences and the longer lines of continuity in non-discursive practices provide Foucault with a powerful and flexible grid of interpretation with which to approach relations of knowledge and power. It should be underlined, however, that this is not a philosophy of history which for some mysterious reason glorifies discontinuity" (p. 9).

13. See Martin Jay, "In the Empire of the Gaze: Foucault and the Denigration of Vision in Twentieth-Century French Thought," in *Foucault: A Critical Reader*, ed. David Couzens Hoy (Oxford: Basil Blackwell, 1986), pp. 175-204. In this essay, Jay attempts to contextualize Foucault's thought by drawing attention to its affiliation with the interrogation of sight "carried out by a wide and otherwise disparate number of French intellectuals beginning perhaps with Bergson." Although it is not exactly true that this motif of Foucault's thought is a "hitherto unexamined one," it does contribute significantly to making "sense of his remarkable work, in particular the source of its puzzling critical impulse": "Beginning with Bergson's critique of the spatialization of time, the French interrogation of sight has tended increasingly to emphasize its more problematic implications. The link between privileging vision and the traditional humanistic subject, capable of rational enlightenment, has been opened to widespread attack. The illusions of imagistic representation and the allegedly disinterested scientific gaze have been subjected to hostile scrutiny. The mystifications of the social imagery and the spectacle of late capitalist culture have been the target of fierce criticism. And the psychological dependence of the ideological 'I' on the totalizing gaze of the 'eye' has been ruthlessly exposed" (p. 178). Unfortunately, as the quoted passage itself suggests, Jay's limitation of the context to the modern French interrogation of visualism—to its origins in Bergson—tends to identify Foucault's discourse with the critique of science and thus obscures his affinities with Heidegger and the larger (historical) context it is the purpose of this chapter to focalize: that which understands the ideological continuity between science and "poetic" humanism. Further, in failing to indicate the degree to which French structuralism (Claude Lévi-Strauss and Gérard Gen-

ette, for example) enhanced the authority of visualism and the spatial model, it also obscures Foucault's poststructuralist project.

14. Michel Foucault, *Surveiller et punir: Naissance de la prison* (Paris: Editions Gallimard, 1975). In the English translation, *Discipline and Punish: The Birth of the Prison*, trans. Alan Sheridan (New York: Pantheon Books, 1977; hereafter cited *DP*), the title obscures the crucial relationship between visual perception and power and thus diverts the reader from making the connection between the metaphysical tradition (and the educational institutions to which it has given rise) and sociopolitical power; i.e., Foucault's kinship with Heidegger and Sartre. Foucault's brilliant genealogy of the modern disciplinary society is an extension and deepening of his "archaeological" analysis of the cultural significance of insanity and disease in the eighteenth century in *Madness and Civilization: A History of Insanity in the Age of Reason*, trans. Richard Howard (New York: Vintage Books, 1973) and *The Birth of the Clinic: An Archaeology of Medical Perception*, trans. A. M. Sheridan Smith (New York: Vintage Books, 1975). The genealogy of discipline is further developed in *The History of Sexuality, Vol. I: An Introduction*, trans. Robert Hurley (New York: Pantheon Books, 1978).

15. Matthew Arnold, "On the Modern Element in Literature," *The Complete Prose Works*, vol. 1, ed. R. H. Super (Ann Arbor: University of Michigan Press, 1974), p. 20.

16. William V. Spanos, "Postmodern Literature and Its Occasion: Retrieving the Preterite Middle," *Repetitions: The Postmodern Occasion in Literature and Culture* (Baton Rouge: Louisiana State University Press, 1987), pp. 200-5. Foucault refers to Vauban and the circular fortress cities, but dismisses them as an architectural geometry intended to facilitate the observation of "external space" (*DP*, p. 172). On the other hand, he invokes Claude-Nicholas Ledoux's (1736-1806) circular saltworks at Arc-et-Senans as a precursor of Bentham's Panopticon: "The perfect disciplinary apparatus would make it possible for a single gaze to see everything constantly. A central point would be both the source of light illuminating everything, and a locus of convergence for everything that must be known: a perfect eye that nothing could escape and a centre towards which all gazes would be turned. This is what Ledoux had imaged when he built Arc-et-Senans; all the buildings were to be arranged in a circle, opening on the inside, at the centre of which a high construction was to house the administrative functions of management, the policing functions of surveillance, the economic functions of control and checking, the religious functions of encouraging obedience and work; from here all order would come, all activities would be recorded, all offences perceived and judged; and this would be done immediately with no other aid than an exact geometry. Among all the reasons for the prestige that was accorded in the second half of the eighteenth century to circular architecture, one must no doubt include the fact that it expressed a certain political utopia" (*DP*, pp. 173-74). See also Foucault, "The Eye of Power," *Power/Knowledge: Selected Interviews and Other Writings 1972-1977*, ed. Colin Gordon (New York: Pantheon Books, 1980), pp. 147-48. What Foucault fails to recognize in emphasizing the "epistemic break" occurring in the Age of the Enlightenment, is that his description and analysis of the function of Ledoux's Arc-et-Senans apply *mutatis mutandi* to, say, Campanella's circular utopian City of the Sun modeled on the orderly circular macrocosm and governed from the center by the Platonic "Metaphysician" (also called "Sun" on the analogy with its planetary counterpart in the Copernican astronomy. Tommaso Campanella, *La Citte del Sole: Dialogo Poetico/The City of the Sun*, bilingual ed. trans. Daniel J. Bonno (Berkeley: University of California Press, 1981), pp. 26ff. The point I am making about the relationship between the circle—the perennial image of beauty and perfection *and* power—is inadvertently made by at least two humanists who have written on the history of the circular city: E. A. Gutkind, *Urban Development in Western Europe: France and Belgium* (New York: Free Press, 1970), vol. 5 of Gutkind, *International History of City Development*, 8 vols.; and Norman J. Johnston, *Cities in the Round* (Seattle: University of Washington Press, 1983). Both, but especially Johnston, interpret the military/disciplinary uses to which the circular/utopian model was increasingly put after the Renaissance as a tragic betrayal of the ideal envisaged by Plato and by the Renaissance humanists, for whom the circular city becomes the worldly manifestation of eternal Cosmic Beauty. However, all the evidence, including that of their own texts, points to them as the historically specific fulfillment of the latent power that theorists of the circular city, both utopians and practicing architects

and engineers, recognized in this totalizing geometry of beauty from the beginning. See, for example, Johnston, *Cities in the Round*, p. 45. For an interesting book (influenced generally by Foucault) on the relationship between Vauban's fortresses and the literature of eighteenth-century France, see Joan Dejean, *Literary Fortifications: Rousseau, Laclos, Sade* (Princeton, N.J.: Princeton University Press, 1984).

17. Campanella, *Citte del Sole*, pp. 54-55.

18. *DP*, p. 174. Although Foucault does not acknowledge it, the immediate source of his phrase is no doubt Jean-Paul Sartre's *le regard* (the look), which, one recalls, like Medusa's eye, transforms the threatening and unpredictable, because ultimately unknowable other, into stone. See *Being and Nothingness: An Essay in Phenomenological Ontology*, trans. Hazel Barnes (New York: The Citadel Press, 1964), p. 406. Sartre's extended phenomenological account of "the look" can be found in *Being and Nothingness*, pp. 228-78. For one of Sartre's many fictional and dramatic instances of "the look," see the Dr. Rogé/Achilles entry in *Nausea*, trans. Lloyd Alexander (New York: New Directions, 1964), pp. 92-96. Ultimately, as Foucault also seems to be aware, the specific image goes back to the commonplace visual depiction of God's all-seeing eye looking down on the vainly concealed sinner in Renaissance emblem books, which is accompanied by the following verse:

> Behinde a fig tree great, him selfe did ADAM hide:
> And thought from GOD hee there might lurke, & should not bee espide.
> Oh foole, no corners seeke, though thou a sinner bee;
> For none but GOD can thee forgive, who all thy waies doth see.

See, for example, Geoffrey Whitney, *A Choice of Emblems* (Leyden, 1586), p. 229.

19. From Foucault's perspective, the term "Enlightenment" assumes an ironical significance. The emphasis on the spatializing eye, which in fact deliberately forgets or conceals temporal being for the sake of power over "it," becomes not simply a blindness, but a blinding insight. For a similar critique of the Enlightenment, see Max Horkheimer and Theodor Adorno, *Dialectic of the Enlightenment*, trans. John Cumming (New York: Herder and Herder, 1972).

20. Of this "new knowledge of man," Marjorie Hope Nicolson, the celebrated humanist literary historian, says nothing in her account of the rise of the technology of optics in *Newton Demands the Muse: Newton's Optics and the Eighteenth Century Poets* (Princeton, N.J.: Princeton University Press, 1946). Indeed, no study of a cultural period demonstrates better, however inadvertently, the complicity of humanism (poetry and literary criticism) with empirical science in its will to power over being.

21. Max Weber, *The Protestant Ethic and the Spirit of Capitalism*, trans. Talcott Parsons (New York: Scribners, 1958), pp. 104-5. Foucault, in fact, alludes to this continuity between the eye of the theo-logos that, in accounting even for the fall of a sparrow, makes every singular thing and event accountable, and the later anthropo-logos that, in the surveillance of detail (difference), makes it serve the hegemonic purposes of the dominant culture (identity). And between theological and anthropological pedagogy: "There is a whole history to be written about 'stone-cutting'—a history of the utilitarian rationalization of detail in moral accountability and political control. The classical age did not initiate it; rather it accelerated it, changed its scale, gave it precise instruments, and perhaps found some echoes for it in the calculation of the infinitely small or in the description of the most detailed characteristics of natural beings. In any case, 'detail' had long been a category of theology and asceticism: every detail is important since in the sight of God no immensity is greater than a detail, nor is anything so small that it was not willed by one of his individual wishes. In this great tradition of the eminence of detail, all the minutiae of Christian education, of scholastic or military pedagogy, all forms of 'training' found their place easily enough. For the disciplined man, as for the true believer, no detail is unimportant, but not so much for the meaning that it conceals within it as for the hold it provides for the power that wishes to seize it" (*DP*, p. 140). For a definitive account of the enabling role played by the Puritan work ethic in the formation of schooling—particularly the goal of reading and writing—in colonial and post-Revolutionary America, see Sandra Jamieson "Rereading Readers" (Ph.D. diss., SUNY-Binghamton, 1991).

22. Though Foucault is referring here specifically to Jean Baptiste de la Salle's "dream" of the ideal classroom in *Conduite des écoles chrétiennes* (B. N. Ms. 11759), it is clear that the reference applies as well to the other disciplinary institutions.

23. According to Foucault, "the power of the Norm appears" with the emergence of the disciplines in the eighteenth century to combine with "other powers—the Law, the Word (*Parole*), and the Text, Tradition"—and with surveillance to become fundamental to the pedagogical economy of power of modern society: "The Normal is established as a principle of coercion in teaching with the introduction of a standardized education and the establishment of the *écoles normales* [teachers' training colleges]. . . . Like surveillance and with it, normalization became one of the great instruments of power at the end of the classical age." (*DP*, p. 184. See also p. 192.)

24. See note 16.

25. I am referring to the fusion of the American Puritan and the classical Roman heritage in the eighteenth century, a fusion already more than intimated by the Puritans, especially Cotton Mather in *Magnalia Christi Americana* (1702), in blending the Biblical and Virgilian narrative of the "saving remnant" to justify their establishment of "the city on the hill." See chapter 1, note 31.

26. Michel Foucault, "The Eye of Power," p. 152. The affiliative relation between Rousseau and Bentham that Foucault points to is also suggested by the fact that Claude-Nicholas Ledoux, the eighteenth-century French architect whose circular manufactory Arc-et-Senans, according to Foucault, prefigured Bentham's Panopticon, was an avowed Rousseauist. See William V. Spanos's "Postmodern Literature and Its Occasion: Retrieving the Preterite Middle," *Repetitions*, pp. 203-5. See also Jean Dejean, "*Julie* and *Emile*: 'Studia la Maternatica'," *Literary Fortifications*, pp. 112-90.

27. Gerald Graff, *Professing Literature: An Institutional History* (Chicago: University of Chicago Press, 1987), pp. 12-13.

28. Graff makes this point insistently in *Professing Literature*, but characteristically, as I will argue in chapter 7, fails to perceive or resists in a disabling way the relationship between ideology and structure.

29. Mikhail Bakhtin, "Epic and Novel: Towards a Methodology for the Study of the Novel," *The Dialogic Imagination: Four Essays*, ed. Michael Holquist and trans. Caryl Emerson and Michael Holquist (Austin: University of Texas Press, 1981), pp. 4-40.

30. The ideology inscribed in this apparently natural organization and distribution of classroom space disclosed itself to me several years ago in a graduate course on contemporary theory. Made acutely conscious of the importance of (antagonistic) dialogue by discourses intended to decolonize the difference colonized by identity privileged by the ontotheological tradition, I began the course (on the advice of a friend) by suggesting that all of us in the class introduce ourselves to each other: to say something about where we were from, our educational backgrounds, our reasons for studying these texts, etc. About halfway through the process, it occurred to me that the students in the first rows were by and large talking to me, that those trying to address others had virtually to break their necks to do so, and that those in the rear of the class were addressing the back of the heads of those in front. With this break in the sedimented referential surface, as Heidegger would put it, the hidden ideological function of the natural(ized) classroom manifested itself: the privileged gaze of the professor/the captivated eyes of the students; the invisible partitions; the contradictions inherent in the spatial paradigm privileged by the liberal discourse of humanism. As a consequence, I suggested that henceforth we all sit in a circle in *full consciousness of the absent center* so that our eyes would meet each other's in the process of conversation. The deconstruction of this classroom space, now recognized as constituted by the dominant culture, transformed my classes. But the degree to which the disciplinary spatial economy of the classroom is inscribed in the student is borne witness to by the easy way students keep drifting back into the traditional arrangement of classroom seating.

31. Paolo Freire, *Pedagogy of the Oppressed*, trans. Myra Bergman Ramos (New York: Seabury Press, 1968).

32. Martin Heidegger, "The Age of the World Picture," *The Question Concerning Technology and Other Essays*, trans. William Lovitt (New York: Harper and Row, 1977), pp. 133-34. In Appendix 10 of

this essay, Heidegger defines "anthropology" as "that interpretation of man that already knows fundamentally what man is and hence can never ask who he may be. For with this question it would have to confess itself shaken and overcome. But how can this be expected of anthropology when the latter has expressly to achieve nothing less than the securing consequent upon the self-secureness of the *subjectum?*" (p. 153). This momentous question, which the anthropological problematic is blind to, is precisely the question that Heidegger, Foucault, Derrida, Althusser—the postmodern countermemory in general—ask. And it is precisely the asking of this question and the ensuing shaking or, in Derrida's term, "solicitation" of *anthropo*logy that has called forth the *ressentiment* of the humanistic establishment, epitomized institutionally by William Bennett and academically by Allan Bloom. See especially Bloom's extraordinary diatribe in the name of the sanctity of reason against the professors and students of the 1960s—one replicating Bennett's in "To Reclaim a Legacy" in an even more contemptuous and irrational rhetoric—in which he draws a parallel between what he interprets as the alliance of craven professors and student mobs against the principle of reason (Socrates) and the university, and the professors (especially Heidegger) and students who destroyed the German university in the 1930s, making it the ideological vehicle for the enhancement of the irrational goals of Hitler and National Socialism: "No longer believing in their higher vocation, both [teachers and students] gave way to a highly ideologized student populace. And the content of the ideology was the same—value commitment. The university had abandoned all claim to study or inform about value—undermining the sense of value of what it taught, while turning over the *decision* about values to the folk, the *Zeitgeist*, the relevant. Whether it be Nuremberg or Woodstock, the principle is the same. As Hegel was said to have died in Germany in 1933, Enlightenment in America came close to breathing its last breath during the sixties" (*The Closing of the American Mind: How Higher Education Has Failed Democracy and Impoverished the Souls of Today's Students* [New York: Simon and Schuster, 1987], pp. 313-14); I will return to Bloom's reactionary account of the 1960s in chapter 6.

33. Martin Heidegger, "The Question Concerning Technology," *The Question Concerning Technology*, pp. 17ff. The parallel between Heidegger's understanding of enframement/standing reserve and Foucault's panopticism/docile bodies is suggested by the following definition of "standing reserve": "Everywhere everything is ordered to stand by, to be immediately at hand, indeed to stand there just so that it may be on call for a further ordering. Whatever is ordered about in this way has its own standing. We call it the standing-reserve [*Bestand*]. The word expresses here something more, and something more essential, than mere 'stock.' The name 'standing-reserve' assumes the rank of an inclusive rubric. It designates nothing less than the way in which everything presences that is wrought upon by the challenging revealing. Whatever stands by in the sense of standing-reserve no longer stands over against us as object" (p. 17). As William Lovitt observes, Heidegger "wishes to stress not the permanency, but the orderability and substitutability of objects."

34. For a more fully articulated version of the point I am making about the equiprimordiality of *Befindlichkeit*, *Verstehen*, and *Rede*, see Alex Argyros, "The Warp of the World: Deconstruction and Hermeneutics," *Diacritics*, vol. 16, 3 (Fall 1986). In a significant qualification of Jacques Derrida's curiously literal reading of Heidegger's hermeneutics, Argyros does not read this tripartite structure, the " 'collective name' of which is *Dasein*" (p. 48), as the agency of disclosing "meaning": the transcendental Truth of Being. It is, rather, the condition that renders *Dasein* always already historical (worldly) and the truth it articulates undecidable, that is, a necessary construction always open to and in need of destruction, the hermeneutic circle: "It is inaccurate . . . to think of meaning as lying 'before' or 'beneath' discourse. Indeed, it is precisely such a temporal or geological model that Heidegger would have us abandon. Meaning does not point to a temporarily obscured sense lurking behind a sign or symbol. Nor is it simply a receptacle enclosing or supporting understanding. The meaning of Being is not a transcendental essence grounding Heidegger's hermeneutic. Meaning is simply that intimation of an answer necessary to any inquiry. As the possibility of investigation, *Dasein* is that entity which, uniquely touched by Being with the gift of curiosity, *is* the hermeneutic circle. And if Heidegger claims that the circle is the only legitimate mode of philosophic inquiry, his position should not be read as normative. To the contrary, meaning, the circularity of any gesture of interpretive investigation, is that prior articulation of *Dasein*'s environment

that radically precludes the possibility of a simple, simply real, or punctual world. The meaning of Being is that meaning's other name, the world, must already have been read before it may be encountered. . . . As opposed to Husserl, for whom the presence of the present is the ultimate guarantor of truth, Heidegger 'grounds' experience in an interpretive bed of meaning which, dispersed as it is in a fore-structure preceding any possible present, is radically unphenomenal. Indeed, since meaning, the possibility of articulation, is always discursive, and insofar as discourse is less a system of constituted signs than the spacing which founds them (as well as other entities), Heidegger posits *Dasein* as that being which is defined by the precomprehension of a world which is itself nothing more than its own precomprehension or interpretation. The meaning of Being, then, would be the 'truth' of Being if by 'truth' is understood a concept that is as deeply historical, as profoundly unbounded, as Derrida's *'differance'* " (pp. 53-54). What is lacking in Argyros's brilliant reading of Heidegger's text is specification of the concept "world." Like Heidegger, he fails to draw out the cultural and sociopolitical implications of his essentially ontological analysis of an understanding of interpretation grounded on the equiprimordiality of state of mind, understanding, and discourse. Thus in the end his reading remains trapped in the base/superstructure model. Nevertheless, it points toward the opening I am undertaking to achieve in my text.

35. See also Michel Foucault, "The Life of Infamous Men," *Power, Truth, Strategy*, ed. Meaghan Morris and Paul Patton, trans. Paul Foss and Meagan Morris (Sydney, Australia: Feral Publications, 1979): The (realistic) novel, according to Foucault, "forms part of the great [panoptic] system of constraint by which the [post-Enlightenment] West compelled the everyday to bring itself into discourse" (p. 91). It would seem that Foucault's genealogy of the novel is at odds with Bakhtin's. But a careful reading of Bakhtin will suggest that he means by "the novel" not the fiction of everyday life accommodated to the logocentrism of the dominant bourgeois culture of the nineteenth century but rather that parodic tradition, originating in the carnivalesque discourses of the folk, epitomized by Rabelais, Cervantes, and Sterne and culminating in the postmodern or postrealist fiction these have influenced. This tradition has always existed to undermine the *logos* and its repressive cultural and sociopolitical allotropes: the law of the father, the symbolic order, the finished *polis*, etc. See Julia Kristeva, "Word, Dialogue and the Novel," *The Kristeva Reader*, ed. Toril Moi (New York: Columbia University Press, 1986), pp. 35-61.

36. For amplifications of Foucault's suggestive genealogy of the modern realist novel, see Mark Seltzer, *Henry James: The Art of Power* (Ithaca, N.Y.: Cornell University Press, 1984), and William V. Spanos, "Percy Lubbock and the Craft of Supervision," *Repetitions*, pp. 149-88.

37. Erich Auerbach, "Figura," *Scenes from the Drama of European Literature: Six Essays*, trans. Ralph Mannheim (New York: Meridian, 1959), pp. 53-54.

38. Michel Foucault, "What Is an Author?" *Language, Counter-Memory, Practice: Selected Essays and Interviews*, trans. Donald F. Bouchard and Sherry Simon, ed. Donald F. Bouchard (Ithaca, N.Y.: Cornell University Press, 1977), pp. 127-28. My emphasis.

39. Jacques Derrida, "Force and Signification," *Writing and Difference*, trans. Alan Bass (Chicago: University of Chicago Press, 1978), pp. 17, 20-21. My emphasis, except *"Before Polyeucte"* and *"duration."* Derrida's "preformationism" is a biological metaphor but his studied reference to Rousset's theological rhetoric and to prefiguration suggest his awareness of the affiliation between providential and preformational history. See also Louis Althusser, " 'On the Young Marx,' " *For Marx*. In this text, Althusser's criticism of humanist Marxists' "analytico-teleological method" for imposing a continuity between the differential texts of the young Marx and the late Marx is analogous to Derrida's criticism of Rousset's "structuralist method" for imposing a continuity between Corneille's early texts and *Polyeucte*, the text that completes the "Corneillean movement": "Just what . . . could we say about [Marx's] thought, considered as what it is, that is, as a whole. Would we regard it as idealist or materialist? Marxist or non-Marxist? Or should we regard its meaning as *in abeyance*, waiting on a stage it has not yet reached? But this is the way Marx's early texts are only too often treated, as if they belonged to a reserved domain, sheltered from the *'basic question'* solely because they *must* develop into Marxism. . . . As if their meaning had been held in abeyance until the end, as if it was necessary to wait on the final synthesis before their elements could be at last absorbed *into the whole*, as if, before this final synthesis, the question of the whole could not

be raised, just because all totalities earlier than the final synthesis have been destroyed? But this brings us to the height of the paradox from behind which this analytico-teleological method breaks out: this method which is constantly *judging* cannot *make the slightest judgment of any totality unlike itself*. Could there be a franker admission that it merely *judges itself, recognizes itself behind the objects it considers*, that it *never moves outside itself*, that the development it hopes to think it cannot definitively think other than as *a development of itself within itself?* And to anyone whose response to the ultimate logic that I have drawn from this method is to say '*that is precisely what makes it dialectical*'—my answer is '*Dialectical, yes, but Hegelian!*' " (p. 60). See also Pierre Macherey's *A Theory of Literary Production*, trans. Geoffrey Wall (London: Routledge and Kegan Paul, 1978), pp. 17-18. For Althusser's definition of "the problematic," see chapter 1, note 53.

40. M. H. Abrams, "Belief and the Suspension of Disbelief," *Literature and Belief*, ed. M. H. Abrams, English Institute Essays, 1957 (New York: 1958), pp. 28-29.

41. Michel Foucault, "Nietzsche, Genealogy, History," *Language, Counter-Memory, Practice*, pp. 160-61.

42. By "degradation," Bakhtin means something quite different from what it means to the dominant culture—that "low" is what a privileged "high" is not: "Degradation and debasement of the higher do not have a formal and relative character in grotesque realism. 'Upward' and 'downward' have here an absolute and strictly topographical meaning. 'Downward' is earth, 'upward' is heaven. Earth is an element that devours, swallows up (the grave, the womb) and at the same time an element of birth, of renascence (the maternal breasts). Such is the meaning of 'upward' and 'downward' in their cosmic aspect, while in their purely bodily aspect, which is not clearly distinct from the cosmic, the upper part is the face or the head and the lower part is the genital organs, the belly, and the buttocks. These absolute topographical connotations are used by grotesque realism, including medieval parody. Degradation here means coming down to earth, the contact with earth as an element that swallows up and gives birth at the same time. To degrade is to bury, to sow, and to kill simultaneously, in order to bring forth something more and better. To degrade also means to concern oneself with the lower stratum of the body, the life of the belly and the reproductive organs; it therefore relates to acts of defecation and copulation, conception, pregnancy, and birth. Degradation digs a bodily grave for a new birth; it has not only a destructive, negative aspect, but also a regenerating one. To degrade an object does not imply merely hurling it into the void of nonexistence, into absolute destruction, but to hurl it down to the reproductive lower stratum, the zone in which conception and a new birth take place. Grotesque realism knows no other lower level; it is the fruitful earth and the womb. It is always conceiving." *Rabelais and His World*, trans. Helen Iswolsky (Cambridge, Mass.: MIT Press, 1968), p. 21. In thus rehabilitating "degradation" against the multiple interdictions of social rank, Bakhtin points forcefully to a series of hierarchized binary oppositions epitomized by the identity/difference (and including the male/female and culture/anarchy) opposition that, as I will suggest in the following chapters, are fundamental to the disciplinary purposes of the discourse of humanism. See especially Bakhtin, "Epic and Novel: Towards a Methodology for the Study of the Novel," *The Dialogic Imagination*, pp. 3-40. See also Peter Stallybrass and Allon White, *The Politics and Poetics of Transgression* (Ithaca, N.Y.: Cornell University Press, 1986).

43. Bakhtin, "Epic and Novel," pp. 19-20.

44. Allan Bloom, *The Closing of the American Mind*, pp. 74-75. See William V. Spanos, "The Uses and Abuses of Certainty," *On Humanism and the University I*, a special double issue of *boundary 2* (vol. 12, 3/13, 1 [Spring/Fall] 1984), 1-12.

45. See, for example, Simon Frith, *Sound Effects: Youth, Leisure and the Politics of Rock and Roll* (New York: Pantheon Books, 1981), originally published in a different form as *The Sociology of Rock* (London: Constable, 1976); Dick Hebdige, *Subculture: The Meaning of Style* (London: Methuen, 1979); and Greil Marcus, *Lipstick Traces: A Secret History of the Twentieth Century* (Cambridge, Mass.: Harvard University Press, 1989). These and other books on rock music and culture emanating from the Birmingham School of Cultural Criticism complicate and sharply qualify the Frankfurt School's (especially Theodor Adorno's) curiously elitist and reductive critique of popular music—jazz and rock—as being wholly in the service of, if not the invention of, consumer capitalism. For the Birmingham critics, as for me, the rock culture, whatever the degree of its assimilation and

co-optation by late capitalism, is, especially in its "degradations" of official high cultural forms and styles, a *symptomatic* expression of the contradiction of and thus a symbolic form of resistance to the disciplinary society and its cultural apparatuses by a number of previously subordinated social constituencies. As Dick Hebdige puts it: "Subcultures are . . . expressive forms but what they express is, in the last instance, a fundamental tension between those in power and those condemned to subordinate positions and second-class lives. The tension is figuratively expressed in the form of subcultural style and it is appropriate that we should turn here to a metaphor for our final definition of subculture. In one of his most influential essays, 'Ideology and Ideological State Apparatuses,' Althusser describes how the different parts of the social formation—the family, education, the mass media, cultural and political institutions—together serve to perpetuate submission to the ruling ideology. However, these institutions do not perform this function through the direct transmission of 'ruling ideas.' Instead, it is the way in which they work together in what Althusser calls a 'teeth-gritting harmony' that the ruling ideology is reproduced 'precisely in its contradictions.' . . . I have interpreted subculture as a form of resistance in which experienced contradictions and objections to this ruling ideology are obliquely represented in style. Specifically I have used the term 'noise' to describe the challenge to symbolic order that such styles are seen to constitute. Perhaps it would be more accurate and more telling to think of this noise as the flip-side to Althusser's 'teeth-gritting harmony' " (pp. 132-33).

46. For a postmodern fictionalized version of the thesis I am arguing—both its exclusionary and its accommodational phases (the repression of Aristotle's "lost manuscript" on comedy and the accommodation of the carnivalesque, especially the *Coena Cyprianus*—see Umberto Eco, *The Name of the Rose*, trans. William Weaver (New York: Harcourt Brace Jovanovich, 1983). The reference to the *Coena Cyprianus* can be found on pp. 437ff.

47. Matthew Arnold, "On the Modern Element in Literature," *The Complete Prose Works*, vol. 1, ed. R. H. Roper (Ann Arbor: University of Michigan Press, 1974), p. 20. My emphasis.

48. Matthew Arnold, "Preface to the First Edition of *Poems*," *The Complete Prose Works*, vol. 1, p. 8.

49. Terry Eagleton, *Literary Theory: An Introduction* (Minneapolis: University of Minnesota Press, 1983), pp. 25-26. See also Chris Baldick, *The Social Mission of English Criticism* (Oxford: Oxford University Press, 1983). The quotation referring to the importance of impressing the people sentimentally or " 'by having the presentations in legend and history of heroic and patriotic examples brought vividly and attractively before them,' " derives from J. C. Collins, *The Study of English Literature* (1891). For further comment on this passage see my discussion of James Bryant Conant's *Education in a Divided World* (1949) in chapter 5.

50. Matthew Arnold, "Numbers; or the Majority and the Remnant," *The Complete Prose Works*, vol. 10, p. 147.

51. M. H. Abrams, *Natural Supernaturalism: Tradition and Revolution in Romantic Literature* (New York: W. W. Norton, 1971), p. 13.

52. Michel Foucault, "Revolutionary Action: 'Until Now,' " *Language, Counter-Memory, Practice*, pp. 221-22.

53. Herman Melville, *Moby-Dick*, ed. Harrison Hayford and Hershel Parker (New York: Norton Critical Editions, 1967), p. 43. Father Mapple, it will be recalled, gives his sermon on Jonah and the whale from a pulpit high above the congregation, after he has pulled up the rope-ladder "step by step, till the whole was deposited within, leaving him impregnable in his little Quebec." In thus gaining this distanced vantage point overlooking the congregation of "fallen" sailors, Father Mapple establishes an exact earthly parallel with his narrative, in which the panoptic eye of God relentlessly tracks the wayward Jonah wherever he goes to escape his calling. Not incidentally, Melville uses this same ironic image in *The Confidence-Man*, this time to thematize the immunity of an anthropological power (that of Emerson and Thoreau) that is beyond the reach of free play: "In short, with all sorts of cavilers [says the confidence man, who exposes the absence behind the confidence of anthropological confidence men] it was best, both for them and everybody, that whoever had the true light should stick behind the secure Malakoff of Confidence, not be tempted forth to hazard skirmishes on the open ground of reason." The reference is to the impregnable Malakoff defended by

the Russians in the Crimean War. *The Confidence-Man: His Masquerade*, ed. Hershel Parker (New York: W. W. Norton, 1971), p. 56.

54. Michel Foucault, "Nietzsche, Genealogy, History," *Language, Counter-Memory, Practice*, p. 152.

55. This ironic reversal, which is recurrent in Nietzsche's texts, is epitomized by his identification of the "Apollonianism" of modern German classicists with "Egyptian rigidity" in *The Birth of Tragedy*, trans. Walter Kaufmann (New York: Vintage Books, 1967): "Lest this Apollonian tendency congeal the form to Egyptian rigidity and coldness . . . the high tide of the Dionysiac destroyed from time to time all those little circles in which the one-sidedly Apollonian 'will' had sought to conquer the Hellenic spirit" (p. 72).

56. Martin Heidegger, "Letter on Humanism," *Basic Writings*, ed. David Farrell Krell (New York: Harper and Row, 1977), pp. 197-99.

3. THE APOLLONIAN INVESTMENT OF MODERN HUMANIST EDUCATIONAL THEORY: THE EXAMPLES OF MATTHEW ARNOLD, IRVING BABBITT, AND I. A. RICHARDS

1. Michel Foucault, *Discipline and Punish: The Birth of the Prison* (New York: Pantheon Books, 1977), p. 209.

2. Friedrich Schiller, *On the Aesthetic Education of Man: In a Series of Letters*, trans. Reginald Snell (New York: Frederick Ungar, 1965): "Art [and aesthetic education] must abandon actuality and soar with becoming boldness above necessity; for Art is a daughter of Freedom, and must receive her commission from the needs of spirits, not from the exigency of matter. But today Necessity is master, and bends a degraded humanity beneath its tyrannous yoke. *Utility* is the great idol of the age, to which all powers must do service and all talents swear allegiance. In these clumsy scales the spiritual service of Art has no weight; deprived of all encouragements, she flees from the noisy mart of our century. The very spirit of philosophical enquiry seizes one province after another from the imagination, and the frontiers of Art are contracted as the boundaries of science are enlarged" (p. 26).

3. See especially Thomas Huxley, "Liberal Education, and Where to Find It," and "Science and Culture" in *Science and Education* (New York: Citadel Press, 1964), pp. 72-100; 120-40.

4. See especially Matthew Arnold, *Culture and Anarchy*, vol. 5, *The Complete Prose Works*, ed. R. H. Super (Ann Arbor: University of Michigan Press, 1965); Irving Babbitt, *Literature and the American College: Essays in Defense of the Humanities* (Boston: Houghton Mifflin, 1908), *The New Laokoön: An Essay on the Confusion of the Arts* (Boston: Houghton Mifflin, 1910), *Rousseau and Romanticism* (Boston: Houghton Mifflin, 1919), *Democracy and Leadership* (Boston: Houghton Mifflin, 1924); Paul Elmer More, *Aristocracy and Justice* (Boston: Houghton Mifflin, 1915); E. M. W. Tillyard, *The Unchained Muse: An Intimate Account of the Revolution in English Studies at Cambridge* (London: Bowes and Bowes, 1958); I. A. Richards, *Principles of Literary Criticism* (London: Routledge and Kegan Paul, 1924), *Practical Criticism: A Study of Literary Judgment* (London: Routledge and Kegan Paul, Trench Trubner, 1929), *How to Read a Page* (New York: W. W. Norton, 1942), *Interpretation in Teaching* (New York: Harcourt, Brace, 1938), *Speculative Instruments* (Chicago: University of Chicago Press, 1955), *So Much Nearer: Essays Towards a World English* (New York: Harcourt, Brace and World, 1968), *General Education in a Free Society: Report of the Harvard Committee* (Cambridge, Mass.: Harvard University Press, 1945); James Bryant Conant, *Education in a Divided World: The Function of the Public Schools in Our Unique Society* (Cambridge, Mass.: Harvard University Press, 1949); Robert Maynard Hutchins, *The Higher Learning in America* (New Haven: Yale University Press, 1936); F. R. Leavis, *Education and the University: A Sketch of an English School* (New York: G. W. Stewart, 1948), *The Common Pursuit* (New York: G. W. Stewart, 1952), *Two Cultures? The Significance of C. P. Snow* (London: Chatto and Windus, 1962), *English Studies in Our Time and the University* (London: Chatto and Windus, 1969), *The Living Principle: English as a Discipline of Thought* (New York: Oxford University Press, 1975); Lionel Trilling, *Matthew Arnold*, 2d ed. (New York: Columbia University Press, 1949); *The Liberal Imagination: Essays in Literature and Society* (New York: Viking Press, 1950), *Beyond Culture: Essays on Literature and Learning* (New York: Viking Press, 1965), *Sincerity and*

Authenticity (Cambridge, Mass.: Harvard University Press, 1972); Jacques Barzun, *Teachers in America* (Garden City, N.Y.: Doubleday Anchor Books, 1954); Gerald Graff, *Literature Against Itself: Literary Ideas in Modern Society* (Chicago: University of Chicago Press, 1979), *Professing Literature: An Institutional History* (Chicago: University of Chicago Press, 1987); Phyllis Keller, *Getting at the Core: Curricular Reform at Harvard* (Cambridge, Mass.: Harvard University Press, 1982); *The Humanities in American Life: Report of the Commission on the Humanities* (Berkeley: University of California Press, 1980); Walter Jackson Bate, *The Burden of the Past and the English Poet* (New York: W. W. Norton, 1972), "The Crisis in English Studies," *Harvard Magazine*, vol. 81, 1 (Sept.-Oct. 1982), 46-53; "Report of the Commission on the Future of the Profession, Spring, 1982," *PMLA*, vol. 97 (Nov. 1982), 941-42; Allan Bloom, *The Closing of the American Mind: How Higher Education Has Failed Democracy and Impoverished the Souls of Today's Students* (New York: Simon and Schuster, 1987); E. D. Hirsch, Jr., *Cultural Literacy: What Every American Needs to Know* (New York: Houghton Mifflin, 1988); Roger Kimball, *Tenured Radicals: How Politics Has Corrupted Our Higher Education* (New York: Harper and Row, 1990); David Lehman, *Signs of the Times: Deconstruction and the Fall of de Man* (New York: Poseidon Press, 1991); Dinesh D'Souza, *Illiberal Education: The Politics of Race and Sex On Campus* (New York: The Free Press, 1991).

5. See especially Martin Heidegger, *Being and Time*, trans. John Macquarrie and Edward Robinson (New York: Harper and Row, 1962), pp. 122ff., 428 ff. I have argued this complicity as it is reflected in literature and critical theory on a number of occasions. See especially "The Detective and the Boundary: Some Notes on the Postmodern Literary Imagination" in *Repetitions: The Postmodern Occasion in Literature and Culture* (Baton Rouge: Louisiana University Press, 1987), pp. 13-49, originally published in *boundary 2*, vol. 1 (Fall 1972); "Breaking the Circle: Hermeneutics as Disclosure," *boundary 2*, vol. 2 (Winter 1977), pp. 421-57; and "Postmodern Literature and Its Occasion: Retrieving the Preterite Middle," *Repetitions*, pp. 189-276.

6. Francis Bacon, *The New Atlantis*, vol. 5, *Works*, ed. James Spedding, Robert L. Ellis, and Douglas D. Heath (New York: Hurd and Houghton, 1872), p. 398.

7. Friedrich Schiller, *On the Aesthetic Education of Man*, pp. 62-63.

8. M. H. Abrams, *Natural Supernaturalism: Tradition and Revolution in Romantic Literature* (New York: W. W. Norton, 1971), p. 13. For an analogous critique of the supplementary relationship between the theological and humanistic *logos*, see Pierre Macherey, *A Theory of Literary Production*, trans. Geoffrey Wall (London: Routledge and Kegan Paul, 1978), pp. 66ff.

9. Jacques Derrida, "Structure, Sign, and Play in the Discourse of the Human Sciences," *Writing and Difference*, trans. Alan Bass (Chicago: University of Chicago Press, 1978), p. 279. See also Martin Heidegger, *Being and Time*, pp. 41ff; and Michel Foucault, "Nietzsche, Genealogy, History," *Language, Counter-Memory, Practice: Selected Essays and Interviews*, trans. Donald F. Bouchard and Sherry Simon (Oxford: Basil Blackwell, 1977), pp. 138-64.

10. Matthew Arnold, "The Function of Criticism at the Present Time," *Lectures and Essays in Criticism*, vol. 3, *Complete Prose Works*, pp. 269-70.

11. Matthew Arnold, *Culture and Anarchy*, pp. 124ff. Hereafter cited in text as *CA*. See also "The Function of Criticism at the Present Time," pp. 266ff.

12. This phrase, which recurs again and again in Irving Babbitt's and I. A. Richards's discourse and becomes a sedimented formula of liberal humanists at large, is, of course, from Matthew Arnold's poem "To A Friend," celebrating (his Apollonian version of) Sophocles's tragic vision: "But be his / My special thanks, whose even-balanced soul / From first youth tested up to extreme old age / Business could not make dull, nor passions wild; / Who saw life steadily, and saw it whole; / The mellow glory of the Attic stage, / Singer of sweet Colonus, and its child" (*Poetical Works*, ed. L. B. Tinker and H. F. Lowry [London: Oxford University Press], p. 2). Since Arnold's mystified formula has become by this time a cliché of humanistic discourse and pedagogy, one of the purposes of this chapter will be to interrogate its usage in order to disclose its figural and ideological origins, which habituation and sedimentation have concealed.

13. Although much could be said about Arnold's ethnocentric humanism at this point, I postpone comment until my discussion of I. A. Richards. For history made Richards far more aware of European

cultural provincialism and thus compelled him to open up the Arnoldian canon to accommodate the best that has been thought and said in other than Western nations.

14. The continuity of Arnold's cultural/political thought with that of the cultural critics of German Romantic classicism becomes evident in comparing this passage with the following in Friedrich Schiller's *On the Aesthetic Education of Man*: "Every individual man, it may be said, carries in disposition and determination a pure ideal man within himself, with whose unalterable unity it is the great task of his existence, throughout all his vicissitudes, to harmonize. This pure human being, who may be recognized more or less distinctly in every person, is represented by the *State*, the objective and, so to say, canonical form in which the diversity of persons endeavours to unite itself" (p. 31).

15. Arnold makes this equation twelve times in the chapter of *Culture and Anarchy* entitled "Doing as One Likes."

16. Arnold deleted the rather gruesome (however caricatured) second paragraph, in which he identifies his own view of the function of the state with his father's "old Roman way of dealing with [rioting]," from the second edition of *Culture and Anarchy* published in 1875. It was not restored until 1932, when, under the editorship of J. Dover Wilson, the original unexpurgated text was reprinted in its entirety by Cambridge University Press. It is important to point out, however, that despite his assertion that "the restoration is by no means of purely antiquarian interest," Wilson's motive was not to call the politics of Arnold's humanism into question but to restore "its original 'vivacities' " that the passage of time—and its achievement of the status of classic—had annulled: "Clearly the principal object of these deletions was to suppress or tone down personal allusions, either in order to remove grounds of offence—Arnold was ever a man of peace—or because the allusions had ceased to be topical and would no longer interest the public. But *Culture and Anarchy* is now a classic; the shrinking flesh flicked on the raw by its original 'vivacities' has long been compounded with the dust; and though many of the names and allusions omitted in 1875 are ten times more forgotten in 1931, the rediscovery of them often gives point to Arnold's argument and helps us to understand the mood in which he wrote," "Editor's Preface," *Culture and Anarchy* (London: Cambridge University Press, 1932), p. vii. It is not irrelevant to add, as the bracketing of this paragraph in my text suggests, that R. H. Super, the editor of the definitive *Complete Prose Works* published by the University of Michigan Press, reprints the expurgated version of *Culture and Anarchy*.

17. When Arnold's editors explain his "topical allusions" (as they are usually called in the notes to their editions of his texts), events such as this one, despite their facticity, are invariably interpreted from Arnold's point of view. This is pervasive, for example, in the Critical and Explanatory Notes to *The Complete Prose Works of Matthew Arnold*, edited by R. H. Super. There is, of course, no way to verify this charge in a footnote, but its validity can be suggested by pointing to Super's insistent, however naive, use of Arnold's pejorative rhetoric in his "factual" account of the events referred to above: "The Reform League organized a monster meeting for Hyde Park on July 23, 1866 . . . " (pp. 384-85); "At one point two companies of the Guards were called out, but the soldiers did not come into actual conflict with the people. Rioting was resumed the next day [there is an incredible—and eloquent—gap between these two casually articulated sentences] and windows in the Athenaeum Club, of which Arnold was a member, were broken" (p. 385); "Edmond Beale (1808-1881) was president of the Reform League during its short and prosperous life (1865-1869) and organizer of the monster rallies on behalf of reform in July, 1866" (p. 420). For a significantly different representation of these same events of July 1866, see Raymond Williams, "A Hundred Years of Culture and Anarchy," *Problems in Materialism and Culture: Selected Essays* (London: New Left Books, 1980), pp. 3-10. What Arnold and his "disinterested" editors call "the monster rallies," for example, Williams refers to in terms of an effort "to establish the right of free assembly" (p. 4).

This question of explanatory notes to historical texts that traditional scholars have naively taken for granted becomes, in the context of an emergent neomaterialist literary criticism, an enormously important issue for scholarship, one that needs intensive interrogation. For, as "new historians" have gone some way to suggest, it is precisely in the historical allusions relegated to "topicality" and to dubiously factual footnotes by traditional humanistic scholars who worry about the contamination of the universality of their texts by the density of particular history, or what I would call their occasion, that we discover the worldliness of the text and its cultural and socio-political affiliations.

18. Edward Said, "Introduction: Secular Criticism," *The World, the Text, and the Critic* (Cambridge, Mass.: Harvard University Press, 1983), p. 11. It should be made clear here that, like Said, I am stressing the negative or repressive function of the panoptic schema rather than its positive or productive function: its construction of the sovereign subject as agency of the production of knowledge for the sake of achieving a more economic political economy of power. Though the latter plays a significant role in Arnold's discourse and should not be overlooked, it is subordinated to the former because, as his insistent reference to "doing as one likes" suggests, the social tensions (contradictions) inhering in the fiction of the sovereign individual were beginning to manifest themselves in Great Britain in the historically specific moment in which Arnold was writing his cultural criticism.

19. In line with the central terms of Arnold's binary metaphorics, the word "cure" and its synonyms recur insistently in his texts, designating him as *pharmakos* and his "disinterested inquiry" as the remedy for the disease of partiality or provincialism and the threat of anarchy. For example, "But now to evince the disinterestedness which culture teaches us. We have seen the narrowness generated in Puritanism by its hole-in-the-corner organization, and we propose to cure it by bringing Puritanism more into contact with the main current of national life. Here we are fully at one with the Dean of Westminster; and, indeed, he and we were trained in the same school to mark the narrowness of Puritanism, and to wish to cure it" (*CA*, p. 245).

20. Irving Babbitt, *Literature and the American College: Essays in Defense of the Humanities* (Boston: Houghton Mifflin, 1908), p. 25. Hereafter cited *LAC*.

21. It is this critique of scientific and emotional humanitarian naturalism—the humanitarian and sentimental impulses—that affiliates Babbitt's New Humanism with the antihumanist humanism of T. E. Hulme, Wyndham Lewis, T. S. Eliot, and ultimately the New Critics, especially Allen Tate and Cleanth Brooks. See especially T. E. Hulme, "Humanism and the Religious Attitude," *Speculations: Essays on Humanism and the Philosophy of Art*, ed. Herbert Read (New York: Harcourt, Brace, 1924), pp. 3-71.

22. Irving Babbitt, *Rousseau and Romanticism* (New York: Meridian Books, 1955), pp. 54-55.

23. Arnold uses the metaphor of expansion in an ambiguous way, implying at times the movement away from the center toward anarchy, and, at others, a process that includes and accommodates wider and wider areas of knowledge as the circumference of the centered circle expands. Babbitt, on the other hand, invariably understands this metaphor, which pervades his discourse, as the second (negative) term of a binary opposition in which the privileged first term is "concentration," an inward movement that, as the etymology suggests, intensifies (and makes more visible) the power and authority of the center over the circumference. This metaphorical opposition is, of course, an extension of Babbitt's insistent polarization of the "concentric" and "eccentric" and of "measure" and "measurelessness."

24. *Rousseau and Romanticism*, pp. 26-27. That Babbitt has Arnold in mind in these passages is made clear in his essay review of Stuart Pratt Sherman's *Matthew Arnold: How to Know Him* in *The Nation*, vol. 105 (1917), 117-21. What he says about Aristotle in *Rousseau and Romanticism* he also—in virtually the same words—says here about Arnold: "But man, Arnold insisted, is the creature of two laws. In addition to his ordinary self of passing impulse and desires he has a permanent self that is felt in its relation to his ordinary self as a power of control. As a matter of experience, man can find happiness only in so far as he exercises this control. To deny such a conflict in man between a law of the spirit and a law of the members is simply to avert one's face from the facts and so to fall short of being completely positive and critical" (Irving Babbitt, *Representative Writings*, ed. George A. Panichas [Lincoln: University of Nebraska Press, 1981], p. 105).

25. *The Dhammapada*, trans. Irving Babbitt (New York: Oxford University Press, 1936).

26. Irving Babbitt, "Buddha and the Occident," *Representative Writings*, pp. 225-27.

27. Ibid., p. 237.

28. Ibid., p. 228.

29. Irving Babbitt, "Appendix: Chinese Primitivism," *Rousseau and Romanticism*, p. 297.

30. Babbitt, *Rousseau and Romanticism*, p. 27. See also pp. 25, 84.

31. Martin Heidegger, *Being and Time*, section 27, pp. 163-68. See also "Letter on Humanism," *Basic Writings*, ed. David Farrell Krell (New York: Harper and Row, 1977), p. 197.

32. Babbitt, *Rousseau and Romanticism*, pp. 62-63.

33. Since Babbitt, like Arnold, makes much of "high seriousness," which he puts insistently in terms of sobriety, it is worth pointing to the possible relationship in his mind, if not the actual etymology, between "hubris (ὕβρις)," that "insolent excess" that violates the law of measure, and "inebriation," that "wantoning of the imagination" (*Rousseau and Romanticism*, p. 57), which is the consequence of devotion to "the god Whirl": " 'Whirl is King,' cried Aristophanes, 'having driven out Zeus.' The modern sophist is even more a votary of the God Whirl than the Greek, for he has added to the mobility of an intellect that has no support in either tradition or insight the mobility of feeling. . . . Even more significant than the cult of vertigo is the closely allied cult of intoxication, 'Man being reasonable,' says Byron, with true Rousseauistic logic, 'must therefore get drunk. The best of life is but intoxication.' The subrational and impulsive self of the man who has got drunk is not only released from the surveillance of reason in any sense of the word, but his imagination is at the same time set free from the limitations of the real" (*Rousseau and Romanticism*, p. 147). Babbitt, in fact, virtually makes this connection between spatial perception and sobriety, on the one hand, and temporal experience and inebriation, on the other, in *Rousseau and Romanticism* (p. 167). "In an absolute sense nobody can see life steadily and see it whole; but we may at least move towards steadiness and wholeness. The aesthete is plainly moving in the opposite direction; he is becoming more and more openly a votary of the god Whirl" (p. 167). That this central metaphorical/ideological opposition—and the characteristically excessive, oversimplified, and remarkably ungenerous rhetoric in which it is presented—is not foreign to the contemporary reformist movement in education should be obvious to anyone who has read Allan Bloom's *Closing of the American Mind*. Compare, for example, the following representative passage on today's students' preference for the rock music that was symptomatic of the irrational dismantling of reason and its institutional apparatuses, such as the core curriculum, in the 1960s: "Only in those great critics of Enlightenment and rationalism, Rousseau and Nietzsche, does music return, and they were the most musical of philosophers. Both thought that the passions—and along with them their ministerial arts—had become thin under the rule of reason and that, therefore, man himself and what he sees in the world have become correspondingly thin. They wanted to cultivate the enthusiastic states of the soul and to re-experience the Corybantic possession deemed a pathology by Plato. Nietzsche, particularly, sought to tap again the irrational sources of vitality, to replenish our dried-up stream from barbaric sources, and thus encouraged the Dionysian and the music derivative from it. This is the significance of rock music. I do not suggest that it has any high intellectual sources. But it has risen to its current heights in the education of the young on the ashes of classical music, and in an atmosphere in which there is no intellectual resistance to attempts to tap the rawest passions. Modern-day rationalists, such as economists, are indifferent to it and what it represents. The irrationalists are all for it. There is no need to fear that 'the blond beasts' are going to come forth from the bland souls of our adolescents. But rock music has one appeal only, a barbaric appeal, to sexual desire—not love, not *eros*, but sexual desire undeveloped and untutored" (p. 73).

34. In explanation of his decision to give up his professorship of history at Harvard University in 1877, Adams writes: "For himself he was clear that the fault lay in the system, which would lead to inertia [read "indifferent or motionless motion"]. Such little knowledge of himself as he preserved warranted him in affirming that his mind required conflict, competition, contradiction, even more than that of the student. He too wanted a rank-list to get his name upon. His reforms of the system would have begun in the lecture-room at his desk. He would have seated a rival assistant professor opposite him, whose business should be strictly limited to expressing opposite views. Nothing short of this would ever interest either the professor or the student: but of all university freaks, no irregularity shocked the intellectual atmosphere as much as contradiction or competition between teachers. In that respect the Nineteenth-century university system was worth the whole teaching

of the modern school.

"All his petty efforts to create conflicts of thought among his students failed for want of system [by which he means an environment sympathetic to his decentered stance]. None met the needs of instruction. In spite of Eliot's reforms and his steady, generous, liberal support, the system remained costly, clumsy and futile. The university—as far as it was represented—produced at great waste of time and money results that were not worth reaching." *The Education of Henry Adams*, ed. Ernest Samuels (New York: Houghton Mifflin, 1973), pp. 303-4.

35. Symptomatically, Babbitt uses the same metaphor from Emerson over ten years later in *Rousseau and Romanticism*, p. 143.

36. Pierre Macherey, *A Theory of Literary Production*, pp. 17-18.

37. Babbitt, *Rousseau and Romanticism*, p. 167: "In an absolute sense nobody can see life steadily and see it whole; but we may at least move towards steadiness and wholeness. The [Romantic] aesthete is plainly moving in an opposite direction; he is becoming more and more openly a votary of the god Whirl."

38. The influence of Babbitt's overview of the Western literary tradition as a continuous whole authorized and presided over by a single, unified, and self-present "humanistic mind" on his recalcitrant pupil, T. S. Eliot, is readily recognizable, despite the latter's greater sophistication and depth of vision, especially in his famous and influential definition of the historical sense: "The historical sense compels a man to write not merely with his generation in his bones, but with a feeling that the whole of the literature of Europe from Homer and within it the whole of the literature of his own country has a simultaneous existence and composes a simultaneous order" ("Tradition and the Individual Talent," *The Sacred Wood* [London: Methuen, 1920], p. 49). Elsewhere in this essay, Eliot refers to this simultaneous order as "the mind of Europe" (p. 51). See also "What Is a Classic?," *On Poetry and Poets* (London: Faber and Faber, 1957), pp. 53-71, for a far less ambiguous statement of Eliot's teleological understanding of the European memory.

39. Martin Heidegger, *Being and Time*, pp. 194-95.

40. Michel Foucault, *The Order of Things: An Archaeology of the Human Sciences*, trans. Alan Sheridan (New York: Vintage Books, 1973), pp. 17-44.

41. Louis Althusser and Etienne Balibar, "Marx's Immense Theoretical Revolution," *Reading Capital*, trans. Ben Brewster (London: New Left Books, 1970), pp. 186-89.

42. R. P. Blackmur, "Humanism and the Symbolic Imagination: Notes on Rereading Irving Babbitt," *The Lion and the Honeycomb: Essays in Solicitude and Critique* (New York: Harcourt, Brace and World, 1955), pp. 146-47.

43. Babbitt, *Rousseau and Romanticism*, p. 130.

44. Irving Babbitt, *Democracy and Leadership* (Boston: Houghton Mifflin, 1924), pp. 246-47.

45. Matthew Arnold, "The Function of Criticism," pp. 266-67. See Edmund Burke, *Works and Correspondence*, 8 vols. (London: R. and J. Rivington, 1852), vol. 4, p. 591: "If a great change is to be made in human affairs, the minds of men will be fitted to it; the general opinions and feelings will draw that way. Every fear, every hope will forward it; and then they who persist in opposing this mighty current in human affairs, will appear rather to resist the decrees of Providence itself, than the mere designs of men. They will not be resolute and firm but perverse and obstinate."

46. Babbitt, *Democracy and Leadership*, pp. 311-12.

47. Blackmur, "Humanism and the Symbolic Imagination," pp. 156-57.

48. Ibid., p. 154.

49. I am appropriating this phrase from Joseph Conrad's *Nostromo*, where it is used insistently to thematize both the hegemonic imperatives of liberal capitalist enterprise and the alienation of being all along its continuum that is the inevitable consequence of its reifications.

50. Herman Melville, *Moby-Dick*, ed. Harrison Hayford and Hershel Parker (New York: Norton Critical Editions, 1967), p. 43.

51. R. P. Blackmur, "The Craft of Herman Melville: A Putative Statement," *The Lion and the Honeycomb*, p. 132. My emphasis.

52. See, for example, Douglas Bush, "Irving Babbitt: Crusader," in *Reappraisals, The American Scholar*, vol. 48 (1979), 515-22; J. David Hoeveler, Jr., *The New Humanism: A Critique of Modern*

America, 1900-1940 (Charlottesville: University Press of Virginia, 1977); George A. Panichas, "Introduction," *Irving Babbitt: Representative Writings*, p. vii-xxxix; Walter Jackson Bate, "To the Editor of *Critical Inquiry*," a response to Stanley Fish's "Profession Despise Thyself: Fear and Self-Loathing in Literary Studies," *Critical Inquiry*, vol. 10 (December 1983), 368. It would, in fact, be quite easy to demonstrate the continuing influence of Babbitt's conservative humanistic discourse on Bate, especially if one focused on the mutual central theme of their writing: originality in a centrifugal era of expansion. Like Babbitt's, Bate's essential thesis in his influential book, *The Burden of the Past and the English Poet* (New York: W. W. Norton, 1970), is that the abandonment of the principle of imitation in favor of the principle of originality by the Romantic poets precipitated a cultural process that has ended in the "neurosis" of the modern period, a neurosis which can only be remedied by the recuperation of the *litterae humaniores*. This thesis, articulated in the context of the disruptions on college campuses during the Vietnam War, is repeated, this time in response to the emergence of theory, principally that of deconstruction, in the 1980s, in his by now notorious essay "The Crisis of English Studies," *Harvard Magazine*, vol. 85 (Sept.-Oct. 1982), calling on university administrators to save "the humanities," which "seem bent on a self-destructive course." Addressing the "centrifugal heterogeneity" (p. 50), which is to say "the crisis of literary studies" precipitated by the obsession for originality, Bate writes: "One of the sadder commonplaces about human nature is the incorrigible tendency (when we face a high enough achievement or something different enough from our individual experience [Bate, of course, is alluding to the thesis of *The Burden of the Past*] to imitate the wrong things—or at least the peripheral rather than the essential things. . . . What is called 'decay' in movements in the arts (since we began to make an idolatry of the idea of 'originality' in the later eighteenth century) is often said to be 'imitation.' This is silly. The scent of decay in the arts comes not from imitation . . . but from an imitation of the wrong, unessential things, the exterior mannerisms" (p. 48). See my essay *"boundary 2* and the Polity of Interest: Humanism, the 'Center Elsewhere,' and Power," *On Humanism and the University I*, a special double issue of *boundary 2* (vol. 12, 3/13, 1 [Spring/Fall 1984]), 182-92.

53. *General Education in a Free Society: Report of the Harvard Committee* (Cambridge, Mass.: Harvard University Press, 1950).

54. In his chapter "A Free, Varied, and Unwasteful Life: I. A. Richards's Speculative Instruments," *Intellectuals in Power: A Critique of Critical Humanism* (New York: Columbia University Press, 1986), Paul Bové offers a parallel reading of Richards's literary criticism that persuasively discloses the integral (synoptic) relationship between Richards's understanding of the disciplinary reading of poetry, especially as it is articulated in *Principles of Literary Criticism* (1929) and in *Practical Criticism* (1931), and university education in general. These, it should not be forgotten, were the two most influential texts in the production of the now theoretically questionable—if still actively and widely practiced—New Critical method of close or intrinsic reading and in the establishment of this rigorous disciplinary spatial hermeneutics as *the* method, not simply of literary study, but of encounter with virtually all semiotic systems in the Anglo-American academy. "What is clear," Bové writes, "is that I. A. Richards and a great deal of Anglo-American academic criticism practiced after him as a discipline, that is, as an accumulative, cooperative project for the production of knowledge, the exercise of power, and the creation of careers, emerges with a degree of self-consciousness from this nineteenth-century problematic [the orientation that authorizes literary criticism to "resist, master and control the mysterious multiplicity of language's inflationary proliferation"] and furthermore that it attempts in its own ways to rebalance what it sees as the disorderly functions of language, to reestablish a linguistic unity through and in a positively productive academic critical discipline that, somewhat belatedly, affiliates itself with and at times tries to master the other positive disciplines such as economics, psychology, medicine, and anthropology. Richards urgently senses that the inflation and differentiation of language and language study is a threat to a balanced, sane, and healthy civilization. To balance the complex machine of language he initiates a realignment of elements of critical method, rhetoric, and practice with the hope of changing the existence of literature as a special sphere of language unavailable to disciplined study" (p. 48). This homologous relationship between Richards's understanding of the discipline of literary interpretation and that of university education is a decisive one that the compartmentalization of

the continuum of knowledge into disciplines has caused literary critics interested only in Richards's poetics to overlook. For, as Bové suggests, it points to the *interest* that ultimately informs the introductory courses in "objective" literary analysis (i.e., close reading) that, despite the New Criticism's loss of theoretical authority, are still more or less universally required for English majors, and which continue to shape the interpretive mindset and judgmental norms of undergraduates, not only in literary study but in other "disciplines" as well. See my essay "Theory in the Undergraduate Curriculum: Towards an Interested Pedagogy," *boundary 2* (vol. 56, 2/3, Winter/Spring, 1989]), 41-70.

55. I. A. Richards, *Speculative Instruments* (Chicago: University of Chicago Press, 1955); hereafter cited as *SI*. The essays collected in this volume were written between 1940 and 1955, during the period of Richards's involvement in the development of the general education program at Harvard. Elsewhere in this essay, Richards refers to this dispersal of knowledge as "an illimitable proliferation . . . of facts, comments, opinions, and mere phrases, too extensive and diverse to form, in any mind not of a rare order, any coherent, much less any directing or confirming, view of essential human purpose" (p. 60). It needs to be said that Richards does not deny such a "directing or confirming view," *only that the ordinary person cannot see it.* Richards does not specify what he means by the "modern scholarship" affiliated with the other agencies of proliferation. Given his theoretical commitment to an ahistorical view of literature, historiography, and so on, and to the autonomy of cultural texts and the impersonality of authorship, one can be certain that at least one significant aspect of this disruptive scholarship is that associated with the emergence of existentialism during World War II.

56. I. A. Richards, *Principles of Literary Criticism*, pp. 249-50. The influence of Richards's definition on the New Critics can be seen in Cleanth Brooks's adoption of the distinction between the exclusive and inclusive poem in *Modern Poetry and the Tradition* (New York: Oxford University Press, 1965), pp. 41-47. The structure of balanced inclusion constitutes Richards's (and the New Critics') ideal model for psyche, poem, culture, socius, state, etc. All these sites are implied in some degree or other in any particular one of his texts, whether such a text is centrally about psychology, the principles of literary criticism, the pedagogy of literary interpretation, the idea of the university, culture, or national or international politics.

Further, Richards's account of the ideal poem (and society) is an updating of Arnold's "disinterestedness," his Apollonian commitment, against intellectual provincialism, to seeing life steadily and seeing it whole. This becomes evident in the pages following his definition of the two kinds of poetry: "The equilibrium of opposed impulses, which we suspect to be the ground-plan of the most valuable aesthetic responses, brings into play far more of our personality than is possible in experiences of a more defined emotion. We cease to be orientated in one definite direction; more facets of the mind are exposed and, what is the same thing, more aspects of things are able to affect us. To respond, not through one narrow channel of interest, but simultaneously and coherently through many, is to be *disinterested* in the only sense of the word which concerns us here. A state of mind which is not disinterested is one which sees things only from one standpoint or under one aspect. At the same time since more of our personality is engaged the independence and individuality of other things becomes greater. We seem to see 'all round' them, to see them as they really are; we see them apart from any one particular interest which they may have for us. Of course without some interest, we should not see them at all, but the less any one particular interest is indispensable, the more *detached* our attitude becomes. And to say that we are *impersonal* is merely a curious way of saying that our personality is more *completely* involved" (pp. 251-52; Richards's emphasis). The seductive paradox informing this passage is disarming. But the crucial qualification, which Richards characteristically *subordinates* ("Of course without some interest we should not see them at all"), is an aporia that deconstructs the authority of the paradoxical definitions of "disinterestedness" and "impersonality." That is to say, it is the colonized voice of *interest* seeking its *own* articulation inside the rigid confines of a constituted binary opposition of an absolutely positive disinterest and an absolutely negative (narrow, provincial, exclusive, i.e., Arnold's "Hebraistic") engagement. Far from exonerating disinterestedness of its complicity with the will to power, Richards's definition bears witness against itself to his affiliation not only with Matthew Arnold's authoritarian discourse but also with the philosophers of the Enlightenment (including Bentham), who, according to Gadamer, reduced interest to *prejudice* and thus institutionalized this binary opposition between disinterested and interested or committed inquiry. Richards's discourse, in other words, reinscribes the reductive terms of the "two cultures" debate initiated at the site of Anglo-American education by Arnold and T. H. Huxley, the debate which it is one of the main purposes of postmodern theory to demystify by demonstrating their affiliative scholarship: their mutual reliance on metaphysical (circular) thinking. It has been Gadamer's hermeneutic project (following Heidegger) to rehabilitate or decolonize prejudice; that is, as the interest that activates inquiry and, in turn, that is always already undermined and transformed by the disclosure of that inquiry. See Hans-Georg Gadamer, *Truth and Method*, trans. and ed. by Garret Barden and J. Cumming (New York: The Seabury Press, 1973): "The overcoming of all prejudice, this global demand of the enlightenment, will prove to be itself a prejudice, the removal of which opens the way to an appropriate understanding of our finitude, which dominates not only our humanity, but also our historical consciousness" (p. 244).

57. Michel Foucault, *Discipline and Punish*, p. 148. See also *The Order of Things*, pp. 73-75.

58. See especially the chapter entitled "Docile Bodies," *Discipline and Punish*, pp. 135-69.

59. Michel Foucault, *Madness and Civilization: A History of Insanity in the Age of Reason*, trans. Richard Howard (New York: Vintage Books, 1965), pp. 241-78.

60. See also "Towards a More Synoptic View," *SI*, p. 122: "And since language is inescapably a social acteevity [sic] which only comes into existence with, and owes its whole character to, mutualities among men and within communities, the study of language, even in the most elementary stages, has to be a dependent of that highest generic taping which may be called ethics. It is concerned— endlessly—with standards and validity. It must be as *normative* through and through as, for example, the study of *medicine*" (Richards's emphasis).

61. Paul Bové, "A Free, Varied, and Unwasteful Life," *Intellectuals in Power*, pp. 67-68. The quotation from Foucault appears in *Discipline and Punish*, p. 183.

62. "Towards a More Synoptic View," *SI*, pp. 113-26, based on a talk given at the Eighth Conference on Cybernetics held under the auspices of the Josiah Macy, Jr., Foundation in New York on March 15, 1951.

63. For Richards's account of his understanding of the hermeneutic circle, see his discussion of "Circular and Feedback Mechanisms" in "Towards a More Synoptic View," pp. 118ff. A comparison with Heidegger's phenomenological understanding of hermeneutic circularity in which the inquirer "leap[s] into the 'circle,' primordially and wholly," i.e., acknowledges temporality as the agency of the disclosure of difference (*Being and Time*, p. 63), reveals the degree to which Richards's "feedforward" mechanism is in fact essentially metaphysical and viciously circular. See also my essay "Heidegger, Kierkegaard, and the Hermeneutic Circle: Towards a Postmodern Theory of Interpretation as Disclosure," *boundary 2*, vol. 4, 2 (Winter 1976), 455-88. Indeed, such a comparison reveals the degree to which Richards's mechanism is what Heidegger would call a cybernetic instrument, i.e., an instrument drained of its ontological content (Martin Heidegger, "The End of Philosophy and the Task of Thinking," *On Time and Being*, trans. Joan Stambaugh [New York: Harper Colophon Books, 1972], pp. 59-60).

64. I derive the word from Robert Creeley ("poetry is the measure of its occasion") and intend it to decolonize the meaning alienated by the privileged first term of the opposition universal/occasional. The retrieved meaning is suggested by its etymology: immediately from the Latin *occasus*, "the setting of the sun," and ultimately from the ablative form of *cadre* (as in *de casibus illustrium virorum*), "to fall," "to perish," "to die." It is also intended to evoke other colonized cognates such as "case" (as in "being-in-the-world is our case"), "accidental," "incidental," "cadence," and, not least, "Occident," from *occidere* ("to go down," "to set"), a correlate of *cadere* and *occasus*). See William V. Spanos, "Postmodern Literature and the Hermeneutic Circle," *Union Theological Review*, vol. 34 (Winter 1979), 127-28; and "Postmodern Literature and Its Occasion," *Repetitions*, pp. 231-37. For Martin Heidegger's version of this occasional measure see especially " . . . Poetically Man Dwells . . . " pp. 221-25.

65. Like Hegel, Richards gives inordinate value to the word "comprehend" precisely because of its etymological connotations (*com* + *prehendre*, "to understand by seizing or grasping *all* [at once]"). Behind this valorization, as I have noted, is the concept of the hermeneutic circle in which Being is the condition for the possibility of temporality. See, for example, "Towards a Theory of Comprehension," *SI*, pp. 17-38.

66. See Frank Kermode, *The Classic: Literary Images of Permanence and Change* (Cambridge, Mass.: Harvard University Press, 1983), pp. 15-80 (originally published by Faber and Faber, 1975). Ostensibly a critique of T. S. Eliot's "imperialistic" or "Virgilian" understanding of the classic and the tradition (the Eternal or "essential") in favor of a "provincial" (the temporal and transient or "dispositional") understanding, Kermode as humanist will not, unfortunately, deny the validity of the idea of the classic. Thus, despite his effort to escape, he remains loyal to the identity or *télos* that his forebears Arnold, Babbitt, and Richards invoke more overtly in their interpretations of literary history. Despite his acknowledgment of the temporality of the historical process, Kermode continues to give ontological priority to being/form/*logos*/presence in interpreting it. Thus remaining caught in the hermeneutic circle by colonizing temporality within the traditional binary structure, he reinstates a hermeneutics of accommodation in the act of trying to displace it and recuperates (if in a naturalized form) an imperialistic view of the classic in the act of trying to call it into question: "It can be argued . . . that to require the classic to speak to us directly in our time, rather than demand of ourselves the effort to speak to the classic in *its* time, is an instance of what Eliot calls 'overestimation of the importance of our own time' and of ourselves. Yet the fact is inescapable that a much humbler tradition than Eliot's [clearly his own anthropological humanism]—working through time, across generations—is the proximate cause of there being any classics—old books which people still read—at all. *And this means that over and over again in time those old books are accommodated to the sense* [common? If not, what?] of readers whose language and culture is different. Here we deal in dispositions, not essences. The paradox—that there is an identity but that it changes—is made more difficult by the certainty that it can in some measure be redeemed from change, by an *effort* of interpretation rather than simple accommodation, the establishment of 'relevance.' It seems that on a just view of the matter the books we call classics possess intrinsic qualities that endure, but possess also an openness to accommodation which keeps them alive under endlessly varying dispositions" (pp. 43-44; my emphasis). Further, Kermode's discussion of the "imperialism" of the classic understood in terms of the tradition to which Eliot belongs and which he would recuperate is virtually devoid of material history: the dense historical conjunctures that precipitate the classic and the sociopolitical implications of its canonization. For Kermode, this "imperialism" is essentially a literary matter.

67. Martin Heidegger, "A Dialogue on Language," *On the Way to Language*, trans. Peter D. Hertz (San Francisco: Harper and Row, 1982), p. 15. This, it is worth emphasizing, is a reiterated motif in Heidegger's late writing on technology and in "The Age of the World Picture." See, for example, "The End of Philosophy": "The End of Philosophy proves to be the triumph of the manipulable arrangement of a scientific-technological world and of the social order proper to this world. The end of philosophy means: the beginning of the world civilization based upon Western European thinking" (p. 59).

68. Edward Said, *Orientalism* (New York: Pantheon Books, 1978), pp. 145-46. Said is referring primarily to Renan's *Histoire générale et système comparé des langues semitique* and *L'Avenir de les sciences: Pensées de 1848*.

69. Quoted in Edward Said, "Secular Criticism," *The World, the Text and the Critic*, p. 12. Said derives this quotation from Philip D. Curtin, ed., *Imperialism* (New York: Walter, 1971), p. 181.

70. Ibid., p. 13.

71. I. A. Richards, "Toward a World English," *So Much Nearer: Essays Toward a World English* (New York: Harcourt, Brace and World, 1968), p. 241. For a characteristic example of this kind of accommodation, see Edward Said's analysis of the 1925 recommendations vis-à-vis the emergent "Orient" of the distinguished French Orientalist, Sylvain Lévi (*Orientalism*, pp. 248-50). In a brief reference to *Mencius on the Mind: Experiments in Multiple Definition* (London: Routledge and Kegan Paul, 1932), however, Said curiously finds Richards's discourse a gratifying exception to this

characteristic Orientalist accommodation of the emergent "East": "My point is that the metamorphosis of a relatively innocuous philological subspeciality into a capacity for managing political movements, administering colonies, making nearly apocalyptic statements representing the White Man's difficult civilizing mission—all this is something at work within a purportedly liberal culture, one full of concern for its vaunted norms of catholicity, plurality, and open-mindedness. In fact, what took place was the opposite of liberal: the hardening of doctrine and meaning, imparted by 'science,' into 'truth.' For if such truth reserved for itself the right to judge the Orient as immutably Oriental in ways I have indicated, the liberality was no more than a form of oppression and mentalistic prejudice.

"The extent of such illiberality has not been—and is not—often recognized from within the culture. . . . It is heartening, nevertheless, that such illiberality has occasionally been challenged [as in Richards's *Mencius*]. . . . Richards's argument advances claims for the exercise of what he calls Multiple Definition, a genuine type of pluralism, with the combativeness of systems definition eliminated" (*Orientalism*, p. 254).

72. Richards apparently made a number of futile efforts during the decade before the Revolution to convince Nationalist Chinese authorities to adopt Basic English in their schools.

73. Paul Bové, "A Free, Varied, and Unwasted Life," *Intellectuals in Power*, p. 73.

74. Michel Foucault, *The Order of Things*, p. 297.

75. Martin Heidegger, "The Concept of the *Logos*," *Being and Time*, pp. 55ff. See also my essay, "Breaking the Circle: Hermeneutics as Dis-closure," *boundary 2*, vol. 2, 2 (Winter 1977), 427ff.

76. Martin Heidegger, "Letter on Humanism," trans. Frank A. Capuzzi and J. Glen Gray in *Basic Writings*, ed. David Farrell Krell (New York: Harper and Row, 1977), pp. 200-201. See also Charles Olson, "Human Universe," *Human Universe and Other Essays*, ed. Donald Allen (New York: Grove Press, 1961); *The Special View of History*, ed. Ann Charters (Berkeley: Oyez, 1970); and my essay "Charles Olson and Negative Capability: A Destructive Interpretation," in William V. Spanos, *Repetitions: The Postmodern Occasion in Literature and Culture* (Baton Rouge: Louisiana State University Press, 1987), pp. 107-47. For an account of Johann J. Winckelmann's enormous influence on British Victorian humanist Hellenism, see Frank M. Turner's *The Greek Heritage in Victorian Britain* (New Haven: Yale University Press, 1981). Turner's ground-breaking study, especially his interpretation of Winckelmann's reading of classical Greek sculpture (*Thoughts on the Imitation of Greek Art in Painting and Sculpture* [1755] and *The History of Ancient Art* [1764]) and its effect on British humanist writers from Joshua Reynolds to Matthew Arnold and after, goes far to corroborate Heidegger's passing reference to Winckelmann's—and the later German writers'—Romanization of Greek art: "[Winckelmann's] interpretation of the classical restraint and harmony in fifth—and fourth—century sculpture derived from his reading of the literature of that period rather than from examination of its sculpture. The statues with which he was actually acquainted were Hellenistic" (p. 40); and again, "Winckelmann had . . . contended . . . that the achievement of ideal beauty had occurred only during the highest stage of Greek art. Following in detail the scheme of art history set forth by Quintilian and Cicero, Winckelmann portrayed four periods in the development of Greek sculpture. . . . British critics later repeated this same pattern in their accounts of the rise and fall of Greek art. Its origin in the ancient [Roman] critics of art, and Winckelmann's repetition of the scheme, convinced them of its validity" (p. 43). In this pointing to the "Romanism" of Winckelmann's classical scholarship, I am taking exception to Philippe Lacoue-Labarthe's identification of Heidegger's "Greece" with the "national aestheticism" of the German tradition of classical scholarship, which, according to Lacoue-Labarthe, culminates in the Nazis' idea of the *polis* as a *Gesamtkunstwerk*. See *Heidegger, Art and Politics*, trans. Chris Turner (Oxford: Basil Blackwell, 1990), pp. 62ff.

77. See, for example, Michel Foucault, *Discipline and Punish: The Birth of the Prison*, pp. 146-47: "One should not forget that, generally speaking, the Roman model, at the Enlightenment, played a dual role: in its republican aspect, it was the very embodiment of liberty; in its military aspect, it was the ideal schema of discipline. The Rome of the eighteenth century and of the Revolution was the Rome of the Senate, but it was also that of the legion; it was the Rome of the Forum, but it was also that of the camps. Up to the empire, the Roman reference transmitted, somewhat ambigu-

ously, the juridical ideal of citizenship and the technique of disciplinary methods. In any case, the strictly disciplinary element in the ancient fable used by the Jesuit colleges came to dominate the [earlier] element of joust and mock warfare. Gradually—but especially after 1762—the educational space unfolds: the class becomes homogeneous, it is no longer made up of individual elements arranged side by side under the master's eye. In the eighteenth century, 'rank' begins to define the great form of distribution of individuals in the educational order: rows or ranks of pupils in the class, corridors, courtyards; rank attributed to each pupil at the end of each task and each examination; the rank he obtains from week to week, month to month, year to year; an alignment of age groups, one after another; a succession of subjects taught and questions treated, according to an order of increasing difficulty." That Foucault is quite aware of the historical relationship between education as *eruditio et institutio in bonas artes* and the extension of territorial hegemony becomes clear in the conclusion of the chapter entitled "Docile Bodies," in which he traces the origins of the Napoleonic regime back through the tactics of eighteenth-century military theorists such as J. A. Guibert to the Roman elision of military discipline, training in citizenship, and empire into a single continuous figure: " 'Discipline must be made national,' said Guibert. 'The state that I depict will have a simple, reliable, easily controlled administration. It will resemble those huge machines which by quite uncomplicated means produce great effects; the strength of this state will spring from its own strength, its prosperity from its own prosperity. Time, which destroys all, will increase its power. It will disprove that vulgar prejudice by which we are made to imagine that empires are subject to an impervious law of decline and ruin' (Guibert, *'Discours préliminaire,' Essai général de tactique*, I, 1772, xxiii-xxiv). . . . The Napoleonic régime was not far off and with it the form of state that was to survive it and, we must not forget, the foundations of which were laid not only by jurists, but also by soldiers, not only by councillors of state, but also junior officers, not only the men of the courts, but also the men of the camps. The Roman reference that accompanied this formation certainly bears with it this double index: citizens and legionnaires, law and manoeuvres" (p. 169). See also Edward Said, *Orientalism* (New York: Vintage Books, 1979), especially pp. 79-92, on the Napoleonic Egyptian expedition in which Said amplifies on Foucault's brief remarks on Napoleonic imperialism by adding textual tactics (knowledge production) to the military discipline and training in good citizenship that are continuous with colonization.

78. Martin Heidegger, *Parmenides*, vol. 54, *Gesamtausgabe* (Frankfurt am Main: Vittorio Klostermann, 1982), pp. 58-60. My translation.

79. Heidegger, *Parmenides*, pp. 60-61. Heidegger's analysis of this developed form of the imperial project, especially of the role played by the operations of power he reiteratively invokes with the German word *heissen*, which not only means "to command, enjoin, bid, order, direct," but also "to name, call, denominate," bears a striking resemblance to Althusser's analysis of ideology as the "interpellation" (or "hailing") of individuals as (subjected) subjects. See "Ideology and Ideological State Apparatuses (Notes Toward an Investigation)," *Lenin and Philosophy, and Other Esssays*, trans. Ben Brewster (New York: Monthly Review Press, 1971), pp. 180-81.

80. According to Heidegger—and here he is developing Nietzsche's genealogy—Greek thinking was determined, not by the modern ideal of truth as correspondence between mind and thing, but as un-concealment. The hardening process that eventually rendered being a total thing (*summum ens*) and thinking a free-floating "philosophy of presence" begins, according to Heidegger, with the Romans' translation of *a-letheía* to *veritas* as "*adequaetio intellectus et rei.*" Whether it is understood as "the correspondence of the matter to knowledge" or "the correspondence of knowledge to the matter," this concept has "continually in view a conforming to . . . and hence think[s] truth as *correctness [Richtigkeit]*" ("On the Essence of Truth," *Basic Writings*, p. 120). When the Romans began to think temporal phenomena on the *basis* or *ground* achieved by originative Greek thinking, "the translation of Greek names into Latin," Heidegger says, "is in no way the innocent process it is considered to this day. Beneath the seeming literal and thus faithful translation there is concealed, rather, a *trans*lation of Greek experience into a different way of thinking. Roman thought emphatically and insistently "*takes over the Greek words without a corresponding, equally original experience of what they say, without the Greek word. The rootlessness of Western thought begins with this translation*" ("The Origin of the Work of Art," *Basic Writings*, p. 154). Hence-

forth, and increasingly, "the ontology that thus arises is ensnared by the tradition, which allows it to sink to the level of the obvious and becomes mere material for reworking (as it was for Hegel). Greek ontology thus uprooted became a fixed body of doctrine" ("Introduction," *Being and Time*, in *Basic Writings*, p. 66).

81. Plutarch, "Cato the Elder," *Makers of Rome*, trans. Ian Scott-Kilvert (Harmondsworth: Penguin, 1965), p. 146. In his essay "From the Prehistory of Novelistic Discourse," *The Dialogic Imagination: Four Essays*, trans. Caryl Emerson and Michael Holquist (Austin: University of Texas Press, 1981), Mikhail Bakhtin observes that "the literary and artistic consciousness of the Romans could not imagine a serious form without its comic equivalent. . . . As in the Saturnalia the clown was the double of the ruler and the slave the double of the master, so such comic doubles were created in all forms of culture and literature. For this reason Roman literature, *and especially the low literature of the folk*, created an immense number of parodic-travestying forms. . . . *It was oral tradition* preeminently that transmitted many of these forms. . . . It was Rome that taught European culture how to laugh and ridicule. But of the rich heritage of laughter that was part of the written tradition of Rome only a minuscule quantity has survived: *those upon whom the transmission of this heritage depended were agelasts [ideologues of 'high seriousness,' from the Greek 'one who doesn't laugh'] who elected the serious word and rejected its comic reflections as a profanation* (as happened, for example, with numerous parodies on Virgil)" (pp. 58-59). Writing from a somewhat different perspective, Bakhtin does not directly address the question of the sociopolitical relationship between the "low" ludic oral literature of the folk and the "high" literature of Roman officialdom. But his emphasis on "the low literature of the folk" and his reference to the grave custodians of Roman letters and what their "high seriousness" allowed to be transmitted suggests where he would stand on this question. This possibility is underscored if, with Michael Holquist, we read Bakhtin's scholarly investigations into the relationship between the ludic and the rise of the novel as a critical commentary on the official (*agelast*) cultural and sociopolitical policies of Stalinism. See Holquist, "Bakhtin and Rabelais: Theory as Praxis," in *Engagements: Postmodernism, Marxism, Politics*, a special double issue (ed. Jonathan Arac) of *boundary 2*, vol. 11, 1/2 (Fall/Winter 1983), 5-19.

82. Sacvan Bercovitch, *The American Jeremiad* (Madison: University of Wisconsin Press, 1978). Bercovitch traces the ideological origin of the historical itinerary of America "from visible saint to American patriot, sacred errand to 'manifest destiny,' colony to republic to imperial power" (p. 92) back to the Puritan biblical exegetes who accommodated Patristic figural or typological interpretation (which was also used to justify the Holy Roman Empire) to legitimate their expansive New England theocracy. As persuasive as his argument is, it nevertheless fails to indicate the degree to which both the medieval exegetes and the American Puritans also resorted to the Roman imperial model; above all to the narrative of the saving remnant embodied in Virgil's *Aeneid*, to justify their "imperial" projects. Thus he also obscures the Federalists' conflation of the imperial Roman with the biblical figural narrative of the saving remnant in their effort to articulate a hegemonic discourse—a discourse of national consensus—vis-à-vis Empire. To focalize what in Bercovitch is merely a suggestion, I quote the following passage on Cotton Mather's influential, indeed enabling text, *Magnalia Christi Americana* (1702), which one finds buried in a footnote in Bercovitch's study: "Mather's millennarianism at this time is worth special emphasis because the *Magnalia* has so often been read as a cry of despair. . . . The significance of those deliverances [which are usually taken to be the expression of despair] are indicated by the title of the last section of this last Book, 'Arma Virosque Cano,' a title that recalls the Virgilian invocation with which Mather opens the History (as well as the numerous echoes from the *Aeneid* thereafter), and so suggests the epic proportions of his narrative. For Mather, of course, New England's story not only parallels but supersedes that of the founding of Rome [by the saving remnant], as his literary 'assistance' from Christ excels the inspiration of Virgil's muse, as the 'exemplary heroes' he celebrates resemble but outshine the men of Aeneas' band—not only as Christians but as seafarers and conquerors of hostile pagan tribes—and, more spectacularly, as the millennium toward which the Reformation is moving provides the far more glorious antitype of the Augustan *Pax Romana*. Undoubtedly, the proper title for Mather's work is the exultant one he gave it: *Magnalia Christi Americana*, 'The Great Acts of Christ in America' " (p. 87).

The recurrence of the Puritan formula—"to build a City on the Hill"—in the public speeches of President Ronald Reagan is thus no accident. However sedimented and trivialized by his hegemonic rhetoric of consensus, the logocentric/imperial narrative it brings to culmination continues to resonate in it.

83. As Frank M. Turner observes in *The Greek Heritage in Victorian Britain*, his monumental history of the uses to which classical Greece was put by Victorian English intellectuals, Homer's epics were, by and large, read in terms of the typological hermeneutics of the Patristic Fathers, sometimes in ways that merely suggest this exegetical model, but often, especially since the Tractarian movement at Oxford, quite consciously and specifically: "The reading of the Homeric epics as 'a secular Bible of mankind' was in part an emulation of the patristic embracing of pagan civilization for Christian purposes. [This mode was probably precipitated by Henry Nelson Coleridge, the nephew and son-in-law of the poet, whose *Introduction to the Study of the Greek Classic Poets* (1830) was the first post-Romantic period study of the subject and may properly be regarded as the earliest Victorian commentary on Homer.] However, this mode of interpretation also reflected the anxiety of Victorian Christians over the secularization of history by non-Christian writers. If portions of Homeric and Greek culture could be drawn into providential history or could be understood as illustrating Christian truth, then all history and not just that recorded in the Bible could be regarded as prescriptively sacred. This effort might well be considered the historical equivalent of Carlyle's metaphysical natural supernaturalism. Just as Carlyle had discerned the wonder and splendor of the supernatural within finite physical nature, so the writers who linked the Greeks and the Hebrews found evidence of divine dispensation and perhaps even of revelation in secular history" (p. 156). Despite the "empirical" scholarship of George Grote, who interpreted the Homeric texts to conform to the liberalism of the utilitarians, this prefigurative hermeneutics prevailed throughout the Victorian era. It informed the scholarship of William E. Gladstone, whose work on Homer constituted "for better or for worse . . . the single most extensive body of Victorian Homeric commentary" (p. 160), and numerous other Anglican scholars; it also influenced a more secular tradition culminating in Gilbert Murray's *The Rise of the Greek Epic* (1907). Turner makes no reference to the importance of Virgil's *Aeneid* in this prefigurative reading of Homer. If, however, the fundamental role this Roman text played in the exegetical practice and politics of the Patristic Fathers is remembered, the mediating function of *The Aeneid* in the Victorian interpretation of Homer will become apparent.

84. The German scholarship on which Arnold relies for his understanding of the Greek spirit is precisely that which, according to Heidegger, remains Roman. See Frank Turner, *The Greek Heritage in Victorian Britain*: "[Arnold's] Greeks were not ancient Hellenes but a version of humanity largely conjured up in the late-eighteenth-century German literary and aesthetic imagination" (p. 21; see also pp. 40-41). According to Turner, Arnold's German interpretation of the Greeks influenced other leading English classicists, among them Richard Jebb, Benjamin Jowett, and R. W. Livingstone (pp. 29-36).

85. Charles Augustin Sainte-Beuve, *Etude sur Virgile, suivre d'une étude sur Quintin de Smyrne* (Paris: Garnier frères, 1857).

86. T. S. Eliot, "Ulysses, Order and Myth," *The Dial* (1923), rpr. in William Van O'Connor, ed., *Forms of Modern Fiction* (Bloomington: Indiana University Press, 1959), p. 123.

87. It should not be overlooked in this respect that Arnold's British humanism is also informed by the racist thought of his time. Derived essentially from German scholarship, this thinking privileged Indo-European over Semitic and other racial stock and was appropriated by European powers to justify their imperial projects. See Frederick E. Faverty, *Matthew Arnold the Ethnologist* (Evanston, Ill.: Northwestern University Press, 1951), pp. 182-85. I am indebted to Gerald Graff for referring me to this text.

88. Frank Kermode, *The Classic: Literary Images of Permanence and Change* (Cambridge, Mass.: Harvard University Press, 1983), p. 19.

89. *The Collected Poems of Wilfred Owen*, ed. C. Day Lewis (New York: New Directions, 1964), p. 55. As the editor notes, "BM [British Museum Manuscript] has two drafts, the earlier of which gives, beneath the title, *To Jessie Pope etc.* (cancelled), and *To a Certain Poetess*. HO [Harold Owen Manu-

script] has two drafts, one subscribed *To Jessie Pope etc.*, the other, *To a Certain Poetess.*" But it is clear from this and from many other poems of Owen that the "you" he addresses here is meant to signify the custodians of the British heritage who have inscribed the hegemonic lie in the mind of a friend who ought to know better.

90. For Eliot's critique of Babbitt, see "The Humanism of Irving Babbitt," and "Second Thoughts about Humanism," *Selected Essays*, (New York: Harcourt, Brace, 1950), pp. 419-28; 429-38. For his critique of Arnold, see "Arnold and Pater," *Selected Essays* (New York: Harcourt, Brace, 1951), pp. 382-93; "Matthew Arnold," *The Use of Poetry and the Use of Criticism* (London: Faber and Faber, 1964), pp. 103-19, and "The Three Senses of Culture," in *Notes Towards the Definition of Culture* (New York: Harcourt, Brace, 1949), pp. 619-32. For his critique of Richards, see "The Modern Mind," *The Use of Poetry and the Use of Criticism*, pp. 121-43.

91. T. S. Eliot, "Virgil and the Christian World," *On Poetry and Poets* (London: Faber and Faber, 1957), p. 124. Hereafter cited "VCW" in the text.

92. T.S. Eliot, "What Is a Classic?" *On Poetry and Poets*, p. 61. Hereafter cited "WC" in the text. The inordinate importance Eliot gives to maturity (and the genetic model) in his formulation of the idea of the classic is suggested in the following passage from "WC": "If there is one word on which we can fix, which will suggest the maximum of what I mean by the term 'a classic,' it is the word *maturity*. . . . A classic can only occur when a civilization is mature; when language and a literature are mature; and it must be the work of a mature mind" (p. 55).

93. I am referring, of course, to the teleological hermeneutics perfected by the Patristic exegetes to accommodate radical temporal/historical transformations to the providential design of the abiding *logos*; more specifically, to accommodate the events of the Old Testament to the New. As I showed a long time ago (without being consciously aware of its coercions and its aporias), this typological or prefigurative method is at the structural core of Eliot's dramas from *Murder in the Cathedral* on, and is also essential to his cultural criticism. See my chapters on Eliot's verse plays in *The Christian Tradition in Modern British Verse Drama: The Poetics of Sacramental Time* (New Brunswick, N.J.: Rutgers University Press, 1967). On figural interpretation, see Erich Auerbach, "Figura," *Scenes from the Dramas of European Literature: Six Essays*, trans. Ralph Mannheim (New York: Meridian Books, 1958), pp. 53-54.

94. Matthew Arnold, "The Modern Element in Modern Literature," *On the Classical Tradition*, p. 31.

95. What Eliot implies about Homer's "immaturity" in his remarks on the *Odyssey* and the *Iliad* is rendered explicit by his Christian humanist colleague C. S. Lewis in "Virgil and the Subject of Secondary Epic," *A Preface to Paradise Lost*, rpr. in *Virgil: A Collection of Critical Essays*, ed. Steele Commager (Englewood Cliffs, N.J.: Prentice-Hall, 1966): "With Virgil European poetry grows up. For there are certain moods in which all that had gone before seems, as it were, boy's poetry, depending both for its charm and for its limitations on a certain naivety, seen alike in its heady ecstasies and in its heady despairs" (p. 66).

96. See also T. S. Eliot, "Virgil's Christian World": "What then does this destiny . . . mean? For Virgil's conscious mind, and for his contemporary readers, it means the *imperium romanum*. This in itself, as Virgil saw it, was a worthy justification of history. . . . You must remember that the Roman Empire was transformed into the Holy Roman Empire. What Virgil proposed to his contemporaries was the highest ideal even for an unholy Roman Empire, for any merely temporal empire. We're all, so far as we inherit the civilization of Europe, still citizens of the Roman Empire, and time has not yet proved Virgil wrong when he writes *nec tempora pono: imperium sine fine dedi*" (p. 130).

97. Elsewhere I have shown that what Eliot posits about Virgil, the tradition, the "mind of Europe," etc., in his cultural and literary criticism, his poetry deconstructs. See my "Repetition in *The Waste Land*: A Phenomenological De-struction," *boundary 2*, vol. 7, 3 (Spring 1979), 225-85, and "Hermeneutics and Memory: Destroying T. S. Eliot's *Four Quartets*", *Genre*, vol. 11 (Winter 1978), 523-73.

4. The Violence of Disinterestedness: A Genealogy of the Educational "Reform" Initiative in the 1980s

1. William J. Bennett, "To Reclaim a Legacy: Report on the Humanities in Education," *Chronicle of Higher Education* (November 28, 1984), 19.
2. Carol Gruber, *Mars and Minerva: World War I and the Uses of the Higher Learning in America* (Baton Rouge: Louisiana State University Press, 1975), p. 241.
3. Ibid., pp. 241-42.
4. Ibid., pp. 243-44. As Gerald Graff observes in *Professing Literature: An Institutional History* (Chicago: University of Chicago Press, 1987), it was not only general education that got its original impulse from "wartime superpatriotism"; it was also American literary studies (pp. 130ff). Hereafter cited *PL* in the text.
5. Harvard Committee, *General Education in a Free Society* (Cambridge, Mass.: Harvard University Press, 1945), p. xiii. Hereafter cited *GEFS*. A similar recuperation of the general education project in the face of specialism and the emergence of ideological conflict was institutionalized at the University of Chicago during and after World War II under the authority of President Robert Maynard Hutchins and Mortimer Adler (who had taught in the general honors course at Columbia after World War I). Among other things, the "Chicago plan" reintroduced the "Great Books" curriculum, which in Adler's terms (borrowed from John Erskine, the founder of the general honors, i.e., "Great Books" course at Columbia after World War I) constituted "a Great Conversation among Great [Western] Thinkers on universal themes." See Gerald Graff, *Professing Literature*, pp. 162-67, and James Sloan Allen, *The Romance of Commerce and Culture, Modernism, and the Chicago-Aspen Crusade for Cultural Reform* (Chicago: University of Chicago Press, 1983).
6. The Harvard Committee consisted of Paul H. Buck (dean of the Faculty of Arts and Sciences and professor of history), John H. Finley, Jr. (professor of Greek), Raphael Demos (professor of philosophy), Leigh Hoardley (professor of zoology and associate dean of the Graduate School of Arts and Sciences), Byron S. Hollenshead (research fellow in education, president of Scranton Keystone Junior College and past president of the American Association of Junior Colleges), William K. Jordon (president of Radcliffe College), Ivor A. Richards (university professor and director of the Commission on English Language Studies), Phillip J. Rulon (professor of education and acting dean of the Graduate School of Education), Arthur M. Schlesinger (professor of history and former president of the American Historical Association), Robert Ulich (professor of education and former minister of education in Saxony, Germany), George Wald (professor of biology), and Benjamin F. Wright (professor of government and chairman of the Department of Government).
7. Gerald Graff, *Professing Literature*, p. 168. Graff misquotes the original text, which reads "preparation for life in the broad sense of completeness as a human being [rather than in the narrower sense of competence in a particular lot]" (p. 4).
8. Daniel Bell, *The Reforming of General Education: The Columbia College Experience in Its Natural Setting* (New York: Columbia University Press, 1966), pp. 212-14.
9. I put "defense" and "survival" in quotation marks to suggest how the discourse of humanism/liberal democracy has encoded ethnocentric aggression in terms that render it benign, thus producing a context for consensual assent. The discourse of *General Education in a Free Society* is in large part determined by this discursive reversal. What is largely unconscious in the educational discourse of the immediate postwar period becomes, as I will suggest later, a deliberate and calculated hegemonic strategy for justifying American aggression during the Vietnam War, not simply in the sphere of politics, but in that of education as well. See especially *The Pentagon Papers* and the numerous defenses of the institutions of learning, especially by university administrations, throughout the decade of the 1960s.
10. Paul Bové, *Intellectuals in Power: A Genealogy of Critical Humanism* (New York: Columbia University Press, 1986), pp. 52-53.
11. As Donald Pease (and other "new Americanists") have recently pointed out in countering the recuperative strategy of post-Vietnam liberal humanist literary Americanists, this Cold War agenda also informed the "field imaginary" that emerged during and especially after World War II by way of

the inaugural master texts of such leading intellectuals as F. O. Matthiessen (*American Renaissance: Art and Expression in the Age of Emerson and Whitman*, 1941); Lionel Trilling (*The Liberal Imagination: Essays on Literature and Society*, 1950); Henry Nash Smith (*Virgin Land*, 1950); R. W. B. Lewis (*The American Adam*, 1955); Richard Chase (*The American Novel and Its Tradition*, 1957); and Harry Levin (*The Power of Blackness: Hawthorne, Poe, Melville*, 1958). Thus, for example, Pease writes in reference to Trilling's project: "Trilling's splitting off of the literary imagination from any public world constitutes the ideological work, what might be called the field-defining *action*, of Trilling's review article [of Matthiessen's *American Renaissance*]. Following this split, the readiness within the reader/writer of American literature to actualize the relationship between a literary idea and a political question itself undergoes a critical transformation. And when *re-experienced* from within this liberal imagination, the willingness *not* to realize the relation between literary idea and the public realm produces for the reader/writer what Trilling calls, after Keats, a negative capability. This ability, best exemplified in James's writing, both negates the reader/writer's need to realize literary ideas in the public realm and enables her experience of the *separation* between what is and what is not literary. The experience of this separation, by which literary possibilities can be realized as determinate actions or as particular referents, in turn results in the internalization of that dialectical contradiction (the yes and no) Trilling earlier defined as the agency of American cultural history. When exercising his liberal imagination, an otherwise politically engaged liberal subject can experience the disconnection between what commits him and the place where commitment can be realized. Thus, Trilling's liberal imagination produces two disconnected realms—the cultural and the public. And in diverting their attention from the 'limited' world of politics (preoccupied by the large and permanent dialectical contradiction that sets, for Trilling, the United States' freedom against the Soviets' totalitarianism) to the densely nuanced, complexly differentiated realm of high modernist culture, American readers/writers experience a surrogate fulfillment of their deepest drives and an ersatz wholeness for their authentic selves. By promising wholeness for selves partitized within the public world and an infinity of private locations for the fulfillment of drives left unrealized in the public realm, the cultural sphere's attraction increases, according to Trilling, in direct proportion to the needs for such compensatory gratifications produced within the public realm." "New Americanists: Revisionist Interventions into the Canon," *boundary 2*, vol. 17, 1 (Spring 1990), 7-8. See also Pease, *Visionary Compacts: American Renaissance Writings in Cultural Context* (Madison: University of Wisconsin Press, 1987).

12. James Bryant Conant, *Education in a Divided World: The Function of the Public Schools in Our Unique Society* (Cambridge, Mass.: Harvard University Press, 1949), pp. 108-9. Hereafter cited *EDW*. In his preface Conant pays a special debt of gratitude to I. A. Richards along with H. A. Cowley of Stanford University and Talcott Parsons of Harvard University for being "unusually helpful" (p. x).

13. Clark Kerr, *The Uses of the University* (Cambridge, Mass.: Harvard University Press, 1963). "Basic to this transformation is the growth of the 'knowledge industry,' which is coming to permeate government and business and to draw into it more and more people raised to higher and higher levels of skill. The production, distribution, and consumption of 'knowledge' in all its forms is said to account for 29 percent of gross national product, according to Fritz Machlup's calculations; and 'knowledge production' is growing at about twice the rate of the rest of the economy. Knowledge has certainly never in history been so central to the conduct of an entire society. What the railroads did for the second half of the last century and the [car] for the first half of this century may be done for the second half of this century by the knowledge industry: that is, to serve as the focal point for national growth. And the university is at the center of the knowledge process" (pp. 86-88).

14. For a useful sourcebook of documents concerning the nature of the protest movement forgotten by those humanist custodians of the "Western tradition" and the educational institutions dedicated to the recuperation of the core curriculum in the aftermath of the Vietnam War, see Immanuel Wallerstein and Paul Starr, eds. *The University Crisis Reader*, 2 vols. (New York: Random House, 1971).

15. Louis Althusser, "Ideology and Ideologist State Apparatuses (Notes Towards an Investigation)," *Lenin and Philosophy and Other Essays*, trans. Ben Brewster (New York: Monthly Review Press, 1971), p. 146. Hereafter cited "IISA"). According to Althusser, "Gramsci is the only one who went

any distance in the road I am taking. He had the 'remarkable' idea that the State could not be reduced to the (Repressive) State Apparatus, but included, as he put it, a certain number of institutions from '*civil* society': The Church, the Schools, the trade unions, etc." (p. 142).

16. The hyphenation of "e-mergence," which points to its etymology, is intended to suggest two related meanings: (1) the difference rising out of and asserting itself against the identity in which it was hitherto submerged; (2) the condition of crisis (emergency) that e-mergence precipitates.

17. Barry O'Connell, "Where Does Harvard Lead Us?" *Toward the Restoration of the Liberal Arts Curriculum: Working Papers*, ed. Joel Colton (New York: The Rockefeller Foundation, June 1979), p. 61; hereafter cited "WDHL." The same point, though from a highly favorable perspective, is also made by Alston Chase in "Skipping Through College: Reflections on the Decline of Liberal Arts Education," *Toward the Restoration of the Liberal Arts Curriculum*: "Thirty-three years ago a prestigious Harvard committee issued a report defining and supporting the concept of a liberal (general) education (the famed 'Redbook'). This report was highly influential. After it was issued, Harvard established its now well-known system of general education, and most of the rest of the community of higher education followed suit. Last March another prestigious Harvard committee, under the direction of Dean Henry Rosovsky, issued a report containing virtually the same message" (p. 82). Both O'Connell and Chase could have added Irving Babbitt's program at the beginning of the century to suggest the continuing conservatism of Harvard educational theory and practice.

18. Report on the Core Curriculum (original version, published on February 15, 1978, by Dean Henry Rosovsky for distribution "to members of the faculty of Arts and Sciences and other members of the Harvard Community"). A slightly edited report which "incorporates modifications called for in the faculty legislation" was published as one of the working papers of the Rockefeller Foundation Conference on *Toward the Restoration of the Liberal Arts Curriculum*. In the following, I will make use of both texts, indicating reference to the first as RCC, o.v., and the second as RCC, r.v. These, with page numbers, will be incorporated in the text in parentheses.

19. Jacques Derrida, "Structure, Sign, and Play in the Discourse of the Human Sciences," *Writing and Difference*, trans. Alan Bass (Chicago: University of Chicago Press, 1978), p. 248.

20. The essential difference between the distribution requirements of the old general education program of the 1940s and the "new" core curriculum lies simply in the addition of history and foreign cultures to the original areas (humanities, social sciences, and natural science), or rather, in the redistribution of the latter into five areas.

21. Richard A. Lanham, *Style: An Anti-Text Book* (New Haven: Yale University Press, 1974), James Berlin, *Rhetoric and Reality: Writing Instruction in American Colleges, 1900-1985* (Carbondale: Southern Illinois University Press, 1987).

22. Richard Ohmann, *English in America: A Radical View of the Profession* (New York: Oxford University Press, 1976).

23. I am referring to the disclosure of the leveling will to power informing the grammar of metaphysics (Heidegger and Gadamer), of the unbridgeable gap between signifier and signified (Saussure, Derrida, and Paul de Man), of the "Law of the Father" informing the discourse of the symbolic order (Lacan, Irigaray, Kristeva), and of the complicity between the (humanist) discourse of truth and power, which is represented as an adversarial relationship (Althusser and Foucault).

24. Richard Ohmann, *English in America*, pp. 205-6. Precisely because it violates the "decorum" of the gentlemanly discourse of academic humanists, it is worth recalling Ohmann's very different style in response to his reading of the memoranda of *The Pentagon Papers*: "What arguments like these have in common is a lunatic incommensurability. Even now, reading these strange documents, I want to shout, 'You destroyed the South Vietnamese people, and talked of piaster spending. You held off from still greater killing only because open debate in America about doing so might encourage the North Vietnamese.' The main point to make, in this context, is that since the suffering of the Vietnamese didn't impinge on the consciousness of the policy-makers as a cost, it had virtually no existence for them—at least not in these memoranda" (p. 202).

25. I. A. Richards, "The Future of the Humanities in General Education," *Speculative Instruments* (Chicago: Chicago University Press, 1955), pp. 58-59.

26. T. S. Eliot, "Tradition and the Individual Talent," *Selected Essays* (New York: Harcourt Brace, 1950), p. 49. The interpretation of Eliot's idea of the tradition to which the Harvard Core Curriculum Report refers is that canonized by I. A. Richards and the New Critical establishment. It is not necessarily the final reading. In fact, Eliot's essay may, if it is read in the context of his poetic practice, be "misread" as precisely a de-struction of the metaphysical interpretation of the New Criticism. See my essay "Repetition in *The Waste Land*: A Phenomenological De-struction," *boundary 2*, vol. 7, 3 (Spring 1979), 225-85.

27. See Lionel Trilling, "On the Teaching of Modern Literature," *Beyond Culture: Essays on Literature and Learning* (New York: The Viking Press, 1965), pp. 3-30.

28. I have discussed the relationship between the tradition and the countertradition in literature (and literary criticism) in the following essays: "Modern Literary Criticism and the Spatialization of Time: An Existential Critique," *JAAC*, vol. 24 (Fall 1970), 87-104; "Modern Drama and the Aristotelian Tradition: The Formal Imperatives of Absurd Time," *Contemporary Literature*, vol. 12 (1971), 345-72; "The Detective and the Boundary: Some Notes on the Postmodern Literary Imagination," *boundary 2*, vol. 1 (Fall 1972), 141-68; "The Un-Naming of the Beasts: The Postmodernity of Jean-Paul Sartre's *La Nausée*," *Criticism*, vol. 20 (Summer 1978), 223-80; "Hermeneutics and Memory: Destroying T. S. Eliot's Four Quartets," *Genre*, vol. 11 (Winter 1978), 523-73; "Repetition in *The Waste Land*: A Phenomenological De-struction," *boundary 2*, vol. 7, 3 (Spring 1979), 225-85. The third and fourth have been reprinted in *Repetitions: The Postmodern Occasion in Literature and Culture* (Baton Rouge: Louisiana University Press, 1987).

29. Thomas Pynchon, *The Crying of Lot 49* (New York: Harper and Row, 1981), p. 181. "Preterition"—the reduction of the force of difference consequent to the quest of reason for certainty and uniformity—is the essential theme of Pynchon fiction, from *V.* through *The Crying of Lot 49* and *Gravity's Rainbow* to *Vineland*. And it is invariably associated with Harvard and its Puritan origins. See *Gravity's Rainbow* (New York: Viking Press, 1973), pp. 267 and 554. All these novels, especially the first two, reveal the immediate influence of *The Education of Henry Adams*.

30. Edward Said, *Orientalism*, p. 12. See also Malek Alloula, *The Colonial Harem*, trans. Myrna Godzich and Wlad Godzich (Minneapolis: University of Minnesota Press, 1986).

31. Edward Said, *Orientalism*, pp. 248-50. Said cites Frederic Lefèvre, "Une Heure avec Sylvain Lévi," in *Mémorial Sylvain Lévi*, ed. Jacques Bacot (Paris: Paul Hartmann, 1937), pp. 123-24, as source of the quotation from Lévi. The emphasis in the passage from Lévi is, as Said points out, Lévi's.

32. I. A. Richards, "Responsibilities in the Teaching of English," *Speculative Instruments*, p. 93.

33. It should not be overlooked that Foucault's analysis of the "regime of Truth" constitutes an extension of, not a departure from, Gramsci's neo-Marxist analysis of capitalist hegemony. As Raymond Williams observes in his brilliant amplification of Gramsci's insight into the operation of power in the Western industrial nations: "[Hegemony] does not equate . . . ["the articulate and formal meanings, values and beliefs which a dominant class develops and propagates"] with consciousness, or rather it does not reduce consciousness to them. Instead it sees the relations of domination and subordination, in their forms as practical consciousness, as in effect a saturation of the whole process of living—not only of political and economic activity, nor only of manifest social activity, but of the whole substance of lived identities and relationships, to such a depth that the pressures and limits of what can ultimately be seen as a specific economic, political, and cultural system seem to most of us the pressures and limits of simple experience and common sense. Hegemony is then not only the articulate upper level of 'ideology,' nor are its forms of control only those ordinarily seen as 'manipulation,' or 'indoctrination.' It is a whole body of practices and expectations, over the whole of living: our senses and assignments of energy, our shaping perceptions of ourselves and our world. It is a lived system of meanings and values—constitutive and constituting—which as they are experienced as practices appear as reciprocally confirming. It is, that is to say, in the strongest sense a "culture," but a culture which has also to be seen as the lived dominance and subordination of particular classes" (*Marxism and Literature* [Oxford: Oxford University Press, 1977], p. 110).

34. The extraordinary importance that Harvard University attributes to the need to recuperate this moral/ethical pedagogy is underscored by President Derek Bok's "President's Report, 1986-87" (to the members of the Board of Overseers), which is entirely devoted to articulating a "comprehensive program of moral education" in the face of its universal neglect. This initiative, I suggest, is also manifest in Bok's administrative efforts to annul the gains made by the exponents of critical legal studies in the Harvard Law School.

35. See Martin Heidegger, "Letter on Humanism," *Basic Writings*, ed. David Farrell Krell (New York: Harper and Row, 1977), pp. 234-35.

36. Ibid., pp. 232-33.

37. See F. R. Leavis's response to C. P. Snow in *Two Cultures? The Significance of C. P. Snow* (London: Chatto and Windus, 1962), and Lionel Trilling, "The Leavis-Snow Controversy," *Beyond Culture: Essays on Literature and Learning* (New York: Viking Press, 1965), pp. 145-77. For background, see also E. M. W. Tillyard, *The Muse Unchained: An Intimate Account of the Revolution in English Studies at Cambridge* (London: Bowes and Bowes, 1958).

38. Martin Heidegger, "The Origin of the Work of Art," *Basic Writings*, pp. 167ff.

39. Phyllis Keller, *Getting at the Core: Curricular Reform at Harvard* (Cambridge, Mass.: Harvard University Press, 1982), p. 41. Hereafter cited *GC*.

40. Michael Foucault, "Nietzsche, Genealogy, History," p. 152.

41. Michael Foucault, "Revolutionary Action: 'Until Now,' " pp. 221-22.

42. Friedrich Nietzsche, "On the Uses and Disadvantages of History in Life," *Untimely Meditations*, trans. R. J. Hollingdale (Cambridge: Cambridge University Press, 1983), pp. 67-72. The disclosure of the self-parodic character of monumental history becomes for Foucault one of the three agencies of the genealogical countermemory (the other two being *dissociation*, "directed against identity" and opposed to "history given as continuity or representative of a tradition," and *sacrifice*, "directed against truth" and opposed to "history as knowledge"): Monumental history is "a history given to reestablishing the high points of historical development and their maintenance in a perpetual presence, given to the recovery of works, actions, and creations through the monogram of their personal essence. But in 1874, Nietzsche accused this history, one totally devoted to veneration, of barring access to the actual intensities and creations of life. The parody of his last texts serves to emphasize that 'monumental history' is itself a parody. Genealogy is history in the form of a concerted carnival." "Nietzsche, Genealogy, History," pp. 160-61.

43. Edward Said, "Secular Criticism," *The World, the Text, the Critic* (Cambridge, Mass.: Harvard University Press, 1983), p. 21.

44. I am, of course, referring to the enabling context of Heidegger's de-structive hermeneutics: "when something ready-to-hand [for the working instrument] is found missing, though its everyday presence has been so obvious that we have never taken any notice of it, this makes a *break* in those referential contexts which circumspection discovers. Our circumspection comes up against emptiness, and now sees for the first time *what* the missing article was ready-to-hand *with*, and *what* it was ready-to-hand *for*. The environment announces itself afresh. What is thus lit up is not itself just one thing ready-to-hand among others; still less is it *something present-at-hand* upon which equipment ready-to-hand is somehow founded: it is the 'there' before anyone had observed or ascertained it. It is itself inaccessible to circumspection, so far as circumspection is always directed towards entities; but in each case it has already been disclosed for circumspection. 'Disclose' and 'disclosedness' will be used as technical terms in the passages that follow, and shall signify 'to lay open' and 'the character of having been laid open.' Thus 'to disclose' never means anything like 'to obtain indirectly by inference' " (*Being and Time*, p. 105). It should not be overlooked that Heidegger's understanding of the totalized world of traditional philosophy as uninterrupted "referential surface," in which the constituted is naturalized, is analogous to more politically articulated accounts of this totalized and naturalized world such as Foucault's (the disciplinary society), in which power is saturated throughout the social body, and Gramsci's (civil society), in which domination is practiced by means of the naturalized discourse of hegemony.

45. Wayne Booth, *Critical Understanding: The Powers and Limits of Pluralism* (Chicago: University of Chicago Press, 1979); E. D. Hirsch, *Cultural Literacy: What Every American Needs to Know* (Bos-

ton: Houghton Mifflin, 1987); Gerald Graff, *Professing Literature: An Institutional History* (Chicago: University of Chicago Press, 1987). See also Giles Gunn, *The Culture and the Criticism of Culture* (Oxford: Oxford University Press, 1987).

46. See Paul de Man, "The Return of Philology," *Times Literary Supplement* (December 10, 1982); Jacques Derrida, "The Principle of Reason: The University in the Eyes of the Pupils," *Diacritics*, vol. 13, 3 (Fall 1983), 3-20; Stanley Fish, "Profession Despise Thyself: Fear and Self-Loathing in Literary Studies," *Critical Inquiry*, vol. 10 (December 1983); Paul Bové, "Closing up the Ranks: Xerxes' Hordes Are at the Pass," *Contemporary Literature*, vol. 26 (Spring 1985); William Spanos, "*boundary 2* and the Polity of Interest: Humanism, the 'Center Elsewhere,' and Power," *boundary 2*, vol. 12, 3/13, 1 (Spring/Fall 1984), 173-214, and "Destruction and the Critique of Ideology: A Polemic Meditation on Marginal Discourse," *Repetitions*, pp. 277-313; Joseph A. Buttigieg, "Introduction: Criticism Without Boundaries," *Criticism Without Boundaries: Directions and Crosscurrents in Postmodern Critical Theory*, ed. Joseph A. Buttigieg (Notre Dame, Ind.: Notre Dame University Press, 1987).

47. William J. Bennett, "To Reclaim a Legacy: A Report on Humanities in Education," *Chronicle of Higher Education* (November 28, 1988), 19.

48. Walter Jackson Bate, "The Crisis in English Studies," *Harvard Magazine*, vol. 85 (September-October 1982), 46-54.

49. Allan Bloom, *The Closing of the American Mind*, p. 313.

50. Transcript of "This Week With David Brinkley," ABC News, December 30, 1990, pp. 8-9.

51. Antonio Gramsci, *Selections from the Prison Notebooks*, ed. and trans. Quentin Hoare and Geoffrey Nowell Smith (New York: International Publishers, 1971), p. 12.

52. In *The Political Responsibility of the Critic* (Ithaca, N.Y.: Cornell University Press, 1987), Jim Merod thematizes the possibility for revolutionary praxis by oppositional intellectuals in the present North American context enabled by Gramsci's recognition that the state intervenes in the domain of culture (hegemony) only at times of crisis: "Gramsci's response to the subordination of intellectuals to state power, to all those apparatuses of ideological and bureaucratic control which permeate social life, posits 'a long war of position' in which revolutionary (his term is 'organic') intellectuals are able to wear down the dominant class by invalidating its cultural and ideological hegemony. If enough teachers and writers resist the assumptions that support the ruling class, Gramsci thought, it will be forced to rely increasingly on repressive means to enforce its rule, and the ensuing crisis not only will expose the bankruptcy of capitalist values but will foster the conditions for change" (p. 60). In amplifying on the relevance of Gramsci to the present educational context, Merod offers Noam Chomsky's extension of his insight into the operations of cultural hegemony to include "international (imperialist) hegemony": "Chomsky's writing shows . . . that militarism, a systematic belligerence and ceaseless preparation for large wars and smaller-scale interventions, is the central tenet of United States' domestic and foreign policy. The constantly rehearsed violence of commercial entertainment (television, movies, professional sports) forms a part of what Chomsky calls 'The Cold War system along with its domestic counterpart, militarization of the economy' " (p. 63).

While I am in sympathy with that aspect of Chomsky's Gramscian project Merod recommends as exemplary practice to oppositional intellectuals in the university, I do not think that Chomsky's (and Merod's) discourse as a whole is adequate to the cultural and sociopolitical conditions that presently obtain in North America. For all his awareness of the constitutedness of the discourse and practice of hegemony, he and Merod remain bound to (and by) the anthropologos ("human nature")—to the principle of the self-present humanist self—and thus fall prey to the ruse of the sovereign subject, the fiction that subsumes every other aspect of the discursive *practice* of cultural hegemony in contemporary North American educational institutions. It is for this reason that, for me, Foucault's appropriation, extension, and modification of Gramsci's Marxist insight—above all, his exposure of the complicity of the concept of "sovereign individual" with hegemony (the disciplinary "microphysics of power")—is more useful to oppositional intellectuals, especially in the context of the university, as an instrument of praxis in the present conjuncture.

In thus opting for Foucault's Gramsci against Chomsky's and Merod's, I am not oblivious to the critique of Foucault, most forcefully articulated by Merod in his chapter entitled "On the Political Use of Cultural Consciousness" (pp. 153-95), maintaining that his discourse on power/knowledge "depreciates the notion of human agency" (p. 164). Merod's critique has its point of departure in Foucault's refusal to understand revolutionary action in terms of "human justice" (since this concept, like "human nature," the "sovereign individual," "the repressive hypothesis," etc., is another dimension of the ruse of the disciplinary society, i.e., the discursive practices of hegemony), and goes on to read Foucault's discourse backwards in terms of this strategic refusal. If, however, one begins with texts such as "Revolutionary Action: 'Until Now' " (1971) or "Intellectuals in Power" (1972), where he writes about the "specific intellectual," one can, as I do in the final chapter of this book, as easily read Foucault's discourse on power/knowledge as one that releases the potential for a kind of revolutionary praxis consonant with the conditions that now pertain from the bondage of the ruse of justice. For the primary texts in this debate, see the exchange between Chomsky and Foucault in *Reflexive Water: The Basic Concerns of Mankind*, interviews conducted and edited by Fons Elders (London: Souvenir Press, 1974), pp. 135-97; Edward Said, "Traveling Theory," *The World, the Text, the Critic*, pp. 226-47; Paul Bové, "Intellectuals at War: Michel Foucault and the Analytics of Power," *Intellectuals in Power*, pp. 209-37; and Jim Merod, "On the Political Use of Critical Consciousness," *The Political Responsibility of the Critic*, pp. 153-95, and Jürgen Habermas, *The Philosophy of Modernity: Twelve Lectures*, trans. Frederick Lawrence (Cambridge, Mass.: MIT Press, 1987).

53. Martin Heidegger, "On the Essence of Truth," *Basic Writings*, p. 134.

5. THE UNIVERSITY IN THE VIETNAM DECADE: THE "CRISIS OF COMMAND" AND THE "REFUSAL OF SPONTANEOUS CONSENT"

1. Martin Heidegger, "Introduction: The Exposition of the Question of the Meaning of Being," trans. Joan Stambaugh and J. Glenn Gray, *Basic Writings*, ed. David Farrell Krell (New York: Harper and Row, 1972), p. 68.

2. Martin Heidegger, *Being and Time*, trans. John Marquarrie and Edward Robinson (New York: Harper and Row, 1962), p. 363.

3. Theodor Adorno, *Minima Moralia: Reflections from a Damaged Life*, trans. E. F. N. Jephcott (London: Verso, 1978): "He who stands aloof runs the risk of believing himself better than others and misusing his critique of society or an ideology for his private interest. While he gropingly forms his own life in the frail image of a true existence, he should never forget its frailty, nor how little the image is substitute for true life. Against such awareness, however, pulls the momentum of the bourgeois within him. The detached observer is as much entangled as the active participant; the only advantage of the former is insight into his entanglement, and the infinitismal freedom that lies in knowledge as such" (p. 26).

4. See, for example, Edward Said, "Criticism Between Culture and System" and "Traveling Theory," *The World, the Text, and the Critic* (Cambridge, Mass.: Harvard University Press, 1983), pp. 78-225, 226-47; Jim Merod, *The Political Responsibility of the Critic* (Ithaca, N.Y.: Cornell University Press, 1987), pp. 153-95; Henry A. Giroux, *Theory and Resistance in Education: A Pedagogy for the Opposition* (So. Hadley, Mass.: Bergin and Garvey, 1983), pp. 138-39; Gerald Graf, "Humanism and the Hermeneutics of Power: Reflections on the Post-Structuralist Two-Step and Other Dances," *boundary 2*, vol. 12, 3/13, 1 (Spring /Fall 1984), 495-505; and Luc Ferry and Alain Renaut, *French Philosophy of the Sixties: An Essay on Anti-Humanism*, trans. Mary Schnackeberg Cattani (Amherst: University of Massachusetts Press, 1990). For the most thorough critique by a humanist that accuses the discourse of postmodernism of denying human agency, see Jürgen Habermas, *The Philosophical Discourse of Modernity* (Cambridge, Mass.: MIT Press, 1987).

5. William V. Spanos, "De-struction and the Critique of Ideology," *Repetitions: The Postmodern Occasion in Literature and Culture* (Baton Rouge: Louisiana State University Press, 1987), p. 288. See also Friedrich Nietzsche's identification of the Apollonian, the Socratic, and the Alexandrian with "theoretical man" in *The Birth of Tragedy*, trans. Walter Kaufmann (New York: Vintage Books, 1967), p. 109.

6. Martin Heidegger, *Being and Time*, pp. 437-38. See also *Being and Time*, pp. 194-95, 362-63 for two other versions of the "hermeneutic circle."

7. Jacques Derrida, "La parole soufflée," *Writing and Difference*, trans. Alan Bass (Chicago: University of Chicago Press, 1978), p. 178.

8. William V. Spanos, "The Detective and the Boundary: Some Notes on the Postmodern Literary Imagination," *Repetitions*, pp. 26-27.

9. See *Crisis at Columbia: Report of the Fact-Finding Commission Appointed to Investigate the Disturbances at Columbia University in April and May 1968* (New York: Vintage Books, 1968); hereafter cited *CC*. This document came to be known as the Cox Commission Report, after its chairman, Archibald Cox, professor of Law, Harvard University.

10. William J. Bennett, "To Reclaim a Legacy: Report on Humanities in Education," *Chronicle of Higher Education* (November 20, 1984), p. 19. Allan Bloom, *The Closing of the American Mind* (New York: Simon and Schuster, 1987), p. 317.

11. See Stanley Aronowitz, "When the New Left Was New," *The 60s Without Apology*, ed. Sohnya Sayres, Anders Stephanson, Stanley Aronowitz, Fredric Jameson (Minneapolis: University of Minnesota Press, in cooperation with *Social Text*, 1985), pp. 18ff.

12. Herbert Marcuse is, of course, a significant exception in respect to the theorization of hegemony. But the influence of his critique of culture was largely limited to the site of Eros. Although his discourse was influential in forwarding the "sexual revolution," its implication for literary culture, gender relations, race, and sociopolitics were by and large not realized.

13. Paul Rockwell, "The Columbia Statement," *The University Crisis Reader*, vol. 1, ed. Immanuel Wallerstein and Paul Starr (New York: Random House, 1971), pp. 32-38.

14. In the words of the Cox Commission Report, the Institute for Defense Analysis was "established by the Department of Defense and Joint Chiefs of Staff in 1955 in order to obtain organized university research and counsel upon such matters as weapons systems and conditions of warfare. To a degree IDA was the Army-Navy counterpart of the Air Force's 'RAND.' At its establishment five universities became institutional sponsors; seven more joined over the next decade. . . . Columbia became an institutional member of IDA in 1959. President Kirk and William A. M. Burden, a Trustee of Columbia University, served on both the IDA Board of Trustees and its Executive Committee. The Executive Committee of which Mr. Burden was Chairman, approved all work conducted by IDA, including classified projects directly related to the prosecution of the Vietnam War" (p. 90).

15. See, for example, *The Dissenting Academy*, ed. Theodore Roszak (New York: Pantheon Books, 1968), especially Louis Kampf, "The Scandal of Literary Scholarship," pp. 43-62.

16. Richard Ohmann, *English in America: A Radical View of the Profession* (New York: Oxford University Press, 1976), pp. 49-50. My emphasis, except for *means*. Cited hereafter as *EA*.

17. George F. Kennan, speech given at Swarthmore College in December 1967, reprinted in Immanuel Wallerstein and Paul Starr, *The University Crisis Reader*, vol. 1, p. 15. Kennan, it should be recalled, was the theoretical architect of American Cold War foreign policy.

18. Ibid., pp. 13-14. The quotations are from Woodrow Wilson's address in 1896 at the time of the Princeton Sesquicentennial.

19. Allan Bloom, *The Closing of the American Mind*, pp. 313-14.

20. Ibid., p. 317. This resort to a discourse that calls the legitimate demands of the disenfranchised minorities "intimidation" is an instant of the narrative of the "saving remnant." One sees it more recently in the intervention of Secretary of Education William Bennett at Stanford University in April, 1988, when, in the wake of a year-long effort on the part of a growing number of minority students to open up the required canonical Western Civilization course (which consisted of texts by "white European males"), the Stanford faculty voted to revise the course—rather minimally—to include some texts representing the points of view of hitherto excluded cultures: "Stanford's decision of March 31 to alter its Western Culture Program was not a product of enlightened debate, but rather an unfortunate capitulation to a campaign of pressure politics and intimidation. Does anyone really doubt that selecting books based on the ethnicity or gender of their authors trivializes the academic enterprise? Does anyone really doubt the political agenda underlying these pro-

visions? The events of the past two years at Stanford, therefore, in my mind strikes as an example of what Allan Bloom has called 'The Closing of the American Mind.' In the name of opening minds, promoting diversity, we have seen in this instance the closing of the Stanford mind. The loudest voices have won, but not through force of argument, but bullying, threatening, and name calling. That's not the way the university should work." Speech sponsored by the Young Republican Club at Stanford, March 31, 1988. Bennett's representation of the events at Stanford as a practice of "political correctness" that uses intimidation to achieve its political agenda has become the fundamental tactic of the National Association of Scholars in its effort to delegitimize the multicultural initiative enabled in part by posthumanist theory. See note 23.

21. Michel Foucault, "Revolutionary Action: 'Until Now,' " *Language, Counter-Memory, Practice: Selected Essays and Interviews*, trans. Donald F. Bouchard and Sherry Simon and ed. Donald F. Bouchard (Oxford: Basil Blackwell, 1972), p. 288.

22. Given the historical elitism and canonicity of the Modern Language Association and its publications, "distinguished scholars" in this text means, above all, those whose published scholarship preserves and enhances the authority of the Occidental, if not entirely the Anglo-American literary heritage.

23. That the chauvinist sentiment expressed in these letters to Professor Kampf is not exceptional is underscored by Ohmann's statistics: "It would be pleasant to dismiss this sort of response as the inevitable squawk of the lunatic fringe, but unfortunately it represents, in all but tone, the widespread opinion of MLA members. Thus, a petition circulated by 24 distinguished scholars from Duke and North Carolina bemoaned the fact that 300 people (roughly the voting majority at the Business Meeting) were able to strike a political stance for the whole MLA, and asked the Executive Council to do what it could to reverse the votes taken in New York. . . . what bears comment here is that in the view of 24 scholars, and the many hundreds who signed their petition, measures taken by a majority of 16 scholars should have precedence over those taken by a majority of between 500 and 600 people voting at an open and legal business meeting."

The parallel between the rationale informing the responses made by traditional humanists in the late 1960s to demands for institutional change and those by traditional humanists in the late 1980s and early 1990s should not be overlooked. Like the former, the latter represent these demands as an unequivocal imposition of a "politically correct" ideology that threatens not only the principle of free speech, but the bodily well-being of those attempting to practice it. Both take the form of intimidation justified by charging the opposition with intimidation, and both call for a policing action against it. One could cite any number of such responses, but to suggest the current pervasiveness of this reactionary initiative I quote from the introduction of a piece written by a member of the National Association of Scholars for the SUNY at Binghamton campus: "I will be making statements which could very well put in motion against me the forces of reprisal. It is now a well-known and documented fact that a new brand of McCarthyism reigns on countless campuses across this nation. Many of my colleagues here on this campus share this view, but admit to me privately their fear of even raising discussion on certain issues which indeed have been all but banished beyond the pale of rational debate and discussion. . . . To debate openly or to question in any way this dogmatism is to be labeled and branded racist, sexist, and/or homophobe, Eurocentric, or logocentric, to be condemned as excommunicate and pariah. (The single label of 'arch-conservative' or 'right winger' serves as a convenient catch-all for all the above.) In many cases dissenters are faced with threats of violence and in some cases administrative punishment" (Michael C. Mittelstadt, "Unity, Diversity, and Rational Discourse," *Forum*, vol. 6, 3 [SUNY at Binghamton], February, 1991, 2).

24. Given his economistic model, it is no accident that Ohmann says virtually nothing by way of interrogating the binary opposition between teacher and student which affiliates the site of traditional pedagogy with all the other repressive oppositions informing the "disinterested" discourse and practice of the humanistic institution. The blindness to this discursive site continues to limit oppositional criticism, even that oriented by postmodern theory. See chapter 7.

25. What I have said about the profession of literary studies in general applies even more precisely to the profession of American literature, the field of studies established as a discipline after World War II. According to the "new Americanists," a growing body of American literary critics who have

developed a 'new historicism' from the interrogations of historical representation by such cultural critics as Antonio Gramsci, Michel Foucault, Walter Benjamin, etc., the "field imaginary" of this discipline is profoundly inscribed by the ideology of the Cold War. See especially Donald Pease, *Visionary Compacts: American Renaissance Writings in Cultural Context* (Madison: University of Wisconsin Press, 1987), and the special issue of *boundary 2* entitled "New Americanists: Revisionist Interventions into the Canon," vol. 17, 1 (Spring 1990), ed. Donald Pease.

26. Hubert L. Dreyfuss and Paul Rabinow, *Michel Foucault: Beyond Structuralism and Hermeneutics* (Chicago: University of Chicago Press, 1982), pp. 129-30.

27. Charles Frankel, *Education and the Barricades* (New York: W. W. Norton, 1968), pp. 72-73.

28. Michel Foucault, "Truth and Power," *Power/Knowledge: Selected Interviews and Other Writings, 1972-1977*, ed. Colin Gordon (New York: Pantheon Books, 1980): "The important thing here, I believe, is that truth isn't outside power, a lacking in power: contrary to a myth whose history and functions would repay further study truth isn't the reward of free spirits, the child of protracted solitude, nor the privilege of those who have succeeded in liberating themselves. Truth is a thing of the world: it is produced only by virtue of multiple forms of constraint. And it induces regular effects of power. Each society has its regime of truth, its 'general politics' of truth: that is, the types of discourse which it accepts and makes function as true; the mechanisms and instances which enable one to distinguish true and false statements, the means by which each is sanctioned; the techniques and procedures accorded value in the acquisition of truth; the status of those who are charged with saying what counts as true" (p. 131). For a tellingly ironic example of the way the emancipatory discourse of Marxism has been disabled at the affiliated site of sexuality by its adherence to the repressive hypothesis—the failure, from its specular perspective, to see that the disciplinary society encourages the production of sexual knowledge (rather than repressing it) in behalf of extending its hegemony—see Michel Foucault, *The History of Sexuality, Vol. I: An Introduction*, trans. Robert Hurley (New York: Pantheon Books, 1978), pp. 5-6.

29. "Introduction," *The Sixties Without Apology*, p. 8.

30. Ibid., pp. 5-7.

31. Sylvia Wynter, "The Ceremony Must Be Found: After Humanism," *On Humanism and the University I*, ed. William V. Spanos, *boundary 2*, vol. 12, 3; 13, 1 (Spring/Fall 1984), 37-38. The references are to David Bradley, "Black and American, 1982," *Esquire* (May, 1982); M. Detienne, ed., *Dionysios Slain* (Baltimore: Johns Hopkins University Press, 1979).

6. THE INTELLECTUAL AND THE POSTHUMANIST OCCASION: TOWARD A DECENTERED *PAIDEIA*

1. Martin Heidegger, *Being and Time*, trans. John Macquarrie and Edward Robinson (New York: Harper and Row, 1962), pp. 194-95. What Heidegger means by coming into the circle in the right way is further amplified later in *Being and Time*: "When one talks of the 'circle' in understanding, one expresses a failure to recognize two things: (1) that understanding as such makes up a basic kind of Dasein's Being, and (2) that this Being is constituted as care ["interestedness"]. To deny the circle, to make a secret of it, or even to want to overcome it means finally to reinforce this failure. We must rather endeavor to leap into the 'circle,' primordially and wholly, so that even at the start of the analysis of Dasein we make sure that we have a full view of Dasein's circular Being. If, in the ontology of Dasein, we 'take our departure' from a worldless 'I' in order to provide this 'I' with an Object and an ontologically baseless relation to that Object, then we have 'presupposed' not too much, but *too little*. . . . The object we have taken as our theme is *artificially and dogmatically curtailed* if 'in the first instance' we restrict ourselves to a 'theoretical subject,' in order that we may then round it out 'on the practical side' by tacking on an 'ethic' " (pp. 363-64).

2. I have adopted the term "transdisciplinary" from Mas'ud Zavarzadeh and Donald Morton, "Theory Pedagogy Politics: The Crisis of 'the Subject' in the Humanities," *boundary 2*, vol. 15 1/2 (Fall 1986/Winter 1987), 9.

3. See Paul Bové, *Mastering Discourses* (Durham, N.C.: Duke University Press, 1992). Recently, however, especially in the wake of and under the pressure of the disclosure of Paul de Man's early

journalistic writing in Belgian collaborationist newspapers, American deconstructive critics have begun to explore the affiliation of deconstruction with radical sociopolitics. See, for example, Christopher Norris, *Paul de Man* (Routledge: New York, 1988).

4. See especially Gayatri Chakravorty Spivak, "A Literary Representation of the Subaltern: A Woman's Text from the Third World," *In Other Worlds: Essays in Cultural Politics* (New York: Methuen, 1987), pp. 241-68. See also Chandra Talpade Mohanty, "Under Western Eyes: Feminist Scholarship and Colonial Discourses," *boundary 2*, vol. 12, 3/13, 1 (Spring/Fall, 1984), 333-58.

5. The problem I am bringing into focus is epitomized by the debate precipitated by Jacques Derrida's essay "Racism's Last Word" in *Cultural Inquiry*, vol. 13 (Autumn 1985), 290-99, in which he engages the historically specific political occasion in South Africa in terms of his interest in the rhetoric of apartheid. From the Left political perspective of Anne McClintock and Rob Nixon, Derrida's text constitutes a transformation of the South African political context into a rarified and free-floating textual matter that finally endorses a liberal capitalist "solution" of the "problem of *Apartheid*" ("No Names Apart: The Separation of Word and History in 'Racism's Last Word,' " *Critical Inquiry*, vol. 13 [Autumn 1986], 140-54). This reductive critique of Derrida's essay, I submit, is the consequence of the disciplinary understanding of theory I am referring to in my text (an understanding, not incidentally, to which unfortunately Derrida himself and especially Paul de Man and other prominent American exponents of deconstruction have contributed). For in putting their interested politics and Derrida's interested textuality in radical opposition, they are blinded to the relay between the two that, despite his specific choice of site, Derrida is pointing to in this and other recent essays. This, without referring to the pedagogical issues that are my present concern, is the point Christopher Fynsk makes in his powerful response to McClintock's and Nixon's critique of Derrida, which thematizes Derrida's understanding of "apartheid" as the last—and self-destructive—name of the Western discourse on essence: "In the word *apartheid* . . . a history comes to speak. A certain Western history, which is the history of a discourse, declares itself in the word. This is an event, Derrida says, a 'singularity'—the end of a discourse on essence is announcing itself, happening in this word. Or so Derrida would have it in his effort to write history by answering to the strange renown of the word and to its 'obsidian power' in declaring *apartheid* the last word of racism.

"Is Derrida separating the word or the name *apartheid* from history as McClintock and Nixon would have it? The answer, most evidently, is that he is not. When Derrida writes, 'But hasn't *apartheid* always been the archival record of the unnameable?', he is suggesting that this word has always already spoken in the Western discourse on essence which dissimulates its own unspeakable violence—unspeakable, that is, until the moment when Western racism accomplishes itself at the moment of its apogee and death and comes to declare itself *as such*. *Apartheid* then speaks as the monument or archive of something that has inhabited Western discourse throughout its instituted memory. Derrida is not separating word from history, he is bringing forth history in the word." "*Apartheid*, Word and History," *boundary 2*, vol. 16, 2, 3 (Winter/Spring 1988), 8.

6. Edward W. Said, "Introduction: Secular Criticism," *The World, the Text, and the Critic* (Cambridge, Mass.: Harvard University Press, 1983), pp. 23-24.

7. Edward W. Said, "Reflections on American 'Left' Literary Criticism," *The World, the Text, and the Critic*, p. 175.

8. Edward Said, "Traveling Theory," *The World, the Text, and the Critic*, pp. 241-42. Said articulates this distinction between "traveling theory" and "critical consciousness" in the process of contrasting Lukács's situated discourse with Lucien Goldmann's de-situated adaption of his predecessor, which "removes from theory its insurrectionary role" (p. 235): "In principle," according to Said's account of Lukács's analysis of capitalist reification, "nothing—no object, person, place, or time—is left out, since everything can be calculated. But there are moments when the qualitative existence of 'things' that lead their lives beyond the purview of economics as misunderstood and neglected things-in-themselves, as use-values . . . suddenly becomes the decisive factor (suddenly, that is, for reified, rational thought). Or rather: these 'laws' fail to function and the reified mind is unable to perceive a pattern in this 'chaos.' At such a moment, then, mind or 'subject' has its one opportunity to escape reification: by thinking through what it is that causes reality to appear

to be only a collection of objects and economic *données*. And the very act of looking for process behind what appears to be eternally given and objectified, makes it possible for the mind to know itself as subject and not as a lifeless object, then to go beyond empirical reality into a putative realm of possibility. . . . Crisis, in short, is converted into criticism of the status quo" (p. 232). What Said, through Lukács's *History of Class Consciousness*, says about the relation between crisis, critical consciousness, and theory is a theoretical way of putting what I have said about the enabling occasion of my critique of modern educational practice: the knowledge explosion (and the various resistances accompanying it) in the 1960s that betrayed the contradictions inhering in the totalizing discursive practices of the liberal humanistic institutions of learning. Said, however, does not say how the "moments" that precipitate the possibility of escaping reification (i.e., critical consciousness) arise, whereas I have been suggesting that they e-merge when the hegemonic imperatives of the totalizing problematic of the dominant culture are fulfilled; have come to their end. For Said, in other words, critical consciousness *tends* to be limited to a spontaneous response to crisis. In his reluctance to theorize the moment of recognition—a reluctance suggested by his uneasiness about, if not resistance to, theory—Said repeats at the level of theory and at the site of the Palestinian question, in some degree at least, the failure of the resistance movements of the Vietnam decade to adequately theorize the crisis of Western humanism and the critical consciousness it precipitated. Said's interrogation of "theory"—especially of its "travelling" manifestations—constitutes a necessary and salutary intervention in a context that has witnessed the all too easy institutionalization of several theoretical discourses: "It may seem an abrupt conclusion to reach, but the kinds of theory I have been discussing can quite easily become cultural dogma. Appropriated to schools or institutions, they quickly acquire the status of authority within the cultural group, guild, or affiliative family. Though of course they are to be distinguished from grosser forms of cultural dogma like racism and nationalism, they are insidious in that their original provenance—their history of adversarial, oppositional derivation—dulls the critical consciousness, convincing it that a once insurgent theory is still insurgent, lively, responsive to history. Left to its own specialists and acolytes, so to speak, theory tends to have walls erected around itself" (p. 247). But his argument—however equivocal his text as a whole renders it—"that we distinguish theory from critical consciousness," constitutes in my opinion a regression from the potentialities for meaningful and effective resistance and change enabled by the emergence of "theory." This is why I prefer to collapse his distinction to the oxymoron "critical theory." It would be a self-serving negligence on my part not to add that it is "critical theory" that Said, in fact, practices in his very consequential writing. For another influential critique of "theory" similar to that of Said, see Frank Lentricchia, *Ariel and the Police: Michel Foucault, William James, Wallace Stevens* (Madison: University of Wisconsin Press, 1988).

9. Michel Foucault, "Intellectuals and Power: A Conversation between Michel Foucault and Gilles Deleuze," *Language, Counter-Memory, Practice: Selected Essays and Interviews*, trans. Daniel F. Bouchard and Sherry Simon and ed. Donald Bouchard (Oxford: Basil Blackwell, 1977), p. 207; hereafter cited "IP" in the text.

10. Paul Bové, *Intellectuals in Power: A Genealogy of Critical Humanism* (New York: Columbia University Press, 1988). Following Foucault, Bové observes, "the leading intellectual has always had a double existence. The various forces of discipline and punishment that shape subjectivities throughout that society also form the intellectual; in addition, though, the leading intellectual is specially determined by the disciplinary operations of the particular discourses and institutions in which he or she has been trained and practices. This particular secondary determination is what gives the leading intellectual a unique role in the extension and development of a disciplinary society. The leading intellectual is essential to the reproduction of the disciplinary apparatus and to the dynastic formation's application of power upon the subjugated" (p. 24). The "leading" or "sublime" intellectual, therefore, is an institutionally produced "visionary," the certified "leader" of others, who "leads" them through a pre-scribed path to a pre-viewed disciplinary end in the name of his/her sublime vision. For Bové, the leading intellectual is not simply the traditional humanist, say I. A. Richards or the early Erich Auerbach, but also the oppositional intellectual, who, like the late

Auerbach, Marshall Hodgson, and even Edward Said, succumbs to the disciplinary society's ruse of the sovereign subject.

11. Michel Foucault, "Truth and Power," *Power/Knowledge: Selected Interviews and Other Writings, 1922-1977*, ed. Colin Gordon (New York: Pantheon Books, 1980), p. 126. See also Paolo Freire's remarkably similar version of the revolutionary function of the intellectual in *Pedagogy of the Oppressed*, trans. Myra Bergman Ramos (New York: The Seabury Press, 1968): "We simply cannot go to the laborers — urban or peasant — in the banking style [of teaching], to give them 'knowledge' or to impose upon them the model of the 'good man' contained in a program whose content we have ourselves organized. Many political and educational plans have failed because their authors designed them according to their own personal views of reality, never once taking into account (except as mere objects of their actions) the *men-in-a-situation* to whom their program was ostensibly directed.

"For the truly humanist educator and the authentic revolutionary, the object of action is the reality to be transformed by them together with other men — not other men themselves. The oppressors are the ones who act upon men to indoctrinate them and adjust them to a reality which must remain untouched. Unfortunately, however, in the desire to obtain the support of the people for revolutionary action, revolutionary leaders often fall for the banking line of planning program content from the top down. They approach the peasant or urban masses with projects which may correspond to their own view of the world, but not to that of the people. . . . One cannot expect positive results from an educational or political action program which fails to respect the particular view of the world held by the people. Such a program constitutes cultural invasion, good intentions notwithstanding" (pp. 83-84). Freire cites Mao Tse-tung as the primary source of this revisionist view of the function of revolutionary intellectuals ("There are two principles here: one is the actual needs of the masses rather than what we fancy they need, and the other is the wishes of the masses, who must make up their minds instead of our making up their minds for them." *Selected Works of Mao Tse-Tung*, vol. 3, "The United Front in Cultural Work" [October 30, 1944] [Peking, 1967], pp. 186-87). Seen in the context of Gramsci, and Foucault and Deleuze (among other Europeans), it suggests how fundamental — and global — this revision of the traditional Marxist view of the function of the oppositional intellectual becomes in the aftermath of the Vietnam War.

12. Antonio Gramsci, *Selections from the Prison Notebooks*, trans. and ed. Quentin Hoare and Geoffrey Nowell Smith (New York: International Publishers, 1971), pp. 5-23.

13. Louis Althusser, "Ideology and Ideological Status Apparatuses (Notes towards an Investigation)," *Lenin and Philosophy and Other Essays*, trans. Ben Brewster (New York: Monthly Review Press, 1971), pp. 156-57.

14. Althusser's seminal though Gramsci-inspired essay, "Ideology and Ideological State Apparatuses," precipitated a host of important left critiques of education in the modern industrialized Western nations in the late 1970s and early 1980s, mostly neo-Marxist. Among the most prominent of these are S. Bowles and H. Gintis, *Schooling in Capitalist America* (New York: Basic Books, 1976); Pierre Bourdieu and Jean-Claude Passeron, *Reproduction: In Education, Society, and Culture*, trans. Richard Nice (London: Sage, 1977); B. Bernstein, *Class, Codes and Control*, vol. 13, *Towards a Theory of Educational Transmission* (London: Routledge and Kegan Paul, 1977); Michael W. Apple, *Ideology and Curriculum* (London: Routledge and Kegan Paul, 1979); Henry Giroux, *Ideology, Culture and the Process of Schooling* (Philadelphia: Temple University Press, 1981), and *Theory and Resistance in Education: A Pedagogy for the Opposition* (So. Hadley, Mass.: Bergin and Garvey, 1983); and Stanley Aronowitz and Henry Giroux, *Education Under Siege* (So. Hadley, Mass.: Bergin and Garvey, 1985). These constitute valuable contributions both to an oppositional discourse that reoriented a Left critique determined by the vulgar Marxist base/superstructure model from the site of economics to that of culture, specifically education, and also to a discourse that sharply qualified Althusser's rather monolithic structuralist analysis, which from Giroux's Frankfurtian perspective "falls prey to an abstract system of power and domination that appears to suffer from the very reification it analyzes. Instead of providing a dialectical understanding of the logic of domination, he enshrined it in a formalistic system that is as insular as it is theoretically demeaning to the notions of struggle and human agency," *Theory and Resistance*, p. 83.

See also Giroux, *Schooling and the Struggle for Public Life: Critical Pedagogy in the Modern Age* (Minneapolis: University of Minnesota Press, 1988); and Aronowitz and Giroux, *Postmodern Education: Politics, Culture, and Social Criticism* (Minneapolis: University of Minnesota Press, 1991). But insofar as all these texts focus inquiry on the inclusive site chosen by Althusser, they repeat his oversight — his abstracting of the historically specific occasion (the student uprising in the late 1960s) that precipitated this oppositional discourse on education. Richard Ohmann's *English in America* is, of course, an exception. But as I have indicated in chapter 5, his critique of university education in America has its point of departure in the professors' experience, and not in that of the students. In overlooking what was being expressed symptomatically by the young, that is, Ohmann's discourse betrays the perspective of the traditional or universal intellectual.

15. See, however, Jim Merod, *The Political Responsibility of the Critic* (Ithaca, N.Y.: Cornell University Press, 1987), the one significant exception to this state of affairs. To the three intellectual constituencies that oppositional theoretical discourses have identified — the traditional intellectual, the specific intellectual, the organic intellectual — Merod would add "a fourth and somewhat strangely unrepresented one. It is the 'provisional' or 'intermediate' and unformed intellectual identity of the college student. I have in mind here undergraduates for the most part, since graduate students, even in their first semester of work, have already made a conscious choice of an intellectual or professional identity and are quickly made aware of the rules of the game by which they all succeed or fail. Most undergraduates, in a large part of their activity in colleges and universities, are very much in personal and professional transition. Their intellectual identities, such as they are, can be thought of as in flux. . . . In the normal run of college activity, undergraduates are seldom if ever invited to think of themselves explicitly as 'intellectuals' but rather are put through numerous, frequently bewildering exercises. I offer this fourth category of intellectual identity, first, because at any one time most people who are actively engaged in studying texts, writing essays, attending (in some form of consciousness) to ideas, are students, not professors or professional writers. This is a fact to be reckoned with not as a by-product or incidental feature of the professional critic's work. Students are not merely the necessary audience (or clientele) for the propagation of knowledge and the continuation of intellectual traditions. They provide immediate access to the future. The purpose of intellectual work is not just to advance theoretical understanding and to enrich intellectual practices but to widen and deepen the social relevance of knowledge — to put ideas into more useful contact with democratic principles, to make all institutions within the Western sphere of influence more democratic, to make democracy as a natural political force (as a cultural ideal) more prominent, less prone to the massive assault of commercially induced apathy. I open the notion of the unformed or 'provisional' intellectual because students are genuinely intellectuals-in-process whether they recognize it or not, even though they are not granted such status in the organization of knowledge itself" (pp. 127-28). Even in Merod's view, however, the emphasis is on the teacher's responsibility to "form" or to facilitate the "formation" of the "unformed" student, rather than on the dialogic reciprocity demanded by the de-authorization of the leading intellectual.

16. Paolo Freire, *Pedagogy of the Oppressed*. Hereafter cited as *PO* in my text. "This myth [which threatens to repeat the oppressor ideology] implies the existence of someone who decrees the ignorance of someone else. The one who is doing the decreeing defines himself and the class to which he belongs as those who know or were born to know; he thereby defines others as alien entities. The words of his own class come to be the 'true' words, which he imposes or attempts to impose on the others: the oppressed, whose words have been stolen from them. Those who steal the words of others develop a deep doubt in the abilities of the others and consider them incompetent. Each time they say their word without hearing the word of those whom they have forbidden to speak, they grow more accustomed to power and acquire a taste for guiding, ordering, and commanding. They can no longer live without having someone to give orders to. Under these circumstances, dialogue is impossible" (p. 129).

17. Sylvia Wynter, "The Ceremony Must Be Found: After Humanism," in *On Humanism and the University I*, a special double issue of *boundary 2*, vol. 12, 3/13, 1 (Spring/Fall 1984), 41.

18. The same critique applies, of course, to the response of the ephebes of Heidegger — especially the so-called orthodox Heideggerians in France — to Farías's elaboration of the extent and depth of

Heidegger's complicity with Nazism. I have chosen to focus on the de Manian response, not to obscure my historical affiliation with Heidegger's thought, but because (1) the de Manians constitute a dominant American school of literary criticism, whereas the orthodox Heideggerians are situated primarily in France, and (2) the defense of Heidegger has been far more complex and critically nuanced, the consequence not of following the master, but, as in the cases of Jacques Derrida, Lacoue-Labarthe, and Gerard Granel (in France) and Christopher Fynsk and Mark Zimmerman among others (in the United States), of a thinking of the question concerning sociopolitics that the tension between his destructive discourse and National Socialist practice raises. The reader may decide on the viability of this assertion by consulting my intervention in the debate, "Heidegger, Nazism and the Repressive Hypothesis," *boundary 2*, vol. 17, 2 (Summer 1990), 198-280.

19. Christopher Norris, "Postscript: On de Man's Early Writings for 'Le Soir,' " *Paul de Man*, pp. 177-98. Geoffrey Hartman, "Blindness and Insight," *New Republic* (March 7, 1988), 26-31.

20. Cynthia Chase, "Letter," *London Review of Books*, vol. 10, 10 (May 19, 1988), 4.

21. William V. Spanos, "De-struction and the Critique of Ideology: A Polemic Meditation on Marginal Discourse," *Repetitions: The Postmodern Occasion in Literature and Culture* (Baton Rouge: Louisiana State University Press, 1987), pp. 277-313.

22. According to Freire, it is the investigation of what he calls "the people's 'thematic universe'—the complex of their 'generative themes' " that "inaugurates the dialogue of education as the practice of freedom" (*PO*, p. 86). For such an investigation activates consciousness of and makes meaningful the interdependent contradictory realities (themes)—from general to specific—imbedded and made permanent in the historically produced and always related "limit situations": the condition resulting from the mythification of reality, i.e., the reduction of the contradictory and dialectically related themes to an inclusive and dominant one. "The fundamental theme of our epoch," in Freire's view, is "that of *domination*, which implies its opposite, the theme of *liberation* as the objective to be achieved." In investigating the complex of generative themes that characterizes a people's thematic universe, then, a pedagogy of the oppressed is a praxis intended to expose (free) the contradictions—the differences—obscured by and contained in a constituted totalized reality, i.e., the discourse of hegemony.

23. By "*logos*," it is important to emphasize, Freire does not mean a Transcendental Signified but, as in the case of the Heidegger of *Being and Time*, a saying (*legein*) that is radically temporal and differential.

24. "Reflection upon situationality is reflection about the very condition of existence: critical thinking by means of which men discover each other to be 'in a situation.' Only as this situation ceases to present itself as a dense, enveloping reality or a tormenting blind alley, and men can come to perceive it as an objective-problematic situation—only then can commitment exist. Men *emerge* from their *submersion* and acquire the ability to *intervene* in reality as it is unveiled. *Intervention* in reality—historical awareness itself—thus represents a step forward from *emergence*, and results from *conscientização* of the situation. *Conscientização* is the deepening of the attitude of awareness characteristic of all emergence" (*PO*, pp. 100-101).

25. Friedrich Nietzsche, "On the Uses and Disadvantages of History in Life," *Untimely Meditations*, trans. R. J. Hollingdale (Cambridge: Cambridge University Press, 1983), pp. 102-3. Needless to say, perhaps, I am taking exception to the pervasive simplistic representation of Nietzsche's call for "active forgetting" as the annihilation of memory, one of the most recent of which occurs in Howard Horwitz, " 'I Can't Remember': Skepticism, Synthetic Histories, Critical Action," *South Atlantic Quarterly*, vol. 87 (Fall 1988). In the process of arguing against the political efficacy of the new historicism, Horwitz accuses its practitioners of "routinely" alluding "to Nietzsche's distinction [between universal history and critical history] without attending to the ramifications of his argument; in fact, his critique of universal history entails a proposition about action that appropriates history by forgetting it. . . . The 'mustness of history and of our place in it, our belief in the necessity of history, must be shattered.' Nietzsche quite predictably upholds untrained youth as symbol of an incompletely fashioned historical sense. . . . But he does have advice for adults. Liberation from history begins with violence against memory. . . . Nietzsche's critical history, then, is

hardly recognizable as historicism. Rather it is the destruction and erasure of history in the violence of forgetting. This violence fathers the strong, great man capable of fathering a new history. We should forget neither the gender nor the possible political implications of this masculinist 'superhistory' " (pp. 806-7). I am also taking exception to Jürgen Habermas's representation of Nietzsche's critique of the "monumental history" of humanism—precisely the passage quoted in my text—as "Dionysian messianism." See "The Entry into Postmodernity: Nietzsche as a Turning Point," *The Philosophical Discourse of Modernity: Twelve Lectures*, trans. Frederick G. Lawrence (Cambridge, Mass.: MIT Press, 1987), pp. 83-105.

26. Friedrich Nietzsche, "On the Uses and Disadvantages of History for Life," pp. 117-18.

27. The continuing failure of postmodern theory to provide a *pedagogical* context that would facilitate the conceptualization of the "unconscious resistance of youth" is most apparent in its institutionally inscribed disciplinary tendency to overlook the scene of undergraduate study in favor of graduate courses in "theory." See my essay, "Theory in the Undergraduate Curriculum: Towards an Interested Pedagogy," *boundary 2*, vol. 16, 2-3 (Winter/Spring 1989), 41-70.

28. See, for example, Walter Jackson Bate, "The Crisis of Literary Studies," *Harvard Magazine*, vol. 85 (September-October, 1982): "The truth is that, with the fading of the Renaissance ideal through progressive stages of specialism, leading to intellectual emptiness, we are left with a potentially suicidal movement among 'leaders of the profession,' while, at the same time, the profession sprawls, without its old center, in helpless disarray. One quickly cited example is the professional organization, the Modern Language Association. . . . Fifteen years ago it was already considered too cumbersome and specialized. . . . A glance at its thick program for its last meeting (1981) shows a massive increase and fragmentation into more than 500 categories! I cite a few examples: 'Deconstruction as Politics,' 'Lesbian Feminist Poetry in Texas,' 'The Trickster Figure in Chicano Poetry in Texas,' or (astonishingly) 'The Absent Father in Fact, Metaphor, and Metaphysics in the Middle Generation of American Poets.' These, mind you, are not specialized papers but topical headings of groups within which the still more specialized papers were to be given. Naturally, the progressive trivialization of topics has made these meetings a laughingstock in the national press" (p. 52). As Stanley Fish has observed, "One begins to see how draconian are the measures that must be taken if the enterprise is to be returned to the state Bate associates with earlier and happier days; any number of worlds and activities will have to be excluded. There will be no blacks, no gays, no Chicanos, no filmmakers, no journalists, no women, no businessmen, and even, in some strange sense, no jobs. Bate, however, cannot mean this literally. He knows as well as anyone else (although it is part of what he laments) that, since the end of World War II, men and women of every religious, ethnic, national, and sexual persuasion from every possible social class have found their way into the world of letters. What he objects to (and in these circumstances, it is all that he *can* object to) is the tendency of these men and women to comport themselves *as* gays, blacks, Chicanos, and so forth rather than as literary persons who just happen to be of certain race, sex, or color. That is, the social diversity of the members of the literary community would be tolerable if their differences were subordinated to some general project, to some ideal that was not particularized in any way that corresponded to the interests and concerns of this or that group." "Profession Despise Thyself: Fear and Self-Loathing in Literary Studies," *Critical Inquiry*, vol. 10 (December, 1983), 355-56. See also William V. Spanos, "*boundary 2* and the Polity of Interest: Humanism, the 'Center Elsewhere,' and Power," in *On Humanism and the University I*, pp. 173-214; and "De-struction and the Critique of Ideology," *Repetitions*, pp. 277-313.

29. This alternative was and continues to be perpetuated by the neo-Marxist Frankfurt School, especially in its critique of Lukács's commitment to realism in favor of a view of modernist art that understands its autonomous aesthetic form as a contradiction and critique of the objective reality of modern capitalist society: "Art is the negative knowledge of the actual world. In analogy to a current philosophical phrase we might speak of the 'aesthetic distance' from existence: only by virtue of this distance, and not by denying its existence, can the work of art become both work of art and valid consciousness. A theory of art which ignores this is at once philistine and ideological" (p. 160). "Reconciliation under Duress," *Aesthetics and Politics: Debates between Ernest Bloch, Georg*

Lukács, Bertolt Brecht, Walter Benjamin, and Theodor Adorno, trans. and ed. Ronald Taylor (London: New Left Books, 1977), p. 160.

30. T. S. Eliot, "Tradition and the Individual Talent," *Selected Essays* (New York: Harcourt, Brace, 1950), p. 6.

31. A debate between William Bennett and President Donald Kennedy, produced by PBS, April 1, 1988. What I am suggesting about the expanding curriculum applies as well to the expanding culture industry in general. For example, the flood of texts—films, novels, documentaries—following the dedication of the memorial to the Vietnam veterans in Washington ten years after the fall of Saigon, which "allowed" the hitherto berated or forgotten "grunt" to tell his own story about the war, is more than simply an inadequate response to the official representations that rendered him an indifferent integer in a specular narrative of body-counting. As a body of texts that *individualizes* the participants in war, this symptomatic expansive gesture of the culture industry is a response that reinscribes itself into a retrospective hegemonic discursive practice that would, if not win the lost war, at least dull the grunts' (and the American public's) consciousness of the all-too-obvious economic and sociopolitical (neocolonialist) motives they were sent to Vietnam to die for. Especially telling in this respect are such enormously popular documentary texts as *Dear America: Letters Home from Vietnam*, ed. Bernard Edelman (New York: Pocketbooks, 1985); *Everything We Had*, ed. Al Santoli (New York: Ballantine, 1982); *Nam: The Vietnam War in the Words of the Men and Women Who Fought There* (New York: William Morrow, 1981). This publishing initiative is paralleled by the large number of films on the Vietnam War produced in the last decade. See also the special issue on "Representations of Vietnam" of *Cultural Critique*, no. 3 (Spring 1986), and John Hellman, *American Myth and the Legacy of Vietnam* (New York: Columbia University Press, 1986).

32. For prominent examples of this kind of reinscription, see Elaine Showalter's reading of Virginia Woolf's writing in *A Literature of Their Own: British Women Novelists from Brontë to Lessing* (Princeton, N.J.: Princeton University Press, 1977), and Joyce A. Joyce, "The Black Canon: Reconstructing Black American Literary Criticism," *New Literary History*, vol. 18, 2 (Winter 1987), 335-44. For critiques of these readings, see Toril Moi, *Sexual/Textual Politics: Feminist Literary Theory* (London: Methuen, 1987), pp. 2-18; and Henry Louis Gates, Jr., " 'What's Love Got to Do with It?': Critical Theory, Integrity, and the Black Idiom," and Houston A. Baker, Jr., "In Dubious Battle," both in *New Literary History*, vol. 18, 2 (Winter 1987), 345-62; 363-70.

33. See Henry A. Giroux, *Theory and Resistance in Education: A Pedagogy for the Opposition*, pp. 216-19.

34. Gerald Graff, *Professing Literature: An Institutional History* (Chicago: University of Chicago Press, 1987), p. 258. Hereafter cited *PL*. See also Graff, "What Should We Be Teaching—Where There's No 'We'?" *The Yale Journal of Criticism*, vol. 1 (Spring 1988), 189-211; and "The University and the Prevention of Culture," *Criticism in the University*, ed. Gerald Graff and Reginald Gibbons (Evanston, Ill.: Northwestern University Press, 1985), pp. 111-23.

35. Graff, *Literature Against Itself: Literary Ideas in Modern Society* (Chicago: University of Chicago Press, 1979), p. 125.

36. See the proceedings of the Symposium on Allan Bloom's *Closing of the American Mind* held at Dartmouth College, May 1988 (available on video cassettes), especially the exchanges between Graff and Paul Bové following the latter's intervention ("Intellectual Arrogance and Cultural Carelessness, or, Why One Cannot Read Allan Bloom") and Graff and me (in the final panel discussion of the issues raised during the symposium).

37. Patrick D. Murphy, "Dialectics or Dialogics: Method and Message in the Classroom," in *The Political Responsibilities of the Critic and Teacher, The GRIP Report*, vol. 8 (1988).

38. I refer the reader to the passage from Heidegger's *Being and Time* quoted on p. 189 of this chapter.

39. Michel Foucault, *Madness and Civilization*, trans. Richard Howard (New York: Random House, 1965). See also Friedrich Nietzsche, *On the Genealogy of Morals*, trans. Walter Kaufmann (New York: Vintage Books, 1969): "While every noble morality develops from a triumphant affirmation of itself, slave morality from the outset says No to what is 'outside,' what is 'different,' what is 'not

itself': and this No is its creative deed. This inversion of the value-positing eye—this *need* to direct one's view outward instead of back to oneself—is the essence of *ressentiment*: in order to exist, slave morality always first needs a hostile external world; it needs, physiologically speaking, external stimuli in order to act at all—its action is fundamentally reaction" (pp. 36-37).

Abrams, Meyer H.: definition of masterpiece, 60; Hegel's influence on, 13, 59, 225 n. 29; *Natural Supernaturalism,* 59-60, 69

Adams, Henry, 85, 144, 242-43 n. 34

Adorno, Theodor, 164, 232 n. 19, 236 n. 45, 259 n. 3

affirmative action programs: and consent, 183-84

Althusser, Louis: and agency, 164; and base/superstructure model, 27; and Derrida, 235-36 n. 39; and Gramsci, 159, 254-55 n. 15; on ideology, 131-32, 236-37 n. 45; on metaphysical history, 228 n. 48; as posthumanist, 189-91; on problematic, 229 n. 52; on schools, 197. *See also* Hegelianism

Apollonianism: of Arnold, 73-78; of Babbitt, 81-87; and disinterestedness, 62-64; domestication of Dionysiac force, 15-17, 35-37, 51-52; as Egyptianism, 61-62, 238 n. 55; and logocentrism, 16-17, 51-52; and maturity, 205-7; of modern literary criticism, 50-52; as Orientalism, 17-18; posthumanist resistance to, 188-90; of Richards, 94-103; and spatial form, 19. *See also* circle, centered; Dionysiac force; eye; panopticism

Argyros, Alex, 234-35 n. 34

Arnold, Matthew: affinities with Schiller, 240 n. 14; *Culture and Anarchy,* 71-78, 240 n. 16; and facticity, 240-41 n. 17; "The Function of Criticism at the Present Time," 70; as general intellectual, 77; on Homeric and Periclean cultures, 115-16; nostalgia for lost origin, 70; racism of, 251 n. 84; reclaiming classical heritage, 56-57; and saving remnant, 58-59; on the state, 74-75; violence of disinterestedness, 75-78; on Virgil, 112, 251 n. 83

Aronowitz, Stanley, 265-66 n. 14

Auerbach, Erich: "Figura," 49; Hegelianism of, 226 n. 31

Augustine, Saint, 17

Babbitt, Irving: and classical canon, 85-86; *Democracy and Leadership,* 90-92; on eccentricity, 79-80, 241 n. 23; on high and low culture, 242 n. 33; influence of, 243 n. 38, 244 n. 52; *Literature and the American College,* 79-89; as Orientalist, 82; and patriarchal cultural memory, 86-87; phallocentrism of, 88-90; recuperation of lost center, 79-80; *Rousseau and Romanticism,* 80-87

Bacon, Francis, 20, 67

Bakhtin, Mikhail, 44, 142, 164, 235 n. 35, 250 n. 81

Barthes, Roland, 229 n. 48

base/superstructure model. *See* Marxism

Bate, Walter Jackson: anxiety over cultural heritage, 223 n. 5; and Babbitt, 244 n. 52; "The Crisis in English Studies," 1-2, 268 n. 28; repression of emergent discourses, 156

be-ing: distinguished from Being, 17, 227 n. 34

Benjamin, Walter, 119, 208

Bennett, William J.: anxiety over cultural heritage, 209-10, 223 n. 5; and modern humanist university, xvii; and other humanist reformers, 233 n. 4; and political correctness, 260-61 n. 20; and protest movement, 3; repression of emergent discourses, 156; "To Reclaim a Legacy," 2, 234 n. 32

Bentham, Jeremy, 39-42. *See also* Panopticon

Bercovitch, Sacvan, 111, 250 n. 82

Bergson, Henri: *Time and Free Will,* 20

Berlin, James, 139

Birmingham School of Cultural Criticism, 236-37 n. 45

Blackmur, R. P.: "Humanism and the Symbolic Imagination," 88, 91-93

Blake, William, 31

Bloom, Allan, 55-56, 156, 175-77, 225-26 n. 29, 234 n. 32, 242 n. 33

Bok, Derek, 1, 133, 151-53

Bové, Paul: critique of Richards, 98, 244-45 n. 54; *Intellectuals in Power*, 125, 195-96; on leading intellectual, 264-65 n. 10

Burke, Edmund, 90-91

Campanella, Tommaso: *The City of the Sun*, 33-35

canon: and accommodation of deviant texts, 56, 142-43; Christian, and modern humanist, 51-53; as ideological instrument of dominant culture, 50-55. *See also* Report on the Core Curriculum

Cervantes, Miguel de: *Don Quixote*, 143

Cheney, Lynne V., 156-58, 223 n. 5

Chomsky, Noam: debate with Foucault, 258-59 n. 52

circle, centered: and ec-centricity, 13; as figure for beauty and perfection, 29; as figure for sociopolitical power, 31-32, 231-32 n. 16; as figure informing poetic humanism and positivist science, 66-68; and periphery, 33; as speculative instrument, 29-30; and supervisory gaze, 11. *See also* culture; Panopticon; spatial form

circle, decentered: and dominant culture, 218-19

circle, hermeneutic, 163, 189, 246 n. 63, 262 n. 1

circular city, 33-36, 104-5, 231-32 n. 16

circularity: of narrative time, and linearity, 10-11

colonization. *See* circle, centered; culture; Roman civilization

Columbia University: April-May 1968 crisis, 166, 168-70, 178-80; connection between War Issues Course and General Honors, 121-23; model for Harvard Redbook, 123, 127

Conant, James Bryant: *Education in a Divided World*, 128-31

countermemory, 3-4, 6, 11, 87

Creeley, Robert, 246 n. 64

critical theory: definition of, 164-65

culture: and colonization, 110; and cultivation, 207-8; opposed to anarchy, xviii, 70-78; opposed to barbarism, 105-10, 127-29. *See also* circle, centered; *paideia;* Roman civilization

Dante, Alighieri, 15, 101, 226 n. 31

Deleuze, Gilles, 194

de Man, Paul: and National Socialism, 201, 267 n. 18; as teacher, 201

Derrida, Jacques: and agency, 164; and Althusser, 235-36 n. 39; on centered structure, 14-15, 69; critique of Apollonianism, 16, 51-52; deconstruction, essential limitation of, 26; "Differance," 224 n. 14; *différance,* and Heidegger's ontological difference, 6, 30-31, 224 n. 14; "Force and Signification," 16-17, 51-52; and Heidegger, 6; on logocentrism, 12, 14-15; as posthumanist, 189-91; "Racism's Last Word," 263 n. 5; "Structure, Sign, and Play in the Discourse of the Human Sciences," 4; on supplementarity, 67

Descartes, René, 6, 14

destruction: and critical theory, 164-65; essential weakness of, 26; and genealogy, xvii, 6-11, 62-64, 188, 191-92; of metaphysical tradition, 6-8, 15-16; of modern humanism, 107-9; not purely negative critique, 217-18; and repetition (*Wiederholen*), 6, 163-64

Dickens, Charles: *Hard Times*, 139

difference: coercion into identity, 8, 29; dissemination of, by time, 6; ontological, and *différance*, 30-31, 224 n. 14

Dionysiac force: as barbarism, 175-76, 199, 242 n. 33; as carnival, 44, 56, 235 n. 35, 250 n. 81; as force of temporal difference, 15-17, 51-52; of protest movement, 185; as youth, 198-99, 205-6. *See also* Apollonianism

disciplinary society: and circular city, 231-32 n. 16; and economy of power, 37-38; Foucault's genealogy of, xvi, 9; and interdisciplinary study, 44, 144; and ontotheology, xvii, 8-10; as panoticism, 42; production of docile and useful bodies, 36-37; and transdisciplinarity, 191-92

disinterestedness: as Apollonianism, 63-64; as Egyptianism, 61-62; and *interesse*, 10; interestedness of, xiv-vx, 7, 75-78; and recollection, 15; as regime of Truth, 159; as tool of repression, 75-78; as will to power over difference, 21-23, 61-64. *See also* humanism

Dostoevsky, Fyodor: *Notes from the Underground*, 139

Eagleton, Terry, 57

Eco, Umberto, 237 n. 46

Eliot, Charles: elective system at Harvard, 84-85, 134

Eliot, T. S., 67-68; and Arnold, 116-17; and Babbitt, 244 n. 52; on maturity, 114-15; and mythical method, 20-21; and New Critics, 256 n. 26; poetry of, 252 n. 97; and Roman imperialism, 101, 111-12, 114-17, 226 n. 31, 247 n. 66, 252 n. 96; "Tradition and the Individual Talent," 142; "Virgil's Christian World," 252 n. 96; "What Is a Classic?" 115-17, 226 n. 31, 252 n. 92

Enlightenment: as blinding insight, 232 n. 19; classical Rome as model, 37-38; and surveillance, 38-39

Europe, Eastern and Central, revolutions in, 23-24

existentialism: limitations of, xx, 168

eye: metaphysical, and spatial perspective, 17, 19-20; objective, of classical realist novelists, 10-11; rational, of classical philosophers, 10; spatializing, and colonization of the "other," 17-18; spatializing, and Western nihilism, 18. *See also* panoptic gaze; panopticism

Fanon, Frantz: and agency, 164

Fielding, Henry: *Tom Jones,* 143

Fish, Stanley, 268 n. 28

Foucault, Michel: affinities with Heidegger, xvii, 8-10, 31-33, 62-64, 188, 191-92, 230 n. 12, 230-31 n. 13, 234 n. 33; and agency, 164; and circular city, 231-32 n. 16; on complicity between *anthropologos* and *theologos,* 22, 232 n. 21; *Discipline and Punish,* 9, 36-42; epistemic break, 22-23, 230 n. 12; "The Eye of Power," 41-42; and Gramsci, 159, 256 n. 33; on language, 103-4; limitations of, xvi, 22-23, 35, 47-48; "Nietzsche, Genealogy, History," 53, 61-62, 257 n. 42; on pedagogical economy of power, 233 n. 23; as posthumanist, 189-91; on realistic novel, 235 n. 35; on regime of Truth, 47, 181; repressive hypothesis, 109, 178-79, 181; "Revolutionary Activity: Until Now," 60-61; and Richards's speculative instrument, 96; Roman reference, 108, 248-49 n. 77; "Truth and Power," 262 n. 28; and Two Cultures debate, xvi, 47-48, 66; "What Is an Author?" 49-51. *See also* disciplinary society; genealogy; panoptic gaze; panopticism; Panopticon

Frank, Joseph: "Spatial Form in Modern Literature," 19, 228 nn. 46, 47

Frankel, Charles, 179-80

Frankfurt School, 196, 236-37 n. 42, 268-69 n. 29

Friere, Paolo, 45, 199, 202-4, 216, 265 n. 11, 266 n. 16, 267 n. 22

Fynsk, Christopher, 263 n. 5

Gadamer, Hans-Georg, 19, 246 n. 56

genealogy: and destruction, xvii, 8-10, 62-64, 188, 191-92; of disciplinary society, xxi, 9, 38-48; of humanism, xv-xvi, 38, 46, 107-8, 127, 160-61

General Education in a Free Society (Harvard Redbook): and Chicago plan, 253 n. 5; and cold war politics, xix, 123-32; and Columbia model, 253 n. 5

Giroux, Henry, 265-66 n. 14

Goldmann, Lucien, 263-64 n. 8

Graff, Gerald: *Professing Literature,* 43, 124-25, 213-17, 253 n. 4

Gramsci, Antonio: and Althusser, 254-55 n. 15; and Chomsky, 258-59 n. 52; on civil and political societies, 158-60, 166; and Foucault, 258-59 n. 52; on hegemony, 158-60; organic intellectual, 195

Gruber, Carol: *Mars and Minerva,* 120-22

Habermas, Jürgen, 268 n. 25

Hartman, Geoffrey, 87

Harvard Core Curriculum Report. *See* Report on the Core Curriculum

Harvard Redbook. *See General Education in a Free Society*

Haussmann, Baron Georges Eugène, 34

Hebdige, Dick, 237 n. 45

Hegel, G. W. F., 17; *Er-innerung,* 13-14, 59

Hegelianism, 226 n. 31; Althusser's critique of, 20, 228-29 n. 48, 235-36 n. 39

Heidegger, Martin: affinities with Foucault, xvii, 8-10, 31-33, 62-64, 188, 191-92, 230 n. 12, 230-31 n. 13, 234 n. 33; "The Age of the World Picture," 14, 46; and agency, 164; and Althusser, 109, 249 n. 79; and anthropological will to power, 148-49, 233-34 n. 32; *Being and Time,* 5, 30, 107, 189, 262 n. 1; on binary logic of metaphysics, 5; and critical theory, 164-65; disclosure, 257 n. 44; "The End of Philosophy," 247 n. 67; enframing (*Ge-stell*), 6, 46, 227 n. 42, 234 n. 33; Europeanization of earth and man, 18, 101; genealogy of humanism, xv-xiv, 38, 46, 107-8, 127, 160-61; *An Introduction to Metaphysics,* 8; "Letter on Humanism," 30-31, 63-64, 107-8; limitations of, xvi, 26, 30-31; on Marxism, 26, 28-29, 31; and

National Socialism, xvi, 30, 267 n. 18; ontological difference, 30-31; on ontology of speech, different from Derrida, 224 n. 13; *Parmenides,* 108-9; as postmodernism theorist, 189-91; "The Question Concerning Technology," 227 n. 42, 234 n. 33; retrieval of truth as *a-lethîa,* xviii, 106, 108-10, 249-50 n. 80; on Roman cultural and political imperialism, xviii, 107-9, 127; *Seinsfrage,* 163, 227 n. 33. *See also* circle, hermeneutic; destruction; repetition

Homer: filtered through Virgil, 111, 251 n. 83

Horwitz, Howard, 267-68 n. 25

Hulme, T. E., 228 n. 47

humanism: as disinterested inquiry, xiii, 62-63; as effort to contain play of difference, 71; and hegemony, 160-61; as naturalized Logos, 61, 63, 68-69, 140; and New World Order, 157-58; and objective science, 62-64; opposed to barbarism, xviii, 107-8, 127-29; as presuppositionless inquiry, 61; as preterition, 65-66; Roman origins of, xviii-xix, 38, 106-17, 127-28, 226 n. 31, 248 n. 76, 252 n. 96. *See also* disinterestedness; posthumanism

Husserl, Edmund, 6, 234-35 n. 34

imperialism. *See* circle, centered; culture; Orientalism; Roman civilization

intellectual, xxi, 265 n. 11, 266 n. 15; leading, 264-65 n. 1; oppositional, 213-221; organic, 195

interesse, 225, n. 24

Irigaray, Luce, 229 n. 4

James, William, 88

Jay, Martin, 230-31 n. 13

Jerome, Saint, 49-51

Johnston, Norman J.: *Cities in the Round,* 231-32 n. 16

Keller, Phyllis: *Getting at the Core,* 150-55

Kennan, George, 174-76

Kermode, Frank: *The Classic,* 112-13, 226 n. 31, 247 n. 66

Kerr, Clark: *The Uses of the University,* 254 n. 13

Kierkegaard, Søren: on Hegel's *Er-innerung,* 13, 228 n. 48; on *interesse,* 225 n. 24

Kristeva, Julia: and agency, 164; as posthumanist, 189-91

Lacan, Jacques, 229 n. 48; as posthumanist, 189-91

Lacoue-Labarthe, Philippe, 248 n. 76

Lanham, Richard, 139

Leavis, F. R., 209

Ledoux, Claude-Nicholas: Arc-et-Senans, as precursor to Panopticon, 34-35, 231-32 n. 16, 233 n. 26

Lévi, Sylvain, 147

Lévi-Strauss, Claude, 21, 229 n. 50

logocentric tradition: as Apollonianism, 16; complicity between *anthropologos* and *theologos,* xiv-xv, 22, 232 n. 21; and philosophy of presence, 7

logos: as origin, 6-7; as permanent presence, 8. *See also* Transcendental Signified

Lukács, Georg, 268-69 n. 29

Macauley, Thomas Babington, 102-3

Machery, Pierre, 86

Macomber, W. B., 224 n. 15

Marcuse, Herbert, 260 n. 12

Marxism: determinism and overdetermination, 27; limitations of, xx, 26, 168-73, 183-84, 229 n. 3, 265-66 n. 14; and social realism, 27-28

masterpiece, 52-55, 142-43. *See also* canon

Mather, Cotton, 233 n. 23, 250 n. 82

maturity: privileged in opposition to youth, 45, 198-99, 204-6

Melville, Herman, 92-92, 236-37 n. 53; *Moby-Dick,* 143

Merod, Jim, 258-59 n. 52, 266 n. 15

metaphysics: binary logic of, 5, 68; identity as condition for possibility of difference, 8-9; interpretation of history from after or above, 8, 228 n. 48; and post-Enlightenment disciplinary practice, 40; privileging of visual perception, 10-12; and spatial form, 19-20; as spatialization of time, 6-8, 19-20; and technology of power, 9; as will to power over difference and temporality, 20-21

Mill, John Stuart, 67

More, Paul Elmer, 93

National Socialism, 234 n. 32; Heidegger's and de Man's complicity with, 267 n. 18

New Americanists, 253-54 n. 11, 261-62 n. 25

New Criticism, 143, 209; and spatial form, 19. *See also* Blackmur, R. P.; Richards, I. A.

new historicism, 47

New World Order, xxiii-xxiv, 157-58, 197, 221

Nietzsche, Friedrich: active forgetting, 267-68
n. 25; critique of maturity, 205-6; on
Egyptianism, 238 n. 55; genealogical
critique of humanist historiography, 6, 18,
61-62; on monumental history, 53, 153,
208, 257 n. 42; *On the Genealogy of Morals*,
269-70 n. 39; and Roman *paideia*, 107

occasion: etymology of, 246 n. 64
O'Connell, Barry: "Where Does Harvard Lead
Us?" 133-34, 138-41, 255 n. 17
Ohmann, Richard, 139-40; *English in America*,
171-74, 177-78; and Vietnam War, 255 n. 24
Olson, Charles, 246 n. 64; "Letter 27," 11
ontotheological tradition, xv; and disciplinary
society, xvii, 6-11; principle of identity, 8-9;
and Western culture, 4-5
Orientalism: and Apollonianism, 17-18; of
Babbitt, 82; of Harvard Core Curriculum
Report, 144-46; and Heidegger's dialogue
with a Japanese interlocutor, 18; and
representational gaze, 17-20; of Richards,
100-4. *See also* Said, Edward
Owen, Wilfred, 113-14, 251-52 n. 89

paideia, humanist: as Apollonian repose, 15;
decentering of, 207-8, 211-13; as regime of
Truth, 160-61; Roman origins of, xvi-xviii,
107-17, 127-30, 251 n. 83; shattered by
protest movement, xiv, 166-67, 185-86. *See
also* culture; pedagogy
panoptic gaze: as economy of power, 36-38;
interrogation of, in context of French
thought, 230-31 n. 13; and metaphysical
perspective, 29, 40; and Protestant God,
37; of teacher, 44-45. *See also* eye
panopticism: constitutive of disciplinary
society, 42; as disciplinary *polis*, 105-6; as
humanistic alternative to positivism, 41-42,
66-67; overseeing and oversight, 46;
relation to enframing, 234 n. 33
Panopticon: and binary logic of metaphysics,
67-68; determinative for both medieval
exegesis and modern literary criticism,
50-51; as diagram of a mechanism of power
reduced to its ideal form, 41-42, 48; and
economy of classroom, 43-45, 233 n. 30;
ontotheological origins of, 40, 45-47. *See
also* circle, centered
parody, 56, 250 n. 81
Patristic Fathers, 48-50
Pease, Donald, 253-54 n. 11

pedagogy, oppositional, xxii, 212-23; brushing
history against the grain, 119, 208, 211-12;
demystification of metaphysical history,
228-29 n. 48; as interested strategy, 202-3,
211-16; opening up the curriculum, 209,
218-19; and refusal of spontaneous consent,
216-17; teacher-student relation, 207-8,
219-20; undermining regime of Truth, 212.
See also Friere, Paolo; *paideia*;
posthumanism
Pentagon Papers, 139-40, 182-83, 255 n. 24
Plato, 6, 10, 12-23, 17; influence of *Republic* on
modern humanists, 95-99, 225-26 n. 29
pluralism: and accommodation, 213-19; in
American university, 43-44; and racism,
168-71
Plutarch, 110
political correctness, xxiii, 185, 210, 219-20,
260-61 n. 20, 261 n. 23
posthumanism: as collaborative practice, 193-
96, 199-200; decentering the *anthropologos*,
188-90; precipitated by protest movement,
185-86; as transdisciplinarity, 191-93. *See
also* humanism; *paideia*; pedagogy
Protestantism, Calvinist, 37
protest movement: and critical theory, 166-67,
185-86; failure of, xx-xxi, 167-74, 177-81,
182-86. *See also* Vietnam decade
Pynchon, Thomas, 65, 144; on preterition, 256
n. 29

Rabinow, Paul, 230 n. 12; and Hubert
Dreyfuss, 179
recollection, 3-4; Abrams and, 59-60;
Althusser's critique of, 225 n. 29, 228 n.
48; Arnold and, 70-72; Babbitt and, 95-96;
Hegel's *Er-innerung*, 13-14, 59, 225 n. 29;
Heidegger's critique of, 227 n. 33; Plato's
recollective memory, 11-13; recuperation of
lost origin, 6-12, 15; relegitimation of
dominant culture, 119; Richards and, 95-96,
99-104. *See also* countermemory; repetition
reform initiatives, liberal: complicity with
conservatism, xiv, 61-62, 120, 158-61, 166-
68, 211. *See also* Two Cultures
Renan, Ernest, 101-2
repetition (*Wiederholen*): as countermemory,
5-6, 227 n. 33; and destruction, 6, 165. *See
also* recollection
Report on the Core Curriculum: and cultural
anarchy of Vietnam decade, xix-xx, 4, 140,
150-52, 154-55; ethnocentrism of, 144-48;
exclusion of popular arts, 141-42; and

ideology, 135; influence on colleges and universities, 1; and panoptic perspective, 137; and saving remnant, 3-4. *See also* Keller, Phyllis

Richards, I. A.: and Apollonian repose, 15; and Arnold, 245-46 n. 56; and cultural imperialism, 147-48; as leading intellectual, 98, 125, 244-45 n. 54; as Orientalist, 101-2, 247-48 n. 71; on proliferation, 245 n. 55; *Speculative Instruments,* 95-102; and synoptic university, 38, 98-102; "Toward a World English," 102-3; understanding of hermeneutic circle, 246 n. 56, 247 n. 65

rock music, 55-56, 242 n. 33

Rockwell, Paul: "The Columbia Statement," 168-70

Roman civilization: and American Puritanism, 233 n. 23, 250-51 n. 82; Arnold's classicism, 111-13; cultural and sociopolitical hegemony of metropolis, 105-6; Eliot's recuperation of, xviii-xix, 111, 114-17, 226 n. 31, 247 n. 66, 252 nn. 95, 96; Greek art, mediated through Rome, 111-17, 127, 248 n. 76, 251 n. 83; imperialism of, 105-10; 116-17, 127; as origin of and model for modern humanism, xviii-xix, 38-39, 107-17, 127-29, 248 n. 76, 249-50 n. 80; as panoptic model, 37-38, 248-49 n. 77; translation of *a-letheia* as *veritas,* xviii, 108-10, 249-50 n. 80. *See also paideia*

Romanticism, 66-69

Rosovsky, Henry. *See* Report on the Core Curriculum

Rousseau, Jean-Jacques, 41-42, 233 n. 26

Rousset, Jean, 51-52

Said, Edward: on affiliation, 31, 192-93; and agency, 164; on Arnold, 77-78; on Lukács, 263-64 n. 8; *Orientalism,* 18, 101, 145-47, 247-48 n. 71; on Richards, 247-48 n. 71; "Secular Criticism," 102-3, 154; "Traveling Theory," 193-94

Sainte-Beuve, Charles Augustin,101; and Virgil, 111-12, 226 n. 31

Sartre, Jean-Paul: the look, 232 n. 18

saving remnant, 58-59, 226 n. 31, 233 n. 23

Schiller, Friedrich, 68-69, 238 n. 2; and pedagogy of Arnold, 240 n. 14

Smart, Barry, 229 n. 3

Sophocles, 113

spatial form: and linear narrative, 19; and metaphysical perspective, 20, 228 n. 47;

and New Criticism, 19; ontological priority of end over temporal process, 228 n. 46

speculative instrument: and coercion of difference, 29

Spivak, Gayatri, 191

Stanford University: debate on Western civilization course, 209-11

Sterne, Laurence: *Tristram Shandy,* 143

structuralism, 21, 51-52, 228 n. 47, 229 n. 50

teacher: civilized, opposed to uncivilized student, 140, 199; mature, opposed to immature student, 204-8; panoptic gaze of, 44-45, 233 n. 30. *See also* Friere, Paolo; pedagogy

teleology: of Biblical exegetes, 48-50; of classical Marxists, 228 n. 48; of modern literary criticism, 50-51; as spatialization of time, 66. *See also* recollection

temporality: of being-in-the-world, 30; as dissemination of difference, 6, 228 n. 46; spatialization of, 6-8, 19-20, 228 nn. 46, 48; and structuralism, 17, 21, 228 n. 47

Transcendental Signified, 22, 31, 52, 61

Trilling, Lionel, 143, 209

truth: as agency of power, xx, 38-39, 262 n. 28; *a-letheia* versus *veritas,* xviii, 87, 106, 108-9, 249-50 n. 80

Turner, Frank M.: *Greek Heritage in Victorian England,* 248 n. 76, 251 n. 83

Two Cultures: as false opposition that reproduces dominant culture, xv-xvi, 20, 23, 67-69, 140-41

university: contemporary, as microcosm of society, xxi, 44, 198-99; as ideological state apparatus, 167, 198-99; liberal, and complicity with disciplinary society, xiii, 120-22; synoptic, 32, 98-100, 102

Vietnam decade: Bush's "Vietnam Syndrome," 157; and culture industry, 269 n. 31; disclosure of contradictions of humanism, xiii-xiv, 140, 155-56, 166; as epistemic break, 4-5; Reagan era, and forgetting, 152-57. *See also* protest movement

Virgil, 101; as classic poet of Western tradition, 111-12, 226 n. 31; and Patristic Fathers, 115; and saving remnant, 226 n. 31. *See also* Eliot, T. S.

Weber, Max: *The Protestant Ethic and the Spirit of Capitalism,* 37

Wiederholen. See repetition

Williams, Raymond: on base/superstructure model, 27-28; on hegemony, 256 n. 33

Winckelmann, Johann J., 248 n. 76

Wynter, Sylvia, 211

William V. Spanos is professor of English and comparative literature at the State University of New York at Binghamton. He was the founder of *boundary 2* and its editor until 1990. He is the author of *Repetitions: The Postmodern Occasion in Literature and Culture* (1987), the editor of *Martin Heidegger and the Question of Literature* (1980), and the coeditor of *The Question of Textuality: Strategies of Reading in Contemporary American Criticism* (1982). His *Heidegger and Criticism: Retrieving the Cultural Politics of Destruction* is forthcoming from Minnesota.